MICROSO

The Essential Reference

for Developing

Data Access Solutions

in Microsoft Access 95

and Microsoft Excel 95

Microsoft® Office 95 Data Access Reference

Microsoft Press

PUBLISHED BY
Microsoft Press
A Division of Microsoft Corporation
One Microsoft Way
Redmond, Washington 98052-6399

Copyright © 1995 by Microsoft Corporation

All rights reserved. No part of the contents of this book may be reproduced or transmitted in any form or by any means without the written permission of the publisher.

Library of Congress Cataloging-in-Publication Data
Microsoft office 95 data access reference / Microsoft Corporation.
    p. cm.
  Includes index.
  ISBN 1-55615-942-0
  1. Integrated software. 2. Microsoft Office.
QA76.76.I57M47 1995
005.74--dc20   95-37448
                                                          CIP

Printed and bound in the United States of America.

1 2 3 4 5 6 7 8 9 MLML 0 9 8 7 6 5

Distributed to the book trade in Canada by Macmillan of Canada, a division of Canada Publishing Corporation.

A CIP catalogue record for this book is available from the British Library.

Microsoft Press books are available through booksellers and distributors worldwide. For further information about international editions, contact your local Microsoft Corporation office. Or contact Microsoft Press International directly at fax (206) 936-7329.

dBASE, dBASE III, dBASE IV, and Paradox are registered trademarks of Borland International, Inc. Btrieve is a registered trademark of Btrieve Technologies, Inc. FoxPro, Microsoft, Microsoft Press, MS, MS-DOS, Visual Basic, and Windows are registered trademarks and Visual C++ and Windows NT are trademarks of Microsoft Corporation in the United States and/or other countries. Unicode is a trademark of Unicode, Inc. ZIP Code is a registered trademark of the United States Postal Service.

Acquisitions Editor: Casey D. Doyle
Project Editor: Brenda L. Matteson

Contents

Introduction

    How to Use This Book 1
    Other Resources 1
    Using Data Access Objects 2
    Using SQL 4

Data Access Objects A–Z Reference 7

SQL A–Z Reference 289

Appendix Data Access Object Hierarchy 359

Introduction

Welcome to the *Microsoft® Office 95 Data Access Reference,* your reference for using data access objects and SQL to create data access applications in Microsoft Access and Microsoft Excel. This book contains information on the data access objects, methods, and properties and the SQL statements and functions available to you when you program in Visual Basic® in Microsoft Access or Microsoft Excel.

Microsoft Access and Microsoft Excel both include the Microsoft Jet database engine. The Jet database engine creates and stores the structure of your database and maintains all the data within it. From Visual Basic, there are two ways to work with the Jet database engine to control the structure and content of your database. You can use either data access objects or Microsoft Jet database engine SQL to create, alter, and delete objects and data in your database.

How to Use This Book

This book is divided into two sections. The first section contains reference information on data access objects and their methods and properties. The second section contains reference information on SQL statements and functions.

Because you may use data access objects or SQL differently in Microsoft Excel than you would in Microsoft Access, many topics contain general information followed by specific information for either or both applications. You will also see general examples demonstrating the use of a particular language element followed by examples showing how you might use it in Microsoft Access and Microsoft Excel.

Other Resources

All the reference topics in this book are available in online Help in Microsoft Access and Microsoft Excel. If you view examples online, you can copy them into your application and run them. You can also search for information in the online index, or ask the Answer Wizard a question if you're not sure what topic you're looking for. Online Help may also include updated or late-breaking information that wasn't available before this book was published.

For more information about Visual Basic programming in Microsoft Access and Microsoft Excel, see the following resources:

- *Building Applications with Microsoft Access for Windows 95*, a guide to designing and creating database applications in Microsoft Access, is available with Microsoft Access.
- *Microsoft Access Language Reference* is available in the Microsoft Access Developer's Toolkit.
- *Microsoft Excel/Visual Basic for Windows 95 Programmer's Guide*, a guide to programming in Visual Basic and creating applications in Microsoft Excel, is published by Microsoft Press®.
- *Microsoft Excel/Visual Basic Language Reference, Second Edition,* is published by Microsoft Press.

Using Data Access Objects

Data access objects provide a way to control your database from Visual Basic. If you are working in Microsoft Access, you can do many of the same things in Visual Basic code that you do from the Microsoft Access interface. Many data access objects have graphical representations in Microsoft Access. For instance, a **TableDef** object corresponds to a Microsoft Access table.

Programming with data access objects gives you a finer degree of control over your application than you have from the Microsoft Access interface, and enables you to adapt your application to changing environments. You don't have to create an entire database from Visual Basic. To speed development, you can create objects in Microsoft Access and write Visual Basic code later to enhance and complete your application.

If you are working in Microsoft Excel, you must use data access objects to manipulate your database, because Microsoft Excel does not have graphical representations of these objects. If you need to control a database from Microsoft Excel, you can create that database graphically in Microsoft Access and write code later to manipulate it from Microsoft Excel. Because both Microsoft Access and Microsoft Excel include the Jet database engine, both applications can use the same database files. Database files are saved with the .MDB filename extension.

Data access objects represent the different components of a database. The objects have a hierarchical relationship to one another; one type of object or collection contains or is contained by another type of object or collection. For a graphical representation of the data access object hierarchy, see "Data Access Object Hierarchy" in the Appendix or in online Help.

DBEngine Object At the top of the hierarchy is the **DBEngine** object. This object represents the Jet database engine. The **DBEngine** object exists whenever you launch Microsoft Access or reference the Microsoft DAO 3.0 Object Library in Microsoft Excel. You don't have to create it explicitly.

Workspace Object The Jet database engine supports multiple sessions, each of which begins when a particular user logs on and ends when that user logs off. Each session is represented by a **Workspace** object. Unless you're programming security into your application, you're usually using the default **Workspace** object implicitly.

Database Object Within a session, you can open one or more databases, each of which is represented by a **Database** object. A **Database** object corresponds to a saved .MDB file. A **Database** object contains all the other objects and the data in your database. If you're working in Microsoft Access, the database that is currently open can be represented by a **Database** object.

TableDef, QueryDef Objects Within a **Database** object are the tables that contain data, represented by **TableDef** objects. **QueryDef** objects represent saved queries of any type and contain combined data from one or more tables. These objects are stored in the database file, so you don't have to recreate them each time you use them. The data in a table or query is organized into fields, represented by **Field** objects.

Index Object An **Index** object corresponds to an index on a table. An index is a cross-reference on one or more fields in a table and enables faster access to data. An index is also useful for defining some rules about data, such as whether the combination of data entered in certain fields must be unique.

Parameter Object A **Parameter** object represents any parameters defined for a query. You can use **Parameter** objects to change the values of query parameters from code before you run the query.

Recordset Object A **Recordset** object represents a set of data, or recordset. A recordset is created using data in a table or query. Unlike tables and queries, however, recordsets are not stored to disk and must be re-created each time you use them. Data in **Recordset** objects is organized into **Field** objects representing fields in the underlying table or query.

You can think of a **TableDef** or **QueryDef** object as an object that defines the structure of a table or query, and a **Recordset** object as the object that represents the data stored in the table or query. To add, delete, or change data in your database, you must create a **Recordset**. You can manipulate data by applying the methods of the **Recordset** and setting and returning its properties.

There are three types of **Recordset** objects: table-type, dynaset-type, and snapshot-type. Not all **Recordset** types are updatable in all situations. To determine when you should use each one, see the topics discussing these objects.

Relation Object A **Relation** object represents a relationship between fields in two tables in a database. Relationships are a key structural component of your database, in that they link like fields in your tables. They also determine how data in one table is affected when corresponding data in another table is changed or deleted.

Container Object A **Container** object represents a type of object in your database. Both Microsoft Access and Microsoft Excel provide the Databases, Tables, and Relations **Container** objects. Microsoft Access also provides Forms, Modules, Reports, and Scripts **Container** objects.

Document Object A **Document** object represents an object of the type defined by its corresponding **Container** object. For instance, each database has at least one Table **Document** object within the Tables **Container** object. You use **Container** and **Document** objects together with **User** and **Group** objects to program security into your application.

User, Group Objects A **User** object represents a user account with certain access permissions. A **Group** object represents a group of user accounts with common access permissions. You use **User** and **Group** objects together with **Container** and **Document** objects to program security into your application.

Error Object An **Error** object stores information about data access errors that have occurred. Several data access errors can occur at the same time; information about each is stored in an **Error** object in the **Errors** collection. The **Errors** collection is cleared each time a new error occurs.

Property Object Every data access object has a set of properties, which are represented by **Property** objects and stored in the **Properties** collection associated with that object.

Using SQL

You can use Microsoft Jet database engine SQL to create and change both the structure of your database and the data within it. Unless you're an experienced SQL programmer, it's easiest to create your database either in Microsoft Access or with data access objects in Microsoft Excel. However, you may need to be familiar with basic SQL when you're working with data access objects. Some objects, such as the **QueryDef** object, include an SQL statement as part of their definition.

If you are working with Microsoft Access, you can create a query in the query design grid and change to SQL view to see the corresponding SQL statement, which Microsoft Access generates for you. This is the easiest way to generate an SQL statement, and is useful if you're not familiar with SQL. You can also write SQL code in SQL view in the Query window, or you can include SQL statements in Visual Basic code.

If you are working with Microsoft Excel, you can only use SQL statements in Visual Basic code. You may want to use Microsoft Access to create a query in the query design grid and save it. You can then open the database from Microsoft Excel and use the corresponding **QueryDef** object. Your code will run faster if you execute a saved query rather than one that you create on the fly.

There are two parts to SQL: the Data Definition Language (DDL) and the Data Manipulation Language (DML). Using DDL, you can create a database or alter the structure of an existing database. Using DML, you can add, change, or delete data in an existing database. Most of the time you will use DML to create SQL statements.

The following DDL statements are available in Jet database engine SQL:

CREATE TABLE statement

CREATE INDEX statement

ALTER TABLE statement

CONSTRAINT clause

DROP statement

SELECT... INTO statement

The following DML statements are available in Jet database engine SQL:

SELECT statement

INSERT INTO statement

UPDATE statement

DELETE statement

TRANSFORM statement

UNION operation

The following SQL clauses and operations are used to extend the basic SELECT statement in Jet database engine SQL:

FROM clause

IN clause

WHERE clause

GROUP BY clause

HAVING clause

ORDER BY clause

ALL, DISTINCT, DISTINCTROW, TOP predicates

PROCEDURE clause

INNER JOIN operation

LEFT JOIN, RIGHT JOIN operations

PARAMETERS declaration

WITH OWNERACCESS OPTION declaration

Jet database engine SQL also includes the SQL aggregate functions, which you can use to perform statistical operations on your data. The aggregate functions include the **Avg**, **Count**, **Min**, **Max**, **StDev**, **StDevP**, **Sum**, **Var**, and **VarP** functions.

PART 1

Data Access Objects A–Z Reference

AbsolutePosition Property

Applies To Dynaset-Type **Recordset** Object, **Recordset** Object, Snapshot-Type **Recordset** Object.

Description Sets or returns the relative record number of a **Recordset** object's current record.

Settings and Return Values The setting or return value is an integer from 0 to one less than the number of records in the **Recordset** object. It corresponds to the ordinal position of the current record in the **Recordset** object specified by the object. The data type is **Long**.

Remarks The **AbsolutePosition** property enables you to position the current record pointer to a specific record based on its ordinal position in a dynaset- or snapshot-type **Recordset** object. You can also determine the current record number by checking the **AbsolutePosition** property setting.

Because the **AbsolutePosition** property value is zero-based (that is, a setting of 0 refers to the first record in the **Recordset** object), it cannot be set to a value greater than or equal to the number of populated records; doing so causes a trappable error. You can determine the number of populated records in the **Recordset** object by checking the **RecordCount** property setting. The maximum allowable setting for the **AbsolutePosition** property is the value of the **RecordCount** property minus 1.

If there is no current record, as when there are no records in the **Recordset** object, –1 is returned. If the current record is deleted, the **AbsolutePosition** property value isn't defined, and a trappable error occurs if it's referenced. New records are added to the end of the sequence.

This property isn't intended to be used as a surrogate record number. Bookmarks are still the recommended way of retaining and returning to a given position and are the only way to position the current record across all types of **Recordset** objects. In particular, the position of a given record changes when one or more records preceding it are deleted. There is also no assurance that a given record will have the same absolute position if the **Recordset** object is re-created again because the order of individual records within a **Recordset** object isn't guaranteed unless it's created with an SQL statement using an ORDER BY clause.

Note The **AbsolutePosition** property isn't available on a forward-only scrolling snapshot type **Recordset** object, or on a **Recordset** object opened from a pass-through query against a remote database.

See Also **PercentPosition** Property, **RecordCount** Property.

10 AbsolutePosition Property

Example

This example positions the current record to the nth record in a dynaset-type **Recordset** object.

```
Function MoveToRecord (intPosition As Long, rstTest As recordset) _
    As Integer
    rstTest.MoveLast
    If rstTest.RecordCount > intPosition Then
        rstTest.AbsolutePosition = intPosition
        MoveToRecord = True
    Else
        MoveToRecord = False
    End If
End Function
```

Example (Microsoft Access)

The following example uses the **AbsolutePosition** property to set the ordinal position of the first record in a dynaset-type **Recordset** object to 1.

```
Sub FirstRecord()
    Dim dbs As Database, rst As Recordset

    ' Return Database variable that points to current database.
    Set dbs = CurrentDb
    Set rst = dbs.OpenRecordset("SELECT * FROM Orders WHERE " & _
        "[ShippedDate] >= #1-1-95#;")
    rst.MoveFirst
    rst.AbsolutePosition = 1
End Sub
```

Example (Microsoft Excel)

This example prompts the user for a record number. The example uses this number to move to a record in the Customer recordset in the NWINDEX.MDB database, and then it copies the values for three specified fields onto Sheet1.

To create the NWINDEX.MDB database, run the Microsoft Excel example for the **CreateDatabase** method.

```
Dim db As Database, rs As Recordset
Sheets("Sheet1").Activate
recordNumber = Application.InputBox(Prompt:="Record number to copy " _
    & "to Sheet1", Title:="Record to copy", Type:=1)
If recordNumber = False Then    ' user cancelled InputBox
    Exit Sub
End If
Set db = Workspaces(0).OpenDatabase(Application.Path & "\NWINDEX.MDB")
Set rs = db.OpenRecordset("Customer", dbOpenSnapshot)
rs.MoveLast
If rs.RecordCount > recordNumber Then
    rs.AbsolutePosition = recordNumber
    ActiveCell.Value = rs.Fields("CONTACT").Value
    ActiveCell.Offset(, 1).Value = rs.Fields("ADDRESS").Value
    ActiveCell.Offset(, 2).Value = rs.Fields("CITY").Value
```

```
Else
    MsgBox "The record #" & recordNumber & " doesn't exist."
End If
rs.Close
db.Close
```

AddNew Method

Applies To Dynaset-Type **Recordset** Object, **Recordset** Object, Table-Type **Recordset** Object.

Description Creates a new record for a table-type or dynaset-type **Recordset** object.

Syntax *object*.**AddNew**

The *object* placeholder represents the name of an open table-type or dynaset-type **Recordset** object to which you want to add a new record.

Remarks The **AddNew** method creates a new record you can edit and add to the **Recordset** object named by *object*. This method sets the fields to **Null** (the default values specified for a table-type **Recordset**) or default values, if any.

After you modify the new record, use the **Update** method to save the changes and add the record to the recordset. No changes are made to the database until you use the **Update** method.

Caution If you issue an **AddNew** and then perform any operation that moves to another record without using **Update**, your changes are lost without warning. In addition, if you close the *object* or end the procedure that declares the *object* or its **Database** object, the new record and the changes made to it are discarded without warning.

When you use **AddNew** and the Microsoft Jet database engine has to create a new 2-kilobyte page to hold the current record, page locking is pessimistic. If the new record fits in an existing page, page locking is optimistic.

If you haven't moved to the last record of your dynaset, records added to base tables may be included if they would be positioned beyond the current record. If you add a record to a dynaset-type **Recordset** using the **AddNew** method, however, the record is visible in the **Recordset** and included in the underlying table where it becomes visible to any new **Recordset** objects.

12 AddNew Method

The position of the new record depends on the type of **Recordset**:

- In a dynaset-type **Recordset** object, records are inserted at the end of the recordset, regardless of any sorting or ordering rules that may have been in effect when the recordset was opened.
- In a table-type **Recordset** object whose **Index** property has been set, records are returned in their proper place in the sort order. If the **Index** property hasn't been set, new records are returned at the end of the recordset.

The record that was current before you used **AddNew** remains current. If you want to make the new record current, you can set the **Bookmark** property to the bookmark identified by the **LastModified** property setting.

See Also

Bookmark Property; **Delete** Method; **Index** Object; **LastModified** Property; **Move** Method; **MoveFirst**, **MoveLast**, **MoveNext**, **MovePrevious** Methods; **Seek** Method.

Specifics (Microsoft Access)

When you use a bookmark in a Microsoft Access module, you must include an **Option Compare Binary** statement in the Declarations section of the module. A bookmark is a **Variant** array of **Byte** data, so the string comparison method for the module must be binary. If a bookmark is evaluated with a text-based string comparison method, such as the **Option Compare Text** statement or the default setting for the **Option Compare Database** statement, the current record may be set to an incorrect record.

Example

This example creates a new record in a table named Customers, enters values, saves the changes, and then moves to and deletes the new record.

```
Dim dbsNorthwind As Database, rstCustomers As Recordset
Set dbsNorthwind = DBEngine.Workspaces(0).OpenDatabase("Northwind.mdb")
' Open table.
Set rstCustomers = dbsNorthwind.OpenRecordset("Customers")
With rstCustomers
    .AddNew                                     ' Create new record.
    !CustomerID = "FINNF"                       ' Set record key.
    !CompanyName = "Finnegan's Foods"           ' Set company name.
    .Update                                     ' Save changes.
    .Bookmark = rstCustomers.LastModified       ' Go to new record
    .Delete                                     ' Delete new record.
    .Close                                      ' Close Table.
End With
dbsNorthwind.Close                              ' Close Database.
```

Example (Microsoft Access)

The following example creates a new record in an Employees table and saves the changes.

```
Sub NewRecord()
    Dim dbs As Database, rst As Recordset
```

```
            ' Return Database variable pointing to current database.
            Set dbs = CurrentDb
            Set rst = dbs.OpenRecordset("Employees")
            With rst
                ' Add new record to end of Recordset object.
                .AddNew
                .[LastName] = "Russell"        ' Add data.
                .[FirstName] = "Peter"
                .Update                        ' Save changes.
            End With
            dbs.Close
    End Sub
```

AllowZeroLength Property

Applies To **Field** Object.

Description Sets or returns a value that indicates whether a zero-length string ("") is a valid setting for the **Value** property of a **Field** object with a Text or Memo data type. For an object not yet appended to the **Fields** collection, this property is read/write.

Settings and Return Values The setting or return value is a Boolean expression that indicates if a value is valid. The data type is Boolean. It returns **True** (-1) if a zero-length string is a valid value.

Remarks For a **Field** object, use of the **AllowZeroLength** property depends on the object that contains the **Fields** collection that the **Field** object is appended to, as the following table shows.

Object appended to	Usage
Index	Not supported
QueryDef	Read-only
Recordset	Read-only
Relation	Not supported
TableDef	Read/write

You can set this property to **False** (0) to make sure you can't use a zero-length string to set the **Value** property of a **Field** object.

You can use this property along with the **Required**, **ValidateOnSet**, or **ValidationRule** property to determine the validity of a value in a field.

See Also **QueryDef** Object, **Required** Property, **TableDef** Object, **ValidateOnSet** Property, **ValidationRule** Property, **ValidationText** Property, **Value** Property.

14 AllPermissions Property

Example (Microsoft Access) The following example creates a new **Field** object and sets its **AllowZeroLength** property to **True**.

```
Sub ZeroLengthField()
    Dim dbs As Database, tdf As TableDef, fld As Field

    ' Return Database variable that points to current database.
    Set dbs = CurrentDb
    Set tdf = dbs.TableDefs!Employees
    ' Create new field in Employees table.
    Set fld = tdf.CreateField("SpouseName", dbText, 15)
    ' Allow zero-length strings in field.
    fld.AllowZeroLength = True
    ' Append Field object.
    tdf.fields.Append fld
End Sub
```

AllPermissions Property

Applies To **Container** Object, **Document** Object.

Description Returns all the permissions that apply to the current **UserName** property of the **Container** or **Document** object, including permissions that are specific to the user as well as the permissions a user inherits from memberships in groups.

Returned Values For any **Container** or **Document** object, the returned values may include the following.

Constant	Description
dbSecReadDef	Can read the table definition including column and index information.
dbSecWriteDef	Can modify or delete the table definition including column and index information.
dbSecRetrieveData	Can retrieve data from the **Document** object.
dbSecInsertData	Can add records.
dbSecReplaceData	Can modify records.
dbSecDeleteData	Can delete records.

AllPermissions Property

In addition, the Databases **Container** object or any **Document** object in a **Documents** collection may include the following.

Constant	Description
dbSecDeleteData	Can delete records.
dbSecDBAdmin	Gives user permission to make a database replicable and change the database password.
dbSecDBCreate	Can create new databases (valid only on the databases **Container** object in the system database [System.mdw]).
dbSecDBExclusive	Exclusive access.
dbSecDBOpen	Can open the database.

Remarks

These constants are listed in the Data Access (DAO) object library in the Object Browser.

This property contrasts with the **Permissions** property, which returns only the permissions that are specific to the user and doesn't include any permissions that the user may also have as a member of groups. If UserName is a group, then **AllPermissions** property returns the same values as **Permissions**.

Specifics (Microsoft Access)

Microsoft Access defines four types of **Container** objects in addition to those defined by the Microsoft Jet database engine. These include the Forms, Reports, Scripts, or Modules **Container** objects. Individual Form, Report, Script and Module **Document** objects belong to the **Documents** collections of these **Container** objects. For these **Container** and **Document** objects, you can also set the **AllPermissions** property to the following constants.

Constant	User or group can
acSecFrmRptReadDef	Open the form or report in Design view but not make any changes.
acSecFrmRptWriteDef	Modify or delete the form or report in Design view.
acSecFrmRptExecute	Open the form in Form view or Datasheet view; print or open the report in Sample Preview or Print Preview.
acSecMacReadDef	Open the Macro window and view a macro without making changes.
acSecMacWriteDef	Modify or delete the macro in the Macro window.
acSecModReadDef	Open the module but not make any changes.
acSecModWriteDef	Modify or delete the contents of a module.
acSecMacExecute	Run the macro.

**Example
(Microsoft Access)**

The following example checks the **AllPermissions** property for the Forms **Container** object and determines whether the user specified by the **UserName** property has full access to forms.

```
Sub CheckAllPermissions()
    Dim dbs As Database, ctr As Container

    ' Return Database variable that points to current database.
    Set dbs = CurrentDb
    ' Return Container object that points to Forms container.
    Set ctr = dbs.Containers!Forms
    ' Print current value of UserName for container.
    Debug.Print ctr.UserName
    ' Check if AllPermissions property includes full access.
    If (ctr.AllPermissions And dbSecFullAccess) Then
        MsgBox "User " & ctr.UserName & " has full access to all forms."
    End If
End Sub
```

Append Method

Applies To   **Documents** Collection; **Fields** Collection; **Groups** Collection; **Indexes** Collection; **Properties** Collection; **QueryDefs** Collection; **Relations** Collection; **TableDefs** Collection; **Users** Collection; **Workspaces** Collection.

Description   Adds a new data access object to a collection.

Syntax   *collection.***Append** *object*

The **Append** method syntax has these parts.

Part	Description
collection	Any collection that can accept new objects (for limitations, see the following table).
object	A variable of an object data type identifying the object being appended, which must be of the same type as the elements of *collection*.

Remarks   Uses of the **Append** method include adding a new table to a database, adding a field to a table, and adding a field to an index.

The appended object becomes a persistent object, stored on disk, until you delete it using the **Delete** method. If the collection is a **Workspaces** collection (which is stored only in memory), the object is active until you remove it using the **Close** method.

The addition of a new object occurs immediately, but you should use the **Refresh** method on any other collections that may be affected by changes to the database structure.

If the object being appended isn't complete (such as when you haven't appended any **Field** objects to a **Fields** collection of an **Index** object before it's appended to an **Indexes** collection) or if the properties set in one or more subordinate objects are incorrect, the **Append** method triggers a trappable error. For example, if you haven't specified a field type and then try to append the **Field** object to the **Fields** collection in a **TableDef** object, the **Append** method triggers a trappable error.

The following table shows some limitations on the use of the **Append** method. The object in the first column is an object containing the collection in the second column. The third column indicates when, if ever, you can append an object to that collection (for example, you can never append a **Container** object to the **Containers** collection of a **Database** object).

Object	Collection	When you can use Append
Workspace	**Databases**	Never; use the **OpenDatabase** method instead
Database	**Containers**	Never
Database	**Recordsets**	Never; use the **OpenRecordset** method instead
Container	**Documents**	Never
Index	**Fields**	When the **Index** object is a new, unappended object
QueryDef	**Fields**	Never
QueryDef	**Parameters**	Never
Recordset	**Fields**	Never
Relation	**Fields**	Never
TableDef	**Fields**	When the **Updatable** property of the **TableDef** is set to **True**
TableDef	**Indexes**	When the **Updatable** property of the **TableDef** is set to **True**
Database, Field, Index, QueryDef, TableDef	**Properties**	When the **Database**, **Field**, **Index**, **QueryDef**, or **TableDef** is persistent

See Also   **Delete** Method, **GetChunk** Method, **Refresh** Method, **Type** Property.

18 Append Method

Example

The following example defines a new field and appends it to a **Fields** collection.

```
Dim dbsBiblio As Database, fldPhone As Field, tdfAuthors As TableDef
                                                ' Open a database.
Set dbsBiblio = DBEngine.Workspaces(0).OpenDatabase("Biblio.mdb")
Set tdfAuthors = dbsBiblio.TableDefs("Authors")
Set fldPhone = dbsBiblio.CreateField()
fldPhone.Name = "Phone"                         ' Set field properties.
fldPhone.Type = dbText
fldPhone.Size = 15
' Append field to collection.
dbsBiblio.tdfAuthors.Fields.Append fldPhone
dbsBiblio.tdfAuthors.Fields.Delete "Phone"
dbsBiblio.Close
```

Example (Microsoft Access)

The following example defines a new **Field** object and appends it to the **Fields** collection of a **TableDef** object.

```
Sub NewField()
    Dim dbs As Database, tdf As TableDef, fld As Field

    ' Return Database variable that points to current database.
    Set dbs = CurrentDb
    Set tdf = dbs.TableDefs!Employees
    ' Create new field in Employees table.
    Set fld = tdf.CreateField("SocialSecurity#", dbText, 15)
    ' Append field to collection.
    dbs.TableDefs!Employees.Fields.Append fld
End Sub
```

Example (Microsoft Excel)

This example creates a new database (NWINDEX.MDB). The example attaches two tables from the C:\Program Files\Common Files\Microsoft Shared\MSquery folder to the database. (On Windows NT™, the two tables are in the \WINDOWS\MSAPPS\MSQUERY folder.)

```
Const sourceDir = "C:\Program Files\Common Files\Microsoft Shared\"

Sub createNWindEx()
    Dim nWindEx As Database, customerTable As TableDef, _
        supplierTable As TableDef
    Dim dataSource As String
    dataSource = "dbase IV;DATABASE=" & sourceDir & "MSquery"
    appPath = Application.Path
    Set nWindEx = Workspaces(0).CreateDatabase(Application.Path _
        & "\NWINDEX.MDB", dbLangGeneral)
    Set customerTable = nWindEx.CreateTableDef("Customer")
    customerTable.Connect = dataSource
    customerTable.SourceTableName = "Customer"
    nWindEx.TableDefs.Append customerTable
    Set supplierTable = nWindEx.CreateTableDef("Supplier")
```

```
            supplierTable.Connect = dataSource
            supplierTable.SourceTableName = "Supplier"
            nWindEx.TableDefs.Append supplierTable
            MsgBox "The database " & nWindEx.Name & " has been created."
            nWindEx.Close
End Sub
```

AppendChunk Method

Applies To **Field** Object.

Description Appends data from a string expression to a Memo or OLE Object **Field** object in the **Fields** collection of a **Recordset** object.

Syntax *recordset*!*field*.**AppendChunk** *source*

The **AppendChunk** method syntax has these parts.

Part	Description
recordset	A variable of an object data type that refers to the **Recordset** object containing the **Fields** collection.
field	The name of a **Field** object whose **Type** property is set to **dbMemo** (Memo), **dbLongBinary** (OLE Object), or the equivalent.
source	A string expression or variable containing the data you want to append to the **Field** object specified by *field*.

Remarks You can use the **AppendChunk** and **GetChunk** methods to access subsets of data in a Memo and OLE Object field.

You can also use these methods to conserve string space when you work with Memo and OLE Object fields. Certain operations (copying, for example) involve temporary strings. If string space is limited, you may need to work with chunks of a field instead of the entire field.

If there is no current record when you use **AppendChunk**, an error occurs.

Note The initial **AppendChunk** (after the first **Edit** method), even if the record already contains data, will simply place the data in the field as the only data. Subsequent **AppendChunk** calls within a single **Edit** session will then add to the data.

See Also **FieldSize** Method, **GetChunk** Method, **Type** Property.

20   AppendChunk Method

Example

This example uses the **GetChunk** method to return consecutive 16K chunks of the Notes field in the Employees table of the database Northwind.mdb. It uses **FieldSize** to determine how many chunks it needs to copy and then copies the chunks to the string array NoteArray() where they can be changed. It then uses **AppendChunk** to copy NoteArray() back to Notes.

```
' This line should be in Declarations section.
Option Base 1

Sub GetNotes
    Const ChunkSize = 16384          ' Set size of chunk.
    Dim intChunks As Integer, lngTotalSize As Long, intX As Integer
    Dim dbsNorthwind As Database, rstEmployees As Recordset
    Set dbsNorthwind = _
        DBEngine.Workspaces(0).OpenDatabase("Northwind.mdb")
                                     ' Open table.
    Set rstEmployees = dbsNorthwind.OpenRecordset("Employees")
    ' Get field size.
    lngTotalSize = rstEmployees![Notes].FieldSize()
    ' How many chunks?
    intChunks = lngTotalSize\ChunkSize - (lngTotalSize Mod ChunkSize _
        <> 0)
    ReDim NoteArray(intChunks) As String * ChunkSize
    ' Get current Notes field.
    For intX = 1 To intChunks
        NoteArray(intX) = rstEmployees![Notes].GetChunk((intX - 1) * _
            ChunkSize, ChunkSize)
    Next intX
    ...                              ' Make changes.
    rstEmployees.Edit                ' Enable editing.
    rstEmployees!Notes = ""          ' Initialize Notes field.
    For intX = 1 To intChunks
        ' Replace with edited Notes.
        rstEmployees![Notes].AppendChunk NoteArray(intX)
    Next intX
    rstEmployees.Update              ' Save changes.
    rstEmployees.Close
    dbsNorthwind.Close               ' Close database.
End Sub
```

Example (Microsoft Access)

The following example appends data to a Notes field in an Employees table. The Notes field is Memo data type. The procedure then returns the contents of the field using the **GetChunk** method, adds to the data, and appends the altered data back to the Notes field using the **AppendChunk** method.

```
Sub AddToMemo()
    Dim dbs As Database, rst As Recordset
    Dim fldNotes As Field, fldFirstName As Field
    Dim lngSize As Long, strChunk As String
```

```
                        ' Return Database variable pointing to current database.
                        Set dbs = CurrentDb
                        ' Create table-type Recordset object.
                        Set rst = dbs.OpenRecordset("Employees")
                        Set fldNotes = rst.Fields!Notes
                        Set fldFirstName = rst.Fields!FirstName
                        rst.MoveLast                    ' Populate Recordset object.
                        rst.MoveFirst                   ' Move to first record.
                        Do Until rst.EOF
                            ' Determine size of field in current record.
                            lngSize = fldNotes.FieldSize
                            If lngSize = 0 Then
                                MsgBox "No text in " & fldNotes.Name & " field!"
                                Exit Do
                            Else
                                ' Return contents of Notes field.
                                strChunk = fldNotes.GetChunk(0, lngSize)
                                ' Alter data.
                                strChunk = strChunk & "  " & fldFirstName.Value & _
                                    " is a terrific employee!"
                                With rst
                                    .Edit                       ' Enable editing.
                                    .[Notes] = ""               ' Initialize field.
                                    .[Notes].AppendChunk strChunk    ' Append altered data.
                                    .Update                     ' Save changes.
                                    .MoveNext                   ' Move to next record.
                                End With
                            End If
                        Loop
                    End Sub
```

Attributes Property

Applies To Field Object, **Relation** Object, **TableDef** Object.

Description Sets or returns a value that indicates one or more characteristics of a **Field** object, a **Relation** object, or a **TableDef** object. For an object not yet appended to a collection, this property is read/write. For an appended **TableDef** object, the property is read/write, although not all of the constants may be set if the object is appended, as noted below.

Settings and Return Values The data type of the setting or return value is **Long**.

22 Attributes Property

For a **Field** object, the value specifies characteristics of the field represented by the **Field** object and can be a sum of these constants.

Constant	Description
dbFixedField	The field size is fixed (default for Numeric fields).
dbVariableField	The field size is variable (Text fields only).
dbAutoIncrField	The field value for new records is automatically incremented to a unique **Long** integer that can't be changed (supported only for Microsoft Jet database tables).
dbUpdatableField	The field value can be changed.
dbDescending	The field is sorted in descending (Z to A or 100 to 0) order (applies only to a **Field** object in a **Fields** collection of an **Index** object). If you omit this constant, the field is sorted in ascending (A to Z or 0 to 100) order (default).
dbSystemField	The field is a replication field (on a **TableDef** object) used on replicable databases and cannot be deleted.

For a **Relation** object, value specifies characteristics of the relationship represented by the **Relation** object and can be a sum of these constants.

Constant	Description
dbRelationUnique	Relationship is one-to-one.
dbRelationDontEnforce	Relationship isn't enforced (no referential integrity).
dbRelationInherited	Relationship exists in a noncurrent database that contains the two attached tables.
dbRelationUpdateCascade	Updates will cascade.
dbRelationDeleteCascade	Deletions will cascade.

Note If you set the **Relation** object's **Attributes** property to activate cascade operations, the Microsoft Jet database engine automatically updates or deletes records in one or more other tables when changes are made to related primary key tables.

For example, suppose you establish a cascade delete relationship between a Customers table and an Orders table. When you delete records from the Customers table, records in the Orders table related to that customer are also deleted. In addition, if you establish cascade delete relationships between the Orders table and other tables, records from those tables are automatically deleted when you delete records from the Customers table.

For a **TableDef** object, value specifies characteristics of the table represented by the **TableDef** object and can be a sum of these **Long** constants.

Constant	Description
dbAttachExclusive	For databases that use the Jet database engine, indicates the table is an attached table opened for exclusive use. This constant can be set on an appended **TableDef** object for a local table, but not for a remote table.
dbAttachSavePWD	For databases that use the Jet database engine, indicates that the user ID and password for the remotely attached table are saved with the connection information. This constant can be set on an appended **TableDef** object for a remote table, but not for a local table.
dbSystemObject	Indicates the table is a system table provided by the Jet database engine. This constant can be set on an appended **TableDef** object.
dbHiddenObject	Indicates the table is a hidden table provided by the Jet database engine. This constant can be set on an appended **TableDef** object.
dbAttachedTable	Indicates the table is an attached table from a non-ODBC database, such as a Microsoft Jet or Paradox® database (read-only).
dbAttachedODBC	Indicates the table is an attached table from an ODBC database, such as Microsoft SQL Server (read-only).

Remarks

These constants are listed in the Data Access (DAO) object library in the Object Browser.

For a **Field** object, use of the **Attributes** property depends on the object that contains the **Fields** collection that the **Field** object is appended to, as shown in the following table.

Object appended to	Usage
Index	Read/write until the **TableDef** object that the **Index** object is appended to is appended to a **Database** object; then the property is read-only
QueryDef	Read-only
Recordset	Read-only
Relation	Not supported
TableDef	Read/write

For a **Relation** object, the **Attributes** property setting is read-only for an object appended to a collection.

24　BeginTrans, CommitTrans, Rollback Methods

When setting multiple attributes, you can combine them by summing the appropriate constants. Any nonmeaningful values are ignored without producing an error. For example, to use the **Attributes** property to make the Text field represented by a new **Field** object variable-sized and changeable, you can use this code:

```
fldLastName.Attributes = dbVariableField + dbUpdatableField
```

Example (Microsoft Access)

The following example checks the **Attributes** property for each table in the current database, and prints the names of system and hidden tables provided by the Microsoft Jet database engine.

Note that the **And** operator performs a bitwise comparison to determine whether an attribute is currently set.

```
Sub CheckAttributes()
    Dim dbs As Database, tdf As TableDef

    ' Return Database variable that points to current database.
    Set dbs = CurrentDb
    For Each tdf In dbs.TableDefs
        ' Compare property setting and constant in question.
        If (tdf.Attributes And dbSystemObject) Or _
            (tdf.Attributes And dbHiddenObject) Then
            Debug.Print tdf.Name
        End If
    Next tdf
End Sub
```

BeginTrans, CommitTrans, Rollback Methods

Applies To　**Workspace** Object.

Description　The transaction methods manage transaction processing during a session defined by a **Workspace** object as follows:

- **BeginTrans** begins a new transaction.
- **CommitTrans** ends the current transaction and saves the changes.
- **Rollback** ends the current transaction and restores the databases in the **Workspace** object to the state they were in when the current transaction began.

Syntax　*workspace*.**BeginTrans** | **CommitTrans** | **Rollback**

The transaction methods have this part.

Part	Description
workspace	A variable of an object data type identifying the **Workspace**.

Remarks

You use these methods with a **Workspace** object when you want to treat a series of changes made to the databases in a session as one unit.

Typically, you use transactions to maintain the integrity of your data when you must update records in two or more tables and make sure changes made are completed (committed) in all tables or none at all (rolled back). For example, if you transfer money from one account to another, you might subtract an amount from one and add the amount to another. If either update fails, the accounts no longer balance. Use the **BeginTrans** method before updating the first record, and then, if any subsequent update fails, you can use the **Rollback** method to undo all of the updates. Use the **CommitTrans** method after you successfully update the last record.

Caution Within one **Workspace** object, transactions are always global to the **Workspace** and aren't limited to only one database or recordset. If you perform operations on more than one database or recordset within a **Workspace** transaction, the **Rollback** method restores all operations on those databases and recordsets.

After you use **CommitTrans**, you can't undo changes made during that transaction unless the transaction is nested within another transaction that is itself rolled back. You can have up to five levels of transactions open at once in a single **Workspace** object by using multiple, nested combinations of **BeginTrans** and **CommitTrans** or **Rollback**. If you nest transactions, you must save or roll back the current transaction before you can save or roll back a transaction at a higher level of nesting. If you want to have simultaneous transactions with overlapping, non-nested scopes, you can create additional **Workspace** objects to contain the concurrent transactions.

If you close a **Workspace** object without saving or rolling back any pending transactions, the transactions are automatically rolled back.

If you use the **CommitTrans** or **Rollback** methods without first using the **BeginTrans** method, an error occurs.

26   BeginTrans, CommitTrans, Rollback Methods

Some databases may not support transactions, in which case the **Transactions** property of the **Database** object or **Recordset** object is **False**. To make sure that the database supports transactions, check the value of the **Transactions** property of the **Database** object before using the **BeginTrans** method. If you are using a **Recordset** object based on more than one database, check the **Transactions** property of the **Recordset** object. If a recordset is based entirely on Microsoft Jet database engine tables, you can always use transactions. Dynaset-type **Recordset** objects based on tables created by other database products, however, may not support transactions. For example, you can't use transactions in a **Recordset** based on a Paradox table. In this case, the **Transactions** property is **False**. If the **Database** or **Recordset** doesn't support transactions, the methods are ignored and no error occurs.

When using external ODBC SQL databases, you can't nest transactions.

Tip In addition to performing transactions to maintain data integrity, you can often improve the performance of your application by breaking operations that require disk access on your database into transaction blocks. This ensures buffering of your operations and may greatly reduce the number of times a disk is accessed.

Note When you begin a transaction, the Jet database engine records its operations in a file kept in the directory specified by the TEMP environment variable on the workstation. If the transaction log file exhausts the available storage on your TEMP drive, the Jet database engine triggers a trappable error (2004). At this point, if you use **CommitTrans**, an indeterminate number of operations are committed but the remaining uncompleted operations are lost, and the operation has to be restarted. Using a **Rollback** method releases the transaction log and rolls back all operations in the transaction.

See Also

Close Method, **CreateWorkspace** Method, **Refresh** Method, **Transactions** Property.

Example

This example changes the job title of all sales representatives in the Employees table of the database. After the **BeginTrans** method starts a transaction that isolates all the changes made to the Employees table, the **CommitTrans** method saves the changes. Notice that you can use the **Rollback** method to undo changes that you saved using the **Update** method.

One or more table pages remain locked while the user decides whether or not to accept the changes. For this reason, this technique isn't recommended but shown only as an example.

```
Sub ChangeTitle
    Dim strName As String, strMessage As String, strPrompt As String
    Dim wspDefault As Workspace, dbsNorthwind As Database
    Dim rstEmployees As Recordset
```

BeginTrans, CommitTrans, Rollback Methods 27

```
        strPrompt = "Change title to Account Executive?"
        Set wspDefault = DBEngine.Workspaces(0)    ' Get default Workspace.
        ' Get current database.
        Set dbsNorthwind = wspDefault.OpenDatabase("Northwind.mdb")
        ' Open table.
        Set rstEmployees = dbsNorthwind.OpenRecordset("Employees", _
            dbOpenTable)
        wspDefault.BeginTrans                ' Start of transaction.
        rstEmployees.MoveFirst
        Do Until rstEmployees.EOF
            If rstEmployees![Title] = "Sales Representative" Then
                strName = rstEmployees![LastName] & ", " & _
                    rstEmployees![FirstName]
                strMessage = "Employee: " & strName & vbCrLf & vbCrLf
                If MsgBox(strMessage & Prompt, vbQuestion + vbYesNo, _
                    "Change Job Title") = YES Then
                    rstEmployees.Edit    ' Enable editing.
                    rstEmployees![Title] = "Account Executive"
                    rstEmployees.Update  ' Save changes.
                End If
            End If
            rstEmployees.MoveNext        ' Move to next record.
        Loop
        If MsgBox("Save all changes?", vbQuestion + vbYesNo, _
            " Save Changes") = YES Then
            wspDefault.CommitTrans       ' Commit changes.
        Else
            wspDefault.Rollback          ' Undo changes.
        End If
        rstEmployees.Close ' Close table.
        dbsNorthwind.Close
    End Sub
```

Example (Microsoft Access)

The following example changes the job title of all sales representatives in an Employees table. After the **BeginTrans** method starts a transaction that isolates all the changes made to the Employees table, the **CommitTrans** method saves the changes. Notice that you can use the **Rollback** method to undo changes that you saved using the **Update** method.

One or more table pages remain locked while the user decides whether or not to accept the changes. Consequently, this technique isn't recommended but only shown as an example.

```
Sub ChangeTitle()
    Dim wsp As Workspace, dbs As Database, rst As Recordset
    Dim strName As String, strMessage As String, strPrompt As String

    strPrompt = "Change title to Account Executive?"
    ' Get default Workspace.
    Set wsp = DBEngine.Workspaces(0)
```

```
' Get current database.
Set dbs = CurrentDb
' Create table-type Recordset object.
Set rst = dbs.OpenRecordset("Employees", dbOpenTable)
' Start of transaction.
wsp.BeginTrans
rst.MoveFirst
Do Until rst.EOF
    If rst![Title] = "Sales Representative" Then
        strName = rst![LastName] & ", " & rst![FirstName]
        strMessage = "Employee: " & strName & vbCrLf & vbCrLf
        If MsgBox(strMessage & strPrompt, vbQuestion + vbYesNo, _
            "Change Job Title") = vbYes Then
            ' Enable editing.
            rst.Edit
            rst![Title] = "Account Executive"
            ' Save changes.
            rst.Update
        End If
    End If
    ' Move to next record.
    rst.MoveNext
Loop
If MsgBox("Save all changes?", vbQuestion + vbYesNo, _
    "Save Changes") = vbYes Then
    wsp.CommitTrans                        ' Commit changes.
Else
    wsp.Rollback                           ' Undo changes.
End If
End Sub
```

BOF, EOF Properties

Applies To   Dynaset-Type **Recordset** Object, **Recordset** Object, Snapshot-Type **Recordset** Object, Table-Type **Recordset** Object.

- **BOF**—returns a value that indicates whether the current record position is before the first record in a **Recordset** object.
- **EOF**—returns a value that indicates whether the current record position is after the last record in a **Recordset** object.

Return Values   The **BOF** property returns **True** (-1) if the current record position is before the first record, and **False** if the current record position is on or after the first record.

BOF, EOF Properties

The **EOF** property returns **True** if the current record position is after the last record, and **False** (0) if the current record position is on or before the last record.

Remarks

The **BOF** and **EOF** properties return values are determined by the location of the current record pointer.

You can use the **BOF** and **EOF** properties to determine whether a **Recordset** object contains records or whether you've gone beyond the limits of a **Recordset** object as you move from record to record.

If either the **BOF** or **EOF** property is **True**, there is no current record.

If you open a **Recordset** object containing no records, the **BOF** and **EOF** properties are set to **True**, and the recordset's **RecordCount** property setting is 0. When you open a **Recordset** object that contains at least one record, the first record is the current record and the **BOF** and **EOF** properties are **False**; they remain **False** until you move beyond the beginning or end of the **Recordset** object using the **MovePrevious** or **MoveNext** method, respectively. When you move beyond the beginning or end of the recordset, there is no current record or no record exists.

If you delete the last remaining record in the **Recordset** object, the **BOF** and **EOF** properties may remain **False** until you attempt to reposition the current record.

If you use the **MoveLast** method on a **Recordset** object containing records, the last record becomes the current record; if you then use the **MoveNext** method, the current record becomes invalid and the **EOF** property is set to **True**. Conversely, if you use the **MoveFirst** method on a **Recordset** object containing records, the first record becomes the current record; if you then use the **MovePrevious** method, there is no current record and the **BOF** property is set to **True**.

Typically, when you work with all the records in a **Recordset** object, your code will loop through the records using the **MoveNext** method until the **EOF** property is set to **True**.

If you use the **MoveNext** method while the **EOF** property is set to **True** or the **MovePrevious** method while the **BOF** property is set to **True**, an error occurs.

This table shows which Move methods are allowed with different combinations of the **BOF** and **EOF** properties.

	MoveFirst, MoveLast	MovePrevious, Move < 0	Move 0	MoveNext, Move > 0
BOF=True, EOF=False	Allowed	Error	Error	Allowed

BOF, EOF Properties

	MoveFirst, MoveLast	MovePrevious, Move < 0	Move 0	MoveNext, Move > 0
BOF=False, EOF=True	Allowed	Allowed	Error	Error
Both **True**	Error	Error	Error	Error
Both **False**	Allowed	Allowed	Allowed	Allowed

Allowing a Move method doesn't mean that the method will successfully locate a record. It merely indicates that an attempt to perform the specified Move method is allowed and won't generate an error. The state of the **BOF** and **EOF** flags may change as a result of the attempted Move.

Effects of specific methods on the **BOF** and **EOF** property settings are as follow:

- An **OpenRecordset** method internally invokes a **MoveFirst** method. Therefore, an **OpenRecordset** method on an empty set of records results in the **BOF** and **EOF** properties being set to **True**. (See the following table for the behavior of a failed **MoveFirst** method.)

- All Move methods that successfully locate a record clear (set to **False**) both the **BOF** and **EOF** properties.

- An **AddNew** method followed by an **Update** method that successfully inserts a new record will clear the **BOF** property, but only if the **EOF** property is already set to **True**. The state of the **EOF** property will always remain unchanged. As defined by the Microsoft Jet database engine, the current record pointer of an empty recordset is at the end of a file, so any new record is inserted after the current record.

- Any **Delete** method, even if it removes the only remaining record from a recordset, won't change the setting of the **BOF** or **EOF** property.

The effect of Move methods that don't locate a record on the **BOF** and **EOF** property settings is shown in the following table.

	BOF	EOF
MoveFirst, MoveLast	**True**	**True**
Move 0	No change	No change
MovePrevious, Move < 0	**True**	No change
MoveNext, Move > 0	No change	**True**

See Also MoveFirst, MoveLast, MoveNext, MovePrevious Methods.

BOF, EOF Properties

Example

This example uses the **BOF** and **EOF** properties to find the beginning and end of an Orders table. The example moves through the records from the beginning of the file to the end and then from the end to the beginning. Notice that there is no current record immediately following the first loop.

```
Set dbsNorthwind = DBEngine.Workspaces(0).OpenDatabase("Northwind.mdb")
Set rstOrders = dbsNorthwind.OpenRecordset("Orders")   ' Open Recordset.
Do Until rstOrders.EOF
    ' Do until end of file.
    rstOrders.MoveNext
    ' Move to next record.
    ...
Loop
rstOrders.MoveLast
    ' Establish a current record.
Do Until rstOrders.BOF
    ' Do until beginning of file.
    rstOrders.MovePrevious
    ' Move to previous record.
    ...
Loop
rstOrders.Close
dbsNorthwind.Close
```

Example (Microsoft Access)

The following example uses the **EOF** property of a **Recordset** object to move the current record pointer past the last record in the **Recordset** object, then uses the **BOF** property to move the current record pointer to before the first record in the **Recordset** object.

```
Sub EndsOfFile()
    Dim dbs As Database, rst As Recordset

    ' Return Database variable that points to current database.
    Set dbs = CurrentDb
    Set rst = dbs.OpenRecordset("Orders")
    ' Do until end of file.
    Do Until rst.EOF
        ' Move to next record.
        rst.MoveNext
        .
        .
        .
    Loop
    ' Move to last record to set a current record.
    rst.MoveLast
    ' Do until beginning of file.
    Do Until rst.BOF
        rst.MovePrevious
```

```
            .
            .
            .
        Loop
        rst.Close
        dbs.Close
End Sub
```

Bookmark Property

Applies To Dynaset-Type **Recordset** Object, **Recordset** Object, Snapshot-Type **Recordset** Object, Table-Type **Recordset** Object.

Description Sets or returns a bookmark that uniquely identifies the current record in a **Recordset** object or sets the current record in a **Recordset** object to a valid bookmark.

Settings and Return Values The setting or returned value is a string expression or variant expression that evaluates to a valid bookmark. (Data type is **Variant** array of **Byte** data.)

Remarks You can use the **Bookmark** property with **Recordset** objects. For a **Recordset** object based entirely on Microsoft Jet database engine tables, the value of the **Bookmarkable** property is **True** and bookmarks can be used. Other database products may not support bookmarks, however. For example, you can't use bookmarks in any **Recordset** object based on an attached Paradox table that has no primary key.

When a **Recordset** object is created or opened, each of its records already has a unique bookmark. You can save the bookmark for the current record by assigning the value of the **Bookmark** property to a variable. To quickly return to that record at any time after moving to a different record, set the **Recordset** object's **Bookmark** property to the value of that variable.

There is no limit to the number of bookmarks you can establish. To create a bookmark for a record other than the current record, move to the desired record and assign the value of the **Bookmark** property to a **String** variable that identifies the record.

To make sure the **Recordset** object supports bookmarks, inspect the value of its **Bookmarkable** property before you use the **Bookmark** property. If the **Bookmarkable** property is **False**, the **Recordset** object doesn't support bookmarks, and using the **Bookmark** property results in a trappable error.

If you create a copy of a **Recordset** object using the **Clone** method, the **Bookmark** property settings for the original and the duplicate **Recordset** objects are identical and can be used interchangeably. However, you can't use bookmarks from different **Recordset** objects interchangeably, even if they were created using the same object or the same SQL statement.

If you set the **Bookmark** property to a value that represents a deleted record, a trappable error occurs.

To refresh the contents of a record, set the **Bookmark** property to itself. (This technique, however, also cancels any pending operations invoked by the **Edit** or **AddNew** methods.) For example:

```
rstCustomers.Bookmark = rstCustomers.Bookmark
```

The value of the **Bookmark** property isn't the same as a record number.

Note The **Bookmark** property doesn't apply to forward-only scrolling snapshots.

See Also   **Bookmarkable** Property, **RecordCount** Property.

Specifics (Microsoft Access)   When you write Visual Basic® code that uses the **Bookmark** property, you must include an **Option Compare Binary** statement in the Declarations section of the module. The **Bookmark** property sets and returns a bookmark, which is a **Variant** array of **Byte** data. The string comparison method for the module must therefore be binary. If a bookmark is evaluated with a text-based string comparison method, such as the **Option Compare Text** statement or the default setting for the **Option Compare Database** statement, the current record may be set to an incorrect record.

Note Don't confuse this property with the Microsoft Access **Bookmark** property, which applies to a **Form** object and stores a bookmark for a particular record in the table or query underlying the form. These two properties do not interfere with each other; you can have separate bookmarks on a form and on a **Recordset** object at the same time.

Example   This example shows how you can save your place in a **Recordset** by saving a bookmark. Once saved, this bookmark can be applied to the **Bookmark** property to reposition the current record pointer to any location in the **Recordset**. The **FindYear** function works with the Biblio.mdb database. It looks up all titles in a given **Recordset** published in a given year, and fills a string array with the bookmarks of any records that match.

```
Function FindYear (intYear As Integer, rstBooks As Recordset, _
    avarRecord() As Variant) As Integer
    Dim intCount As Integer
    rstBooks.FindFirst "[Year Published] = " & intYear
```

34 Bookmark Property

```
            If (rstBooks.NoMatch = True) Or (rstBooks.Bookmarkable = False) _
                Then
                FindYear = 0
                Exit Function
            Else
                Do Until rstBooks.NoMatch = True
                    avarRecord(intCount) = rstBooks.Bookmark
                    rstBooks.FindNext "[Year Published] = " & intYear
                    intCount = intCount + 1
                Loop
            End If
            FindYear = intCount
        End Function
```

Example (Microsoft Access)

The following example moves through the records of the Employees table from the beginning of the file to the end and stores the value of the **Bookmark** property for each record in an array.

```
' Include this statement in the Declarations section of the module.
Option Compare Binary

Sub RecordPositions()
    Dim dbs As Database, rst As Recordset, fld As Field
    Dim intI As Integer
    ' Declare array to hold bookmarks.
    Dim varRecord() As Variant

    ' Return Database variable that points to current database.
    Set dbs = CurrentDb
    ' Open a table-type Recordset object.
    Set rst = dbs.OpenRecordset("Employees")
    Set fld = rst.Fields!LastName
    ' Populate the Recordset object.
    rst.MoveLast
    rst.MoveFirst
    ' Redimension array with value of RecordCount as upper bound.
    ReDim varRecord(0 To rst.RecordCount - 1)
    intI = 0
    ' Check Bookmarkable property of Recordset object.
    If rst.Bookmarkable Then
        Do Until rst.EOF
            ' Populate array with bookmarks.
            varRecord(intI) = rst.Bookmark
            ' Increment counter.
            intI = intI + 1
            rst.MoveNext
        Loop
    End If
End Sub
```

Example **(Microsoft Excel)**	This example prompts the user for a two-letter abbreviation for a state. The example uses this value to find up to 101 matching records in the Customer recordset in the NWINDEX.MDB database. It then marks each record with a bookmark and copies the values of the first and third fields onto Sheet1. To create the NWINDEX.MDB database, run the Microsoft Excel example for the **CreateDatabase** method.

```
Dim Found(100)
i = 0
Set db = Workspaces(0).OpenDatabase(Application.Path & "\NWINDEX.MDB")
Set rs = db.OpenRecordset("Customer")
Sheets("Sheet1").Activate
region = Application.InputBox("What state do you want data from?", _
    "Specify two letters (e.g. 'WA')", Type:=2)
If region = False Then         ' user cancelled InputBox
    Exit Sub
End If
criteria = "[REGION] = '" & region & "'"
rs.FindFirst criteria
If rs.NoMatch Or rs.Bookmarkable = False Then
    MsgBox "No records for this state"
    Exit Sub
Else
    Do Until rs.NoMatch = True
        i = i + 1
        Found(i) = rs.Bookmark
        rs.FindNext criteria
    Loop
End If
For n = 1 To i
    rs.Bookmark = Found(n)
    Cells(n + 1, 1).Value = rs.fields(0).Value
    Cells(n + 1, 2).Value = rs.fields(2).Value
Next
MsgBox "There are " & i & " records from this region"
rs.Close
db.Close
```

Bookmarkable Property

Applies To	Dynaset-Type **Recordset** Object, **Recordset** Object, Snapshot-Type **Recordset** Object, Table-Type **Recordset** Object.
Description	Returns **True** (-1) if the **Recordset** object supports bookmarks, which you can set using the **Bookmark** property.

Remarks

You can use the **Bookmarkable** property with **Recordset** objects.

Check the **Bookmarkable** property setting before you attempt to set or check the **Bookmark** property to make sure that the **Recordset** object supports bookmarks.

For a **Recordset** object based entirely on Microsoft Jet database engine tables, the value of the **Bookmarkable** property is **True**, and bookmarks can be used. Other database products may not support bookmarks, however. For example, you can't use bookmarks in any **Recordset** object based on an attached Paradox table that has no primary key.

Note The **Bookmarkable** property doesn't apply to forward-only scrolling snapshots.

See Also

Bookmark Property, **RecordCount** Property.

Example

See the **Bookmark** property example.

Example (Microsoft Excel)

See the **Bookmark** property example (Microsoft Excel).

CacheSize, CacheStart Properties

Applies To

Dynaset-Type **Recordset** Object, **Recordset** Object.

- **CacheSize**—sets or returns a value that specifies the number of records in a dynaset-type **Recordset** object containing data to be locally cached from an ODBC data source.
- **CacheStart**—sets or returns a value that specifies the bookmark of the first record in the **Recordset** object to be cached.

Settings and Returned Values

The setting or return value is a number or string expression. The setting for **CacheSize** specifies the number of records and must be between 5 and 1200, but not greater than available memory. A typical value is 100. A setting of 0 turns off caching. (Data type is **Long**.) The setting for **CacheStart** specifies a bookmark. (Data type is **String**.)

Remarks

Data caching improves the performance of an application that retrieves data from a remote server through dynaset-type **Recordset** objects. A cache is a space in local memory that holds the data most recently retrieved from the server in the event that the data will be requested again while the application is running. When data is requested, the Microsoft Jet database engine checks the cache for the requested data first rather than retrieving it from the server, which takes more time. Data that doesn't come from an ODBC data source isn't saved in the cache.

Any ODBC data source, such as an attached table, can have a local cache. To create the cache, open a **Recordset** object from the remote data source, set the **CacheSize** and **CacheStart** properties, and then use the **FillCache** method or step through the records using the Move methods.

The **CacheSize** property setting can be based on the number of records your application can work with at one time. For example, if you're using a **Recordset** object as the source of the data to be displayed on screen, you could set its **CacheSize** property to 20 to display 20 records at one time.

The **CacheStart** property setting is the bookmark of the first record in the **Recordset** object to be cached. You can use the bookmark of any record to set the **CacheStart** property. Make the record you want to start the cache with the current record, establish a bookmark for that record, and set the **CacheStart** property to the bookmark.

The Jet database engine requests records within the cache range from the cache, and it requests records outside the cache range from the server.

Notes
- Records retrieved from the cache don't reflect changes made concurrently to the source data by other users.
- To force an update of all the cached data, set the **CacheSize** property of the **Recordset** object to 0, set it to the size of the cache you originally requested, and then use the **FillCache** method.

See Also

Bookmark Property, **Bookmarkable** Property, **FillCache** Method.

Specifics (Microsoft Access)

When you use the **CacheStart** property in a Microsoft Access module, you must include an **Option Compare Binary** statement in the Declarations section of the module. The bookmark set or returned by the **CacheStart** property is a **Variant** array of **Byte** data, so the string comparison method for the module must be binary. If a bookmark is evaluated with a text-based string comparison method, such as the **Option Compare Text** statement or the default setting for the **Option Compare Database** statement, the current record may be set to an incorrect record.

Example (Client/Server)

This example moves through all records in a **Recordset** twice; once with no cache and once with a 50 record cache. The example then displays the performance statistics for the uncached and cached runs through the **Recordset**.

```
Dim wspDefault As Workspace, dbsPubs As Database
Dim tdfPerformanceTest As TableDef, rstRemote As Recordset
Dim strNoCache As String, strCache As String

Set wspDefault = DBEngine.Workspaces(0)
Set dbsPubs = wspDefault.OpenDatabase("PUBLISH.mdb")
Set tdfPerformanceTest = dbsPubs.CreateTableDef("TestData")
```

38 CacheSize, CacheStart Properties

```
            tdfPerformanceTest.Connect = _
                "ODBC;DATABASE=pubs;UID=sa;PWD=;DSN=Publishers"
            tdfPerformanceTest.SourceTableName = "dbo.roysched"
            dbsPubs.TableDefs.Append tdfPerformanceTest
            ConnectSource = True
            Set rstRemote = dbsPubs.OpenRecordset("TestData")

            MsgBox "This example moves through all records in the Recordset " & _
                "twice; once with no cache and once with a 50 record cache."
            ' Start uncached run
            tmStart = Timer
            For i% = 1 To 2
                rstRemote.MoveFirst
                While Not rstRemote.EOF
                    v = rstRemote(0)
                    rstRemote.MoveNext
                Wend
            Next i%
            tmEnd = Timer
            strNoCache = "Time without caching: " & Format$(tmEnd - tmStart) & _
                Chr$(13) & Chr$(10)
            ' Start cached run
            rstRemote.MoveFirst
            rstRemote.CacheStart = rstRemote.Bookmark
            rstRemote.CacheSize = 50
            tmStart = Timer
            For i% = 1 To 2
                rstRemote.MoveFirst
                While Not rstRemote.EOF
                    v = rstRemote(0)
                    rstRemote.MoveNext
                Wend
            Next i%
            tmEnd = Timer
            strCache = "Time with 50 record cache: " & Format$(tmEnd - tmStart) & _
                Chr$(13) & Chr$(10)
            ' Display performance results
            MsgBox "Caching Performance Results:" & Chr$(13) & Chr$(10) & _
                strNoCache & strCache
            rstRemote.Close
            dbsPubs.Close
```

Example (Microsoft Access)

The following example opens a **Recordset** object from an attached Orders table that is stored on an ODBC server. The procedure next sets the **CacheSize** and **CacheStart** properties, and then uses the **FillCache** method to cache data from the server to the database.

```
            Sub CacheData()
                Dim rst As Recordset, dbs As Database
```

```
                        ' Return Database variable pointing to current database.
                        Set dbs = CurrentDb
                        ' Open local dynaset-type Recordset object.
                        Set rst = dbs.OpenRecordset("Orders", DbOpenDynaset)
                        ' Locate record with OrderID of 11000.
                        rst.FindFirst "OrderID = 11000"
                        ' Start caching records beginning with OrderID 11000.
                        rst.CacheStart = rst.Bookmark
                        rst.CacheSize = 12              ' Set cache size to 12 records.
                        rst.FillCache                   ' Fill cache.
                        ' Display rows.
                           .
                           .
                           .
                        End Sub
```

CancelUpdate Method

Applies To Dynaset-Type **Recordset** Object, **Recordset** Object, Table-Type **Recordset** Object.

Description Cancels any pending updates for the **Recordset** object represented by the *object* placeholder.

Syntax *object*.**CancelUpdate**

The *object* placeholder represents an object expression that evaluates to an object in the Applies To list.

Remarks The **CancelUpdate** method cancels any pending updates due to an **Edit** or **AddNew** operation. For example, if a user invokes the **Edit** or **AddNew** method and hasn't yet invoked the **Update** method, **CancelUpdate** cancels any changes made after **Edit** or **AddNew** was invoked.

Note Using the **CancelUpdate** method has the same effect as moving to another record without using the **Update** method except that the current record doesn't change, and various properties, such as **BOF** and **EOF**, aren't updated.

Use the **EditMode** property to determine if there is a pending operation that can be canceled.

See Also **AddNew** Method; **BOF**, **EOF** Properties; **EditMode** Property.

40   Clone Method

Example (Microsoft Access)

The following example creates a new record in an Employees table, enters values, and prompts the user to save the changes. If the user chooses not to save the changes, the **Update** method is canceled.

```
Sub NewRecord()
    Dim dbs As Database, rst As Recordset

    ' Return Database variable pointing to current database.
    Set dbs = CurrentDb
    Set rst = dbs.OpenRecordset("Employees")
    With rst
        ' Add new record to end of Recordset object.
        .AddNew
        .[LastName] = "Christopher"          ' Add data.
        .[FirstName] = "Kevin"
    End With
    ' Prompt user to save changes.
    If MsgBox("Save these changes?", vbYesNo) = vbNo Then
        ' If user chooses No, cancel changes.
        rst.CancelUpdate
    Else
        ' If user chooses Yes, save changes.
        rst.Update
    End If
    dbs.Close
End Sub
```

Clone Method

Applies To   Dynaset-Type **Recordset** Object, **Recordset** Object, Snapshot-Type **Recordset** Object, Table-Type **Recordset** Object.

Description   Creates a duplicate **Recordset** object that refers to the original object.

Syntax   **Set** *duplicate* = *original*.**Clone( )**

The **Clone** method syntax has these parts.

Part	Description
duplicate	A variable of an object data type identifying the duplicate **Recordset** object you're creating.
original	A variable of an object data type identifying the **Recordset** object you want to duplicate.

Clone Method 41

Remarks Use the **Clone** method to create multiple, duplicate **Recordset** objects. Each recordset can have its own current record. Using **Clone** by itself doesn't change the data in the objects or in their underlying structures. Using the **Clone** method, you can share bookmarks between two or more recordsets because their bookmarks are interchangeable.

Note When used on a table-type **Recordset** object, the **Index** property setting is not cloned on the new copy of the **Recordset**. You must copy the **Index** property setting manually.

You can use **Clone** when you want to perform an operation on a recordset that requires multiple current records. This is faster and more efficient than creating a second recordset.

A recordset you create with **Clone** initially lacks a current record. To make a record current before you use the recordset object specified by *duplicate*, you must set the **Bookmark** property or use one of the Move methods, one of the Find methods (for dynaset- and snapshot-type **Recordset** objects only), or the **Seek** method (for table-type **Recordset** objects only).

Cloning a recordset that resulted from running a **QueryDef** object doesn't run the query again.

Using the **Close** method on either the original or duplicate object doesn't affect the other object. For example, using **Close** on the original **Recordset** does not close the clone.

Note You can't use the **Clone** method with forward-only-scrolling snapshots.

See Also **Bookmark** Property.

Specifics (Microsoft Access) If you use the **Bookmark** property of a **Recordset** object in a Microsoft Access module, you must include an **Option Compare Binary** statement in the Declarations section of the module. A bookmark is a **Variant** array of **Byte** data, so the string comparison method for the module must be binary. If a bookmark is evaluated with a text-based string comparison method, such as the **Option Compare Text** statement or the default setting for the **Option Compare Database** statement, the current record may be set to an incorrect record.

Example This example creates a **Recordset** object based on the Orders table in the Northwind database and uses the **Clone** method to create a second **Recordset** object. Each **Recordset** object has its own current record that can be moved independently of the other. A bookmark is used to initially make the same record current in both **Recordset** objects.

```
Dim dbsNorthwind As DatabaseDim rstOriginal As Recordset, rstDuplicate _
    As RecordsetDim strPosition As String
```

42 Clone Method

```
Set dbsNorthwind = DBEngine.Workspaces(0).Databases("Northwind.mdb")
' Create first Recordset.
Set rstOriginal = dbsNorthwind![Orders].OpenRecordset(dbOpenDynaset)
strPosition = rstOriginal.Bookmark   ' Save current record position.
rstDuplicate = rstOriginal.Clone ()  ' Create duplicate.
Recordset.rstDuplicate.Bookmark = strPosition          ' Go to same record.
```

**Example
(Microsoft Access)**

The following example creates a **Recordset** object using an SQL statement on an Employees table and then uses the **Clone** method to create a clone of the **Recordset** object so that bookmarks can be shared between the two objects. This technique is especially useful when you have to compare the results of a query from more than one point at the same time.

The following function creates a dynaset-type **Recordset** object on an Employees table, then creates a clone of that **Recordset** object. The function reads and stores in a string variable the value of the **Bookmark** property for the current record, in this case the second record in the original **Recordset** object. The **Bookmark** property of the duplicate **Recordset** object is set to this string, making the second record the current record in this **Recordset** object as well. The current values of the LastName field for both recordsets are identical, as you can see once they are printed in the Debug window.

```
Sub CreateClone()
    Dim dbs As Database
    Dim rstEmployees As Recordset, rstDuplicate As Recordset
    Dim fldName As Field, strBook As String

    ' Return Database variable that points to current database.
    Set dbs = CurrentDb
    ' Open dynaset-type Recordset object.
    Set rstEmployees = dbs.OpenRecordset("SELECT * FROM Employees " & _
        " ORDER by [LastName]")
    ' Clone Recordset object.
    Set rstDuplicate = rstEmployees.Clone
    Set fldName = rstEmployees.Fields!LastName
    ' Set current record.
    rstEmployees.MoveFirst
    ' Move to second record.
    rstEmployees.MoveNext
    ' Get Bookmark value and print current field value.
    If rstEmployees.Bookmarkable Then
        strBook = rstEmployees.Bookmark
        Debug.Print fldName.value
    Else
    ' If Recordset object doesn't support bookmarks, exit procedure.
        Exit Sub
    End If
    ' Set Bookmark property of clone to obtained value.
```

```
            rstDuplicate.Bookmark = strBook
            Debug.Print fldName.value
        End Sub
```

**Example
(Microsoft Excel)**

This example displays a custom dialog box containing the lists of data from the CONTACTS and CUSTMR_ID fields in the Customer recordset of the NWINDEX.MDB database.

To create the NWINDEX.MDB database, run the Microsoft Excel example for the **CreateDatabase** method.

```
Dim db As Database
Dim rs1 As Recordset, rs2 As Recordset
Set db = Workspaces(0).OpenDatabase(Application.Path & "\NWINDEX.MDB")
Set rs1 = db.OpenRecordset("SELECT * FROM Customer" _
    & " WHERE [REGION] = 'WA' ORDER BY [CUSTMR_ID];")
Set theDialog = DialogSheets.Add
Set list1 = theDialog.ListBoxes.Add(78, 42, 84, 80)
Set list2 = theDialog.ListBoxes.Add(183, 42, 84, 80)
Set rs2 = rs1.Clone()
rs2.MoveFirst
Do Until rs1.EOF
    list1.AddItem (rs1.Fields("CONTACT").Value)
    rs1.MoveNext
Loop
Do Until rs2.EOF
    list2.AddItem (rs2.Fields("CUSTMR_ID").Value)
    rs2.MoveNext
Loop
rs1.Close
rs2.Close
db.Close
```

Close Method

Applies To   **Database** Object, Dynaset-Type **Recordset** Object, **Recordset** Object, Snapshot-Type **Recordset** Object, Table-Type **Recordset** Object, **Workspace** Object.

Description   Closes an open data access object.

Syntax   *object*.**Close**

The *object* placeholder represents the name of an open **Database**, **Recordset**, or **Workspace** object.

Close Method

Remarks

Closing an open object removes it from the collection to which it's appended. Any attempt to close the default workspace is ignored.

To remove objects from collections other than the **Databases**, **Recordsets**, and **Workspaces** collections, use the **Delete** method on those collections.

Caution Use the **Update** method (if there are pending edits) and the **Close** method on all open recordset objects before you close a database. If you exit a procedure that declares recordset or **Database** objects, the database is closed, any unsaved changes are lost, all pending transactions are rolled back, and any pending edits to your data are lost.

If you try to close a **Database** object while any recordset objects are open, or if you try to close a **Workspace** object while any **Database** objects belonging to that specific **Workspace** are open, those **Recordset** objects will be closed and any pending updates or edits will be rolled back.

If you try to close a **Workspace** object while any **Database** objects belonging to it are open, the operation closes all **Database** objects belonging to that specific **Workspace** object which may result in **Recordset** objects being closed and pending edits lost.

If the **Database** object is defined outside the scope of the procedure, and you exit the procedure without closing it, the **Database** object will remain open until explicitly closed or the module in which it is defined is out of scope.

If the **Database**, **Recordset**, or **Workspace** object named by *object* is already closed when you use **Close**, a trappable error occurs.

Using the **Close** method on either the original or duplicate object doesn't affect the other object. For example, using **Close** on the original **Recordset** does not close the clone.

See Also

Clone Method, **Delete** Method, **OpenDatabase** Method, **OpenRecordset** Method.

Specifics (Microsoft Access)

If a Visual Basic procedure contains an object variable that represents the database currently open in Microsoft Access, using the **Close** method on that object will cause the variable to go out of scope. The **Close** method will not affect the database that is open in the Microsoft Access Database window.

Example

This example opens and then closes a database and a table-type **Recordset** object for the Customers table in the database.

```
Dim dbsNorthwind As Database, rstCustomers As Recordset
' Open database.
Set dbsNorthwind = DBEngine.Workspaces(0).OpenDatabase("Northwind.mdb")
' Open table.
Set rstCustomers = dbsNorthwind.OpenRecordset("Customers")
```

```
    ...
    rstCustomers.Close           ' Close recordset.
    dbsNorthwind.Close           ' Close database.
```

Example (Microsoft Access)

The following example creates a **Database** object that points to the current database and opens a table-type **Recordset** object based on a Customers table in the database. It then uses the **Close** method on these object variables, which causes them to go out of scope and frees the memory resources they have been using.

```
Sub UseClose()
    Dim dbs As Database, rst As Recordset

    ' Return Database object that represents current database.
    Set dbs = CurrentDb
    ' Create table-type Recordset.
    Set rst = dbs.OpenRecordset("Customers")
    .
    .
    .
    rst.Close                                    ' Close recordset.
    dbs.Close                                    ' Close database.
End Sub
```

Example (Microsoft Excel)

This example opens the Customer recordset of the NWINDEX.MDB database, counts how many records are available, and enters the result on Sheet1.

To create the NWINDEX.MDB database, run the Microsoft Excel example for the **CreateDatabase** method.

```
Dim db As Database, rs As Recordset
Set db = Workspaces(0).OpenDatabase(Application.Path & "\NWINDEX.MDB")
Set rs = db.OpenRecordset("Customer")
Set resultsSheet = Sheets("Sheet1")
resultsSheet.Activate
With resultsSheet.Cells(1, 1)
    .Value = "Records in " & rs.Name & " table:"
    .Font.Bold = True
    .EntireColumn.AutoFit
End With
rs.MoveLast
resultsSheet.Cells(1, 2).Value = rs.RecordCount
rs.Close
db.Close
```

Clustered Property

Applies To **Index** Object.

Description Sets or returns a value that indicates whether an **Index** object represents a clustering index for a table. This property setting is read/write for a new **Index** object not yet appended to a collection and read-only for an existing **Index** object in an **Indexes** collection.

Settings and Return Values The setting or return value is **True** if the **Index** object represents a clustering index. The data type is Boolean.

Remarks A clustering index consists of one or more nonkey fields that, taken together, arrange all records in a table in a predefined order. A clustering index provides efficient access to records in a table in which the index values may not be unique.

Notes
- The **Clustered** property is ignored for databases that use the Microsoft Jet database engine because the Jet database engine doesn't support clustering indexes.
- For ODBC databases, the **Clustered** property always returns **False** (0); it does not detect whether the ODBC database has a clustering index or not.
- You don't have to create indexes for tables, but in large, unindexed tables, accessing a specific record can take a long time. The **Attributes** property of each **Field** object in the **Index** object determines the order of records and consequently determines the access techniques to use for that index.

See Also **Attributes** Property, **Primary** Property, **Unique** Property.

CollatingOrder Property

Applies To **Database** Object, **Field** Object.

Description Returns a value that specifies the sequence of the sort order in text for string comparison or sorting. This property setting is read-only.

CollatingOrder Property

Return Values The possible return values are:

Values	Description
dbSortGeneral	Use the General (English, French, German, Portuguese, Italian, and Modern Spanish) sort order.
dbSortArabic	Use the Arabic sort order.
dbSortCyrillic	Use the Russian sort order.
dbSortCzech	Use the Czech sort order.
dbSortDutch	Use the Dutch sort order.
dbSortGreek	Use the Greek sort order.
dbSortHebrew	Use the Hebrew sort order.
dbSortHungarian	Use the Hungarian sort order.
dbSortIcelandic	Use the Icelandic sort order.
dbSortJapanese	Use the Japanese sort order.
dbSortNeutral	Use the neutral sort order.
dbSortNorwdan	Use the Norwegian or Danish sort order.
dbSortPDXIntl	Use the Paradox International sort order.
dbSortPDXNor	Use the Paradox Norwegian or Danish sort order.
dbSortPDXSwe	Use the Paradox Swedish or Finnish sort order.
dbSortPolish	Use the Polish sort order.
dbSortSpanish	Use the Spanish sort order.
dbSortSwedFin	Use the Swedish or Finnish sort order.
dbSortTurkish	Use the Turkish sort order.
dbSortUndefined	The sort order is undefined or unknown.

Remarks These constants are listed in the Data Access (DAO) object library in the Object Browser.

For a **Field** object, the **CollatingOrder** property depends on the object that contains the **Fields** collection, as shown in the following table.

Object appended to	Usage
Index	Not supported
QueryDef	Read-only
Recordset	Read-only
Relation	Not supported
TableDef	Read only

The **CollatingOrder** property setting corresponds to the *locale* argument of the **CreateDatabase** method when the database was created or the **CompactDatabase** method when the database was most recently compacted.

Check the **CollatingOrder** property setting of a **Database** or **Field** object to find out the string comparison method for the database or field. You can set the **CollatingOrder** property of a new **Field** object if you want the setting of the **Field** object to differ from that of the **Database** object that contains it.

The **CollatingOrder** and **Attributes** property settings of a **Field** object in a **Fields** collection of an **Index** object together determine the sequence and direction of the sort order in an index. However, you can't set a collating order for an individual index—only for an entire table.

See Also **Attributes** Property.

Example (Microsoft Access) The following example checks the **CollatingOrder** property for the current database.

```
Sub SetSortOrder()
    Dim dbs As Database

    ' Return Database variable that points to current database.
    Set dbs = CurrentDb
    ' Check CollatingOrder property for database.
    Debug.Print dbs.CollatingOrder
End Sub
```

CommitTrans Method

See BeginTrans, CommitTrans, Rollback Methods.

CompactDatabase Method

Applies To **DBEngine** Object.

Description Copies, compacts, and gives you the option of changing the version, collating order, and encryption of a closed database.

Syntax **DBEngine.CompactDatabase** *olddb*, *newdb* [, *locale* [, *options* [, ↳ **;pwd=***password*]]]

CompactDatabase Method

The **CompactDatabase** method syntax has these parts.

Part	Description
olddb	A string expression that identifies an existing, closed database. It can be a full path and filename, such as "C:\MYDB.mdb". If the filename has an extension, you must specify it. If your network supports it, you can also specify a network path, such as "\\MYSERVER\MYSHARE\MYDIR\MYDB.mdb".
newdb	A string expression that is the full path of the compacted database that you're creating. You can also specify a network path as with *olddb*. You can't use the *newdb* argument to specify the same database file as *olddb*.
locale	A string expression used to specify collating order for creating *newdb*, as specified in Settings. If you omit this argument, the locale of *newdb* is the same as *olddb*.
options	An integer that indicates one or more options, as specified in Settings. You can combine options by summing the corresponding constants.
password	An optional string argument containing a password, if the database is password protected. The string ";pwd=" must precede the actual password.

Settings

You can use one of the following constants for the *locale* argument to specify the **CollatingOrder** property for string comparisons of text.

Constant	Collating order
dbLangGeneral	English, German, French, Portuguese, Italian, and Modern Spanish
dbLangArabic	Arabic
dbLangCyrillic	Russian
dbLangCzech	Czech
dbLangDutch	Dutch
dbLangGreek	Greek
dbLangHebrew	Hebrew
dbLangHungarian	Hungarian
dbLangIcelandic	Icelandic
dbLangNordic	Nordic languages (Microsoft Jet database engine version 1.0 only)
dbLangNorwdan	Norwegian and Danish

50   CompactDatabase Method

Constant	Collating order
dbLangPolish	Polish
dbLangSpanish	Traditional Spanish
dbLangSwedfin	Swedish and Finnish
dbLangTurkish	Turkish

You can use one of the following constants in the *options* argument to specify whether to encrypt or to decrypt the database as it's compacted.

Constant	Description
dbEncrypt	Encrypt the database while compacting.
dbDecrypt	Decrypt the database while compacting.

If you omit an encryption constant or if you include both **dbDecrypt** and **dbEncrypt**, newdb will have the same encryption as olddb.

You can use one of the following constants in the *options* argument to specify the version of the data format for the compacted database. This constant affects only the version of the data format of *newdb* and doesn't affect the version of any Microsoft Access-defined objects, such as forms and reports.

Constant	Description
dbVersion10	Creates a database that uses the Microsoft Jet database engine version 1.0 while compacting.
dbVersion11	Creates a database that uses the Jet database engine version 1.1 while compacting.
dbVersion20	Creates a database that uses the Jet database engine version 2.0 while compacting.
dbVersion30	Creates a database that uses the Jet database engine version 3.0 while compacting.

You can specify only one version constant. If you omit a version constant, *newdb* will have the same version as *olddb*. You can compact *newdb* only to a version that is the same or later than that of *olddb*.

Remarks

As you change data in a database, the database file can become fragmented and use more disk space than necessary. Periodically, you can compact your database to defragment the database file. The compacted database is usually smaller and often runs faster. You can also choose to change the collating order, the encryption, or the version of the data format while you copy and compact the database.

The **CompactDatabase** method copies all the data and the security permissions settings from the database specified by *olddb* to the database specified by *newdb*. In the process, the data in the compacted database is organized contiguously to recover disk space.

You must close *olddb* before you compact it. In a multiuser environment, other users can't have *olddb* open while you're compacting it. If *olddb* isn't closed or isn't available for exclusive use, an error occurs.

Because **CompactDatabase** creates a copy of the database, you must have enough disk space for both the original and the duplicate databases. The compact operation fails if there isn't enough disk space available. The *newdb* duplicate database doesn't have to be on the same disk as *olddb*. After successfully compacting a database, you can delete the *olddb* file and rename the compacted *newdb* file to the original filename.

See Also **CollatingOrder** Property, **CreateDatabase** Method, **Database** Object.

Specifics (Microsoft Access) The **CompactDatabase** method won't completely convert a Microsoft Access database from one version to another. Only the data format is converted. Microsoft Access-defined objects, such as forms and reports, aren't converted.

Use the Convert Database command on the File menu to convert Microsoft Access databases from an earlier version to the current version.

Example This example uses **CompactDatabase** to compact a database and keeps a backup copy of the original database. The new database has the same locale as the source database, but is encrypted.

```
DBEngine.CompactDatabase "C:\Biblio.mdb","C:\BibNew.mdb","",dbEncrypt
...
Kill "C:\Biblio.BAK"
Name "C:\Biblio.mdb" As "C:\BIBLIO.BAK"
Name "C:\BibNew.mdb" As "C:\Biblio.mdb"
```

This example copies a database named Northwind.mdb and keeps a new, compacted copy named COPY.NEW. The new database is encrypted.

```
DBEngine.CompactDatabase "C:\Northwind.mdb", "C:\Copy.NEW","",dbEncrypt
```

ConflictTable Property

Applies To **TableDef** Object.

Description Returns the name of a side table containing the database records that conflicted during the synchronization of two replicas. The property is read-only and returns a zero-length string if there is no side table or the database is non-replicable.

ConflictTable Property

Remarks

If two users at two separate replicas each make a change to the same record in the database, the changes made by one user will fail to be applied to the other replica. Consequently, the user with the failed change must address the problem in a process called "conflict resolution."

Conflict occurs at the record level, not between fields. For example, if one user changes the Address field and another updates the Phone field in the same record, then one change is rejected. Because conflict occurs at the record level, the rejection occurs even though the successful change and the rejected change are unlikely to result in a true conflict of information.

The exchange mechanism handles the record conflicts by creating conflict tables, which contain the information that would have been placed in the table, if the change had been successful. As a DAO programmer, you examine these conflict tables and work through them row by row, fixing whatever is appropriate.

All side tables are named *table*_conflict, where *table* is the original name of the table, truncated to the maximum table name length.

Note The **ConflictTable** property can be used only if your application has Microsoft Access with Briefcase Replication installed.

Example

This example finds the name of the conflict table containing the records that were not updated during the replica synchronization, calls a custom routine for resolving the conflicts, deletes the record in the conflict table, and deletes the table after all records have been processed.

```
Sub Resolve (dbsResolve As Database)
    Dim tdfTest As TableDef, rstConflict As Recordset
    For Each tdfTest In dbsResolve.TableDefs
        If (tdfTest.ConflictTable <> " ") Then
            Set rstConflict = dbsResolve.OpenRecordset _
                (tdfTest.ConflictTable)
            rstConflict.MoveFirst      ' Process each record
            While Not rstConflict.EOF
                .
                .                      ' Do conflict resolution
                .
                rstConflict.Delete     ' Remove conflicting
                rstConflict.MoveNext
            Wend
            rstConflict.Close
        End If
    Next tdfTest
End Sub
```

Connect Property

Applies To Database Object, **QueryDef** Object, **TableDef** Object.

Description Sets or returns a value that provides information about the source of an open database, a database used in a pass-through query, or an attached table. For **QueryDef** objects, **Database** objects, attached tables, and **TableDef** objects not yet appended to a collection, this property setting is read/write. For a base table, this property is read-only.

Syntax *object*.**Connect** = [*databasetype*;[*parameters*;]]

The **Connect** property syntax has these parts.

Part	Description
object	An object expression that evaluates to an object in the Applies To list.
databasetype	A string expression that specifies a database type. For Microsoft Jet databases, exclude this argument; if you specify *parameters*, use a semicolon (;) as a placeholder. The data type is **String**.
parameters	A string expression that specifies additional parameters to pass to ODBC or installable ISAM drivers. Use semicolons to separate parameters. The data type is **String**.

Settings The **Connect** property setting is a **String** composed of a database type specifier and zero or more parameters separated by semicolons. The **Connect** property is used to pass additional information to ODBC and certain ISAM drivers as needed. It isn't used for Jet databases, except for those containing attached tables, to allow SQL pass-through queries.

To perform an SQL pass-through query on a table attached to your .mdb file, you must first set the **Connect** property of the attached table's database to a valid ODBC connect string.

For a **TableDef** object that represents an attached table, the **Connect** property setting consists of one or two parts (a database type specifier and a path to the database), each of which ends with a semicolon.

The path as shown in the following table is the full path for the directory containing the database files and must be preceded by the identifier "DATABASE=". In some cases (as with Jet, Btrieve®, and Microsoft Excel databases) a specific filename is included in the database path argument.

Connect Property

The following table shows possible database types and their corresponding database specifiers and paths for the **Connect** property setting.

Database type	Specifier	Path
Database using the Jet database engine	"[*database*];"	"*drive:\path\filename.mdb*"
dBASE III®	"dBASE III;"	"*drive:\path*"
dBASE IV®	"dBASE IV;"	"*drive:\path*"
dBASE 5	"dBASE 5;"	"*drive:\path*"
Paradox 3.*x*	"Paradox 3.*x*;"	"*drive:\path*"
Paradox 4.*x*	"Paradox 4.*x*;"	"*drive:\path*"
Paradox 5.*x*	"Paradox 5.*x*;"	"*drive:\path*"
Btrieve	"Btrieve;"	"*drive:\path\filename.ddf*"
FoxPro® 2.0	"FoxPro 2.0;"	"*drive:\path*"
FoxPro 2.5	"FoxPro 2.5;"	"*drive:\path*"
FoxPro 2.6	"FoxPro 2.6;"	"*drive:\path*"
Excel 3.0	"Excel 3.0;"	"*drive:\path\filename.xls*"
Excel 4.0	"Excel 4.0;"	"*drive:\path\filename.xls*"
Excel 5.0	"Excel 5.0;"	"*drive:\path\filename.xls*"
Excel 7.0	"Excel 7.0;"	"*drive:\path\filename.xls*"
Text	"Text;"	"*drive:\path*"
ODBC	"ODBC; DATABASE=*defaultdatabase*; UID=*user*; PWD=*password*; DSN=*datasourcename* LOGINTIMEOUT=*seconds*" (This may not be a complete connection string for all servers; it's just an example.)	None

Remarks

If the specifier is only "ODBC;", a dialog box listing all registered ODBC data source names is displayed by the ODBC driver so the user can select a database.

If a password is required but not provided in the **Connect** property setting, a login dialog box is displayed the first time a table is accessed by the ODBC driver and again if the connection is closed and reopened.

For Jet database base tables, the **Connect** property setting is a zero-length string ("").

You can set the **Connect** property for a **Database** object by providing a *source* argument to the **OpenDatabase** method. You can check the setting to determine the type, path, user ID, Password, or ODBC data source of the database.

For a **QueryDef** object, you use the **Connect** property with the **ReturnsRecords** property to create an ODBC SQL pass-through query. The *databasetype* of the connection string is "ODBC;", and the remainder of the string contains information specific to the ODBC driver used to access the remote data. For more information, see the documentation for the specific driver.

Note The **Connect** property must be set before the **ReturnsRecords** property is set.

See Also
OpenDatabase Method, **ReturnsRecords** Property.

Example
This example creates a **TableDef** object in the specified database; sets its **Connect**, **Name**, and **SourceTableName** properties; and then appends it to the **TableDefs** collection.

```
Function ConnectSource () As Integer
    Dim dbsLocal As Database, tdfPDXAuthor As TableDef
    Set dbsLocal = DBEngine.Workspaces(0).OpenDatabase("Northwind.mdb")
    Set tdfPDXAuthor = dbsLocal.CreateTableDef("PDXAuthor")
    ' Attach Paradox table Author in database C:\PDX\PUBLISH.
    tdfPDXAuthor.Connect = "Paradox 4.x;DATABASE=C:\PDX\PUBLISH"
    tdfPDXAuthor.SourceTableName = "Author"
    dbsLocal.TableDefs.Append tdfPDXAuthor    ' Attach table.
    ConnectSource = True
End Function
```

Example (Microsoft Access)
The following example creates a **TableDef** object in the specified database. The procedure then sets its **Connect**, **Name**, and **SourceTableName** properties and appends the object to the **TableDefs** collection.

```
Sub ConnectSource()
    Dim dbs As Database, tdf As TableDef

    ' Return Database variable that points to current database.
    Set dbs = CurrentDb
    Set tdf = dbs.CreateTableDef("PDXAuthor")
    ' Attach Paradox table Author in database C:\PDX\Publish.
    tdf.Connect = "Paradox 4.x;DATABASE=C:\PDX\Publish"
    tdf.SourceTableName = "Author"
    dbs.TableDefs.Append tdf
End Sub
```

Example **(Microsoft Excel)**	This example attaches the table PRODUCT.DBF (a dBASE IV table located in the \Program Files\Common Files\Microsoft Shared\MSquery folder) to the NWINDEX.MDB database. (On Windows NT, PRODUCT.DBF is located in the \WINDOWS\MSAPPS\MSQUERY folder.) To create the NWINDEX.MDB database, run the Microsoft Excel example for the **CreateDatabase** method.

```
Const sourceDir = "C:\Program Files\Common Files\Microsoft Shared\"
Dim nWindEx As Database, tDef As TableDef
Dim dataSource As String
dataSource = "dbase IV;DATABASE=" & sourceDir & "MSquery"
Set nWindEx = Workspaces(0).OpenDatabase(Application.Path _
    & "\NWINDEX.MDB")
Set tDef = nWindEx.CreateTableDef("Product")
tDef.Connect = dataSource
tDef.SourceTableName = "Product"
nWindEx.TableDefs.Append tDef
nWindEx.Close
```

Container Object

Description	A **Container** object groups similar types of **Document** objects together—for example, one container might have Tables documents. Applications can define their own document types and corresponding containers.
Remarks	Each **Database** object has a **Containers** collection consisting of built-in **Container** objects. Some of these **Container** objects are defined by the Microsoft Jet database engine while others may be defined by other applications. The following table lists the name of each **Container** object defined by the Jet database engine and what type of information it contains.

Container name	Contains information about
Databases	Containing database
Tables	Saved tables and queries
Relations	Saved relationships

Note Don't confuse the particular types of **Container** objects listed in the preceding table with the collection types of the same name. The Databases type of **Container** object refers to all saved objects of the specified type, but the **Databases** collection refers only to open objects of the specified type.

Container Object 57

Each **Container** object has a **Documents** collection that contains a **Document** object for each instance of the type of object it describes. You typically use a **Container** object with one of the **Document** objects in the **Documents** collection, so you can consider a **Container** object to be an intermediate link to the information that the **Document** object contains.

Because **Container** objects are built-in, you can't create new **Container** objects or delete existing ones. Using the properties of an existing **Container** object, you can:

- Determine the predefined names an object has by checking its **Name** property setting.
- Determine or specify the owner of the **Container** object by checking or setting its **Owner** property. To set the **Owner** property, you must have write permission for the **Container** object, and you must set the property to the name of an existing **User** or **Group** object.
- Set access permissions for the **Container** object using the **Permissions** and **UserName** properties; any **Document** object created in the **Documents** collection of a **Container** object inherits these access permission settings.

You can refer to a **Container** object in a collection by its ordinal number or by its **Name** property setting, using either of the following syntax forms:

Containers(0)

Containers("*name*")

Properties   **AllPermissions** Property, **Inherit** Property, **Name** Property, **Owner** Property, **Permissions** Property, **UserName** Property.

See Also   **User** Object; Appendix, "Data Access Object Hierarchy."

Specifics (Microsoft Access)   In addition to the **Container** objects defined by the Microsoft Jet database engine, the following four **Container** objects are defined by Microsoft Access.

Container name	Contains information about
Forms	Saved forms
Modules	Saved modules
Reports	Saved reports
Scripts	Saved macros

The **Container** objects defined by Microsoft Access are Microsoft Access database objects, not data access objects. These **Container** objects provide the Jet database engine with information about Microsoft Access objects. The Jet database engine uses this information to implement security on Microsoft Access database objects in the same way it does for data access objects.

Container Object

The **Container** objects defined by Microsoft Access and the **Container** objects defined by the Jet database engine are all included in the **Containers** collection in Microsoft Access.

The **Documents** collection of a **Container** object contains **Document** objects representing the individual objects of the type described by the **Container** object. For example, the Forms **Container** object has a **Documents** collection that might include a **Document** object corresponding to a form named Orders.

You can use **Container** objects to establish and enforce permissions for Microsoft Access database objects. To set permissions for a **Container** object, set the **UserName** property of the **Container** object to the name of an existing **User** or **Group** object. Then set the **Permissions** property for the **Container** object.

Note Don't confuse the particular types of **Container** objects with the collection types of the same name. The Forms and Reports **Container** objects each contain **Documents** collections, which include individual **Document** objects representing each saved form or report. The **Forms** and **Reports** collections refer only to open forms or reports.

Example

This example enumerates the properties of all the **Container** and **Document** objects in the current database.

```
Function EnumerateDocuments () As Integer
    Dim dbsCurrent As Database
    Dim conTest As Container, docTest As Document
    Dim intC As Integer, intD As Integer
    Set dbsCurrent = _
        DBEngine.Workspaces(0).OpenDatabase("Northwind.mdb")
    For intC = 0 To dbsCurrent.Containers.Count - 1
        Set conTest = dbsCurrent.Containers(intC)
        Debug.Print ">> Container: "; conTest.Name;
        Debug.Print "  Owner: "; conTest.Owner
        Debug.Print "  UserName: "; conTest.UserName;
        Debug.Print "  Permissions: "; conTest.Permissions
        Debug.Print
        For intD = 0 To conTest.Documents.Count - 1
            Set docTest = conTest.Documents(intD)
            Debug.Print " > Document: "; docTest.Name;
            Debug.Print "  Owner: "; docTest.Owner;
            Debug.Print "  Container: "; docTest.Container
            Debug.Print "  UserName: "; docTest.UserName;
            Debug.Print "  Permissions: "; docTest.Permissions
            Debug.Print "  DateCreated: "; docTest.DateCreated;
            Debug.Print "  LastUpdated: "; docTest.LastUpdated
            Debug.Print
        Next intD
```

```
            Next intC
            EnumerateDocuments = True
        End Function
```

**Example
(Microsoft Access)**

The following example grants programmers full access to all modules in a database, and grants all other users read-only permissions on modules.

```
Sub SetModulePermissions()
    Dim dbs As Database, wrk As Workspace, ctr As Container
    Dim grp As Group

    Set wrk = DBEngine.Workspaces(0)
    ' Return Database object pointing to current database.
    Set dbs = CurrentDb
    Set ctr = dbs.Containers!Modules
    wrk.Groups.Refresh
    For Each grp In wrk.Groups
        ctr.UserName = grp.Name
        If ctr.UserName = "Programmers" Then
                ctr.Permissions = ctr.Permissions Or dbSecFullAccess
        Else
                ctr.Permissions = ctr.Permissions Or acSecModReadDef
        End If
    Next grp
End Sub
```

Container Property

Applies To	**Document** Object.
Description	Returns the name of the **Container** object to which a **Document** object belongs.
Return Values	This property's return value is a **String** data type.
See Also	**Container** Object.
Example	This example determines the name of the **Container** object to which a **Document** object belongs.

```
Sub Doc_Analyzer(docUnknown As Document)
    Dim strContainerName As String
    strContainerName = docUnknown.Container
    Select Case strContainerName
        Case "Tables"
            ...
        Case "Databases"
            ...
```

Container Property

```
            Case "Forms"
                ...
            Case Else
                ...
        End Select
End Sub
```

Example (Microsoft Access)

The following example determines the name of the **Container** object to which a **Document** object belongs, and sets permissions accordingly for the specified group account. Remember that you must denote a particular user or group account before you set permissions for an object. The following example assumes that you have defined a Marketers group.

Note that Microsoft Access defines additional **Container** objects beyond those defined by the Microsoft Jet database engine. These include the Form, Report, Script, and Module **Container** objects.

```
Sub DocAnalyzer(docUnknown As Document)
    Dim strContainerName As String
    ' Set UserName property to valid existing group account.
    docUnknown.UserName = "Marketers"
    ' Get value of Container property.
    strContainerName = docUnknown.Container
    Select Case strContainerName
        Case "Forms"
            ' Set permissions for Form Document object.
            docUnknown.Permissions = docUnknown.Permissions Or _
                acSecFrmRptWriteDef
        Case "Reports"
            ' Set permissions for Report Document.
            docUnknown.Permissions = docUnknown.Permissions Or _
                acSecFrmRptExecute
        Case "Scripts"
            ' Set permissions for Script Document.
            docUnknown.Permissions = docUnknown.Permissions Or _
                acSecMacWriteDef
        Case "Modules"
            ' Set permissions for Module Document object.
            docUnknown.Permissions = docUnknown.Permissions Or _
                acSecModReadDef
        Case Else
            Exit Sub
    End Select
End Sub
```

Containers Collection

Description A **Containers** collection contains all of the **Container** objects that are defined in a database.

Remarks Each **Database** object has a **Containers** collection consisting of built-in **Container** objects. Some of these **Container** objects are defined by the Microsoft Jet database engine while others may be defined by other applications.

Properties **Count** Property.

Methods **Refresh** Method.

See Also Appendix, "Data Access Object Hierarchy."

Specifics (Microsoft Access) See the **Container** object example (Microsoft Access).

Example See the **Container** object example.

Example (Microsoft Access) See the **Container** object example (Microsoft Access).

CopyQueryDef Method

Applies To Dynaset-Type **Recordset** Object, **Recordset** Object, Snapshot-Type **Recordset** Object.

Description Returns a **QueryDef** object which is a copy of the **QueryDef** used to create the **Recordset** object represented by the *object* placeholder.

Syntax Set <*querydefobject*> = <*object*>.**CopyQueryDef**

The <*querydefobject*> is an object variable declared as a **QueryDef**.

Remarks You must first open a **Recordset** with the **OpenRecordset** method before using the **CopyQueryDef** method. **CopyQueryDef** creates a new **QueryDef** that is a duplicate of the **QueryDef** used to create the **Recordset**. If a **QueryDef** wasn't used to create this **Recordset**, you'll see a message that the feature is not available.

See Also **QueryDef** Object.

62 Count Property

Example **(Microsoft Access)**	The following example uses the **CopyQueryDef** method to return a copy of a **QueryDef** object representing an Invoices query, and prints the **SQL** property of that **QueryDef** object.

```
Sub GetQueryDefCopy()
    Dim dbs As Database, rst As Recordset
    Dim qdfOriginal As QueryDef, qdfCopy As QueryDef

    ' Return Database variable pointing to current database.
    Set dbs = CurrentDb
    ' Return QueryDef variable pointing to Invoices query.
    Set qdfOriginal = dbs.QueryDefs!Invoices
    ' Open dynaset-type Recordset object.
    Set rst = qdfOriginal.OpenRecordset
    ' Get copy of original QueryDef object.
    Set qdfCopy = rst.CopyQueryDef
    ' Print value of SQL property for copy.
    Debug.Print qdfCopy.SQL
End Sub
```

Count Property

Applies To	**Containers** Collection, **Databases** Collection, **Documents** Collection, **Errors** Collection, **Fields** Collection, **Groups** Collection, **Indexes** Collection, **Parameters** Collection, **Properties** Collection, **QueryDefs** Collection, **Recordsets** Collection, **Relations** Collection, **TableDefs** Collection, **Users** Collection, **Workspaces** Collection.
Description	Returns the number of objects in a collection.
Return Value	This property's return value is a **Long** integer data type.
Remarks	Because members of a collection are numbered starting with 0, loops are always coded starting with the 0 member; for example: `    For I = 0 to Databases.Count - 1` The **Count** property setting is never **Null**. If its value is 0, there are no objects in the collection.
See Also	**Append** Method, **Delete** Method, **Refresh** Method.

Example	This example lists the names and total number of **TableDef** and **QueryDef** objects in the current database.
	
	`Dim dbsLocal As Database, intCount As Integer`
	`Set dbsLocal = DBEngine.Workspaces(0).OpenDatabase("Northwind.mdb")`

```
For intCount = 0 To dbsLocal.TableDefs.Count - 1
    Debug.Print dbsLocal.TableDefs(intCount).Name
Next intCount
Debug.Print dbsLocal.TableDefs.Count
For intCount = 0 To dbsLocal.QueryDefs.Count - 1
    Debug.Print dbsLocal.QueryDefs(intCount).Name
Next intCount
Debug.Print dbsLocal.QueryDefs.Count
```

Example (Microsoft Access)

The following example prints the names and total number fields in an Orders table.

```
Sub CountFields()
    Dim dbs As Database, tdf as TableDef
    Dim intI As Integer

    ' Return Database variable that points to current database.
    Set dbs = CurrentDb
    Set tdf = dbs.TableDefs!Orders
    ' Count fields in Fields collection of TableDef object.
    Debug.Print tdf.Fields.Count
    ' List names of all fields.
    For Each fld In tdf.Fields
        Debug.Print fld.Name
    Next fld
End Sub
```

Example (Microsoft Excel)

This example displays the number of recordsets in the NWINDEX.MDB database and then enters the names on Sheet1.

To create the NWINDEX.MDB database, run the Microsoft Excel example for the **CreateDatabase** method.

```
Dim db As Database, i As Integer
Sheets("Sheet1").Activate
Set db = Workspaces(0).OpenDatabase(Application.Path & "\NWINDEX.MDB")
Cells(1, 1).Value = "TableDef list for " & db.Name
Cells(1, 1).EntireColumn.AutoFit
For i = 0 To db.TableDefs.Count - 1
    Cells(i + 2, 1).Value = db.TableDefs(i).Name
Next i
MsgBox "There are " & db.TableDefs.Count & " TableDefs"
db.Close
```

CreateDatabase Method

Applies To **Workspace** Object.

Description Creates a new **Database** object, saves the database on disk and returns an opened **Database** object.

Syntax **Set** *database* = *workspace*.**CreateDatabase** (*databasename*, *locale* [, *options*])

The **CreateDatabase** method syntax has these parts.

Part	Description
database	A variable of an object data type that references the **Database** object you're creating.
workspace	A variable of an object data type that represents the existing **Workspace** object that will contain the database. If you omit the *workspace* part, the default **Workspace** is used.
databasename	A string expression that is the name of the database file that you're creating. It can be the full path and filename, such as "C:\MYDB.mdb". If you don't supply a filename extension, .mdb is appended. If your network supports it, you can also specify a network path, such as "\\MYSERVER\MYSHARE\MYDIR\MYDB". Only .mdb database files can be created using this method.
locale	A string expression used to specify collating order for creating the database. You must supply this argument or an error will occur. See the table that lists *locale* constants later in this topic.
options	An integer that indicates one or more options, as specified in Settings. You can combine options by summing the corresponding constants.

Settings You can use one of the following constants for the *locale* argument to specify the **CollatingOrder** property of text for string comparisons.

Constant	Collating order
dbLangGeneral	English, German, French, Portuguese, Italian, and Modern Spanish
dbLangArabic	Arabic
dbLangCyrillic	Russian
dbLangCzech	Czech

CreateDatabase Method

Constant	Collating order
dbLangDutch	Dutch
dbLangGreek	Greek
dbLangHebrew	Hebrew
dbLangHungarian	Hungarian
dbLangIcelandic	Icelandic
dbLangNordic	Nordic languages (Microsoft Jet database engine version 1.0 only)
dbLangNorwdan	Norwegian and Danish
dbLangPolish	Polish
dbLangSpanish	Traditional Spanish
dbLangSwedfin	Swedish and Finnish
dbLangTurkish	Turkish

You can use one or more of the following constants in the *options* argument to specify which version the data format should have and whether or not to encrypt the database.

Constant	Description
dbEncrypt	Creates an encrypted database.
dbVersion10	Creates a database that uses the Jet database engine version 1.0.
dbVersion11	Creates a database that uses the Jet database engine version 1.1.
dbVersion20	Creates a database that uses the Jet database engine version 2.0.
dbVersion30	Creates a database that uses the Jet database engine version 3.0.

If you omit the encryption constant, an unencrypted database is created. You can specify only one version constant. If you omit a version constant, a database that uses the Jet database engine version 3.0 is created.

Remarks The **CreateDatabase** method creates and opens a new, empty database and returns the **Database** object. You must complete its structure and content using additional data access objects. If you want to make a partial or complete copy of an existing database, you can use the **CompactDatabase** method to make a copy that you can customize.

See Also **CollatingOrder** Property, **CompactDatabase** Method, **Database** Object, **DBEngine** Object, **OpenDatabase** Method.

66 CreateDatabase Method

Specifics (Microsoft Access) You can use the **CreateDatabase** method to create a new database from Visual Basic. The new database is immediately opened, appended to the **Databases** collection, and saved to disk. However, only the current database is open in the Microsoft Access Database window. To open a database that you have created with **CreateDatabase** in the Database window, you must click Open Database on the File menu.

Example This example uses **CreateDatabase** to create a new, encrypted **Database** object. The example customizes some properties of the new database, completes its structure, and then closes it.

```
Dim wspDefault As Workspace, dbsDefault As Database, dbsNew As Database
Set wspDefault = DBEngine.Workspaces(0)
Set dbsDefault = wspDefault.OpenDatabase("Northwind.mdb")
If Dir$("NewDB.mdb") <> "" Then
    Kill "NewDB.mdb"
Set dbsNew = wspDefault.CreateDatabase("NewDB.mdb", dbLangGeneral, _
    dbEncrypt)
dbsNew.QueryTimeout = dbsDefault.QueryTimeout
...
' Complete structure of dbsNew, possibly using structure of dbsDefault.
...
dbsNew.Close
dbsDefault.Close
```

Example (Microsoft Access) The following example uses **CreateDatabase** to create a new, encrypted database named Newdb.mdb.

```
Sub NewDatabase()
    Dim wspDefault As Workspace, dbsNew As Database

    Set wspDefault = DBEngine.Workspaces(0)
    ' Create new, encrypted database.
    Set dbsNew = wspDefault.CreateDatabase ("Newdb.mdb", _
        dbLangGeneral, dbEncrypt)
    ' Create and append tables to new database.
    .
    .
    .
    dbsNew.Close
End Sub
```

**Example
(Microsoft Excel)**

This example creates a new database (NWINDEX.MDB). The example attaches two tables from the C:\Program Files\Common Files\Microsoft Shared\MSquery folder to the database. (On Windows NT, the two tables are in the \WINDOWS\MSAPPS\MSQUERY folder.)

```
Const sourceDir = "C:\Program Files\Common Files\Microsoft Shared\"

Sub createNWindEx()
    Dim nWindEx As Database, customerTable As TableDef, _
        supplierTable As TableDef
    Dim dataSource As String
    dataSource = "dbase IV;DATABASE=" & sourceDir & "MSquery"
    appPath = Application.Path
    Set nWindEx = Workspaces(0).CreateDatabase(Application.Path _
        & "\NWINDEX.MDB", dbLangGeneral)
    Set customerTable = nWindEx.CreateTableDef("Customer")
    customerTable.Connect = dataSource
    customerTable.SourceTableName = "Customer"
    nWindEx.TableDefs.Append customerTable
    Set supplierTable = nWindEx.CreateTableDef("Supplier")
    supplierTable.Connect = dataSource
    supplierTable.SourceTableName = "Supplier"
    nWindEx.TableDefs.Append supplierTable
    MsgBox "The database " & nWindEx.Name & " has been created."
    nWindEx.Close
End Sub
```

CreateField Method

Applies To   **Index** Object, **Relation** Object, **TableDef** Object.

Description   Creates a new **Field** object.

Syntax   **Set** *variable* = *object*.**CreateField**([*name*[, *type* [, *size*]]])

The **CreateField** method syntax has these parts.

Part	Description
variable	A variable declared as an object data type **Field**.
object	The variable name of the **Index**, **Relation**, or **TableDef** object you want to use to create the new **Field** object.
name	A **String** variable that uniquely names the new **Field** object. See the **Name** property for details on valid **Field** names.
type	An **Integer** constant that determines the data type of the new **Field** object. See the **Type** property for valid data types.

68 CreateField Method

Part	Description
size	An integer that indicates the maximum size, in bytes, of a **Field** object that contains text. See the **Size** property for valid *size* values. This argument is ignored for numeric and fixed-width fields.

Remarks If you omit one or more of the optional parts when you use **CreateField**, you can use an appropriate assignment statement to set or reset the corresponding property before you append the new object to a collection. After you append the new object, you can alter some but not all of its property settings. See the individual property topics for more details.

Note The *type* and *size* arguments apply only to **Field** objects in a **TableDef** object. These arguments are ignored when a **Field** object is associated with **Index** and **Relation** objects.

If *name* refers to an object that is already a member of the collection, a trappable error occurs when you use the **Append** method.

To remove a **Field** object from a collection, use the **Delete** method on the collection. You can't delete a **Field** object from a **TableDef** object's **Fields** collection once an index has been created that references the field.

See Also **Append** Method, **Delete** Method, **Field** Object, **Name** Property, **Size** Property, **Type** Property.

Example This example creates a new **Field** object.

```
Dim dbsNorthwind As Database
Dim tdfEmployees As TableDef
Dim fldPhone As Field
Set dbsNorthwind = DBEngine.Workspaces(0).OpenDatabase("Northwind.mdb")
Set tdfEmployees = dbsNorthwind.TableDefs("Employees")
' Create new Field object.
Set fldPhone = tdfEmployees.CreateField("Phone", dbText)
' Set another property of fldPhone.
fldPhone.Size = 25    ' Greater than longest phone number.
' Save fldPhone definition by appending it to Fields collection.
tdfEmployees.Fields.Append fldPhone
dbsNorthwind.Close
```

Example (Microsoft Access) The following example creates a new **Field** object and appends it to an Employees table.

```
Sub NewField()
    Dim dbs As Database, tdf As TableDef
    Dim fld As Field

    ' Return Database variable pointing to current database.
```

```
            Set dbs = CurrentDb
            Set tdf = dbs.TableDefs!Employees
            ' Create new Field object.
            Set fld = tdf.CreateField("Phone", dbText)
            ' Set another property of field.
            fld.Size = 25
            ' Append new field to Fields collection.
            tdf.Fields.Append fld
        End Sub
```

CreateGroup Method

Applies To   **User** Object, **Workspace** Object.

Description   Creates a new **Group** object.

Syntax   **Set** *variable* = *object*.**CreateGroup**([*name*[, *pid*]])

The **CreateGroup** method syntax has these parts.

Part	Description
variable	A variable declared as object data type **Group**.
object	The variable name of the **User** or **Workspace** object you want to use to create the new **Group** object.
name	A **String** variable that uniquely names the new **Group** object. See the **Name** property for details on valid **Group** names.
pid	A **String** variable containing the PID of a group account. The identifier must contain from 4 to 20 alphanumeric characters. See the **PID** property for more information on valid personal identifiers.

Remarks   If you omit one or both of the optional parts when you use **CreateGroup**, you can use an appropriate assignment statement to set or reset the corresponding property before you append the new object to a collection. After you append the object, you can alter some but not all of its property settings. See the individual property topics for more details.

If *name* refers to an object that is already a member of the collection, a trappable error occurs when you use the **Append** method.

To remove a **Group** object from a collection, use the **Delete** method on the collection.

See Also   **Append** Method, **Delete** Method, **Group** Object, **Name** Property, **PID** Property.

Specifics (Microsoft Access)   Once you have created a new **Group** object and appended it to the **Groups** collection of a **Workspace** or **User** object, you can verify that the new group exists by examining the Name drop-down list box on the Groups tab of the User And Group Accounts dialog box. This dialog box is available by pointing to Security on the Tools menu and then clicking User And Group Accounts.

Example   This example creates a new **Group** object.

```
Dim grpManagers As Group, strManagersPID As String
strManagersPID = "2222abc"
' Create new Group object.
Set grpManagers = DBEngine.Workspaces(0).CreateGroup("Managers", _
    strManagersPID)
' Create new group in workgroup by appending it to Groups collection.
Workspaces(0).Groups.Append grpManagers
```

CreateIndex Method

Applies To   **TableDef** Object.

Description   Creates a new **Index** object.

Syntax   **Set** *variable* = *tabledef*.**CreateIndex**([*name*])

The **CreateIndex** method syntax has these parts.

Part	Description
variable	A variable declared as object data type **Index**.
tabledef	The variable name of the **TableDef** object you want to use to create the new **Index** object.
name	A **String** variable that uniquely names the new **Index** object. See the **Name** property for details on valid **Index** names.

Remarks   If you omit the optional *name* part when you use **CreateIndex**, you can use an appropriate assignment statement to set or reset the **Name** property before you append the new object to a collection. After you append the object, you may or may not be able to set its **Name** property, depending on the type of object the **Indexes** collection resides in. See the **Name** property topic for more details.

If *name* refers to an object that is already a member of the collection, a trappable error occurs when you use the **Append** method.

To remove an **Index** object from a collection, use the **Delete** method on the collection.

See Also   **Append** Method, **Delete** Method, **Index** Object, **Name** Property.

Example   This example creates a new **Index** object.

```
Dim idxAnother As Index, fldLastName As Field
Dim tdfEmployees As TableDef, dbsNorthwind As Database
Set dbsNorthwind = DBEngine.Workspaces(0).OpenDatabase("Northwind.mdb")
Set tdfEmployees = dbsNorthwind.TableDefs("Employees")
' Create new Index object.
Set idxAnother = tdfEmployees.CreateIndex("Another")
Set fldLastName = idxAnother.CreateField("LastName")
idxAnother.Primary = False
idxAnother.Required = True
idxAnother.Fields.Append fldLastName
' Save Index definition by appending it to Indexes collection.
tdfEmployees.Indexes.Append idxAnother
tdfEmployees.Indexes.Delete "Another"
dbsNorthwind.Close
```

**Example
(Microsoft Access)**

The following example creates a new **Index** object on an Employees table. The new index consists of two fields, LastName and FirstName.

```
Sub NewIndex()
    Dim dbs As Database, tdf As TableDef
    Dim idx As Index, rst As Recordset
    Dim fldLastName As Field, fldFirstName As Field

    ' Return Database variable pointing to current database.
    Set dbs = CurrentDb
    Set tdf = dbs.TableDefs!Employees
    ' Return Index object that points to new index.
    Set idx = tdf.CreateIndex("FullName")
    ' Create and append index fields.
    Set fldLastName = idx.CreateField("LastName", dbText)
    Set fldFirstName = idx.CreateField("FirstName", dbText)
    idx.Fields.Append fldLastName
    idx.Fields.Append fldFirstName
    ' Append Index object.
    tdf.Indexes.Append idx
End Sub
```

CreateProperty Method

Applies To   **Database** Object, **Field** Object, **Index** Object, **QueryDef** Object, **TableDef** Object.

CreateProperty Method

Description Creates a new user-defined **Property** object.

Syntax **Set** *variable* = *object*.**CreateProperty**([*name*[, *type*[, *value*[, *fDDL*]]]])

The **CreateProperty** method syntax has these parts.

Part	Description
variable	A variable declared as an object data type **Property**.
object	The variable name of the **Database**, **Field**, **Index**, **QueryDef**, or **TableDef** object you want to use to create the new **Property** object.
name	A **String** variable that uniquely names the new **Property** object. See the **Name** property for details on valid **Property** names.
type	An **Integer** constant that defines the data type of the new **Property** object. See the **Type** property for valid data types.
value	A **Variant** variable containing the initial property value. See the **Value** property for details.
fDDL	A Boolean variable indicating whether or not the **Property** is a DDL object. The default is **False**. If the *fDDL* is **True**, this **Property** object can't be changed or deleted unless the user has **dbSecWriteDef** permission.

Remarks You can create a user-defined **Property** object only in the **Properties** collection of an object that is persistent (that is, already stored on disk).

If you omit one or more of the optional parts when you use **CreateProperty**, you can use an appropriate assignment statement to set or reset the corresponding property before you append the new object to a collection. After you append the object, you can alter some but not all of its property settings. See the individual property topics for more details.

If *name* refers to an object that is already a member of the collection, a trappable error occurs when you use the **Append** method.

To remove a user-defined **Property** object from the collection, use the **Delete** method on the **Properties** collection. You can't delete built-in properties.

Note If you omit the *fDDL* part, it defaults to **False** (non-DDL). Because no corresponding DDL property is exposed, you must delete and re-create a **Property** object you want to change from DDL to non-DDL.

See Also **Append** Method, **Delete** Method, **Name** Property, **Type** Property, **Value** Property.

Specifics (Microsoft Access) Microsoft Access defines a number of properties on data access objects. These properties are not automatically recognized by the Microsoft Jet database engine. In order to set or return values for a Microsoft Access-defined property in Visual Basic, you must specifically add the property to the **Properties** collection of the object to which it applies. You can do this by using the **CreateProperty** method to create the property and then appending it to the **Properties** collection.

A Microsoft Access-defined property is automatically added to the **Properties** collection when it is first set from the Microsoft Access window. If the property has already been set in this way, then you don't need to add it to the **Properties** collection.

When you write code to set a Microsoft Access-defined property, you should include an error-handling routine that creates a **Property** object representing that property and appends it to the **Properties** collection if it does not already exist in the collection.

When you refer to a Microsoft Access-defined property in Visual Basic, you must explicitly refer to the **Properties** collection. For example, you would refer to the **AppTitle** property in the following manner, once it exists within the **Properties** collection of a **Database** object representing the current database.

```
Dim dbs As Database
Set dbs = CurrentDb
dbs.Properties!AppTitle = "Northwind Traders"
```

Note You need to create and append only the Microsoft Access properties that apply to data access objects. You can set other Microsoft Access properties in Visual Basic using the standard *object.property* syntax.

Example This example creates a new **Property** object.

```
Dim prpPrivilege As Property
Dim dbsNorthwind As Database
Set dbsNorthwind = DBEngine.Workspaces(0).OpenDatabase("Northwind.mdb")
' Create new Property object.
Set prpPrivilege = dbsNorthwind.CreateProperty("Privilege")
' Set other properties of prpPrivilege.
prpPrivilege.Type = dbBoolean
prpPrivilege.Value = True
' Save Property definition by appending it to Properties collection.
dbsNorthwind.Properties.Append prpPrivilege
```

74 CreateProperty Method

**Example
(Microsoft Access)**

The following example sets the **Subject** property. The **Subject** property is a database property that can also be set on the Summary tab of the Database Properties dialog box, available by clicking Database Properties on the File menu.

The **Subject** property applies to a data access object—the SummaryInfo **Document** object. However, it is defined by Microsoft Access, so the Microsoft Jet database engine does not automatically recognize it. Therefore, you must specifically add this property to the **Properties** collection of the **Document** object before you can set it. If the property does not exist in the **Properties** collection, Microsoft Access will generate an error when you attempt to set it.

In the following example, if Microsoft Access generates an error upon trying to set the **Subject** property, the error-handling routine creates the property and appends it to the **Properties** collection.

```
Sub SetAccessProperty()
    Dim dbs As Database, ctr As Container, doc As Document
    Dim prp As Property

    ' Enable error handling.
    On Error GoTo ErrorHandler
    ' Return Database variable pointing to current database.
    Set dbs = CurrentDb
    ' Return Container variable pointing to Databases container.
    Set ctr = dbs.Containers!Databases
    ' Return Document variable pointing to SummaryInfo document.
    Set doc = ctr.Documents!SummaryInfo
    ' Attempt to set Subject property.
    doc.Properties!Subject = "Business Contacts"
    Exit Sub

ErrorHandler:
    ' Check number of error that has occurred.
    If Err.Number = 3270 Then
        ' Create Subject property and set its value.
        Set prp = doc.CreateProperty("Subject", dbText, _
            "Business Contacts")
        ' Append property.
        doc.Properties.Append prp
        ' Resume main procedure.
        Resume Next
    Else
        ' If different error has occurred, display message.
        MsgBox "Unknown error!", vbCritical
    End If
End Sub
```

CreateQueryDef Method

Applies To **Database** Object.

Description Creates a new **QueryDef** object in a specified database.

Syntax **Set** *querydef* = *database*.**CreateQueryDef**([*name*][, *sqltext*])

The **CreateQueryDef** method syntax has these parts.

Part	Description
querydef	A variable of an object data type that references the **QueryDef** object you want to create.
database	A variable of an object data type that references the open **Database** object that contains the new **QueryDef**.
name	A string expression identifying the new **QueryDef**.
sqltext	A string expression (a valid SQL statement) that defines the **QueryDef**. If you omit this argument, you can define the **QueryDef** by setting its **SQL** property before or after you append it to a collection.

Remarks If you include *name* but omit *sqltext* or include both *name* and *sqltext,* the **QueryDef** is automatically saved when you create or change it.

If the object specified by *name* is already a member of the **QueryDefs** collection, a trappable error occurs.

You can create a temporary **QueryDef** by setting the **Name** property of a newly created **QueryDef** to a zero-length string ("") or by using a zero-length string for the *name* argument when you execute the **CreateQueryDef** method. You can't append a temporary **QueryDef** to any collection because a zero-length string isn't a valid name for a permanent **QueryDef**. You can set the **Name** and **SQL** properties of the newly created **QueryDef** and subsequently append the **QueryDef** to the **QueryDefs** collection where it's stored in the database. If you provide anything other than a zero-length string for the name when you create a **QueryDef**, the resulting **QueryDef** object is automatically appended to the **QueryDefs** collection.

To remove a **QueryDef** object from a **QueryDefs** collection, use the **Delete** method on the collection.

To run the SQL statement in a **QueryDef** object, use the **Execute** method.

Using a **QueryDef** object is the preferred way to perform SQL pass-through queries with ODBC databases. See the **QueryDef** object for more information.

See Also **Append** Method, **Connect** Property, **CreateProperty** Method, **Delete** Method, **LogMessages** Property, **Name** Property, **OpenRecordset** Method, **QueryDef** Object, **ReturnsRecords** Property, **SQL** Property, **Type** Property, **Value** Property.

76　CreateQueryDef Method

Example

This example creates a **QueryDef** named All Pubs with an SQL statement, and then creates a dynaset-type **Recordset** based on the query.

```
Dim dbsBiblio As Database, qdfAllPubs As QueryDef
Dim rstAllPubs As Recordset
' Open a database.
Set dbsBiblio = DBEngine.Workspaces(0).OpenDatabase("Biblio.mdb")
' Create a QueryDef.
Set qdfAllPubs = dbsBiblio.CreateQueryDef("All Pubs", _
    "SELECT * FROM Publishers;")
' Create Recordset from query.
Set rstAllPubs = qdfAllPubs.OpenRecordset
...
```

Example (Microsoft Access)

The following example creates a new **QueryDef** object, then opens the query in Datasheet view.

```
Sub NewQuery()
    Dim dbs As Database, qdf As QueryDef, strSQL As String

    ' Return Database variable pointing to current database.
    Set dbs = CurrentDb
    strSQL = "SELECT * FROM Employees WHERE [HireDate] >= #1-1-95#"
    Set qdf = dbs.CreateQueryDef("RecentHires", strSQL)
    DoCmd.OpenQuery qdf.Name
End Sub
```

Example (Microsoft Excel)

This example creates a new query based on the Customer recordset in the NWINDEX.MDB database. The query selects a snapshot of all customers in the state of Washington and then copies it onto Sheet1.

To create the NWINDEX.MDB database, run the Microsoft Excel example for the **CreateDatabase** method.

```
Dim db As Database, qDef As QueryDef, rs As Recordset
Set db = Workspaces(0).OpenDatabase(Application.Path & "\NWINDEX.MDB")
Set qDef = db.CreateQueryDef("WA Region")
qDef.SQL = "SELECT * FROM Customer WHERE [Region] = 'WA';"
Set rs = db.OpenRecordset("WA Region")
numberOfRows = Sheets("Sheet1").Cells(1, 1).CopyFromRecordset(rs)
Sheets("Sheet1").Activate
MsgBox numberOfRows & " records have been copied."
rs.Close
db.Close
```

CreateRelation Method

Applies To **Database** Object.

Description Creates a new **Relation** object.

Syntax Set *variable* = *database*.**CreateRelation**([*name*[, *table*[, *foreigntable*[, ↳ *attributes*]]]])

The **CreateRelation** method syntax uses these parts.

Part	Description
variable	A variable declared as an object data type **Relation**.
database	The variable name of the **Database** object you want to use to create the new **Relation** object.
name	A **String** variable that uniquely names the new **Relation** object. See the **Name** property for details on valid **Relation** names.
table	A **String** variable that names the primary table in the relation. If the table doesn't exist before you append the **Relation** object, a trappable error occurs.
foreigntable	A **String** variable that names the foreign table in the relation. If the table doesn't exist before you append the **Relation** object, a trappable error occurs.
attributes	A **Long** variable that contains information about the relationship type. See the **Attributes** property for details.

Remarks The **Relation** object relays information to the Microsoft Jet database engine about the relationship between fields in two **TableDef** or **QueryDef** objects. The Jet database engine can provide referential integrity through the **Attributes** property.

If you omit one or more of the optional parts when you use **CreateRelation**, you can use an appropriate assignment statement to set or reset the corresponding property before you append the new object to a collection. After you append the object, none of its property settings can be altered. See the individual property topics for more details.

Before you can use the **Append** method on a **Relation** object, you must append the appropriate **Field** objects to define the primary and foreign key relationship tables.

If *name* refers to an object that is already a member of the collection or if the **Field** object names provided in the subordinate **Fields** collection are invalid, a trappable error occurs when you use the **Append** method.

To remove a **Relation** object from a collection, use the **Delete** method on the collection.

78 CreateRelation Method

See Also **Append** Method, **Attributes** Property, **Delete** Method, **Name** Property, **TableDef** Object.

Example This example creates a new **Relation** object. In this case, the Customers table is related to a ValidStates table. Once established, the relationship requires that an entry exist in the ValidStates table corresponding to the Customers.CustState field before it can be added to the Customers table. Any changes to the State field that violate this relationship trigger a trappable error.

By setting the **dbRelationUpdateCascade** attribute, the Microsoft Jet database engine changes the Primary table Customers.CustState if a corresponding value changes in the ValidStates table. For example, if the ValidState entry TR was changed to TX, all Customers records having TR as a CustState code would be changed to TX.

```
Dim relTableOne As Relation
Dim dbsNorthwind As Database
Dim fldCustState As Field
Set dbsNorthwind = DBEngine.Workspaces(0).OpenDatabase("Northwind.mdb")
' Create new Relation object.
Set relTableOne = dbsNorthwind.CreateRelation("TableRelationOne")
relTableOne.Table = "Customers"            'Name the Primary Table.
relTableOne.ForeignTable = "ValidStates"   'Name the Foreign Table.
relTableOne.Attributes = dbRelationUpdateCascade
Set fldCustState = relTableOne.CreateField("CustState")
fldCustState.ForeignName = "StateCode"
relTableOne.Fields.Append fldCustState
' Save Relation definition by appending it to Relations collection.
dbsNorthwind.Relations.Append relTableOne
```

Example (Microsoft Access) The following example creates a new **Relation** object that defines a relationship between a Categories table and a Products table. The Categories table is the primary table in the relationship, and the Products table is the foreign table. The CategoryID field is the primary key in the Categories table, and a foreign key in the Products table.

To test this example in the Northwind database, click Relationships on the Tools menu, and delete the relationship between the Categories table and the Products table. Close the Relationships window, saving the current configuration at the prompt. Run the following procedure. Then view the Relationships window again to see the new relationship.

```
Sub NewRelation()
    Dim dbs As Database, rel As Relation, fld As Field

    ' Return Database variable pointing to current database.
    Set dbs = CurrentDb
```

```
                ' Create new Relation object and specify foreign table.
                Set rel = dbs.CreateRelation("CategoryID", "Categories", "Products")
                ' Set attributes to enforce referential integrity.
                rel.Attributes = dbRelationUpdateCascade + dbRelationDeleteCascade
                ' Create field in relation.
                Set fld = rel.CreateField("CategoryID")
                ' Specify field name in foreign table.
                fld.ForeignName = "CategoryID"
                ' Append Field object to Fields collection of Relation object.
                rel.Fields.Append fld
                ' Append Relation object to Relations collection.
                dbs.Relations.Append rel
            End Sub
```

CreateTableDef Method

Applies To **Database** Object.

Description Creates a new **TableDef** object.

Syntax Set *variable* = *database*.**CreateTableDef**([*name*[, *attributes*[, *source*[, ↪ *connect*]]]])

The **CreateTableDef** method syntax has these parts.

Part	Description
variable	A variable declared as an object data type **TableDef**.
database	The variable name of the **Database** object you want to use to create the new **TableDef** object.
name	A **String** variable that uniquely names the new **TableDef** object. See the **Name** property for details on valid **TableDef** names.
attributes	A **Long** variable that indicates one or more characteristics of the new **TableDef** object. See the **Attributes** property for more information.
source	A **String** variable containing the name of a table in an external database that is the original source of the data. The *source* string becomes the **SourceTableName** property setting of the new **TableDef** object.
connect	A **String** variable containing information about the source of an open database, a database used in a pass-through query, or an attached table. See the **Connect** property for more information on valid connection strings.

80 CreateTableDef Method

Remarks If you omit one or more of the optional parts when you use **CreateTableDef**, you can use an appropriate assignment statement to set or reset the corresponding property before you append the new object to a collection. After you append the object, you can alter some but not all of its properties. See the individual property topics for more details.

If *name* refers to an object that is already a member of the collection or you specify an invalid property in the **TableDef** or **Field** object you're appending, a trappable error occurs when you use the **Append** method.

To remove a **TableDef** object from a collection, use the **Delete** method on the collection.

See Also **Append** Method, **Attributes** Property, **Connect** Property, **Delete** Method, **Name** Property, **TableDef** Object.

Example This example creates a new **TableDef** object in the Biblio.mdb database.

```
Dim tdfTitleDetail As TableDef, fldComments As Field
Dim dbsBiblio As Database
Set dbsBiblio = DBEngine.Workspaces(0).OpenDatabase("Biblio.mdb")
' Create new TableDef.
Set tdfTitleDetail = dbsBiblio.CreateTableDef("Title Detail")
' Add field to tdfTitleDetail.
Set fldComments = tdfTitleDetail.CreateField("Comments",dbMemo)
tdfTitleDetail.Fields.Append fldComments
' Save TableDef definition by appending it to TableDefs collection.
dbsBiblio.TableDefs.Append tdfTitleDetail
```

Example (Microsoft Access) The following example creates a new **TableDef** object and appends it to the **TableDefs** collection of the current database.

```
Sub NewTable()
    Dim dbs As Database, tdf As TableDef, fld As Field

    ' Return Database variable pointing to current database.
    Set dbs = CurrentDb
    ' Return TableDef object variable that points to new table.
    Set tdf = dbs.CreateTableDef("Contacts")
    ' Define new field in table.
    Set fld = tdf.CreateField("ContactName", dbText, 40)
    ' Append Field object to Fields collection of TableDef object.
    tdf.Fields.Append fld
    ' Append TableDef object to TableDefs collection of database.
    dbs.TableDefs.Append tdf
End Sub
```

Example (Microsoft Excel) See the **CreateDatabase** method example (Microsoft Excel).

CreateUser Method

Applies To **Group** Object, **Workspace** Object.

Description Creates a new **User** object.

Syntax **Set** *variable* = *object*.**CreateUser**([*name*[, *pid* [, *password*]]])

The **CreateUser** method syntax has these parts.

Part	Description
variable	A variable declared as an object data type **User**.
object	The variable name of the **Group** or **Workspace** object you want to use to create the new **User** object.
name	A **String** variable that uniquely names the new **User** object. See the **Name** property for details on valid **User** names.
pid	A **String** variable containing the PID of a user account. The identifier must contain from 4 to 20 alphanumeric characters. See the **PID** property for more information on valid personal identifiers.
password	A **String** variable containing the password for the new **User** object. The password can be up to 14 characters long and can include any characters except the ASCII character 0 (null). See the **Password** property for more information on valid passwords.

Remarks If you omit one or more of the optional parts when you use **CreateUser**, you can use an appropriate assignment statement to set or reset the corresponding property before you append the new object to a collection. After you append the object, you can alter some but not all of its property settings. See the individual property topics for more details.

If *name* refers to an object that is already a member of the collection, a trappable error occurs when you use the **Append** method.

To remove a **User** object from a collection, use the **Delete** method on the collection.

See Also **Append** Method, **Delete** Method, **Name** Property, **Password** Property, **PID** Property, **User** Object.

Specifics (Microsoft Access) Once you have created a new **User** object and appended it to the **Users** collection of a **Workspace** or **Group** object, you can verify that the new user exists by examining the Name drop-down list box on the Users tab of the User And Group Accounts dialog box. This dialog box is available by pointing to Security on the Tools menu and then clicking User And Group Accounts.

Example This example creates a new **User** object.

```
Dim usrPartner As User
Dim strManagersPID As String
```

```
strManagersPID = "1122aabb"
' Create new user account.
Set usrPartner = DBEngine.Workspaces(0).CreateUser("Partner", _
    strManagersPID)
' Set other properties of usrPartner.
usrPartner.Password = "NewPassword"
' Save user account definition by appending it to Users collection.
DBEngine.Workspaces(0).Users.Append usrPartner
' Re-create usrPartner and append to Groups collection
Set usrPartner = DBEngine.Workspaces(0).CreateUser("Partner")
DBEngine.Workspaces(0).Groups(0).Users.Append usrPartner
```

CreateWorkspace Method

Applies To **DBEngine** Object.

Description Creates a new **Workspace** object.

Syntax **Set** *variable* = **CreateWorkspace**(*name*, *user*, *password*)

The **CreateWorkspace** method syntax has these parts.

Part	Description
variable	A variable declared as object data type **Workspace**.
name	A **String** variable that uniquely names the new **Workspace** object. See the **Name** property for details on valid **Workspace** names.
user	A **String** variable that identifies the owner of the new **Workspace** object. See the **UserName** property for more information.
password	A **String** variable containing the password for the new **Workspace** object. The password can be up to 14 characters long and can include any characters except ASCII character 0 (null). See the **Password** property for more information on valid passwords.

Remarks Unlike the other methods you use to create data access objects, **CreateWorkspace** requires that you provide all of its parts. In addition, **Workspace** objects aren't permanent and can't be saved. Once you create a **Workspace** object, you can't alter any of its property settings.

You don't have to append the new **Workspace** object to a collection before you can use it. You append a newly created **Workspace** object only if you need to be able to refer to it through the **Workspaces** collection.

If *name* refers to an object that is already a member of the **Workspaces** collection, a trappable error occurs.

Data Access Constants

Once you use **CreateWorkspace** to create a new **Workspace** object, a **Workspace** session is started, and you can refer to the **Workspace** object in your application.

To remove a **Workspace** object from the **Workspaces** collection, close all open databases and then use the **Close** method on the **Workspace** object.

See Also **Close** Method, **Name** Property, **Password** Property, **UserName** Property, **Workspace** Object.

Example This example creates a new **Workspace** object named Special, and sets its UserName property to "guest."

```
Dim wspSpecial As Workspace
' Create new workspace.
Set wspSpecial = DBEngine.CreateWorkspace("Special","guest", "")
```

Data Access Constants

Description You can use the Object Browser to view a list of built-in constants. From the View menu, choose Object Browser, select the appropriate library, and then select the Constants object. Scroll the list in the Methods/Properties box to see the complete list of constants.

The data access objects provide built-in constants that you can use with methods or properties. These constants all begin with the letters **db** and are documented with the method or property to which they apply.

Attributes Property Constants

Field.Attributes Property

Constant	Description
dbFixedField	Read/write. Field size fixed (default for Numeric fields).
dbVariableField	Read/write. Field size variable (Text fields only).
dbAutoIncrField	Read/write. New record field value incremented to unique Long integer (Counter type).
dbUpdatableField	Read-only. Field is updatable.
dbDescending	Read/write. Field sorted in descending order.
dbSystemField	Read-only. The field is a replication field (on a **TableDef** object).

Relation.Attributes Property

Constant	Description
dbRelationUnique	Read/write. One-to-one relationship.
dbRelationDontEnforce	Read/writeRelationship not enforced (no referential integrity).
dbRelationInherited	Read-only. Relationship exists in the database containing the two attached tables.
dbRelationUpdateCascade	Read/write. Updates cascade.
dbRelationDeleteCascade	Read/write. Deletions cascade.

TableDef.Attributes Property

Constant	Description
dbAttachExclusive	Read/write. Attached Microsoft Jet database engine table opened for exclusive use.
dbAttachSavePWD	Read/write. Save user ID and password for attached remote table.
dbSystemObject	Read-only. System table.
dbHiddenObject	Read/write. Hidden table (for temporary use).
dbAttachedTable	Read-only. Attached non-ODBC database table.
dbAttachedODBC	Read-only. Attached ODBC database table.

CollatingOrder Property Constants

All of the following constants are read/write.

Constant	Description
dbSortArabic	Arabic collating order.
dbSortCyrillic	Russian collating order.
dbSortCzech	Czech collating order.
dbSortDutch	Dutch collating order.
dbSortGeneral	English, German, French, and Portuguese collating order.
dbSortGreek	Greek collating order.
dbSortHebrew	Hebrew collating order.
dbSortHungarian	Hungarian collating order.

Data Access Constants

Constant	Description
dbSortIcelandic	Icelandic collating order.
dbSortJapanese	Japanese collating order.
dbSortNeutral	Neutral collating order.
dbSortNorw	Norwegian and Danish collating order.
dbSortPDXIntl	Paradox international collating order.
dbSortPDXNor	Paradox Norwegian and Danish collating order.
dbSortPDXSwe	Paradox Swedish and Finnish collating order.
dbSortPolish	Polish collating order.
dbSortSpanish	Spanish collating order.
dbSortSwedFin	Swedish and Finnish collating order.
dbSortTurkish	Turkish collating order.
dbSortUndefined	Collating order undefined or unknown.

EditMode Property Constants

All of the following constants are read-only.

Constant	Description
dbEditNone	No editing operation in effect.
dbEditInProgress	**Edit** method invoked.
dbEditAdd	**AddNew** method invoked.

Permissions Property Constants

Container.Permissions Property

All of the following constants are read/write.

Constant	Description
dbSecNoAccess	No access to the object.
dbSecFullAccess	Has full access to the object.
dbSecDelete	Can delete the object.
dbSecReadSec	Can read the object's security-related information.
dbSecWriteSec	Can alter access permissions.
dbSecWriteOwner	Can change the **Owner** property setting.

Databases Container.Permissions Property

All of the following constants are read/write.

Constant	Description
dbSecDBAdmin	Gives user permission to make a database replicable and change the database password.
dbSecDBCreate	Can create new databases (valid only on the databases **Container** object in the system database).
dbSecDBOpen	Can open the database.
dbSecDBExclusive	Has exclusive access.

Tables Container.Permissions Property

All of the following constants are read/write.

Constant	Description
dbSecCreate	Create new tables (valid only with a **Container** object that represents a table or with the databases **Container** object in the system database).
dbSecReadDef	Read the table definition, including column and index information.
dbSecWriteDef	Modify or delete table definition, including column and index information.
dbSecRetrieveData	Retrieve data from the document.
dbSecInsertData	Add records.
dbSecReplaceData	Modify records.
dbSecDeleteData	Delete records.

Document.Permissions Property

All of the following constants are read/write.

Constant	Description
dbSecCreate	Create new tables (valid only with a **Container** object that represents a table).
dbSecDBCreate	Can create new databases (valid only on the databases **Container** object in the system database).
dbSecDelete	Can delete the object.

Constant	Description
dbSecDBOpen	Can open the database.
dbSecDBExclusive	Has exclusive access.
dbSecDelete	Can delete the object.
dbSecDeleteData	Delete records.
dbSecFullAccess	Has full access to the object.
dbSecInsertData	No access to the object.
dbSecReadDef	Read the table definition, including column and index information.
dbSecReadSec	Can read the object's security-related information.
dbSecReplaceData	Modify records.
dbSecRetrieveData	Retrieve data from the document.
dbSecWriteDef	Modify or delete table definition, including column and index information.
dbSecWriteSec	Can alter access permissions.
dbSecWriteOwner	Can change the **Owner** property setting.

Type Property Constants

Field.Type Property, Parameter.Type Property, Property.Type Property

All of the following constants are read/write.

Constant	Description
dbBoolean	Boolean (True/False) data.
dbByte	Byte (8-bit) data.
dbInteger	Integer data.
dbLong	Long Integer data.
dbCurrency	Currency data.
dbSingle	Single-precision floating-point data.
dbDouble	Double-precision floating-point data.
dbDate	Date value data.
dbText	Text data (variable width).
dbLongBinary	Binary data (bitmap).
dbMemo	Memo data (extended text).
dbGUID	GUID data.

QueryDef.Type Property

All of the following constants are read-only.

Constant	Description
dbQSelect	SELECT query.
dbQAction	Action query.
dbQCrosstab	Crosstab query.
dbQDelete	DELETE query.
dbQUpdate	UPDATE query.
dbQAppend	APPEND query.
dbQMakeTable	Make-table query.
dbQDDL	Data definition language (DDL) query.
dbQSQLPassThrough	SQL pass-through query.
dbQSetOperation	Set operation query.
dbQSPTBulk	Bulk operation query.

Recordset.Type Property

All of the following constants are read-only.

Constant	Description
dbOpenTable	Open table-type **Recordset**.
dbOpenDynaset	Open dynaset-type **Recordset**.
dbOpenSnapshot	Open snapshot-type **Recordset**.

CompactDatabase, CreateDatabase Methods

The following constants are for the *locale* argument. All are read/write.

Constant	Description
dbLangArabic	Arabic collating order.
dbLangCyrillic	Russian collating order.
dbLangCzech	Czech collating order.
dbLangDutch	Dutch collating order.
dbLangGeneral	English, German, French, Portuguese, Italian, and Modern Spanish collating order.
dbLangGreek	Greek collating order.
dbLangHebrew	Hebrew collating order.
dbLangHungarian	Hungarian collating order.
dbLangIcelandic	Icelandic collating order.
dbLangJapanese	Japanese collating order.

Data Access Constants

Constant	Description
dbLangNeutral	Neutral collating order.
dbLangNordic	Nordic collating order.
dbLangNorwdan	Norwegian and Danish collating order.
dbLangPolish	Polish collating order.
dbLangSpanish	Spanish collating order.
dbLangSwedfin	Swedish and Finnish collating order.
dbLangTurkish	Turkish collating order.

CompactDatabase Method

The following constants are for the *options* argument. All are read/write.

Constant	Description
dbDecrypt	Decrypt database while compacting.
dbEncrypt	Encrypt database.
dbVersion10	Microsoft Jet database engine version 1.0.
dbVersion11	Microsoft Jet database engine version 1.1.
dbVersion20	Microsoft Jet database engine version 2.0.
dbVersion30	Microsoft Jet database engine version 3.0.

CreateDatabase Method

The following constants are for the *options* argument. All are read/write.

Constant	Description
dbEncrypt	Encrypt database.
dbVersion10	Microsoft Jet database engine version 1.0.
dbVersion11	Microsoft Jet database engine version 1.1.
dbVersion20	Microsoft Jet database engine version 2.0.
dbVersion30	Microsoft Jet database engine version 3.0.

Execute Method

The following constants are for the *options* argument. All are read/write.

Constant	Description
dbDenyWrite	Deny write permission to other users.
dbInconsistent	Inconsistent updates.
dbConsistent	Consistent updates.
dbSQLPassThrough	SQL pass-through. Causes the SQL statement to be passed to an ODBC database for processing.
dbFailOnError	Rolls back updates if an error occurs.
dbSeeChanges	Generates a run-time error if another user is changing data you are editing.

Idle Method

The following constant is for the optional argument.

Constant	Description
dbFreeLocks	Read/write. Delay processing until all read locks are released.

OpenRecordset Method

The following constants are for the *type* argument. All are read/write.

Constants	Description
dbOpenTable	Open table-type **Recordset**.
dbOpenDynaset	Open dynaset-type **Recordset**.
dbOpenSnapshot	Open snapshot-type **Recordset**.

The following constants are for the *options* argument. All are read/write.

Constant	Description
dbDenyWrite	Other users can't change **Recordset** records.
dbDenyRead	Other users can't read **Recordset** records.
dbReadOnly	Open the **Recordset** as read-only.
dbAppendOnly	You can add new records to the dynaset, but you can't read existing records.
dbInconsistent	Updates apply to all dynaset fields, even if other records are affected.
dbConsistent	Updates apply only to those fields that will not affect other records in the dynaset.
dbSQLPassThrough	Sends an SQL statement to an ODBC database.
dbForwardOnly	Create a forward-only scrolling snapshot-type **Recordset**.

MakeReplica Method

The following constant is for the optional argument.

Constant	Description
dbRepMakeReadOnly	Read/Write. Replicable elements of new database are read-only.

Synchronize Method

The following constants are for the *exchange* argument.

Constant	Description
dbRepExportChanges	Read/Write. Send changes from current database to target database.
dbRepImportChanges	Read/Write. Receive changes from target database.

Database Object

Description A **Database** object represents an open database.

Remarks You manipulate an open database using a **Database** object and its methods and properties. You can examine the collections in a **Database** object to learn about its tables, queries, and relationships. You can also use its collections to modify or create tables, queries, recordsets, and relationships. For example, you can:

- Use the **Execute** method to run an action **QueryDef** object or pass an SQL string to an ODBC database.
- Use the **OpenRecordset** method to create a new **Recordset** object directly from the **Database** object.
- Use the **Close** method to close an open database.

You use the **CreateDatabase** method to create a new, persistent **Database** object and append it to the **Databases** collection, thereby saving it to disk. After you create a new database, you must create new tables to hold your data. You can also create new indexes and table relationships, attach existing external tables, or establish a protection scheme using permissions, groups, and users.

To open an existing **Database** object, use the **OpenDatabase** method, which appends the object to the **Databases** collection. The **OpenDatabase** method applies to the **Workspace** object. You can use the **OpenDatabase** method on the default **Workspace**(0) object, or on a different opened **Workspace** object.

When you use one of the transaction methods (**BeginTrans**, **CommitTrans**, or **Rollback**) on the **Workspace** object, these transactions apply to all databases opened on the **Workspace** from which the **Database** object was opened. If you want to use independent transactions, you must first open an additional **Workspace** object, and then open another **Database** object in that **Workspace** object. For example, the following creates two independent **Database** objects:

```
Dim dbsThisOne As Database, dbsThatOne As Database
Dim wspFirst As Workspace, wspSecond As Workspace
Dim strUserName As String
Set wspFirst = Workspaces(0)   ' Use the default Workspace.
Set dbsThisOne = wspFirst.OpenDatabase("Biblio.mdb")

' Get UserName of default Workspace.
strUserName = wspFirst.UserName
' Create new Workspace.
Set wspSecond = DBEngine.CreateWorkspace("Special", strUserName, _
    "SpecialPW")
Set dbsThatOne = wspSecond.OpenDatabase("Biblio.mdb")
```

You don't need to specify the **DBEngine** object when using the **OpenDatabase** method. If you need to open a **Database** object in a separate transaction context, then you must reference a specific **Workspace** object. For example, the following statements are equivalent:

```
Set dbsBiblio = DBEngine.Workspaces(0).OpenDatabase("Biblio.mdb")
Set dbsBiblio = Workspaces(0).OpenDatabase("Biblio.mdb")
Set dbsBiblio = OpenDatabase("Biblio.mdb")
```

Opening a database with attached tables doesn't automatically establish links to the specified external files or external ODBC databases; either the table's **TableDef** or **Field** objects must be referenced, or a **Recordset** object opened on it. If links to these tables can't be established, a trappable error occurs. You may also need permission to access the database, or the database may already be open for exclusive use by another user. In these cases, trappable errors occur.

You can also open an external database (such as FoxPro, dBASE, and Paradox) directly instead of opening a Microsoft Jet database that has links to its tables. See the **OpenDatabase** method for more information.

For example, to open a FoxPro database, you could use the following code.

```
Dim dbsFoxFiles As Database
Set dbsFoxFiles = Workspaces(0).OpenDatabase("C:\FoxFiles", _
    False,False,"FoxPro 2.5")
```

Note Opening a **Database** object directly on an ODBC data source such as Microsoft SQLServer is not recommended because query performance is much slower than when using linked tables. Performance is not a problem with opening a **Database** object on an external ISAM database, such as FoxPro, Paradox, etc.

You use the **Close** method to remove a **Database** object from the **Databases** collection without deleting it from disk. Any open **Recordset** objects in the database are closed automatically when the **Database** object is closed.

When a procedure that declares a **Database** object completes execution, these local **Database** objects are closed along with any open **Recordset** objects. Any pending updates are lost and any pending transactions are rolled back, but no trappable error occurs. You should explicitly complete any pending transactions or edits and close **Recordset** objects and **Database** objects before exiting procedures that declare these object variables locally.

The first database opened is **Databases**(0). The **Name** property setting of a database is a string that specifies the path of the database file. The **Connect** property specifies the database type and any other parameters used to connect to external databases. You can refer to any **Database** object by its **Name** property setting using this syntax:

Databases("*name*")

You can also refer to the object by its ordinal number using this syntax (which refers to the first member of the **Databases** collection):

Databases(0)

Properties	**CollatingOrder** Property, **Connect** Property, **Name** Property, **QueryTimeout** Property, **RecordsAffected** Property, **Replicable** Property, **ReplicaID** Property, **Transactions** Property, **Updatable** Property, **Version** Property.
Methods	**Close** Method, **CreateProperty** Method, **CreateQueryDef** Method, **CreateRelation** Method, **CreateTableDef** Method, **Execute** Method, **MakeReplica** Method, **NewPassword** Method, **OpenRecordset** Method, **Synchronize** Method.
See Also	**OpenDatabase** Method; Appendix, "Data Access Object Hierarchy."
Specifics (Microsoft Access)	When working with data access objects from Microsoft Access, you will often need a **Database** object variable that represents the current database. Use the **CurrentDb** function to return a **Database** object for the database that is currently open. This **Database** object is automatically appended to the **Databases** collection.

For example, suppose you are currently working with the Northwind sample database in Microsoft Access. You can create a **Database** object that refers to that database by first declaring a **Database** object variable, then pointing it to the **Database** object returned by the **CurrentDb** function.

```
Dim dbs As Database
Set dbs = CurrentDb
```

You don't need to know the name of the database or its position in the **Databases** collection in order to use the current database. If you do want to know the name of the current database, check the **Name** property of the **Database** object, which contains the path and filename of the database. To find its position in the **Databases** collection, enumerate through the collection.

You can open only one database at a time in the Microsoft Access window. From Visual Basic code, however, you can create multiple independent **Database** object variables to represent multiple open databases. In this way, you can manipulate more than one database at a time from code. You can also create multiple **Database** object variables and point them to the current database.

Database Object

Note In your Visual Basic code, use the **CurrentDb** function to return a **Database** object that refers to the current database, rather than the **DBEngine**(0)(0) syntax. The **CurrentDb** function creates another instance of the current database, while the **DBEngine**(0)(0) syntax refers to the open copy of the current database. Using the **CurrentDb** function enables you to create more than one variable of type **Database** that refers to the current database. Microsoft Access still supports the **DBEngine**(0)(0) syntax, but you should consider making this modification to your code in order to avoid possible conflicts in a multiuser environment.

Example

This example creates a new **Database** object and opens it (thereby appending it to the **Databases** collection) in the default **Workspace** object. Then it enumerates all the collections contained by each **Database** object and the properties of the new **Database** object and closes the new **Database**.

```
Function EnumerateDatabase () As Integer
    Dim wrkDefault As Workspace
    Dim dbsEnum As Database, dbsTemp As Database
    Dim intOBJ As Integer, intDB As Integer
    Set wrkDefault = Workspaces(0)
    Set dbsEnum = wrkDefault.CreateDatabase("Northwind.mdb", _
        dbLangGeneral)
' Enumerate all open databases.
    For intDB = 0 To wrkDefault.Databases.Count - 1
        Set dbsTemp = wrkDefault.Databases(intDB)
        Debug.Print
        Debug.Print "Enumeration of Databases: "; dbsTemp.Name
        Debug.Print
' Enumerate containers.
        Debug.Print "Container: Name, Owner"
        For intOBJ = 0 To dbsTemp.Containers.Count - 1
            Debug.Print "  "; dbsTemp.Containers(intOBJ).Name;
            Debug.Print ", "; dbsTemp.Containers(intOBJ).Owner
        Next intOBJ
        Debug.Print
' Enumerate query definitions.
        Debug.Print "QueryDef: Name"
        For intOBJ = 0 To dbsTemp.QueryDefs.Count - 1
            Debug.Print "  "; dbsTemp.QueryDefs(intOBJ).Name
        Next intOBJ
        Debug.Print
' Enumerate Recordsets.
' No output because no Recordset is open.
        Debug.Print "Recordset: Name"
        For intOBJ = 0 To dbsTemp.Recordsets.Count - 1
            Debug.Print "  "; dbsTemp.Recordsets(intOBJ).Name
        Next intOBJ
        Debug.Print
```

Database Object

```
' Enumerate relationships.
        Debug.Print "Relation: Name, Table, ForeignTable"
        For intOBJ = 0 To dbsTemp.Relations.Count - 1
            Debug.Print "   "; dbsTemp.Relations(intOBJ).Name;
            Debug.Print ", "; dbsTemp.Relations(intOBJ).Table;
            Debug.Print ", "; dbsTemp.Relations(intOBJ).ForeignTable
        Next intOBJ
        Debug.Print
' Enumerate table definitions.
        Debug.Print "TableDef: Name, DateCreated"
        For intOBJ = 0 To dbsTemp.TableDefs.Count - 1
            Debug.Print "   "; dbsTemp.TableDefs(intOBJ).Name;
            Debug.Print ", "; dbsTemp.TableDefs(intOBJ).DateCreated
        Next intOBJ
        Debug.Print
    Next intDB
' Enumerate built-in properties of dbsEnum.
    Debug.Print " dbsEnum.Name: "; dbsEnum.Name
    Debug.Print " dbsEnum.CollatingOrder: "; dbsEnum.CollatingOrder
    Debug.Print " dbsEnum.Connect: "; dbsEnum.Connect
    Debug.Print " dbsEnum.QueryTimeout: "; dbsEnum.QueryTimeout
    Debug.Print " dbsEnum.Transactions: "; dbsEnum.Transactions
    Debug.Print " dbsEnum.Updatable: "; dbsEnum.Updatable
    Debug.Print
    dbsEnum.Close   ' File remains on disk.
    EnumerateDatabase = True
End Function
```

Example (Microsoft Access)

The following example show three ways to return a **Database** object in Microsoft Access. The procedure returns a **Database** object representing the current database, which is open in the Microsoft Access window. Next, the procedure creates another database called Newdb.mdb and saves it to disk. Then it opens an existing database called Another.mdb. Finally, it enumerates all **Database** objects in the **Databases** collection.

```
Sub ReferenceDatabases()
    Dim wsp As Workspace
    Dim dbsCurrent As Database, dbsNew As Database,
    Dim dbsAnother As Database, dbs As Database

    ' Return Database object pointing to current database.
    Set dbsCurrent = CurrentDb
    ' Return Workspace object pointing to current workspace.
    Set wsp = DBEngine.Workspaces(0)
    ' Create new Database object.
    Set dbsNew = wsp.CreateDatabase("Newdb.mdb", dbLangGeneral)
    ' Open database other than current database.
    set dbsAnother = wsp.OpenDatabase("Another.mdb", dbLangGeneral)
    ' Enumerate all open databases.
```

```
        For Each dbs in wsp.Databases
            Debug.Print dbs.Name
        Next dbs
End Sub
```

Databases Collection

Description	A **Databases** collection contains all open **Database** objects opened or created in a **Workspace** object of the Microsoft Jet database engine.
Remarks	When you open an existing **Database** object or create a new one from a **Workspace**, it is automatically appended to the **Databases** collection. When you close a **Database** object with the **Close** method, it is removed from the **Databases** collection but not deleted from disk. You should close all open **Recordset** objects before closing a **Database** object.
	The first database that is opened is appended to the collection as **Databases**(0). The **Name** property setting of a database is a string that specifies the path of the database file. You can refer to any **Database** object in a collection by its **Name** property using this syntax:
	Databases("*name*")
	You can also refer to the object by its ordinal number using this syntax (which refers to the first member of the **Databases** collection):
	Databases(0)
Properties	**Count** Property.
Methods	**Refresh** Method.
See Also	Appendix, "Data Access Object Hierarchy."
Specifics (Microsoft Access)	See the **Database** object specifics (Microsoft Access).
Example	See the **Database** object example.
Example (Microsoft Access)	See the **Database** object example (Microsoft Access).

DataUpdatable Property

Applies To **Field** Object.

Description Returns a value that indicates whether the data in the field represented by a **Field** object is updatable. Returns a **True** (-1) if the data in the field is updatable.

Remarks Use this property to determine whether you can change the **Value** property setting of a **Field** object. The **DataUpdatable** property is always read-only. It is not supported on **Field** objects appended to the **Fields** collection of **Index** and **Relation** objects.

See Also **Updatable** Property, **Value** Property.

Example (Microsoft Access) The following example creates two **Recordset** objects, a dynaset-type **Recordset** object and a snapshot-type **Recordset** object, from the same table. The procedure then checks the **DataUpdatable** property for the LastName field in each **Recordset** object. The value of the **DataUpdatable** property is **True** (-1) for the dynaset-type **Recordset** object, and **False** (0) for the snapshot-type **Recordset** object.

```
Sub CheckUpdatable()
    Dim dbs As Database
    Dim rstDynaset As Recordset, rstSnapshot As Recordset
    Dim fldDynaset As Field, fldSnapshot As Field

    ' Return Database variable that points to current database.
    Set dbs = CurrentDb
    ' Open dynaset-type Recordset object.
    Set rstDynaset = dbs.OpenRecordset("Employees", dbOpenDynaset)
    ' Open snapshot-type Recordset object.
    Set rstSnapshot = dbs.OpenRecordset("Employees", dbOpenSnapshot)
    ' Get Field object variables pointing to field in each Recordset
    'object.
    Set fldDynaset = rstDynaset.Fields!LastName
    Set fldSnapshot = rstSnapshot.Fields!LastName
    ' Get current record.
    rstDynaset.MoveFirst
    rstSnapshot.MoveFirst
    ' Display value of DataUpdatable property for each Recordset object.
    Debug.Print "DataUpdatable (Dynaset-type Recordset): "; _
        fldDynaset.DataUpdatable
    Debug.Print "DataUpdatable (Snapshot-type Recordset): "; _
        fldSnapshot.DataUpdatable
End Sub
```

DateCreated, LastUpdated Properties

Applies To   Document Object, QueryDef Object, Recordset Object, Table-Type Recordset Object, TableDef Object.

- **DateCreated**—returns the date and time that the object was created (or the base table if the object is a table-type **Recordset** object).
- **LastUpdated**—returns the date and time of the most recent change made to the object (or the base table if the object is a table-type **Recordset** object).

Return Values   This property returns a Date/Time data type.

Remarks   You can use the **DateCreated** and **LastUpdated** properties with **Recordset**, **TableDef**, **QueryDef**, and **Document** objects.

For table-type **Recordset** objects, the date and time settings are derived from the computer on which the base table was created or last updated. For other objects, this property returns the date and time that the object was created or last updated. In a multiuser environment, users should get these settings directly from the file server to avoid discrepancies in the **DateCreated** and **LastUpdated** property settings.

Example   This example determines the date and time when the Employees table was created and last updated.

```
Dim varCreation As Variant, varDesignChange As Variant
Dim rstEmployees As Recordset, dbsNorthwind As Database
Set dbsNorthwind = DBEngine.Workspaces(0).OpenDatabase("Northwind.mdb")
Set rstEmployees = dbsNorthwind.OpenRecordset("Employees", dbOpenTable)
varCreation = rstEmployees.DateCreated
varDesignChange = rstEmployees.LastUpdated
```

Example (Microsoft Access)   The following example enumerates through all **QueryDef** objects in the database and lists those which have been created or changed within the last week.

```
Sub TimeUpdated()
    Dim dbs As Database, tdf As TableDef, qdf As QueryDef
    Dim strList As String, intI As Integer
    Dim dteWeek As Date

    ' Return Database variable that points to current database.
    Set dbs = CurrentDb
    dteWeek = Now - 7
     intI = 0
    ' Enumerate through QueryDefs collection.
    For Each qdf In dbs.QueryDefs
        ' Evaluate LastUpdated and DateCreated properties.
        If (qdf.LastUpdated > dteWeek) Or (qdf.DateCreated > dteWeek) _
           Then
           ' Create list.
```

```
                    strList = strList & Chr(13) & Chr(10) & qdf.Name
                End If
                intI = intI + 1
        Next qdf
        MsgBox strList
End Sub
```

Example (Microsoft Excel)

This example displays the dates and times when the Customer recordset in the NWINDEX.MDB database was created and last updated.

To create the NWINDEX.MDB database, run the Microsoft Excel example for the **CreateDatabase** method.

```
Dim creation As Variant, changed As Variant
Dim db As Database, td As TableDef
Set db = Workspaces(0).OpenDatabase(Application.Path & "\NWINDEX.MDB")
Set td = db.TableDefs("Customer")
creation = td.DateCreated
changed = td.LastUpdated
MsgBox "The " & td.Name & " table was created on " & creation _
    & " and updated on " & changed
db.Close
```

DBEngine Object

Description

The **DBEngine** object represents the Microsoft Jet database engine. As the top-level object, it contains and controls all other objects in the hierarchy of data access objects.

Remarks

Use the **DBEngine** object to control the Jet database engine, manipulate its properties, and perform tasks on temporary objects that aren't elements of collections. For example, you can:

- Use the **Version** property to obtain the version number of the Jet engine, the **LoginTimeout** property to obtain or set the ODBC login timeout, and the **RegisterDatabase** method to provide ODBC information to the Jet engine.
- Use the **Idle** method to enable the Jet engine to complete any pending tasks and the **CompactDatabase** and **RepairDatabase** methods to maintain database files.
- Use the **CreateWorkspace** method to create a new session.
- Use the **Errors** collection to examine data access error details.

DBEngine Object

The **DBEngine** object is a predefined object; you can't create additional **DBEngine** objects. To refer to a collection that belongs to the **DBEngine** object, or to refer to a method or property that applies to this object, use this syntax:

[**DBEngine.**][*collection* | *method* | *property*]

The **DBEngine** object isn't an element of any collection.

Properties
: **DefaultUser**, **DefaultPassword** Properties; **IniPath** Property; **LoginTimeout** Property; **Version** Property.

Methods
: **CompactDatabase** Method, **CreateWorkspace** Method, **Idle** Method, **RegisterDatabase** Method, **RepairDatabase** Method.

See Also
: Appendix, "Data Access Object Hierarchy."

Specifics (Microsoft Access)
: Microsoft Access provides a means of manipulating data access objects from other applications through OLE Automation. If you are controlling Microsoft Access from another application, such as Visual Basic or Microsoft Excel, you can use the **DBEngine** property of the Microsoft Access **Application** object to return a reference to the **DBEngine** object. All data access objects and collections are then accessible through the **DBEngine** object.

Example
: This example enumerates the collections of the **DBEngine** object. See the methods and properties of **DBEngine** for additional examples.

```
Function EnumerateDBEngine () As Integer
    Dim wrkEnum As Workspace, intWSP As Integer
    Debug.Print "Enumeration of DBEngine"
    Debug.Print
    ' Enumerate all workspaces.
    Debug.Print "Workspaces: Name, UserName"
    For intWSP = 0 To Workspaces.Count - 1
        Set wrkEnum = Workspaces(intWSP)
        Debug.Print "  "; wrkEnum.Name;
        Debug.Print ", "; wrkEnum.UserName
    Next intWSP
    Debug.Print
    ' Enumerate built-in properties.
    Debug.Print "DBEngine.Version: "; DBEngine.Version
    Debug.Print "DBEngine.LoginTimeout: "; DBEngine.LoginTimeout
    EnumerateDBEngine = True
End Function
```

Example (Microsoft Access)
: The following example prints all the properties of the **DBEngine** object.

```
Sub EngineProperties()
    Dim prp As Property
```

```
        For Each prp In DBEngine.Properties
            Debug.Print prp.Name
        Next prp
End Sub
```

DefaultUser, DefaultPassword Properties

Applies To **DBEngine** Object.

- **DefaultUser**—sets the user name used by the Microsoft Jet database engine when it is initialized.
- **DefaultPassword**—sets the password used by the Microsoft Jet database engine when it is initialized.

Settings The setting for user name can be 1–20 characters long and can include alphabetic characters, accented characters, numbers, spaces, and symbols except for: " (quotation marks), / (forward slash), \ (backslash), [ ] (brackets), : (colon), | (pipe), < (less-than sign), > (greater-than sign), + (plus sign), = (equal sign), ; (semicolon), , (comma), ? (question mark), * (asterisk), leading spaces, and control characters (ASCII 00 to ASCII 31).

The setting for password can be up to 14 characters long and can contain any character except ASCII 0. The data type is **String**.

Remarks User names aren't usually case-sensitive; however, if you're re-creating a user account that was deleted or created in a different workgroup, the user name must be an exact case-sensitive match of the original name. Passwords are case-sensitive.

Typically, the **CreateWorkspace** method is used to create a **Workspace** object with a given user name and password. However, for backward compatibility with earlier versions and for convenience when secured databases aren't being used, the Jet engine automatically creates a default **Workspace** object when needed if one isn't already open. In this case, the **DefaultUser** and **DefaultPassword** property values define the user and password for the default **Workspace** object.

By default, the **DefaultUser** property is set to "admin" and the **DefaultPassword** property is set to a zero-length string ("").

For this property to take effect, it should be set before any data access functions are called.

DefaultValue Property

Applies To Field Object.

Description Sets or returns the default value of a **Field** object. For a **Field** object not yet appended to the **Fields** collection, this property is read/write.

Settings and Return Values The setting or return value for this property is a string expression, which can contain a maximum of 255 characters. It can be either text or an expression. If the property setting is an expression, it can't contain user-defined functions; Microsoft Jet database engine SQL aggregate functions; or references to queries, forms, or other Field objects.

> **Note** You can also set the **DefaultValue** property of a **Field** object on a **TableDef** object to a special value called "GenUniqueId( )". This causes a random number to be assigned to this field whenever a new record is added or created. The field's **Type** property must be **Long**.

Remarks Use of the **DefaultValue** property depends on the parent object of the **Field** objects, as shown in the following table.

Object appended to	Usage
Index	Not supported
QueryDef	Read-only
Recordset	Read-only
Relation	Not supported
TableDef	Read/write

When a new record is created, the **DefaultValue** property setting is automatically entered as the value for the field. You can change the field value by setting its **Value** property.

The **DefaultValue** property doesn't apply to Counter and OLE Object fields.

See Also **AllowZeroLength** Property, **QueryDef** Object, **Required** Property, **TableDef** Object, **ValidateOnSet** Property, **ValidationRule** Property, **ValidationText** Property, **Value** Property.

Specifics (Microsoft Access) If the **DefaultValue** property setting is an expression, it can't contain user-defined functions, Microsoft Access domain aggregate functions, SQL aggregate functions, the **CurrentUser** function, the **Eval** function, or references to queries, forms, or other **Field** objects.

**Example
(Microsoft Access)**

The following example creates a new **Field** object and sets its **DefaultValue** property. The procedure then appends the new object to the **Fields** collection of the Employees table in the **TableDefs** collection of the database.

```
Sub NewField()
    Dim dbs As Database, tdf As TableDef
    Dim fld As Field

    ' Return Database object that points to current database.
    Set dbs = CurrentDb
    ' Return TableDef variable pointing to Employees table.
    Set tdf = dbs.TableDefs!Employees
    ' Create Field object.
    Set fld = tdf.CreateField("DaysOfVacation", dbText, 20)
    ' Set field properties.
    fld.DefaultValue = "10"
    ' Append fld to Fields collection.
    tdf.Fields.Append fld
End Sub
```

Delete Method

Applies To

Dynaset-Type **Recordset** Object, **Fields** Collection, **Groups** Collection, **Indexes** Collection, **Properties** Collection, **QueryDefs** Collection, **Recordset** Object, **Relations** Collection, Table-Type **Recordset** Object, **TableDefs** Collection, **Users** Collection, **Workspaces** Collection.

- **Recordset** objects—deletes the current record in an open dynaset-type or table-type **Recordset** object.
- Collections—deletes a stored object from a collection.

Syntax

recordset.**Delete**

collection.**Delete** *objectname*

The **Delete** method syntax has these parts.

Part	Description
recordset	A variable of an object data type identifying an open dynaset-type or table-type **Recordset** object containing the record you want to delete.
collection	A variable of an object data type identifying a collection.
objectname	A **String** that is the **Name** property setting of an object in *collection*.

104 Delete Method

Remarks

You can use the **Delete** method to delete a current record from a recordset or a member from a collection, such as a stored table from a database, a stored field from a table, and a stored index from a table.

Recordsets

When you delete records from a recordset, the *recordset* must contain a current record before you use **Delete**; otherwise, a trappable error occurs.

In table- and dynaset-type **Recordset** objects, **Delete** removes the current record and makes it inaccessible. Although you can't edit or use the deleted record, it remains current. Once you move to another record, however, you can't make the deleted record current again. Subsequent references to a deleted record in a **Recordset** are invalid and produce an error.

You can undelete a record if you use transactions and the **Rollback** method.

If the base table is the primary table in a cascade delete relationship, deleting the current record may also delete one or more records in a foreign table.

Collections

You can use the **Delete** method to delete a persistent object. However, if the collection is a **Databases**, **Recordsets**, or **Workspaces** collection (each of which is stored only in memory), you can remove an open or active object only by closing that object using the **Close** method.

The deletion of a stored object occurs immediately, but you should use the **Refresh** method on any other collections that may be affected by changes to the database structure.

When you delete a **TableDef** object from the **TableDefs** collection, you delete the table definition and the data in the table.

The following table shows some limitations on the use of the **Delete** method. The object in the first column contains the collection in the second column. The third column indicates when, if ever, you can delete an object from that collection (for example, you can never delete a **Container** object from the **Containers** collection of a **Database** object).

Object	Collection	When you can use Delete method
DBEngine	**Workspaces**	Never; use the **Close** method instead
Workspace	**Databases**	Never; use the **Close** method instead
Database	**Containers**	Never
Database	**Recordsets**	Never; use the **Close** method instead
Container	**Documents**	Never

Object	Collection	When you can use Delete method
Index	**Fields**	On new objects that haven't been appended to the database
QueryDef	**Fields**	Never
QueryDef	**Parameters**	Never
Recordset	**Fields**	Never
Relation	**Fields**	On new objects that haven't been appended to the database
TableDef	**Fields**	On new objects that haven't been appended to the database or when the **Updatable** property of the **TableDef** is set to **True**
TableDef	**Indexes**	On new objects that haven't been appended to the database or when the **Updatable** property of the **TableDef** is set to **True**
Database, **Field, Index, QueryDef, TableDef**	**Properties**	When the property is user-defined

See Also

AddNew Method, **Append** Method, **Close** Method, **Count** Property, **Name** Property, **Refresh** Method.

Example

This example finds a record in a **Recordset** and deletes it.

```
' Find the record you want to delete.
rstPublications.FindFirst "PubNum = 9"
If Not rstPublications.NoMatch Then    ' Check if record found.
    rstPublications.Delete             ' Delete the record.
End If
```

This example adds and then deletes an **Index** from a **TableDef**.

```
Dim dbsBiblio As Database
Dim tdfAuthors As TableDef
Dim idxAuthorName As Index, fldAuthor As Field
' Open the database.
Set dbsBiblio = DBEngine.Workspaces(0).OpenDatabase("Biblio.mdb")
' Set the TableDef.
Set tdfAuthors = dbsBiblio.TableDefs("Authors")
Set idxAuthorName = tdfAuthors.CreateIndex("Author Name")
Set fldAuthor = idxAuthorName.CreateField("Author")
idxAuthorName.Fields.Append fldAuthor    ' Add Field to Index.
' Append Index to TableDef.
tdfAuthors.Indexes.Append idxAuthorName
tdfAuthors.Indexes.Delete "Author Name"  ' Delete the Index.
```

**Example
(Microsoft Access)**

The following example creates a field in a table and then deletes the field.

```
Sub DeleteField()
    Dim dbs As Database, tdf As TableDef
    Dim fldInitial As Field, fld As Field

    ' Return Database variable pointing to current database.
    Set dbs = CurrentDb
    Set tdf = dbs.TableDefs!Orders
    ' Create new Field object, specifying name, type, and size.
    Set fldInitial = tdf.CreateField("MiddleInitial", dbText, 2)
    ' Append new Field object.
    tdf.Fields.Append fldInitial
    ' Enumerate through Fields collection to find new Field object.
    For Each fld In tdf.Fields
        If fld.Name = "MiddleInitial" Then
            ' Delete new Field object.
            tdf.Fields.Delete fld.Name
            MsgBox "Field deleted."
        End If
    Next fld
End Sub
```

**Example
(Microsoft Excel)**

This example adds a new record to PRODUCT.DBF (a dBASE IV table located in the C:\Program Files\Common Files\Microsoft Shared\MSquery folder) and then deletes it. (On Windows NT, PRODUCT.DBF is located in the \WINDOWS\MSAPPS\MSQUERY folder.)

```
Const sourceDir = "C:\Program Files\Common Files\Microsoft Shared\MSQuery"
Dim db As Database, rs As Recordset
Sheets("Sheet1").Activate
Set theID = ActiveSheet.Cells(1, 2)
Set theCategory = ActiveSheet.Cells(2, 2)
theID.Value = 200
theCategory.Value = "BEVR"
Set db = OpenDatabase(sourceDir, False, False, "dBASE IV")
Set rs = db.OpenRecordset("PRODUCT.DBF", dbOpenTable)
rs.AddNew
rs("PRODUCT_ID") = theID.Value
rs("CATEGORY") = theCategory.Value
rs.Update
MsgBox "The new record has been created with " & theID.Value _
    & " and " & theCategory.Value
rs.Move 0, rs.LastModified
rs.Delete
MsgBox "The record you just created has been deleted"
rs.Close
db.Close
```

Description Property

Applies To **Error** Object.

Description Returns a descriptive string associated with an error.

Remarks The **Description** property comprises a short description of the error. Display this property to alert the user to an error that you cannot or do not want to handle.

See Also **HelpContext**, **HelpFile** Properties; **Number** Property; **Source** Property.

Specifics (Microsoft Access) The data access **Description** property applies to the **Error** object and returns a string associated with an error. You can set it only from Visual Basic.

> **Note** Don't confuse this property with the Microsoft Access **Description** property, which describes a table or query and its fields. This property applies to a **TableDef** object, a **QueryDef** object, or a **Field** object in the **Fields** collection of a **TableDef** or **QueryDef** object.

Example This example forces an error, traps it, and displays the **Description**, **Number**, and **Source** properties of the resulting **Error** object.

```
Sub ForceError()
    Dim dbsTest As Database
    On Error GoTo TestErrorHandler
    Set dbsTest = OpenDatabase("DoesNotExist")
    Exit Sub

TestErrorHandler:
    Dim strError As String
    Dim errObj As Error
    strError = " "
    For Each errObj in DBEngine.Errors
        strError = strError & Format$(errObj.Number)
        strError = strError & " : " & errObj.Description
        strError = strError & " (" & errObj.Source & ") . "
        strError = strError & Chr$(13) & Chr$(10)
    Next
    MsgBox strError
    Resume Next
End Sub
```

DesignMasterID Property

Applies To **Database** Object.

Description Sets or returns a 16-byte, OLE 2 **GUID**, created by the Microsoft Jet database engine, that uniquely identifies the Design Master in a replica set.

Remarks The **DesignMasterID** property setting is stored in the MSysReplicas system table. Setting the **DesignMasterID** property gives a specific replica in the replica set design-master status. The **DesignMasterID** property can be set only if you are at the current Design Master. Under extreme circumstances, for example, the loss of the original Design Master, you can set the value at another replica. However, setting this value at a replica, when there is already another Design Master, might partition your replica set into two irreconcilable sets and prevent any further synchronization of data.

Warning This property should be set only at the current Design Master. Setting this property at a replica, when there is already another Design Master, can partition your replica set into two irreconcilable sets and prevent any further synchronization of data. You can set the property at another replica only if the original Design Master is lost or erased. This will designate the current replica as the new Design Master.

See Also **ReplicaID** Property.

Example This example sets the **DesignMasterID** property to the **ReplicaID** property setting of another database giving that database design-master status in the replica set.

```
' Open current Design Master in exclusive mode.
Set dbs = DBEngine(0).OpenDatabase(strOldDM, True)
' Open new Design Master.
set newdmdb = DBEngine(0).OpenDatabase(strNewDB)

dbs.DesignMasterID = newdmdb.ReplicaID
dbs.Synchronize strNewDB,dbRepImpExpChanges

dbs.Close
newdmdb.Close
```

DistinctCount Property

Applies To **Index** Object.

Description Returns a value that indicates the number of unique values for the **Index** object that are included in the associated table.

Return Values This property returns a **Long** data type.

Remarks Check the **DistinctCount** property to determine the number of unique values, or keys, in an index. Any key is counted only once, even though there may be multiple occurrences of that value if the index permits duplicate values. This information is useful in applications that attempt to optimize data access by evaluating index information. The number of unique values is also known as the *cardinality* of an **Index** object.

The **DistinctCount** property won't always reflect the actual number of keys at a particular time. For example, a change caused by a transaction rollback won't be reflected immediately in the **DistinctCount** property. The number will be accurate immediately after using the **CreateIndex** method.

Example This example checks the **DistinctCount** property of an **Index** of a **TableDef** object opened on a table in the database.

```
Dim dbsNorthwind As Database, tdfCustomers As TableDef
Dim idxCurrent As Index
Set dbsNorthwind = DBEngine.Workspaces(0).OpenDatabase("Northwind.mdb")
Set tdfCustomers = dbsNorthwind!Customers
Set idxCurrent = tdfCustomers.Indexes(0)
Debug.Print idxCurrent.DistinctCount
```

Example (Microsoft Access) The following example prints the number of unique values in the indexes on the OrderID and OrderDate fields of an Orders table. Note that the **DistinctCount** property is guaranteed to return the number of unique values in an index only immediately after an index has been created with the **CreateIndex** method, or after a database has been compacted or converted using the **CompactDatabase** method.

```
Sub CountKeys()
    Dim dbs As Database, tdf As TableDef
    Dim idx As Index, fldOrderID As Field, fldOrderDate As Field

    ' Return Database variable that points to current database.
    Set dbs = CurrentDb
    ' Return TableDef object pointing to Orders table.
    Set tdf = dbs.TableDefs!Orders
    ' Create new index.
    Set idx = tdf.CreateIndex("OrderIDDate")
    ' Create and append index fields.
    Set fldOrderID = idx.CreateField("OrderId", dbLong)
```

```
            Set fldOrderDate = idx.CreateField("OrderDate", dbDate)
            idx.Fields.Append fldOrderID
            idx.Fields.Append fldOrderDate
            ' Append new index.
            tdf.Indexes.Append idx
            ' Refresh Indexes collection.
            tdf.Indexes.Refresh
            ' Print value of DistinctCount property for new index.
            Debug.Print idx.DistinctCount
        End Sub
```

Document Object

Description

A **Document** object includes information about one instance of a type of object. The object can be a database, saved table, query, or relationship.

Remarks

Each **Container** object has a **Documents** collection containing **Document** objects that describe instances of built-in **Container** types. The following table lists the type of object each **Document** describes, the name of its **Container** object, and what type of information **Document** contains.

Document	Container	Contains information about
Database	Databases	Containing database
Table or query	Tables	Saved table or query
Relationship	Relations	Saved relationship

Note Don't confuse the particular types of **Container** objects with the collection types of the same name. For example, the Databases **Container** object refers to all saved objects of the specified type, but the **Databases** collection refers only to open objects of the specified type.

Because a **Document** object corresponds to an existing object, you can't create new **Document** objects or delete existing ones. Using the properties of an existing **Document** object, you can:

- Determine the name that a user or the Microsoft Jet database engine gave to the object when it was created by checking the **Name** property setting.
- Determine or specify the owner of the object by checking or setting the **Owner** property. To set the **Owner** property, you must have write permission for the **Document** object, and you must set the property to the name of an existing **User** or **Group** object.

- Determine the name of the **Container** object that contains the **Document** object by checking the **Container** property setting.
- Determine or specify the access permissions of a user or group for the object by checking or setting the **UserName** or **Permissions** property. To set these properties, you must have write permission for the **Document** object, and you must set the **UserName** property to the name of an existing **User** or **Group** object.
- Determine the date and time when the **Document** object was created and last modified by checking the **DateCreated** and **LastUpdated** property settings.

You can refer to a **Document** object by its **Name** property setting using this syntax:

cntApplication.**Documents**("*name*")

Properties **AllPermissions** Property; **Container** Property; **DateCreated**, **LastUpdated** Properties; **Name** Property; **Owner** Property; **Permissions** Property; **UserName** Property.

See Also **User** Object; Appendix, "Data Access Object Hierarchy."

Specifics (Microsoft Access) In addition to the **Document** objects defined by the Microsoft Jet database engine, the following **Document** objects are defined by Microsoft Access.

Document	Container	Contains information about
Form	Forms	Saved form
Macro	Scripts	Saved macro
Module	Modules	Saved module
Report	Reports	Saved report
SummaryInfo	Databases	Database document summary
UserDefined	Databases	User-defined properties

The **Document** objects defined by Microsoft Access are Microsoft Access database objects, not data access objects. These **Document** objects provide the Jet database engine with information about Microsoft Access objects. The Jet database engine uses this information to implement security on Microsoft Access database objects in the same way it does for data access objects.

The **Documents** collection of a **Container** object contains **Document** objects representing the individual objects of the type described by the **Container** object. For example, the Forms **Container** object has a **Documents** collection that might include a **Document** object corresponding to a form named Orders.

Microsoft Access defines two **Document** objects in the Databases **Container** object—SummaryInfo and UserDefined.

Document Object

The SummaryInfo **Document** object provides programmatic access to document summary properties—including **Title**, **Subject**, **Author**, **Keywords**, **Comments**, **Manager**, **Company**, and **Category**. You can also set these properties on the Summary tab of the Database Properties dialog box, available by clicking Database Properties on the File menu.

To set these properties in Visual Basic, you must create them and append them to the **Properties** collection of the SummaryInfo **Document** object if they have not already been set in the Database Properties dialog box. Once a property has been created, you must explicitly refer to the **Properties** collection to set it. In the following example, doc is an object variable pointing to the SummaryInfo **Document** object.

```
doc.Properties!Title = "Northwind Traders"
```

For more information on creating and setting Microsoft Access-defined properties, see the topics for the **Property** object and **CreateProperty** method.

The UserDefined **Document** object provides programmatic access to user-defined properties defined on the Custom tab of the Database Properties dialog box. You can also create these properties in Visual Basic and append them to the **Properties** collection of the UserDefined **Document** object.

Note Don't confuse properties defined in the **Properties** collection of a **Database** document with properties defined in the **Properties** collection of a **Database** object. You can create user-defined properties in either **Properties** collection, but only those defined on the SummaryInfo or UserDefined **Document** objects can be set from the Database Properties dialog box.

You can use **Document** objects to establish and enforce permissions for individual Microsoft Access database objects. To set permissions for a **Document** object, set the **UserName** property of the **Document** object to the name of an existing **User** or **Group** object. Then set the **Permissions** property for the **Document** object.

Note Don't confuse the particular types of **Container** objects with the collection types of the same name. The Forms and Reports **Container** objects each contain **Documents** collections, which include individual **Document** objects representing each saved form or report. The **Forms** and **Reports** collections refer only to open forms or reports.

Example

See the **Container** object example.

**Example
(Microsoft Access)**

The following example prints the name of each Form **Document** object in the current database and the date it was last modified.

```
Sub DocumentModified()
    Dim dbs As database, ctr As container, doc As Document

    ' Return Database variable pointing to current database.
    Set dbs = CurrentDb
    ' Return Container variable pointing to Forms container.
    Set ctr = dbs.Containers!Forms
    ' Enumerate through Documents collection of Forms container.
    For Each doc In ctr.Documents
        ' Print Document object name and value of LastUpdated property.
        Debug.Print doc.Name; "    "; doc.LastUpdated
    Next doc
End Sub
```

Documents Collection

Description A **Documents** collection contains all of the **Document** objects for a specific type of object.

Remarks Each **Container** object has a **Documents** collection containing **Document** objects that describe instances of built-in **Container** types property settings.

You can refer to a **Document** object in a collection by its **Name** property setting using this syntax:

cntApplication.**Documents**("*name*")

Properties **Count** Property.

Methods **Refresh** Method.

See Also Appendix, "Data Access Object Hierarchy."

**Specifics
(Microsoft Access)** See the **Document** object specifics (Microsoft Access).

Example See the **Container** object example.

**Example
(Microsoft Access)** See the **Document** object example (Microsoft Access).

Dynaset-Type Recordset Object

Description A dynaset-type **Recordset** object is a type of **Recordset** object you can use to manipulate data in an underlying database table or tables. A dynaset-type **Recordset** object is a dynamic set of records that can contain fields from one or more tables or queries in a database and may be updatable.

Remarks To create a dynaset-type **Recordset** object, use the **OpenRecordset** method on an open database, against another dynaset- or snapshot-type **Recordset** object, or on a **QueryDef** object.

A dynaset-type **Recordset** object is different from a snapshot-type **Recordset** object because only a unique key for each record is brought into memory, instead of actual data. As a result, a dynaset is normally updated with changes made to the source data, while the snapshot is not. Like the table-type **Recordset** object, a dynaset's current record is fetched only when its fields are referenced.

If you request a dynaset-type **Recordset** object and the Microsoft Jet database engine is unable to gain read-write access to the records, the Jet database engine may create a read-only, dynaset-type **Recordset** object. If the **Recordset** object created isn't updatable, its **Updatable** property setting is **False** (0).

As base table data changes due to updates made by your application or by other users, current data is available to your application when you reposition the current record. In a multiuser database, more than one user can open a dynaset-type **Recordset** object referring to the same records. Because a dynaset-type **Recordset** object is dynamic, when one user changes a record, other users have immediate access to the changed data. However, if one user adds a record, other users aren't notified until they use the **Requery** method on the **Recordset** object. If a user deletes a record, other users are notified when they try to access it.

Records added to the database don't become a part of your dynaset-type **Recordset** object unless you add them using the **AddNew** method. For example, if you use an action query containing an INSERT INTO SQL statement to add records, the new records aren't included in your dynaset-type **Recordset** object until you either use the **Requery** method or you rebuild your **Recordset** object using the **OpenRecordset** method.

To maintain data integrity, dynaset- and table-type **Recordset** objects are locked during **Edit** (pessimistic locking) and **Update** methods operations (optimistic locking) so that only one user can update a particular record at a time. When the Jet database engine locks a record, it locks the entire 2K page containing the record.

Optimistic and pessimistic locking are also used with non-ODBC tables. When you access external tables using ODBC you should always use optimistic locking. The locking conditions in effect during editing are determined by the **LockEdits** property.

Dynaset-Type Recordset Object 115

Not all fields can be updated in all dynaset-type **Recordset** objects. To determine whether you can update a particular field, check the **Updatable** property setting of the **Field** object.

A dynaset-type **Recordset** object may not be updatable if:

- There isn't a unique index on the ODBC or Paradox table or tables.
- The data page is locked by another user.
- The record has changed since you last read it.
- The user doesn't have permission.
- One or more of the tables or fields are set to read-only.
- The database is opened as read-only.
- The **Recordset** object was either created from multiple tables without a JOIN statement or the query was too complex.

The order of dynaset-type **Recordset** object or **Recordset** data doesn't necessarily follow any specific sequence. If you need to order your data, use an SQL statement with an ORDER BY clause to create the **Recordset** object. You can also use this technique to filter the records so that only certain records are added to the **Recordset** object. For example, the following code selects only titles that were published between 1993 and 1994 and sorts the resulting records by title.

```
Dim dbsBiblio As Database, rstTitles As Recordset
Dim strSelect As String
Set dbsBiblio = Workspaces(0).OpenDatabase("Biblio.mdb")
strSelect = "SELECT * FROM Titles  " _
    & " WHERE [Year Published] BETWEEN 1993 AND 1994 " _
        & " ORDER BY ISBN;"
Set rstTitles = dbsBiblio.OpenRecordset(strSelect, dbOpenDynaset)
```

Using this technique instead of using the **Filter** or **Sort** properties or testing each record individually generally results in faster access to your data.

Properties **AbsolutePosition** Property; **BOF, EOF** Properties; **Bookmark** Property; **Bookmarkable** Property; **CacheSize, CacheStart** Properties; **EditMode** Property; **Filter** Property; **LastModified** Property; **LockEdits** Property; **Name** Property; **NoMatch** Property; **PercentPosition** Property; **RecordCount** Property; **Restartable** Property; **Sort** Property; **Transactions** Property; **Type** Property; **ValidationRule** Property; **ValidationText** Property.

Methods **CancelUpdate** Method; **Clone** Method; **Close** Method; **CopyQueryDef** Method; **Edit** Method; **FillCache** Method; **FindFirst, FindLast, FindNext, FindPrevious** Methods; **GetRows** Method; **Move** Method; **MoveFirst, MoveLast, MoveNext, MovePrevious** Methods; **OpenRecordset** Method; **Requery** Method; **Update** Method.

Dynaset-Type Recordset Object

See Also **OpenRecordset** Method; **Recordset** Object; **Updatable** Property; Appendix, "Data Access Object Hierarchy."

Example This example creates a new dynaset-type **Recordset** object and opens it, appending it to the **Recordsets** collection in the default database. It then edits the record(s).

```
Function ChangeSQL () As Integer
    Dim dbsBiblio As Database, rstTitles As Recordset
    Dim strSelect As String
    Set dbsBiblio = DBEngine.Workspaces(0).OpenDatabase("Biblio.mdb")
    strSelect = "Select * From Titles Where Title = 'Using SQL' "
    Set rstTitles = dbsBiblio.OpenRecordset(strSelect, dbOpenDynaset)
    If rstTitles.RecordCount > 0 and rstTitles.Updatable Then
        Do Until rstTitles.EOF
            With rstTitles
                .Edit
                ![Year Published] = 1994   ' Change year published.
                .Update
                .MoveNext
            End With
        Loop
    Else
        Debug.Print "No such title or table not updatable"
    End If
    dbsBiblio.Close
    ChangeSQL = True
End Function
```

Example (Microsoft Access) The following example creates a dynaset-type **Recordset** object, then checks the **Updatable** property of the **Recordset** object.

```
Sub RecentHires()
    Dim dbs As Database, rst As Recordset
    Dim strSQL As String

    ' Return Database object pointing to current database.
    Set dbs = CurrentDb
    strSQL = "SELECT * FROM Employees WHERE HireDate >= #1-1-95#;"
    Set rst = dbs.OpenRecordset(strSQL, dbOpenDynaset)
    Debug.Print rst.Updatable
End Sub
```

Edit Method

Applies To	Dynaset-Type **Recordset** Object, **Recordset** Object, Table-Type **Recordset** Object.
Description	Copies the current record from a dynaset-type or table-type **Recordset** object to the copy buffer for subsequent editing.
Syntax	*recordset*.**Edit**
	The *recordset* placeholder represents the name of an open, updatable **Recordset** object that contains the record you want to edit.
Remarks	Once you use the **Edit** method, changes made to the current record's fields are copied to the copy buffer. After you make the desired changes to the record, use the **Update** method to save your changes.

Caution If you edit a record and then perform any operation that moves to another record without first using **Update**, your changes are lost without warning. In addition, if you close *recordset* or end the procedure which declares the recordset or the parent **Database** object, your edited record is discarded without warning.

When the **Recordset** object's **LockEdits** property setting is **True** (pessimistically locked) in a multiuser environment, the record remains locked from the time **Edit** is used until the updating is complete. If the **LockEdits** property setting is **False** (optimistically locked), the record is locked and compared with the pre-edited record just before it's updated in the database. If the record has changed since you used the **Edit** method, the **Update** operation fails with a trappable error (3197).

Note Optimistic locking is always used on external database formats, such as ODBC and installable ISAM.

The current record remains current after you use **Edit**.

To use **Edit**, there must be a current record. If there is no current record or if *recordset* doesn't refer to an open table-type or dynaset-type **Recordset** object, an error occurs.

Using **Edit** produces an error under the following conditions:

- There is no current record.
- The database or recordset is read-only.
- No fields in the record are updatable.
- The database or recordset was opened for exclusive use by another user.
- Another user has locked the page containing your record.

See Also AddNew Method, Delete Method, LockEdits Property.

Example This example finds the first record in a **Recordset** object that matches the search criteria and opens it for editing. Then it changes the value in the Title field and saves the change using the **Update** method.

```
Dim strCriteria As String, strNewTitle As String
strCriteria = "Title = 'My Right Hand'"      ' Create the criteria.
strNewTitle = "My Right Foot"                ' Create a new title.
rstTitles.FindFirst strCriteria              ' Make record current.
Do While Not rstTitles.NoMatch
    rstTitles.Edit                           ' Open record.
    rstTitles.Fields("Title") = strNewTitle  ' Enter new title.
    rstTitles.Update                         ' Save changes.
    rstTitles.FindNext strCriteria
Loop
```

The following example achieves the same effect without using the **Edit** method.

```
' Create the criteria string.
strSQLQuery = "UPDATE Titles SET Title = 'My Right Foot'" & _
    " WHERE Title = 'My Right Hand';"
dbsPublishers.Execute strSQLQuery  ' Execute the query.
```

This example opens a **Recordset** object and locates each record whose Title field satisfies the search criteria and copies it to the copy buffer. The example then prepares the record for subsequent editing, changes the job title, and saves the change using the **Update** method.

```
Dim dbsNorthwind As Database, rstEmployees As Recordset
Dim strCriteria As String, strNewTitle As String
' Set search criteria.
strCriteria = "Title = 'Sales Representative'"
strNewTitle = "Account Executive"    ' Set new job title.
Set dbsNorthwind = DBEngine.Workspaces(0).OpenDatabase("Northwind.mdb")
' Create dynaset.
Set rstEmployees = dbsNorthwind.OpenRecordset("Employees", _
    dbOpenDynaset)
rstEmployees.FindFirst strCriteria   ' Find first occurrence.
' Loop until no matching records.
Do Until rstEmployees.NoMatch
    With rstEmployees
        .Edit                        ' Enable editing.
        !Title = strNewTitle         ' Change title.
        .Update                      ' Save changes.
        .FindNext strCriteria        ' Find next occurrence.
    End With
Loop                                 ' End of loop.
```

Tip Using an update query to change job titles might be more efficient. For example, you could use the following code to achieve the same results:

```
strSQL = "Update Employees Set Title = 'Account Executive' " & _
    "WHERE Title = 'Sales Representative' "
dbsNorthwind.Execute strSQL
```

Example (Microsoft Access)

The following example opens a **Recordset** object and locates each record satisfying the search criteria for the Title field. The procedure then uses the **Edit** method to prepare the record for subsequent editing, changes the job title, and saves the change.

```
Sub ChangeTitle()
    Dim dbs As Database, rst As Recordset
    Dim strCriteria As String, strNewTitle As String

    ' Return Database variable pointing to current database.
    Set dbs = CurrentDb
    ' Set search criteria.
    strCriteria = "Title = 'Sales Representative'"
    strNewTitle = "Account Executive"
    ' Create dynaset-type Recordset object.
    Set rst = dbs.OpenRecordset("Employees", dbOpenDynaset)
    ' Find first occurrence.
    rst.FindFirst strCriteria
    ' Loop until no matching records.
    Do Until rst.NoMatch
        With rst
            .Edit                         'Enable editing.
            !Title = strNewTitle          'Change title.
            .Update                       'Save changes.
            .FindNext strCriteria         'Find next occurrence.
        End With
    Loop
End Sub
```

Tip Using an update query to alter data is more efficient. For example, you can use the following code to achieve the same results.

```
strSQL = "Update Employees Set Title = 'Account Executive' " & _
    "WHERE Title = 'Sales Representative' "
dbs.Execute strSQL
```

EditMode Property

Applies To Dynaset-Type **Recordset** Object, **Recordset** Object, Snapshot-Type **Recordset** Object, Table-Type **Recordset** Object.

Description Returns a value that indicates the state of editing for the current record.

Return Values The return value is an integer that indicates the state of editing. The data type is **Integer**.

The possible return values are:

Value	Description
dbEditNone	No editing operation is in progress.
dbEditInProgress	**Edit** method has been invoked, and the current record is in the copy buffer.
dbEditAdd	**AddNew** method has been invoked, and the current record in the copy buffer is a new record that hasn't been saved in the database.

These constants are listed in the Data Access (DAO) object library in the Object Browser.

Remarks The **EditMode** property is most useful when you want to depart from the default functionality of a **Data** control. You can check the value of the **EditMode** property and the value of the *action* parameter in the Validate event procedure to determine whether to invoke the **UpdateRecord** method.

You can also check to see if the **LockEdits** property setting is **True** (-1) and the **EditMode** property setting is **dbEditInProgress** to determine whether the current data page is locked.

See Also **CancelUpdate** Method, **LockEdits** Property.

Example This example checks the **EditMode** property of a **Recordset** object and completes the update if the **AddNew** method has been invoked or the object is being edited.

```
Function PostChange(rstTarget as Recordset) As Integer
    If (rstTarget.EditMode = dbEditAdd) or _
            (rstTarget.EditMode = dbEditInProgress) Then
        rstTarget.Update
        PostChange = True
    Else
        PostChange = False
    End If
End Function
```

Error Object   121

Example (Microsoft Excel)

This example checks to see whether the Customer recordset in the NWINDEX.MDB database can be edited. If so, the example updates the value of the first field of the first record with the value in cell C3 on Sheet1.

To create the NWINDEX.MDB database, run the Microsoft Excel example for the **CreateDatabase** method.

```
Dim db As Database, rs As Recordset
Set db = Workspaces(0).OpenDatabase(Application.Path & "\NWINDEX.MDB")
Set rs = db.OpenRecordset("Customer")
If Not ((rs.EditMode = dbEditAdd) Or _
        (rs.EditMode = dbEditInProgress)) Then
    rs.Edit
    rs.Fields(0).Value = Worksheets(1).Cells(3, 3).Value
    rs.Update
Else
    MsgBox ("Cannot update database with cell value")
End If
rs.Close
db.Close
```

EOF Property

See BOF, EOF Properties.

Error Object

Description

The **Error** object contains details about data access errors, each of which pertains to a single operation involving data access objects (DAO).

Remarks

Any operation involving data access objects can generate one or more errors. As each error occurs, one or more **Error** objects are placed in the **Errors** collection of the **DBEngine** object.

When another DAO operation generates an error, the **Errors** collection is cleared, and the new **Error** object is placed in the **Errors** collection. DAO operations that don't generate an error have no effect on the **Errors** collection.

Elements of the **Errors** collection aren't appended as they typically are with other collections. The set of **Error** objects in the **Errors** collection describes one error. The first **Error** object is the lowest level error, the second the next higher level, and so forth. For example, if an ODBC error occurs while trying to open a **Recordset** object, the last **Error** object contains the DAO error indicating that the object couldn't be opened. The first error object contains the lowest level ODBC error; subsequent errors contain the ODBC errors returned by the various layers of ODBC. In this case, the driver manager, and possibly the driver itself, return separate **Error** objects.

Note If you use the **New** keyword to create an object that subsequently causes an error before that object has been appended to a collection, the **DBEngine Errors** collection will not contain an entry for that object's error (because it might still contain information from a previous error).

To determine if the error information in the **Errors** collection is valid, compare the **Number** property of the first element of the **Errors** collection (**DBEngine.Errors**(0)) with the value of the Visual Basic **Err** object.

Error handling code should examine the **Errors** collection whenever you anticipate a data access error. If you are writing a centralized error handler, test the Visual Basic **Err** object. If it matches the **Errors**(0) object, you can then use a series of **Select Case** statements to identify the particular data access error or errors that occurred.

Properties   **Description** Property; **HelpContext**, **HelpFile** Properties; **Number** Property; **Source** Property.

See Also   Appendix, "Data Access Object Hierarchy."

Example   See the **Description** property example.

Example (Microsoft Access)   The following example generates an error by attempting to open a **Recordset** object on a non-existent Students table. Information about the error is stored in both the data access **Error** object and the Visual Basic **Err** object. The procedure prints the value of the **Description**, **Source**, and **Number** properties of the **Error** object. Then it prints the values of the corresponding properties of the **Err** object.

Note that the first **Error** object in the **Errors** collection, Errors(0), should always refer to the same error as the **Err** object. If it doesn't, information in the **Errors** collection may be outdated. Use the **Refresh** method to ensure that the **Errors** collection includes the most recent error information.

```
Sub CheckError()
    Dim dbs As Database, tdf As TableDef, rst As Recordset
    Dim prp As Property
    ' Declare Error variable for enumeration of Errors collection.
    Dim errX As Error
```

```
        ' Ignore errors.
        On Error Resume Next
        ' Clear error in Err object.
        Err.Clear
        ' Refresh Errors collection.
        Errors.Refresh
        ' Return Database variable pointing to current database.
        Set dbs = CurrentDb
        ' Attempt to open Recordset object on nonexistent table.
        Set rst = dbs.OpenRecordset("Students")
        Debug.Print "DAO Error Object:"
        ' Print number of errors in Errors collection.
        Debug.Print ">>>Number of errors: "; Errors.Count
        ' Enumerate Errors collection and key properties.
        For Each errX In DBEngine.Errors
            Debug.Print errX.Description
            Debug.Print errX.Source
            Debug.Print errX.Number
        Next errX
        Debug.Print
        Debug.Print "VBA Err Object:"
        ' Display corresponding properties of Err object.
        Debug.Print Err.Description
        Debug.Print Err.Source
        Debug.Print Err.Number
    End Sub
```

Errors Collection

Description The **Errors** collection contains all stored **Error** objects, each of which pertains to a single operation involving data access objects (DAO).

Remarks Any operation involving data access objects can generate one or more errors. As each error occurs, one or more **Error** objects are placed in the **Errors** collection of the **DBEngine** object. When another DAO operation generates an error, the **Errors** collection is cleared, and the new **Error** object is placed in the **Errors** collection. DAO operations that don't generate an error have no effect on the **Errors** collection.

Elements of the **Errors** collection aren't appended as they typically are with other collections.

124　Execute Method

The set of **Error** objects in the **Errors** collection describes one error. The first **Error** object is the lowest level error, the second the next higher level, and so forth. For example, if an ODBC error occurs while trying to open a **Recordset** object, the last **Error** object contains the DAO error indicating that the object couldn't be opened. The first error object contains the lowest level ODBC error; subsequent errors contain the ODBC errors returned by the various layers of ODBC. In this case, the driver manager, and possibly the driver itself, return separate **Error** objects.

Note　If you use the **New** keyword to create an object that causes an error either before or while being placed into the **Errors** collection, the collection doesn't contain error information about that object (because it might contain information from a previous error).

The error information is available in the Visual Basic **Err** object.

Properties	**Count** Property.
Methods	**Refresh** Method.
See Also	Appendix, "Data Access Object Hierarchy."
Example (Microsoft Access)	See the **Error** object example (Microsoft Access).

Execute Method

Applies To　　**Database** Object, **QueryDef** Object.

Description　　Runs an action query or executes an SQL statement on a specified **Database** object.

Syntax　　*database*.**Execute** *source*[, *options*]

querydef.**Execute** [*options*]

For a **Database** object, the **Execute** method syntax has these parts.

Part	Description
database	The name of the **Database** object on which the query will run.
source	The SQL statement or **QueryDef** object.
options	An integer constant that determines the data integrity characteristics of the query, as specified in Settings.

For a **QueryDef** object, the **Execute** method syntax has these parts.

Part	Description
querydef	The name of the **QueryDef** object whose **SQL** property setting specifies the SQL statement to execute.
options	An integer constant that determines the data integrity characteristics of the query, as specified in Settings.

Settings

You can use the following constants for the *options* part.

Constant	Description
dbDenyWrite	Deny write permission to other users.
dbInconsistent	(Default) Inconsistent updates.
dbConsistent	Consistent updates.
dbSQLPassThrough	SQL pass-through. Causes the SQL statement to be passed to an ODBC database for processing.
dbFailOnError	Rolls back updates if an error occurs.
dbSeeChanges	Generates a run-time error if another user is changing data you are editing.

Remarks

The **Execute** method is valid only for action queries. If you use **Execute** with another type of query, an error occurs. Because an action query doesn't return any records, **Execute** doesn't return a recordset.

Tips

- Given a syntactically correct SQL statement and proper permissions, the **Execute** method won't fail—even if not a single row can be modified or deleted. Therefore, always use the **dbFailOnError** option when using the **Execute** method to run an update or delete query. This option generates a trappable error and rolls back all successful changes if any of the records affected are locked and can't be updated or deleted.

- For best performance, especially in a multiuser environment, nest the **Execute** method inside a transaction: Use the **BeginTrans** method on the current **Workspace** object, then use the **Execute** method, and complete the transaction by using the **CommitTrans** method on the **Workspace**. This saves changes on disk and frees any locks placed while the query was running.

Use the **RecordsAffected** property of the **Database** or **QueryDef** object to determine the number of records affected by the most recent **Execute** method. For example, **RecordsAffected** contains the number of records deleted, updated, or inserted when executing an action query. When you use the **Execute** method to run a **Querydef**, the **RecordsAffected** property of the **QueryDef** object is set to the number of records affected.

126 Field Object

If both **dbInconsistent** and **dbConsistent** are included or if neither is included, the result is the default.

Using **Execute** on a query that selects records produces an error.

Execute doesn't return a recordset.

See Also **RecordsAffected** Property.

Example This example uses a **Data** control to execute an action query that updates all titles that have no value in the ISBN column in the Titles table. If there is an error, all changes are rolled back.

```
Dim strSQL as String
strSQL = "DELETE FROM Titles WHERE ISBN IS NULL"
dbsBiblio.Execute strSQL, dbFailOnError
```

Example (Microsoft Access) The following example executes an action query and prints the number of records affected.

```
Sub RecordsUpdated()
    Dim dbs As Database, qdf As QueryDef
    Dim strSQL As String

    ' Return Database variable pointing to current database.
    Set dbs = CurrentDb
    strSQL = "UPDATE Employees SET Title = " & _
        "'Senior Sales Representative' " & _
            "WHERE Title = 'Sales Representative';"
    ' Create new QueryDef.
    Set qdf = dbs.CreateQueryDef("UpdateTitles", strSQL)
    ' Execute QueryDef.
    qdf.Execute
    Debug.Print qdf.RecordsAffected
End Sub
```

Field Object

Description A **Field** object represents a column of data with a common data type and a common set of properties.

Remarks The **Fields** collections of **Index**, **QueryDef**, **Relation**, and **TableDef** objects contain the specifications for the fields those objects represent. The **Fields** collection of a **Recordset** object represents the **Field** objects in a row of data, or in a record. You use the **Field** objects in a **Recordset** object to read and set values for the fields in the current record of the **Recordset** object.

You manipulate a field using a **Field** object and its methods and properties. For example, you can:

- Get or set the presentation order of the **Field** object in a **Fields** collection using the **OrdinalPosition** property.
- Read the **SourceField** and **SourceTable** property settings to determine the original source of the data.
- Read or set the **ForeignName** property setting for a field in a **Relation** object.
- Read or set the **AllowZeroLength**, **DefaultValue**, **Required**, **ValidateOnSet**, **ValidationRule**, or **ValidationText** property setting to find or specify validation conditions.
- Read or set the **Value** property of a **Recordset** object.
- Use the **AppendChunk**, **FieldSize**, and **GetChunk** methods to get or set a value in an OLE Object or Memo field of a **Recordset** object.

You can refer to the **Value** property of a **Field** object that you create and append to a **Fields** collection by its **Name** property setting using following syntax:

Fields("*name*")

Note Fields that have names with embedded spaces must be delimited with brackets ([ ]), for example [Part Number], or enclosed in single quotation marks (' ') or double quotation marks (" "), as in 'Part Number' or "Part Number".

You can also refer to the **Value** property of a **Field** object that you create and append to a **Fields** collection by its position in the **Fields** collection using this syntax:

Fields(0)

To create a new **Field** object in an **Index**, **TableDef**, or **Relation** object, use the **CreateField** method.

When the **Field** object is accessed as part of a **Recordset** object, data from the current record is visible in the **Field** object's **Value** property. To manipulate data in the **Recordset** object, you don't usually reference the **Fields** collection directly; instead you indirectly reference the **Value** property of the **Field** object in the **Fields** collection of the **Recordset** object, as in the following example.

```
Dim dbsCatalog As Database, rstParts As Recordset
Dim strSelect As String

Set dbsCatalog = Workspaces(0).OpenDatabase("Catalog.mdb")
strSelect = "SELECT [Part Name], Size, " _
    & "[Part Type], [Part Age] AS Age FROM Parts"
Set rstParts = dbsCatalog.OpenRecordset(strSelect)
```

128 Field Object

```
'Return Part Name field in Recordset object.
Debug.Print rstParts.Fields(0).Value
' Otherwise, use indirect coding.
Debug.Print rstParts(0)            ' Return value of Part Name field.
Debug.Print rstParts![Part Name]   ' Also return Part Name field value.
Debug.Print rstParts![Part Type]   ' Return Part Type field.
Debug.Print rstParts!Age           ' Return Part Age field aliased as Age.
```

Properties **AllowZeroLength** Property; **Attributes** Property; **CollatingOrder** Property; **DataUpdatable** Property; **DefaultValue** Property; **ForeignName** Property; **Name** Property; **OrdinalPosition** Property; **Required** Property; **Size** Property; **SourceField**, **SourceTable** Properties; **Type** Property; **V1xNullBehavior** Property; **ValidateOnSet** Property; **ValidationRule** Property; **ValidationText** Property; **Value** Property.

Methods **AppendChunk** Method, **CreateProperty** Method, **FieldSize** Method, **GetChunk** Method.

See Also **CreateField** Method; Appendix, "Data Access Object Hierarchy."

Specifics (Microsoft Access) In addition to the properties defined by the Microsoft Jet database engine, a **Field** object in the **Fields** collection of a **QueryDef** object or a **TableDef** object may also contain the following Microsoft Access application-defined properties.

Example This example creates a **TableDef** object and a **Field** object, appends the **Field** to the **Fields** collection in the new **TableDef**, and appends the **TableDef** to the **TableDefs** collection in the current database. The example enumerates all the fields in the new **TableDef** object and all the properties of the new **Field**. See the methods and properties listed in the **Field** summary topic for additional examples.

```
Function EnumerateField () As Integer
    Dim dbsNorthwind As Database
    Dim tdfTest As TableDef
    Dim fldTest As Field
    Dim I As Integer
    Set dbsNorthwind =_
        DBEngine.Workspaces(0).OpenDatabase("Northwind.mdb")
    Set tdfTest = dbsNorthwind.CreateTableDef("MyTable")
    Set fldTest = tdfTest.CreateField("MyField", dbDate)
    tdfTest.Fields.Append fldTest
    dbsNorthwind.TableDefs.Append tdfTest
' Get database name.
    Debug.Print
    Debug.Print "Database Name: "; dbsNorthwind.Name
    Debug.Print
' Enumerate all fields in tdfTest.
    Debug.Print "TableDefs: Name; Fields: Name"
    For I = 0 To tdfTest.Fields.Count - 1
        Debug.Print "   "; tdfTest.Name;
```

Field Object

```
            Debug.Print "; "; tdfTest.Fields(I).Name
        Next I
        Debug.Print
    ' Enumerate built-in properties of fldTest.
        Debug.Print "fldTest.Name: "; fldTest.Name
        Debug.Print "AllowZeroLength: "; fldTest.AllowZeroLength
        Debug.Print "Attributes: "; fldTest.Attributes
        Debug.Print "CollatingOrder: "; fldTest.CollatingOrder
        Debug.Print "DefaultValue: "; fldTest.DefaultValue
        Debug.Print "OrdinalPosition: "; fldTest.OrdinalPosition
        Debug.Print "Required: "; fldTest.Required
        Debug.Print "Size: "; fldTest.Size
        Debug.Print "SourceField: "; fldTest.SourceField
        Debug.Print "SourceTable: "; fldTest.SourceTable
        Debug.Print "Type: "; fldTest.Type
        Debug.Print "ValidationRule: "; fldTest.ValidationRule
        Debug.Print "ValidationText: "; fldTest.ValidationText
        EnumerateField = True
    End Function
```

Example (Microsoft Access)

The following example creates a new **Field** object, sets some of its properties, and appends it to the **Fields** collection of a **TableDef** object. The procedure then enumerates all fields in the **Fields** collection of the **TableDef** object.

```
Sub NewField()
    Dim dbs As Database, tdf As TableDef
    Dim fld As Field

    ' Return Database variable that points to current database.
    Set dbs = CurrentDb
    Set tdf = dbs.TableDefs!Employees
    ' Create new Field object.
    Set fld = tdf.CreateField("SSN#")
    ' Set Type and Size properties of Field object.
    fld.Type = dbText
    fld.Size = 11
    ' Append field.
    tdf.Fields.Append fld
    ' Enumerate all fields in Fields collection of TableDef object.
    For Each fld in tdf.Fields
        Debug.Print fld.Name
    Next fld
End Sub
```

Fields Collection

Description	A **Fields** collection contains all stored **Field** objects of an **Index**, **QueryDef**, **Recordset**, **Relation**, or **TableDef** object.
Remarks	The **Fields** collections of the **Index**, **QueryDef**, **Relation**, and **TableDef** objects contain the specifications for the fields those objects represent. The **Fields** collection of a **Recordset** object represents the **Field** objects in a row of data, or in a record. You use the **Field** objects in a **Recordset** object to read and to set values for the fields in the current record of the **Recordset** object.

You can refer to the **Value** property of a **Field** object that you create and append to a **Fields** collection by its **Name** property setting using the following syntax:

Fields("*name*")

Fields that have names with embedded spaces must be delimited with brackets ([ ]) or enclosed in double quotation marks (" "), using either of the following syntax forms:

Fields("*long name*")

You can refer to the **Value** property of a **Field** object that you create and append to a **Fields** collection by its position in the **Fields** collection using this syntax:

Fields(0)

Properties	**Count** Property.
Methods	**Append** Method, **Delete** Method, **Refresh** Method.
See Also	Appendix, "Data Access Object Hierarchy."
Specifics (Microsoft Access)	See the **Field** object specifics (Microsoft Access).
Example	See the **Field** object example.
Example (Microsoft Access)	See the **Field** object example (Microsoft Access).

FieldSize Method

Applies To	**Field** Object.

FieldSize Method

Description Returns the number of bytes used in the database (rather than in memory) of a Memo or an OLE Object **Field** object in the **Fields** collection of a **Recordset** object.

Syntax *varname* = *recordset* ! *field*.**FieldSize**( )

The **FieldSize** method syntax has these parts.

Part	Description
varname	The name of a **Long** or **Variant** variable.
recordset	A variable of an object data type that specifies the **Recordset** object containing the **Fields** collection.
field	The name of a **Field** object whose **Type** property is set to **dbMemo** (Memo), **dbLongBinary** (OLE Object), or the equivalent.

Remarks Because the size of an OLE Object field or Memo field can exceed 64K, you should assign the value returned by **FieldSize** to a variable large enough to store a **Long** variable.

You can use **FieldSize** with the **AppendChunk** and **GetChunk** methods to manipulate large fields.

Note To determine the size of a **Field** object (except Memo and Long Binary types), use the **Size** property.

See Also **AppendChunk** Method, **GetChunk** Method, **Size** Property, **Type** Property.

Specifics (Microsoft Access) The data access **FieldSize** method is different from the Microsoft Access **FieldSize** property, which is set in table Design view. The data access **FieldSize** method returns the number of bytes in a **Field** object of type Memo data type or OLE Object data type.

You set the Microsoft Access **FieldSize** property in order to limit the size of a field in a table. The **FieldSize** property is only available in table Design view. From Visual Basic, use the **Size** property to set the size of a field in a table.

Example See the **AppendChunk** method example.

Example (Microsoft Access) The following example uses the **FieldSize** method to return the size in bytes of two fields in an Employees table. The Notes field is Memo data type and the Photo field is Binary data type.

```
Sub GetFieldSize()
    Dim dbs As Database, rst As Recordset
    Dim fldNotes As Field, fldPhoto As Field
    Dim strSQL As String
```

```
                ' Return Database variable pointing to current database.
                Set dbs = CurrentDb
                ' Construct SQL statement to return Notes and Photo fields.
                strSQL = "SELECT Notes, Photo FROM Employees;"
                ' Create dynaset-type Recordset object.
                Set rst = dbs.OpenRecordset(strSQL)
                Set fldNotes = rst.Fields!Notes
                Set fldPhoto = rst.Fields!Photo
                ' Move to first record.
                rst.MoveFirst
                Debug.Print "Size of Notes:"; "    "; "Size of Photo:"
                ' Print sizes of fields for each record in Recordset object.
                Do Until rst.EOF
                    Debug.Print fldNotes.FieldSize; "         "; fldPhoto.FieldSize
                    rst.MoveNext
                Loop
            End Sub
```

FillCache Method

Applies To Dynaset-Type **Recordset** Object, **Recordset** Object.

Description Fills all or a part of a local cache for a **Recordset** object that contains data from an ODBC data source.

Syntax *recordset*.**FillCache** [*rows*[, *start*]]

The **FillCache** method syntax has these parts.

Part	Description
recordset	A **Recordset** object created from an ODBC data source, such as a **TableDef** representing an attached table or a **QueryDef** object derived from such a **TableDef**.
rows	An **Integer** specifying the number of rows to fill in the cache. If you omit this argument, the value is determined by the **CacheSize** property setting.
start	A string specifying a bookmark. The cache is filled starting from the record indicated by this bookmark. If you omit this argument, the cache is filled starting from the record indicated by the **CacheStart** property.

FillCache Method

Remarks

Caching improves the performance of an application that retrieves, or fetches, data from a remote server. A cache is space in local memory that holds the data most recently fetched from the server on the assumption that the data will probably be requested again while the application is running. When data is requested, the Microsoft Jet database engine checks the cache for the data first rather than fetching it from the server, which takes more time. Data that doesn't come from an ODBC data source isn't saved in the cache.

Rather than waiting for the cache to be filled with records as they are fetched, you can explicitly fill the cache at any time using the **FillCache** method. This is a faster way to fill the cache because **FillCache** fetches several records at once instead of one at a time. For example, while each screenful of records is being displayed, you can have your application use **FillCache** to fetch the next screenful of records.

Any ODBC database accessed with **Recordset** objects can have a local cache. To create the cache, open a **Recordset** object from the remote data source, and then set the **CacheSize** and **CacheStart** properties of the **Recordset**.

If *rows* and *start* create a range of records that is partly or wholly outside the range of records specified by the **CacheSize** and **CacheStart** properties, the portion of the *recordset* outside this range is ignored and isn't loaded into the cache.

If **FillCache** requests more records than remain in the remote data source, only the remaining records are fetched, and no error occurs.

Notes

- Records fetched from the cache don't reflect changes made concurrently to the source data by other users.
- **FillCache** fetches only records not already cached. To force an update of all the cached data, set the **CacheSize** property of the **Recordset** to 0, set it to the size of the cache you originally requested, and then use **FillCache**.

See Also

Bookmark Property; **Bookmarkable** Property; **CacheSize**, **CacheStart** Properties.

Specifics (Microsoft Access)

When you use a bookmark in a Microsoft Access module, you must include an **Option Compare Binary** statement in the Declarations section of the module. A bookmark is a **Variant** array of **Byte** data, so the string comparison method for the module must be binary. If a bookmark is evaluated with a text-based string comparison method, the current record may be set to an incorrect record. The **Option Compare Text** statement denotes a text-based comparison method, as does the default setting for the **Option Compare Database** statement.

Example (Client/Server)

See the **CacheSize**, **CacheStart** properties example.

Filter Property

Example (Microsoft Access)	See the **CacheSize**, **CacheStart** properties example (Microsoft Access).

Filter Property

Applies To	Dynaset-Type **Recordset** Object, **Recordset** Object, Snapshot-Type **Recordset** Object.
Description	Sets or returns a value that determines the records included in a subsequently opened **Recordset** object.
Settings and Return Values	A string expression that contains the WHERE clause of an SQL statement without the reserved word WHERE. The data type is **String**.
Remarks	Use the **Filter** property to apply a filter to a dynaset- or Snapshot-Type **Recordset** object.
	You can use the **Filter** property to restrict the records returned from an existing object when a new **Recordset** object is opened based on an existing **Recordset** object.
	The following example shows how the **Filter** property can be used to return only the records for customers who live in a particular region:

```
rstCustomers.Filter = "Region = 'NY'"
Set rstNYCustomers = rstCustomers.OpenRecordset()
```

Notes

- In many cases, it's faster to open a new **Recordset** object using an SQL statement that includes a WHERE clause.
- Use the U.S. date format (month-day-year) when you filter fields containing dates, even if you're not using the U.S. version of the Microsoft Jet database engine; otherwise, the data may not be filtered as you expect. You can use the Visual Basic **Format** function to make this easier. For example:

  ```
  rstEmployees.Filter = "HireDate > #" & Format(mydate, "m/d/yy") & "#"
  ```

See Also	**OpenRecordset** Method, **Sort** Property.
Specifics (Microsoft Access)	The data access **Filter** property applies a filter to a **Recordset** object. You can set it only from Visual Basic.

Filter Property   135

Note The Microsoft Access **Filter** property applies a filter to a form. You can set it in a form's property sheet in form Design view, in a macro, or from Visual Basic.

Example

This example creates a dynaset-type **Recordset** that contains only records for orders shipped to the United Kingdom.

```
Dim dbsNorthwind As Database
Dim rstOrders As Recordset, rstFiltered As Recordset
Set dbsNorthwind = DBEngine.Workspaces(0).OpenDatabase("Northwind.mdb")
' Create dynaset-type Recordset.
Set rstOrders = dbsNorthwind.OpenRecordset("Orders", dbOpenDynaset)
rstOrders.Filter = "ShipCountry = 'UK'"      ' Set filter condition.
' Create filtered dynaset.
Set rstFiltered = rstOrders.OpenRecordset()
```

Note To change the contents of rstOrders, you must set its **Filter** property, and then open a second **Recordset** object based on rstOrders.

Tip In some situations, it may be more efficient to create the second **Recordset** object with the conditions you want in one step. As a general rule, when you know the data you want to select, it's usually more efficient to create a **Recordset** with an SQL statement. This example shows how you can create just one **Recordset** and obtain the same results as in the preceding example:

```
Dim dbsNorthwind As Database, rstOrders As Recordset
Set dbsNorthwind = DBEngine.Workspaces(0).OpenDatabase("Northwind.mdb")
Set rstOrders = dbsNorthwind.OpenRecordset("SELECT * FROM Orders " & _
    "WHERE ShipCountry = 'UK';")
```

Example (Microsoft Access)

The following example prompts the user to enter the name of a country on which to filter, and then sets the **Filter** property of a dynaset-type **Recordset** object. For example, if the user enters "Italy," the filtered recordset will contain only those records in which the ShipCountry field contains the value "Italy."

Note that you first create a dynaset-type **Recordset** object and set its **Filter** property, then open a second dynaset-type **Recordset** object based on the first. Setting the **Filter** property of the first **Recordset** object doesn't actually affect the records that it contains, so you need to create a second **Recordset** object in order to see the effects of the filter.

```
Sub SetRecordsetFilter()
    Dim dbs As Database, strInput As String
    Dim rstOrders As Recordset, rstFiltered As Recordset
```

136 Filter Property

```
    ' Return Database variable that points to current database.
    Set dbs = CurrentDb
    ' Prompt for value on which to filter.
    strInput = InputBox("Enter name of country on which to filter.")
    ' Create dynaset-type Recordset object.
    Set rstOrders = dbs.OpenRecordset("Orders", dbOpenDynaset)
    ' Set filter condition.
    rstOrders.Filter = "[ShipCountry] = '" & strInput & "'"
    ' Create filtered dynaset-type Recordset object.
    Set rstFiltered = rstOrders.OpenRecordset()
    ' Populate recordset.
    rstFiltered.MoveLast
    ' Second Recordset object is now subset of the first.
    Debug.Print rstFiltered.RecordCount
End Sub
```

Tip In most situations, it is more efficient to create the second **Recordset** object with the desired conditions in one step. When you know what data you want to select, it's generally more efficient to create a recordset with an SQL statement. The following example shows how you can create just one recordset and obtain the same results as in the preceding example.

```
Dim dbs As Database, rstOrders As Recordset, strInput As String
Set dbs = CurrentDb
strInput = InputBox("Enter name of country on which to filter.")
Set rstOrders = dbs.OpenRecordset("SELECT * FROM Orders " & _
    "WHERE [ShipCountry] = '" & strInput & "';")
```

Example (Microsoft Excel)

This example creates a new recordset containing records of the Supplier recordset in the NWINDEX.MDB database, and then it copies the recordset contents onto Sheet1. These records contain only data on suppliers located in Canada. The example copies a new, sorted recordset into Microsoft Excel.

To create the NWINDEX.MDB database, run the Microsoft Excel example for the **CreateDatabase** method.

```
Dim db As Database, rs As Recordset, sortedSet As Recordset
Set db = Workspaces(0).OpenDatabase(Application.Path & "\NWINDEX.MDB")
Set rs = db.OpenRecordset("Supplier", dbOpenDynaset)
rs.Filter = "[COUNTRY] = 'Canada'"
Set sortedSet = rs.OpenRecordset()
Sheets("Sheet1").Activate
ActiveCell.CopyFromRecordset sortedSet
sortedSet.Close
rs.Close
db.Close
```

FindFirst, FindLast, FindNext, FindPrevious Methods

Applies To Dynaset-Type **Recordset** Object, **Recordset** Object, Snapshot-Type **Recordset** Object.

Description Locates the first, last, next, or previous record in a dynaset- or Snapshot-Type **Recordset** object that satisfies the specified criteria and makes that record the current record.

Syntax *recordset*.{**FindFirst** | **FindLast** | **FindNext** | **FindPrevious**} *criteria*

The Find methods have these parts.

Part	Description
recordset	The name of an existing dynaset- or Snapshot-Type **Recordset** object.
criteria	A string expression (like the WHERE clause in an SQL statement without the word WHERE) used to locate the record.

Remarks If you want to include all the records in your search—not just those that meet a specific condition—use the Move methods to move from record to record. To locate a record in a table-type **Recordset**, use the **Seek** method.

If a record matching the criteria isn't located, the current record pointer is undetermined, and the **NoMatch** property is set to **True**. If *recordset* contains more than one record that satisfies the criteria, **FindFirst** locates the first occurrence, **FindNext** locates the next occurrence, and so on.

Caution If you edit the current record, be sure you save the changes using the **Update** method before you move to another record. If you move to another record without updating, your changes are lost without warning.

Each of the Find methods begins its search from the location and in the direction specified in the following table.

Find methods	Begin	Search direction
FindFirst	Beginning of recordset	End of recordset
FindLast	End of recordset	Beginning of recordset
FindNext	Current record	End of recordset
FindPrevious	Current record	Beginning of recordset

When you use the **FindLast** method, the Microsoft Jet database engine fully populates your recordset before beginning the search, if this hasn't already been done.

Using one of the Find methods isn't the same as using a Move method, however, which simply makes the first, last, next or previous record current without specifying a condition. You can follow a Find operation with a Move operation.

Always check the value of the **NoMatch** property to determine whether the Find operation has succeeded. If the search succeeds, **NoMatch** is set to **False**. If it fails, **NoMatch** is set to **True** and the current record isn't defined. In this case, you must position the current record pointer back to a valid record, as shown in the following example.

```
Dim Here as Variant
Here = rstCustomers.Bookmark
rstCustomers.Find "Name = 'Ms. Schmidt'"   'Search for a name in the
                                           ' recordset.
If rstCustomers.NoMatch then               'Was it found?
    rstCustomers.Bookmark = Here           'If not, go back to
                                           ' previously current record.
Else
    .                                      'Match found.
    ...
    ...
End If
```

Using the Find methods with ODBC-accessed recordsets can be inefficient. You may find that rephrasing your *criteria* to locate a specific record is faster, especially when working with large recordsets.

You should use the U.S. date format (month-day-year) when you search for fields containing dates, even if you're not using the U.S. version of the Jet database engine; otherwise, the data may not be found. Use the Visual Basic **Format** function to convert the date. For example:

```
rstEmployees.FindFirst "HireDate > #" & Format(mydate, 'm/d/yy' ) & "#"
```

When working with ODBC databases and large dynasets, you might discover that using the Find methods or using the **Sort** or **Filter** properties is slow. You can improve performance by using SQL queries with customized ORDER BY or WHERE clauses, parameter queries, or **QueryDef** objects that retrieve specific indexed records.

Note You can't use the Find methods with forward-only-scrolling snapshots.

See Also   **AbsolutePosition** Property; **Move** Method; **MoveFirst, MoveLast, MoveNext, MovePrevious** Methods; **NoMatch** Property; **Seek** Method.

Specifics (Microsoft Access)   When specifying criteria for the **Find** methods, you must be careful to reference fields and controls properly, and to construct the criteria string correctly.

FindFirst, FindLast, FindNext, FindPrevious Methods

When you use a bookmark in a Microsoft Access module, you must include an **Option Compare Binary** statement in the Declarations section of the module. A bookmark is a **Variant** array of **Byte** data, so the string comparison method for the module must be binary. If a bookmark is evaluated with a text-based string comparison method, such as the **Option Compare Text** statement or the default setting for the **Option Compare Database** statement, the current record may be set to an incorrect record.

You should use the the month-day-year format when you search for fields containing dates, even if the Regional Settings of the Windows® Control Panel is set to a different format; otherwise, the data may not be found. You can use the Visual Basic **Format** function to make this easier. The following code requests a date from the user and constructs a string on which to search.

```
dim dteAny As Date
dteAny = InputBox ("Please enter a date in month-day-year format.")
rstOrders.FindFirst "[OrderDate] > #" & Format(dteAny, "m/d/yy") & "#"
```

Example

This example uses **FindFirst** to find the first record matching the specified criteria in a **Recordset** object and then uses **FindNext** to find the next matching record.

```
Dim strCriteria As String
strCriteria = "State = 'NY'"              ' Set the criteria.
rstAddress.FindFirst strCriteria          ' Find first matching record.
If rstAddress.NoMatch = False Then        ' Check if record is found.
    rstAddress.FindNext strCriteria       ' Find next matching record.
...
```

This example creates a dynaset-type **Recordset** object and then uses **FindFirst** to locate the first record satisfying the title condition.

```
Dim strCriteria As String
Dim dbsBiblio As Database, rstPublishers As Recordset
strCriteria = "State = 'NY'"              ' Define search criteria.
Set dbsBiblio = DBEngine.Workspaces(0).OpenDatabase("Biblio.mdb")
' Create a dynaset-type Recordset based on Publishers table.
Set rstPublishers = dbsBiblio.OpenRecordset("Publishers",dbOpenDynaset)
rstPublishers.FindFirst strCriteria       ' Find first matching record.
If rstPublishers.NoMatch = False Then     ' Check if record is found.
    rstPublishers.FindNext strCriteria    ' Find next matching record.
...
```

Example (Microsoft Access)

The following example creates a dynaset-type **Recordset** object and then uses the **FindFirst** method to locate the first record satisfying the specified criteria. The procedure then finds the remaining records that satisfy the criteria.

```
Sub FindRecord()
    Dim dbs As Database, rst As Recordset
    Dim strCriteria As String
```

```
        ' Return Database variable pointing to current database.
        Set dbs = CurrentDb
        ' Define search criteria.
        strCriteria = "[ShipCountry] = 'UK' And [OrderDate] >= #1-1-95#"
        ' Create a dynaset-type Recordset object based on Orders table.
        Set rst = dbs.OpenRecordset("Orders", dbOpenDynaset)
        ' Find first matching record.
        rst.FindFirst strCriteria
        ' Check if record is found.
        If rst.NoMatch Then
            MsgBox "No record found."
        Else
            ' Find other matching records.
            Do Until rst.NoMatch
                Debug.Print rst!ShipCountry; "    "; rst!OrderDate
                rst.FindNext strCriteria
            Loop
        End If
End Sub
```

Foreign Property

Applies To **Index** Object.

Description Returns a value that indicates whether an **Index** object represents a foreign key in a table. This property setting is read-only and returns **True** (-1) if the **Index** object represents a foreign key.

Remarks A foreign key consists of one or more fields in a foreign table that uniquely identify all rows in a primary table.

The Microsoft Jet database engine creates an **Index** object for the foreign table and sets the **Foreign** property when you create a relationship that enforces referential integrity.

See Also **Primary** Property, **TableDef** Object.

Example (Microsoft Access) The following example prints the value of the **Foreign** property for each index in an Orders table.

```
Sub CheckForeign()
    Dim dbs As Database, tdf As TableDef, idx As Index

    ' Return Database variable that points to current database.
    Set dbs = CurrentDb
    Set tdf = dbs.TableDefs!Orders
```

```
    ' Enumerate through Indexes collection of Orders table.
    For Each idx In tdf.Indexes
        ' Print value of Foreign property.
        Debug.Print idx.Name; "      "; idx.Foreign
    Next idx
End Sub
```

ForeignName Property

Applies To **Field** Object.

Description Sets or returns a value that, in a relationship, specifies the name of the **Field** object in a foreign table that corresponds to a field in a primary table.

Settings and Return Values The setting or return value is a string expression that evaluates to the name of a **Field** in the associated **TableDef** object's **Fields** collection.

Remarks Only a **Field** object that belongs to a **Fields** collection contained by a **Relation** object can support the **ForeignName** property. If the **Relation** isn't appended to the **Database**, but the **Field** is appended to the **Relation**, you can still change the **ForeignName** property. Once the **Relation** object is appended to the database, the properties of the **Field** object are read-only.

The **Name** and **ForeignName** property *value* settings for a **Field** object specify the names of the corresponding fields in the primary and foreign tables of a relationship. The **Table** and **ForeignTable** property *value* argument settings of a **Relation** object determine the primary and foreign tables of a relationship.

For example, if you had a list of valid part codes (in a field named PartNo) stored in a ValidParts table, you could establish a relationship with an OrderItem table such that if a part code was entered into the OrderItem table it must exist in the ValidParts table. If the part code did not exist in the ValidParts table and you had not indicated no enforcement of referential integrity in the **Attributes** property, a trappable error would occur.

In this case, the ValidParts table would be an example of a Primary table, so the **ForeignTable** property of the **Relation** object would be set to OrderItem and the **Table** property of the **Relation** object would be set to ValidParts. The **Name** property and **ForeignName** property of the **Field** object would both be PartNo.

See Also **ForeignTable** Property, **Name** Property, **Table** Property.

Example

This example shows how you can use the **ForeignName**, **ForeignTable**, and **Table** properties when you create a relationship between two existing tables—in this case, Table1 (the primary table) and Table2 (the foreign table) in the specified database. Field1 is the primary key in Table1, and Field2 is a foreign key in Table2. The relationship is one-to-many and referential integrity is enforced.

```
Function ForeignNameTable () As Integer
    Dim dbsDefault As Database
    Dim fldLocal As Field, relForeign As Relation
' Get database.
    Set dbsDefault = _
        DBEngine.Workspaces(0).OpenDatabase("Northwind.mdb")
' Create new relationship and set its properties.
    Set relForeign = dbsDefault.CreateRelation("MyRelation")
    relForeign.Table = "Table1"
    relForeign.ForeignTable = "Table2"
' Create field and set its properties.
    Set fldLocal = relForeign.CreateField("Field1")
    fldLocal.ForeignName = "Field2"
' Append field to relation and relation to database.
    relForeign.Fields.Append fldLocal
    dbsDefault.Relations.Append relForeign
    dbsDefault.Close
End Function
```

Example (Microsoft Access)

The following example shows how you can use the **ForeignName**, **ForeignTable**, and **Table** properties when you create a relationship between two existing tables—in this case, Employees (the primary table) and Orders (the foreign table) in the current database. EmployeeID is the primary key in the Employees table, and also a foreign key in the Orders table. The relationship is one-to-many and referential integrity is enforced.

To test the following example in Microsoft Access, open the Northwind database and click Relationships on the Tools menu. Delete the relationship between the Employees table and the Orders table. Close the Relationships window, saving the current configuration when prompted. Then run the following procedure from a standard module, and view the Relationships window again to see the new relationship.

```
Sub ForeignNameTable()
    Dim dbs As Database
    Dim fld As Field, rel As Relation

    ' Return Database variable that points to current database.
    Set dbs = CurrentDb
    ' Create new relationship and set its properties.
    Set rel = dbs.CreateRelation("EmployeesRelation")
    ' Denote primary table.
    rel.Table = "Employees"
```

```
        ' Denote foreign table.
        rel.ForeignTable = "Orders"
        rel.Attributes = dbRelationUpdateCascade + dbRelationDeleteCascade
        ' Create field in Fields collection of Relation.
        Set fld = rel.CreateField("EmployeeID")
        ' Provide name of foreign key field.
        fld.ForeignName = "EmployeeID"
        ' Append field to Relation and Relation to database.
        rel.Fields.Append fld
        dbs.Relations.Append rel
End Sub
```

ForeignTable Property

Applies To	**Relation** Object.
Description	Sets or returns the name of the foreign table in a relationship. This property setting is read/write for a new **Relation** object not yet appended to a collection and read-only for an existing **Relation** object in the **Relations** collection.
Settings and Return Values	The setting or return value is a string expression that evaluates to the name of a table in the **Database** object's **TableDefs** collection. The data type is **String**.
Remarks	The **ForeignTable** property setting of a **Relation** object is the **Name** property setting of the **TableDef** or **QueryDef** object that represents the foreign table or query; the **Table** property setting is the **Name** property setting of the **TableDef** or **QueryDef** object that represents the primary table or query.
	For example, if you had a list of valid part codes (in a field named PartNo) and stored in a ValidParts table, you could establish a relationship with an OrderItem table such that if a part code was entered into the OrderItem table, it must exist in the ValidParts table. If the part code did not exist in the ValidParts table and you had not indicated no enforcement of referential integrity in the **Attributes** property, a trappable error would occur.
	In this case, the ValidParts table would be an example of a foreign table, so the **ForeignTable** property of the **Relation** object would be set to ValidParts and the **Table** property of the **Relation** object would be set to OrderItem. The **Name** property and **ForeignName** property of the **Field** object would both be set to PartNo.
See Also	**ForeignName** Property, **Name** Property, **QueryDef** Object, **Table** Property, **TableDef** Object.
Example	See the **ForeignName** property example.

GetChunk Method

Example (Microsoft Access) See the **ForeignName** property example (Microsoft Access).

GetChunk Method

Applies To **Field** Object.

Description Returns all or a portion of the contents of a Memo or an OLE Object **Field** object in the **Fields** collection of a **Recordset** object.

Syntax *stringvar* = *recordset*!*field*.**GetChunk**(*offset*, *numbytes*)

The **GetChunk** method syntax has these parts.

Part	Description
stringvar	The name of a **String** variable or **Variant** that receives the data from the **Field** object named by *field*.
recordset	A variable of an object data type that specifies the **Recordset** object containing the **Fields** collection.
field	The name of a **Field** object whose **Type** property is set to **dbMemo** (Memo) or **dbLongBinary** (OLE Object).
offset	A numeric expression that is the number of bytes to skip before copying begins.
numbytes	A numeric expression that is the number of bytes you want to return.

Remarks Assign the bytes returned by **GetChunk** to *stringvar*. Use **GetChunk** to return a portion of the total data value at a time. You can use the **AppendChunk** method to reassemble the pieces.

If *offset* is 0, **GetChunk** begins copying from the first byte of the field.

If *numbytes* is greater than the number of bytes in the field, the actual number of bytes in the field is returned.

Note Use a Memo-type field for human-readable textual data, and put binary data only in OLE-type fields. Doing otherwise will cause undesirable results.

See Also **AppendChunk** Method, **FieldSize** Method, **Type** Property.

Specifics (Microsoft Access) After assigning the results of the **GetChunk** method to a string variable, you can use the Visual Basic **Len** function to determine the number of characters in the string. Or you can use the **LenB** function to determine the number of bytes used to represent that string.

Example	See the **AppendChunk** method example.
Example (Microsoft Access)	See the **AppendChunk** method example (Microsoft Access).

GetRows Method

Applies To	Dynaset-Type **Recordset** Object, **Recordset** Object, Snapshot-Type **Recordset** Object, **Table-Type Recordset** Object.
Description	Retrieves multiple rows of a **Recordset** into an array.
Syntax	*varArray* = *object*.**GetRows** (*numrows*)

The **GetRows** Method syntax has the following parts.

Part	Description
varArray	The name of a **Variant** type variable to store the returned data.
object	An object expression that evaluates to an object in the Applies To list.
numrows	The number of rows to retrieve.

Remarks   Use the **GetRows** method to copy one or more entire records from a **Recordset**. **GetRows** returns a two-dimensional array. The first subscript identifies the field and the second identifies the row number, as follows:

```
avarRecords(intField, intRecord)
```

To get the first field value in the second row returned, use the following:

```
field1 = avarRecords(0,1)
```

To get the second field value in the first row, use the following:

```
field2 = avarRecords(1,0)
```

If more rows are requested than are available, then only the number available are returned. Use **Ubound** to determine how many rows were actually fetched, as the array is sized to fit how many rows were returned. For example, if you returned the results into a variant called varA, you could determine how many rows were actually returned by using:

```
numReturned = Ubound(varA,2) + 1
```

The "+ 1" is used because the first data returned is in the 0 element of the array. The number of rows that can be fetched is constrained by available memory and should be chosen to suit your application—don't expect to use **GetRows** to bring your whole table into an array if it is a large table.

Because all fields of the recordset are returned in the array, including long memo and binary fields, you might want to use a query that restricts the columns returned.

After a call to **GetRows**, the current record is positioned at the next unread row. That is, **GetRows** has an equivalent positioning effect to **Move** *numrows*.

If you are trying to fetch all the rows using multiple **GetRows** calls, use the **EOF** property to be sure that you're at the end of the **Recordset**. **GetRows** returns less than the number requested either at the end of the **Recordset**, or if it cannot fetch a row in the range requested. For example, if a fifth record cannot be retrieved in a group of ten records that you're trying to fetch, **GetRows** returns four records and leaves currency on the record that caused a problem. It will not generate a run-time error. This situation might occur if a record in a dynaset has been deleted by another user.

See Also   **FillCache** Method, **Move** Method, **Value** Property.

Example   The following example uses an SQL statement to retrieve three fields from an Employees table into a **Recordset** object. It then uses the **GetRows** method to retrieve the first three records of the **Recordset**, and stores the selected records in a two-dimensional array. Each record is then printed, one field at a time, using the two array indexes to select specific fields and records.

Note   To clearly illustrate how the array indexes are used, the example uses a separate statement to identify and print each field of each record. In practice, it would be more reliable to use two loops, one nested in the other, and provide integer variables for the indexes, to step through both dimensions of the array.

```
Sub GetRows_Test()

    Dim dbsCurrent As Database, rstEmployees As Recordset
    Dim varRecords As Variant

    Set dbsCurrent = CurrentDB()
    Set rstEmployees = dbsCurrent.OpenRecordset("SELECT FirstName, " & _
        "LastName, Title FROM Employees", dbOpenSnapshot)

    varRecords = rstEmployees.GetRows(3)

    Debug.Print "First Name", "Last Name", "Title"
    Debug.Print varRecords(0, 0),
    Debug.Print varRecords(1, 0),
    Debug.Print varRecords(2, 0)
```

```
            Debug.Print varRecords(0, 1),
            Debug.Print varRecords(1, 1),
            Debug.Print varRecords(2, 1)
            Debug.Print varRecords(0, 2),
            Debug.Print varRecords(1, 2),
            Debug.Print varRecords(2, 2)

        End Sub
```

Example (Microsoft Access)

The following example uses the **GetRows** method to return a two-dimensional array containing the first ten rows of data in a **Recordset** object.

```
Sub RowsArray()
    Dim dbs As Database, rst As Recordset, strSQL As String
    Dim varRecords As Variant, intI As Integer, intJ As Integer

    ' Return Database variable pointing to current database.
    Set dbs = CurrentDb
    ' Build SQL statement that returns specified fields.
    strSQL = "SELECT [FirstName], [LastName], [HireDate] " & _
        "FROM [Employees]"
    ' Open dynaset-type Recordset object.
    Set rst = dbs.OpenRecordset(strSQL)
    ' Return first ten rows into array.
    varRecords = rst.GetRows(10)
    ' Find upper bound of second dimension.
    For intI = 0 To UBound(varRecords, 2)
        Debug.Print
            ' Find upper bound of first dimension.
            For intJ = 0 To UBound(varRecords, 1)
                ' Print data from each row in array.
                Debug.Print varRecords(intJ, intI)
            Next intJ
    Next intI
End Sub
```

Example (Microsoft Excel)

This example copies records from a selection of the Customer recordset in the NWINDEX.MDB database to Sheet1.

To create the NWINDEX.MDB database, run the Microsoft Excel example for the **CreateDatabase** method.

```
Dim db As Database, rs As Recordset
Dim data As Variant
Set db = Workspaces(0).OpenDatabase(Application.Path & "\NWINDEX.MDB")
Set rs = db.OpenRecordset("SELECT CUSTMR_ID, CONTACT FROM Customer;")
data = rs.GetRows(6)
Sheets("Sheet1").Activate
For r = 1 to UBound(data, 2) + 1
```

```
            For c = 1 to 2
                Cells(r, c).Value = data(c - 1, r - 1)
            Next
    Next
    rs.Close
    db.Close
```

Group Object

Description A **Group** object represents a group of user accounts that have common access permissions when a **Workspace** object operates as a secure workgroup.

Remarks You create **Group** objects and then use their names to establish and enforce access permissions for your databases, tables, and queries using the **Document** objects that represent the database and database objects (tables and queries) you're working with.

You can append an existing **Group** object to the **Groups** collection in a **User** object to establish membership of a user account in that **Group** object. Alternatively, you can append a **User** object to the **Users** collection in a **Group** object to give a user account the global permissions of that group. If you use a **Groups** or **Users** collection other than the one to which you just appended an object, you may need to use the **Refresh** method to refresh the collection with current information from the database.

Using the properties of a **Group** object, you can:

- Check the **Name** property setting of an existing **Group** object to determine its name. You can't check the **PID** property setting of an existing **Group** object.
- Set the **Name** and **PID** properties of a newly created, unappended **Group** object to establish the identity of that **Group** object.

The Microsoft Jet database engine predefines three **Group** objects named Admins, Users, and Guests.

You can refer to a **Group** object that you create and append to a **Groups** collection by its **Name** property setting using this syntax:

Groups("*name*")

To create a new **Group** object, use the **CreateGroup** method on a **User** or **Workspace** object.

Properties **Name** Property, **PID** Property.

Methods **CreateUser** Method.

See Also   CreateGroup Method; Appendix, "Data Access Object Hierarchy."

Specifics (Microsoft Access)   You can create **Group** objects to establish and enforce permissions for Microsoft Access database objects as well as for data access objects. For example, you can set security for forms, reports, macros, and modules.

A **Group** object has a **Name** property that you can use in setting permissions for a **Container** or **Document** object. For example, you can assign the value of a **Group** object's **Name** property to the **UserName** property of a **Container** or **Document** object. You can then set the **Permissions** property of the **Container** or **Document** object to establish permissions for the group of users defined by the **UserName** property. Or you can read the **Permissions** property to determine existing permissions for that group.

Example   This example illustrates the use of the **Group** and **User** objects and the **Groups** and **Users** collections. First, it creates a new **User** object with the **Name**, **PID**, and **Password** property settings of "Pat Smith," "abc123DEF456," and "My Secret," and appends the object to the **Users** collection of the default **Workspace** object. Next, it creates a new **Group** object with the **Name** and **PID** property settings of "Accounting" and "UVW987xyz654" and appends the object to the **Groups** collection of the default **Workspace** object. Then the example adds user Pat Smith to the Accounting group. Finally, it enumerates the **User** and **Group** objects in the collections of the default **Workspace** object.

```
Function EnumerateUserGroup () As Integer
    Dim wrkDefault As Workspace
    Dim usrPatSmith As User, usrTemp As User, usrGroupUser As User
    Dim grpAccount As Group, grpTemp As Group, grpMember As Group
    Dim intI As Integer, intJ As Integer

    Set wrkDefault = DBEngine.Workspaces(0)

' Create and append new user.
    Set usrPatSmith = wrkDefault.CreateUser("Pat Smith", _
        "abc123DEF456", "My Secret")
    wrkDefault.Users.Append usrPatSmith

' Create and append new group.
    Set grpAccount = wrkDefault.CreateGroup("Accounting", _
        "UVW987xyz654")
    wrkDefault.Groups.Append grpAccount

' Add new user to new group or converse; do one or the other, not both.
' Use Refresh because both collections are referred to in following
' code.
'     wrkDefault.Groups![Accounting].Users.Append usrGroupUser
'     wrkDefault.Users![Pat Smith].Groups.Refresh

' Or add group to user and refresh group.
```

150　Group Object

```
    ' Create new group object for user Pat Smith
        Set grpMember = usrPatSmith.CreateGroup("Accounting")

    '   wrkDefault.Users![Pat Smith].Groups.Append grpMember
    '   wrkDefault.Groups![Accounting].Users.Refresh

    ' Enumerate all users.
        For intJ = 0 To wrkDefault.Users.Count - 1
            Set usrTemp = wrkDefault.Users(intJ)
            Debug.Print
            Debug.Print "Enumeration of Users: "; usrTemp.Name
            Debug.Print
    ' Enumerate groups.
            Debug.Print " Groups: "
            For intI = 0 To usrTemp.Groups.Count - 1
                Debug.Print "    "; usrTemp.Groups(intI).Name
            Next intI
        Next intJ

    ' Enumerate all groups.
        Debug.Print "-----------------------------------"
        For intJ = 0 To wrkDefault.Groups.Count - 1
            Set grpTemp = wrkDefault.Groups(intJ)
            Debug.Print
            Debug.Print "Enumeration of Groups: "; grpTemp.Name
            Debug.Print
    ' Enumerate users.
            Debug.Print " Users: "
            For intI = 0 To grpTemp.Users.Count - 1
                Debug.Print "    "; grpTemp.Users(intI).Name
            Next intI
        Next intJ
        EnumerateUserGroup = True
    End Function
```

**Example
(Microsoft Access)**

The following example creates a new **User** object and appends it to the **Users** collection of a **Workspace** object. It then creates a new **Group** object and appends it to the **Groups** collection of the **Workspace** object. The new **Group** object is also appended to the **Groups** collection of the **User** object. The new group is then given modify and delete permissions for modules.

Note that in order to assign users to groups, you must either append a **User** object to the **Users** collection of a **Group** object, or append a **Group** object to the **Groups** collection of a **User** object. It doesn't matter which option you choose; either will result in the specified user being included in the specified group.

```
Sub NewModulesGroup()
    Dim wsp As Workspace, dbs As Database
    Dim usr As User, grp As Group, grpMember As Group
```

```
        Dim ctr As Container, doc As Document

        ' Get default Workspace object.
        Set wsp = DBEngine.Workspaces(0)
        ' Return Database variable pointing to current database.
        Set dbs = CurrentDb
        ' Create User object and append to Users collection
        ' of Workspace object.
        Set usr = wsp.CreateUser("Pat Smith", "123abc789xyz", "Password")
        wsp.Users.Append usr
        ' Create Group object and append to Groups collection
        ' of Workspace object.
        Set grp = wsp.CreateGroup("Programmers", "321xyz987abc")
        wsp.Groups.Append grp
        ' Append Group object to Groups collection of User object.
        Set grpMember = usr.CreateGroup("Programmers")
        usr.Groups.Append grpMember
        ' Refresh Groups collection of User object.
        usr.Groups.Refresh
        ' Return Container object.
        Set ctr = dbs.Containers!Modules
        ' Set UserName property of Container object.
        ctr.UserName = grpMember.Name
        'Add modify and delete permissions for new group on all modules.
        ctr.Permissions = ctr.Permissions Or acSecModWriteDef
    End Sub
```

Groups Collection

Description A **Groups** collection contains all stored **Group** objects of a **Workspace** or user account.

Remarks You can append an existing **Group** object to the **Groups** collection in a **User** object or a **Workspace** object to establish membership of a user account in that **Group** object. Alternatively, you can append a **User** object to the **Users** collection in a **Group** object to give a user account the global permissions of that group. If you use a **Groups** or **Users** collection other than the one to which you just appended an object, you may need to use the **Refresh** method to refresh the collection with current information from the database.

You can refer to a **Group** object that you create and append to a **Groups** collection by its **Name** property setting using this syntax:

Groups("*name*")

To create a new **Group** object, use the **CreateGroup** method.

Properties	**Count** Property.
Methods	**Append** Method, **Delete** Method, **Refresh** Method.
See Also	Appendix, "Data Access Object Hierarchy."
Specifics (Microsoft Access)	See the **Group** object specifics (Microsoft Access).
Example	See the **Group** object example.
Example (Microsoft Access)	See the **Group** object example (Microsoft Access).

HelpContext, HelpFile Properties

Applies To	**Error** Object.
	- **HelpContext**— returns a context ID, as a **Long** variable, for a topic in a Microsoft Windows Help file.
	- **HelpFile**— returns a fully qualified path to the Help file.
Remarks	If a Microsoft Windows Help file is specified in **HelpFile**, the **HelpContext** property is used to automatically display the Help topic it identifies.
	Note You should write routines in your application to handle typical errors. When programming with an object, you can use the Help supplied by the object's Help file to improve the quality of your error handling, or to display a meaningful message to your user if the error is not recoverable.
See Also	**Description** Property, **Number** Property, **Source** Property.
Specifics (Microsoft Access)	The data access **HelpContext** and **HelpFile** properties apply to the **Error** object. You can set it only from Visual Basic.
	Note Don't confuse these properties with the Microsoft Access **HelpContextID** and **HelpFile** properties. These properties are similar, but they apply only to forms, reports, and controls. You can set them from Visual Basic, in a macro, or in the property sheet within form Design view or report Design view.

Example

This example uses the **HelpContext** and **HelpFile** properties of an **Error** object to start the Microsoft Windows Help system. By default, the **HelpFile** property contains the name of the Microsoft Jet database engine error message Help file.

```
On Error Resume Next    ' Suppress errors for demonstration purposes.
Err.Raise 3005    ' Use VBA to generate "Invalid database name" error.
Msg = "Press F1 or Help to see " & Errors(0).HelpFile & _
    " topic for this error"
MsgBox Msg, , "Error: " & Errors(0).Description & _
    Errors(0).HelpFile & Errors(0).HelpContext
```

Idle Method

Applies To   **DBEngine** Object.

Description   Suspends data processing, enabling the Microsoft Jet database engine to complete any pending tasks such as memory optimization or page timeouts.

Syntax   **DBEngine.Idle [dbFreeLocks]**

Remarks   You use the **Idle** method to provide the Jet database engine with the opportunity to perform background tasks that may not be up-to-date because of intense data processing. This is often true in multiuser, multitasking environments in which there isn't enough background processing time to keep all records in a recordset current.

Usually, read locks are removed and data in local dynaset-type **Recordset** objects is updated only when no other actions (including mouse movements) are occurring. If you periodically use the **Idle** method, you provide the database engine with time to catch up on background processing tasks by releasing unneeded read locks. If you specify the **dbFreeLocks** constant as an argument, processing is delayed until all read locks are released.

This method isn't needed in single-user environments unless multiple instances of an application are running. The **Idle** method may increase performance in a multiuser environment because it forces the database engine to flush data to disk, releasing locks on memory.

You can also release read locks by making operations part of a transaction. For example:

```
wspSession.BeginTrans
Set rstEmployees = rstEmployees.OpenRecordset("Employees")
wspSession.CommitTrans
```

```
        Do Until rstEmployees.EOF
            ...
            ...
            ...
            rstEmployees.MoveNext
        Loop
```

IgnoreNulls Property

Applies To **Index** Object.

Description Sets or returns a value that indicates whether records that have **Null** values in their index fields have index entries. This property is read/write for a new **Index** object not yet appended to a collection and read-only for an existing **Index** object in an **Indexes** collection.

Settings and Return Values This property is a Boolean expression that indicates index entries. The data type is Boolean. **True** (-1) indicates that the fields with **Null** values don't have an index entry.

Remarks To make searching for records using a field faster, you can define an index for the field. If you allow **Null** entries in an indexed field and expect many of the entries to be **Null**, you can set the **IgnoreNulls** property for the **Index** object to **True** to reduce the amount of storage space that the index uses.

The **IgnoreNulls** property setting and the **Required** property setting together determine whether a record with a **Null** index value has an index entry, as the following table shows.

IgnoreNulls	Required	Null in index field
True	**False**	**Null** value allowed; no index entry added
False	**False**	**Null** value allowed; index entry added
True or **False**	**True**	**Null** value not allowed; no index entry added

See Also **Required** Property.

Example (Microsoft Access) The following example adds a new index to a **TableDef** object, makes that index the current index, and invokes the **Seek** method based on that index. The names of the **Field** objects created and appended to the **Fields** collection of the **Index** object correspond to the names of current fields in the table.

```
Sub NewIndex()
    Dim dbs As Database, tdf As TableDef
    Dim idx As Index, fldID As Field, fldName As Field
```

```
            ' Return Database variable that points to current database.
            Set dbs = CurrentDb
            Set tdf = dbs.TableDefs!Products
            ' Return Index object that points to new index.
            Set idx = tdf.CreateIndex("IDName")
            ' Create and append index fields.
            Set fldID = idx.CreateField("ProductID")
            Set fldName = idx.CreateField("ProductName")
            idx.Fields.Append fldID
            idx.Fields.Append fldName
            ' Set index properties.
            idx.IgnoreNulls = True
            idx.Unique = True
            ' Append the new Index object to the Indexes collection.
            tdf.Indexes.Append idx
        End Sub
```

Index Object

Description   **Index** objects specify the order of records accessed from database tables and whether or not duplicate records are accepted. **Index** objects also provide efficient access to data. For external databases, **Index** objects describe the indexes established for external tables.

Remarks   The Microsoft Jet database engine maintains all base table indexes automatically. Indexes are updated whenever you add, change, or delete records from the base table. Once the database is created, use the **CompactDatabase** method periodically to bring index statistics up-to-date.

The Jet database engine uses indexes when it joins tables and creates **Recordset** objects. Indexes determine the order of records returned by table-type **Recordset** objects, but they don't determine the order in which records are stored in the base table or the order of records returned from any other type of recordset.

When accessing a table-type **Recordset** object, you specify the order of records using the object's **Index** property. Set this property to the **Name** property setting of an existing **Index** object in the **Indexes** collection. This collection is contained by the **TableDef** object underlying the **Recordset** object that you're populating. For example, to order your table-type **Recordset** object by the ZIP_INDEX index, you could use the following code.

```
Set dbsBiblio = Workspaces(0).OpenDatabase("Biblio.mdb")
Set rstPublishers = dbsBiblio.OpenRecordset("Publishers", dbOpenTable)
rstPublishers.Index = "ZIP_INDEX"
```

> **Tip** You don't have to create indexes for a table, but for large, unindexed tables, accessing a specific record or processing joins can take a long time. Conversely, having too many indexes can slow down updates to the database as each of the table indexes is amended.

The **Attributes** property of each **Field** object in the index determines the order of records returned and consequently determines which access techniques to use for that index.

Each **Field** object in the **Fields** collection of an **Index** object is a component of the index. You define a new **Index** object by setting its properties before you append it to a collection, which makes the **Index** object available for subsequent use.

> **Note** You can modify the **Name** property setting of an existing **Index** object only if the **Updatable** property setting of the containing **TableDef** object is **True**.

Using an **Index** object and its properties, you can:

- Use the **Required** property to determine whether the **Field** objects in the index require values that are not **Null**, then use the **IgnoreNulls** property to determine whether the **Null** values have index entries.
- Use the **Primary** and **Unique** properties to determine the ordering and uniqueness of the **Index** object.

When you set a primary key for a table, the Jet database engine automatically defines it as the primary index. A primary index consists of one or more fields that uniquely identify all records in a table in a predefined order. Because the primary index field must be unique, the Jet database engine automatically sets the **Unique** property of the primary **Index** object to **True**. If the primary index consists of more than one field, each field can contain duplicate values, but the combination of values from all the indexed fields must be unique. A primary index consists of a key for the table and is always made up of the same fields as the primary key.

> **Important** Make sure your data complies with the attributes of your new index. If your index requires unique values, make sure that there are no duplicates in existing data records. If duplicates exist, the Jet database engine can't create the index, resulting in a trappable error when you attempt to use the **Append** method on the new index.

Index Object 157

When you create a relationship that enforces referential integrity, the Jet database engine automatically creates an index with the **Foreign** property, set as the foreign key in the referencing table. After you've established a table relationship, the Jet database engine prevents additions or changes to the database that violate that relationship. If you set the **Attributes** property of the **Relation** object to allow cascade update and cascade delete operations, the Jet database engine updates or deletes records in related tables automatically.

Note The **Clustered** property is ignored for databases that use the Jet database engine, which doesn't support clustered indexes.

Properties **Clustered** Property, **DistinctCount** Property, **Foreign** Property, **IgnoreNulls** Property, **Name** Property, **Primary** Property, **Required** Property, **Unique** Property.

Methods **CreateField** Method, **CreateProperty** Method.

See Also **Attributes** Property; **CreateIndex** Method; **Index** Property, **OrdinalPosition** Property; Appendix, "Data Access Object Hierarchy."

Example This example creates a new **TableDef** object and two new **Field** objects, appends the **Field** objects to the **Fields** collection in the new **TableDef**, and appends the **TableDef** to the **TableDefs** collection in the database. Then it creates a new primary **Index** object, includes the two **Field** objects in it, and appends the **Index** to the **Indexes** collection of the **TableDef**. Finally, the example enumerates the **Index** objects in the current database.

```
Function EnumerateIndex () As Integer
    Dim  dbsDefault As Database, tdfTest As TableDef
    Dim fldOne As Field, fldTwo As Field, idxPrimary As Index
    Dim I As Integer
    ' Get workspace and database.
    Set dbsDefault = _
        DBEngine.Workspaces(0).OpenDatabase("Northwind.mdb")
    ' Create table with two fields.
    Set tdfTest = dbsDefault.CreateTableDef("MyTable")
    Set fldOne = tdfTest.CreateField("Field1", dbLong)
    fldOne.Required = True      ' No Null values allowed.
    tdfTest.Fields.Append fldOne
    Set fldTwo = tdfTest.CreateField("Field2", dbLong)
    fldTwo.Required = True      ' No Null values allowed.
    tdfTest.Fields.Append fldTwo
    dbsDefault.TableDefs.Append tdfTest
    ' Create primary index for those two fields.
    Set idxPrimary = tdfTest.CreateIndex("MyIndex")
    idxPrimary.Primary = True
    Set fldOne = tdfTest.CreateField("Field1")
    idxPrimary.Fields.Append fldOne
```

158　Index Object

```
    Set fldTwo = tdfTest.CreateField("Field2")
    idxPrimary.Fields.Append fldTwo
    tdfTest.Indexes.Append idxPrimary
    ' Enumerate index and its fields.
    Debug.Print "Index: "; idxPrimary.Name
    Debug.Print "  Required: "; idxPrimary.Required
    Debug.Print "  IgnoreNulls: "; idxPrimary.IgnoreNulls
    Debug.Print "  Primary: "; idxPrimary.Primary
    Debug.Print "  Clustered: "; idxPrimary.Clustered
    Debug.Print "  Unique: "; idxPrimary.Unique
    Debug. Print "  Foreign: "; idxPrimary.Foreign
    Debug.Print
    Debug.Print "Fields in Index: ";
    For I = 0 To idxPrimary.Fields.Count - 1
        Debug.Print " "; idxPrimary.Fields(I).Name;
    Next I
    Debug.Print
    EnumerateIndex = True
End Function
```

This example opens a table-type **Recordset** and selects an index for the **Recordset**. By setting an index, the Microsoft Jet database engine returns records in the order specified by the index. Without an index, table-type **Recordset** objects return records from the database table in no particular order.

```
Dim dbsDefault As Database
Dim rstTitles as Recordset
' Get workspace and database.
Set dbsDefault = _
    DBEngine.Workspaces(0).OpenDatabase("Northwind.mdb")
Set rstTitles = dbsDefault.OpenRecordset("Titles")
rstTitles.Index = "MyIndex"
    .
    .
    .
```

**Example
(Microsoft Access)**

The following example creates a new index on an Employees table.

```
Sub NewIndex()
    Dim dbs As Database, tdf As TableDef, idx As Index
    Dim fld As Field

    ' Return Database object pointing to current database.
    Set dbs = CurrentDb
    Set tdf = dbs.TableDefs!Employees
    Set idx = tdf.CreateIndex("LastNameIndex")
    Set fld = idx.CreateField("LastName")
    idx.Fields.Append fld
    tdf.Indexes.Append idx
End Sub
```

Index Property

Applies To Recordset Object, Table-Type **Recordset** Object.

Description Sets or returns a value that indicates the name of the current **Index** object in a table-type **Recordset** object.

Settings and Return Values The setting or return value is a string expression that evaluates to the name of an **Index** object in the **Indexes** collection of the **Table** or table-type **Recordset** object's **TableDef** object. The data type is **String**.

Remarks Records in base tables aren't stored in any particular order. Setting the **Index** property changes the order of records returned from the database; it doesn't affect the order in which the records are stored.

For example, to set the **Index** property prior to using the **Seek** method on the Titles table:

```
Dim rstTitles as Recordset, dbsBiblio as Database
Set dbsBiblio = Workspaces(0).OpenDatabase("Biblio.mdb")
Set rstTitles = dbsBiblio.OpenRecordset("Titles",dbOpenTable)
rstTitles.Index = "PubID"
rstTitles.Seek "=", 3
```

The specified **Index** object must already be defined. If you set the **Index** property to an **Index** object that doesn't exist or if the **Index** property isn't set when you use the **Seek** method, a trappable error occurs.

Examine the **Indexes** collection of a **TableDef** object to determine what **Index** objects are available to table-type **Recordset** objects created from that **TableDef** object.

You can create a new index for the table by creating a new **Index** object, setting its properties, appending it to the **Indexes** collection of the underlying **TableDef** object, and then reopening the **Recordset** object.

Records returned from a table-type **Recordset** object can be ordered only by the indexes defined for the underlying **TableDef** object. To sort records in some other order, you can open a dynaset- or Snapshot-Type **Recordset** object using an SQL statement with an ORDER BY clause.

Tips

- You don't have to create indexes for tables, but in large, unindexed tables, accessing a specific record or creating a **Recordset** object can take a long time. On the other hand, creating too many indexes slows down update, append, and delete operations as all indexes are automatically updated.
- Records read from tables without indexes are returned in no particular sequence.
- The **Attributes** property of each **Field** object in the **Index** object determines the order of records and consequently determines the access techniques to use for that index.
- A unique index helps optimize finding records.
- Indexes don't affect the physical order of a base table—indexes affect only how the records are accessed by the table-type **Recordset** object when a particular index is chosen or when the Microsoft Jet database engine creates **Recordset** objects.

See Also **Append** Method, **Index** Object, **Primary** Property, **Seek** Method, **Sort** Property, **TableDef** Object.

Example This example adds a new index to a **TableDef** object in the Biblio.mdb database, makes that index the current index, and invokes the **Seek** method based on that index. The names of the **Field** objects created and appended to the **Fields** collection of the **Index** object correspond to the names of current fields in the table.

```
Dim rstPublishers As Recordset, dbsBiblio As Database
Dim idxPubIDName As Index, fldPubID As Field, fldName As Field
Set dbsBiblio = DBEngine.Workspaces(0).OpenDatabase("Biblio.mdb")
Set idxPubIDName = dbsBiblio.TableDefs("Publishers").CreateIndex _
    ("PubID Name")
Set fldPubID = idxPubIDName.CreateField("PubID")
idxPubIDName.Fields.Append fldPubID
Set fldName = idxPubIDName.CreateField("Name")
idxPubIDName.Fields.Append fldName
idxPubIDName.Unique = True
Debug.Print idxPubIDName.Fields     ' Show Fields property.
' Append the new Index to the Indexes collection.
dbsBiblio.TableDefs("Publishers").Indexes.Append idxPubIDName
'Open the table.
Set rstPublishers = dbsBiblio.OpenRecordset("Publishers",dbOpenTable)
rstPublishers.Index = "PubID Name"    ' Set table's current index.
rstPublishers.Seek "=", "27", "Yourdon Press"  ' Look for Publisher.
If rstPublishers.NoMatch Then
    rstPublishers.MoveFirst
    Debug.Print "Not found"
Else
    Debug.Print rstPublishers!Name
End If
```

```
rstPublishers.Close
```

This example sets the index for rstOrders to the primary key. (PrimaryKey is the default name of an **Index** object if the primary key is set in the table's Design view.) Next, it locates the record with a matching key field value of 10,050. Notice that the current index must be set before certain operations, such as the **Seek** method, can be performed.

```
Dim dbsNorthwind As Database, rstOrders As Recordset
Set dbsNorthwind =  DBEngine.Workspaces(0).OpenDatabase("Northwind.mdb")
Set rstOrders = dbsNorthwind.OpenRecordset("Orders", dbOpenTable)
rstOrders.Index = "PrimaryKey"      ' Set current index.
rstOrders.Seek "=", 10050           ' Locate record.
...
rstOrders.Close                     ' Close recordset.
dbsNorthwind.Close                  ' Close database.
```

Example (Microsoft Access)

The following example sets the index for a table-type **Recordset** object to the primary key. "PrimaryKey" is the default name of an **Index** object if the index corresponds to the primary key set in table Design view. Next, the procedure asks the user for a value to search on and locates the record with a matching key field value. Note that the current index must be set before certain operations, such as the **Seek** method, can be performed on a table-type **Recordset** object.

```
Sub UsePrimaryKey()
    Dim dbs As Database, rst As Recordset
    Dim fld as Field, strInput as String

    ' Return Database variable that points to current database.
    Set dbs = CurrentDb
    Set rst = dbs.OpenRecordset("Orders", dbOpenTable)
    ' Set current index.
    rst.Index = "PrimaryKey"
    strInput = InputBox("Enter the OrderID on which to search.")
    ' Locate record.
    rst.Seek "=", strInput
    If Not rst.NoMatch Then
        For Each fld in rst.Fields
            Debug.Print fld.Name; "    "; fld.Value
        Next fld
    End If
    ' Close Recordset object.
    rst.Close
End Sub
```

Indexes Collection

Description	An **Indexes** collection contains all the stored **Index** objects of a **TableDef** object.
Remarks	Once created, a new **Index** object should be added to the **TableDef** object's **Indexes** collection using the **Append** method.

When accessing a table-type **Recordset** object, you specify the order of records using the object's **Index** property. Set this property to the **Name** property setting of an existing **Index** object in the **Indexes** collection. This collection is contained by the **TableDef** object underlying the **Recordset** object that you're populating. For example, to order your table-type **Recordset** by the ZIP_INDEX index, you could use the following code.

```
Set dbsBiblio = Workspaces(0).OpenDatabase("Biblio.mdb")
Set rstPublishers = dbsBiblio.OpenRecordset("Publishers", dbOpenTable)
rstPublishers.Index = "ZIP_INDEX"
```

Note You can use the **Append** or **Delete** method on an **Indexes** collection only if the **Updatable** property setting of the containing **TableDef** object is **True**.

If you attempt to create an **Index** object and your data doesn't comply with the attributes specified for the index, such as nonunique or **Null** values in an indexed field, a trappable error results when you attempt to use the **Append** method on the new index.

Properties	**Count** Property.
Methods	**Append** Method, **Delete** Method, **Refresh** Method.
See Also	Appendix, "Data Access Object Hierarchy."
Example	See the **Index** object example.
Example (Microsoft Access)	See the **Index** object example (Microsoft Access).

Inherit Property

Applies To	**Container** Object.
Description	Determines whether new **Document** objects will inherit a default **Permissions** property setting.

Inherit Property 163

Return Values The return values are Boolean data type.

Remarks Use the **Inherit** property in conjunction with the **Permissions** property to define what permissions new documents will automatically be given when they're created. If you set the **Inherit** property to **True** (-1), and then set a permission on a container, then whenever a new document is created in that container, that permission will be set on the new document. This is a very convenient way of presetting permissions on an object.

Setting the **Inherit** property will not affect existing documents in the container— you can't modify all the permissions on all existing documents in a container by setting the **Inherit** property and a new permission. It will affect only new documents that are created after the **Inherit** property is set.

See Also **Document** Object, **Permissions** Property.

Example This example sets the Table container's **Inherit** property to True, and then sets the **Permissions** property to allow users to alter the security settings of documents.

```
Dim dbsNorthwind As Database, conTables As Container
Set dbsNorthwind = DBEngine.Workspaces(0).OpenDatabase("Northwind.mdb")
Set conTables = dbsNorthwind.Containers("Tables")
conTables.Inherit = True
conTables.Permissions = dbSecWriteSec
dbsNorthwind.Close
```

Example (Microsoft Access) The following example sets the **Inherit** property of the Forms **Container** object to **True** (-1), and then sets the **Permissions** property to give users full security access to all forms. All new **Document** objects of the Form type will inherit these permissions. The procedure then creates a new **Form** object and displays the permissions for that object.

Note that the Forms **Container** object is different from the **Forms** collection. The Forms **Container** object includes all Form **Document** objects in the database; the **Forms** collection contains only currently open forms.

```
Sub FormPermissions()
    Dim dbs As Database, ctrForms As Container
    Dim docForm As Document, frmNew As Form

    ' Return Database variable that points to current database.
    Set dbs = CurrentDb
    ' Return Container variable pointing to Forms Container object.
    Set ctrForms = dbs.Containers!Forms
    ' Set Inherit property.
    ctrForms.Inherit = True
    ' Set permissions to be inherited.
    ctrForms.Permissions = ctrForms.Permissions Or acSecFrmRptWriteDef
    ' Create new form.
    Set frmNew = CreateForm()
```

```
          ' Save form.
          DoCmd.Save , "OrderForm"
          ' Return Document object associated with new form.
          Set docForm = ctrForms.Documents!OrderForm
          ' Compare permissions for Container and Document objects.
          If docForm.Permissions <> ctrForms.Permissions Then
              MsgBox "Error!"
          Else
              MsgBox "Permissions successfully inherited."
          End If
End Sub
```

Inherited Property

Applies To	**Property** Object.
Description	Returns a value that indicates whether a **Property** object is inherited from an underlying object. This property setting is read-only. **True** (-1) indicates that the Property object is inherited. For built-in **Property** objects that represent predefined properties, **False** (0) is the only possible return value.
Remarks	You can use the **Inherited** property to determine whether a user-defined property was created for the object it applies to or whether the property was created for another object. For example, suppose you create a property for a **QueryDef** object and then open a **Recordset** object from the **QueryDef** object. This property will be part of the **Recordset** object's **Properties** collection, and its **Inherited** property will be set to **True** because the property was created for the **QueryDef** object, not the **Recordset** object.
See Also	**CreateProperty** Method, **QueryDef** Object.
Specifics (Microsoft Access)	Microsoft Access defines a number of properties which apply to data access objects. Because these properties are defined by Microsoft Access, the Microsoft Jet database engine doesn't recognize them automatically. To set one of these properties in Visual Basic, you must first create the property using the **CreateProperty** method and then append it to the **Properties** collection of the object. For more information, search the online index for the **Property** object topic.
	When you create an object based on another object, the derived object inherits the properties of the original object. You can use the **Inherited** property to determine whether one of these properties was created for the object it is applied to, or if the property was inherited from another object.

Inherited Property

For example, suppose you want to set the Microsoft Access **DatasheetFontName** property for a **TableDef** object. If you are setting this property for the first time, you will need to create a corresponding **Property** object and append it to the **Properties** collection of the **TableDef** object. The **Inherited** property of the new **Property** object returns **False**.

If you then create a new **QueryDef** object based on the table corresponding to the **TableDef** object, the **DatasheetFontName** property will be included in the **Properties** collection of the **QueryDef** object. The **Inherited** property of a **Property** object corresponding to this property returns **True**.

Example

This example creates a **Recordset** object from a **QueryDef** object, creates a new property, and indicates whether the property is inherited. Then the example prints the name of each field in the **Recordset** and, for each property of each field, it prints the **Name**, **Type**, **Value**, and **Inherited** property *value* settings.

```
Dim dbsDefault As Database, qdfTest As QueryDef
Dim rstTest As Recordset, prpMoose As Property
Dim intField As Integer, intProp As Integer
Set dbsDefault = DBEngine.Workspaces(0).OpenDatabase("Northwind.mdb")
Set qdfTest = dbsDefault.QueryDefs(0)
Set prpMoose = qdfTest.CreateProperty("Moose",dbBoolean, True)
qdfTest.Properties.Append prpMoose
Set rstTest = qdfTest.OpenRecordset()
Debug.Print "Is qdfTest.Properties(""Moose"")inherited? "
Debug.Print qdfTest.Properties("Moose").Inherited
Debug.Print "Is rstTest.Properties(""Moose"")inherited? "
Debug.Print rstTest.Properties("Moose").Inherited
For intField = 0 To rstTest.Fields.Count - 1
    Debug.Print rstTest.Fields(intField).Name
    On Error Resume Next
    For intProp = 0 To rstTest.Fields(intField).Properties.Count - 1
        Debug.Print rstTest.Fields(intField).Properties(intProp).Name
        Debug.Print rstTest.Fields(intField).Properties(intProp).Type
        Debug.Print rstTest.Fields(intField).Properties(intProp).Value
        Debug.Print _
            rstTest.Fields(intField).Properties(intProp).Inherited
    Next intProp
Next intField
dbsDefault.Close
```

Example (Microsoft Access)

The following example creates a **Property** object in the **Properties** collection of a **TableDef** object, and then creates a new **QueryDef** object based on the same table. The **Property** object automatically exists in the **Properties** collection of the new **QueryDef** object. Next, the procedure checks the **Inherited** property for the **Property** objects in the **Properties** collections of both the **TableDef** and the **QueryDef** objects.

166   IniPath Property

In the following example, the Microsoft Access **DatasheetFontItalic** property is created and appended to the **Properties** collection of the **TableDef** object. The **DatasheetFontItalic** property is defined by Microsoft Access rather than by the Microsoft Jet database engine. However, the property applies to data access objects. Therefore, in order to set it from Visual Basic code, you must first create a **Property** object corresponding to that property and append it to the **Properties** collection of the data access object. It is necessary to create the property only the first time you set it.

```
Sub CheckInherited()
    Dim dbs As Database, tdfOrders As TableDef, qdfOrders As QueryDef
    Dim prpTableDef As Property, prpQueryDef As Property
    Dim strSQL As String

    ' Return Database variable that points to current database.
    Set dbs = CurrentDb
    Set tdfOrders = dbs.TableDefs!Orders
    ' Create Property object and append to Properties collection.
    Set prpTableDef = tdfOrders.CreateProperty("DatasheetFontItalic", _
        dbBoolean, True)
    tdfOrders.Properties.Append prpTableDef
    Debug.Print prpTableDef.Inherited
    ' Create QueryDef based on Orders table.
    strSQL = "SELECT * FROM Orders WHERE ShipCountry = 'USA'"
    Set qdfOrders = dbs.CreateQueryDef("USAOrders", strSQL)
    ' Return Property object pointing to property.
     Set prpQueryDef = qdfOrders.Properties!DatasheetFontItalic
     Debug.Print prpQueryDef.Inherited
End Sub
```

IniPath Property

Applies To	**DBEngine** Object.
Description	Sets or returns the Microsoft Jet database part of the Windows Registry file. This is a change from earlier versions in which options were set in .ini files.
Settings and Return Values	The setting or return value is a string expression that points to a user-supplied portion of the Registry key containing Microsoft Jet database engine settings or parameters needed for installable ISAM databases. The data type is **String**.
Remarks	The Microsoft Jet engine can be configured with the Registry file. You can use the Registry to set options, such as installable ISAM DLLs.

For this option to have any effect, the **IniPath** property must be set before any other data access functions are invoked by your application. The scope of this setting is limited to your application and can't be changed without restarting your application.

You also use the Registry to provide initialization parameters for some installable ISAM database drivers. For example, to use Paradox version 4.0, set the **IniPath** property to a part of the Registry containing the appropriate parameters.

This property recognizes either HKEY_LOCAL_MACHINE or HKEY_LOCAL_USER. If no root key is supplied, the default is HKEY_LOCAL_MACHINE.

Example

This example sets the path in the **IniPath** property to an application's key in the Windows Registry.

```
Sub SetPathFirst()
Dim strPath As String
strPath = "HKEY_LOCAL_MACHINE\SOFTWARE\Microsoft\MyApp\3.0\KeyFolder"
DBEngine.IniPath = strPath
End Sub
```

IsolateODBCTrans Property

Applies To **Workspace** Object.

Description Sets or returns a value that indicates whether multiple transactions that involve the same ODBC database are isolated.

True (-1) indicates to isolate transactions involving the same ODBC database. **False** (0) (the default) indicates not to isolate transactions involving the same ODBC database.

Remarks In some situations, you need to have multiple simultaneous transactions pending on the same ODBC database. To do this, you need to open a separate **Workspace** for each transaction. Although each **Workspace** can have its own ODBC connection to the database, this slows system performance. Because transaction isolation isn't normally required, ODBC connections from multiple **Workspace** objects opened by the same user are shared by default.

Example This example opens a **Workspace** and sets **IsolateODBCTrans** to **True** before starting a transaction.

```
Dim wrkDefault As Workspace
Set wrkDefault = DBEngine.Workspaces(0)
wrkDefault.IsolateODBCTrans = True
wrkDefault.BeginTrans
```

```
' Execute query to ODBC database and complete transaction.
...
...
```

KeepLocal Property

Applies To QueryDef Object, TableDef Object.

Description Sets or returns a value on a **TableDef** or **QueryDef** object, or a table, query, form, report, macro, or module that you do not want made replicable when the database is converted to a replicable form.

Setting and Return Value You set this property to the text string "T" to keep the object local while all other objects are made replicable when the database is made replicable. The **KeepLocal** property cannot be applied to objects after they have been converted into a replicable form.

Remarks Local objects remain at the replica where they were created and are not propagated around the replica set. Each time you make a new replica in the set, all the replicable objects at the source replica are included in that new replica, but none of the local objects are included.

The object on which you are setting the **KeepLocal** property might have already inherited that property from another object. However, the value set by the other object has no affect on the behavior of the object you want to **KeepLocal**. You must directly set the property for each object.

See Also **Replicable** Property.

LastModified Property

Applies To Dynaset-Type **Recordset** Object, **Recordset** Object, Table-Type **Recordset** Object.

Description Returns a bookmark indicating the most recently added or changed record.

Return Values The return value is a **Variant** array of Byte data.

Remarks You can use **LastModified** property to move to the most recently added or updated record. Use the **LastModified** property with **Recordset** objects. A record must be modified in the **Recordset** object itself in order for **LastModified** property to have a value.

LastModified Property 169

See Also **Bookmark** Property; **Bookmarkable** Property; **DateCreated**, **LastUpdated** Properties.

Specifics (Microsoft Access) When you use the **LastModified** property in a Microsoft Access module, you must include an **Option Compare Binary** statement in the Declarations section of the module. The bookmark returned by the **LastModified** property is a **Variant** array of **Byte** data, so the string comparison method for the module must be binary. If a bookmark is evaluated with a text-based string comparison method, such as the **Option Compare Text** statement or the default setting for the **Option Compare Database** statement, the current record may be set to an incorrect record.

Example See the **AddNew** method example.

Example (Microsoft Access) The following example prints the value of the OrderDate field for the most recently modified record in a recordset.

```
' Include this statement in the Declarations section of the module.
Option Compare Binary

Sub LastChangedRecord()
    Dim dbs As Database, rst As Recordset, varBook As Variant

    ' Return Database variable that points to current database.
    Set dbs = CurrentDb
    ' Create Dynaset-Type Recordset object.
    Set rst = dbs.OpenRecordset("SELECT * FROM Orders " & _
        "ORDER BY [ShipCountry]")
    With rst
        ' Populate recordset.
        .MoveLast
        ' Move to first record and search.
        .MoveFirst
        .FindFirst "[ShipCountry] = 'UK'"
        ' Alter record and save changes.
        .Edit
        .[ShipCountry] = "USA"
        .Update
    End With
    ' Check to see if recordset supports bookmarks.
    If rst.Bookmarkable Then
        ' Set bookmark to most recently modified record.
        varBook = rst.LastModified
        ' Set currency to last modified record.
        rst.Bookmark = varBook
        ' Display changed value.
        Debug.Print rst.Fields!ShipCountry
    End If
End Sub
```

LastUpdated Property

See DateCreated, LastUpdated Properties.

LockEdits Property

Applies To	Dynaset-Type **Recordset** Object, **Recordset** Object, Table-Type **Recordset** Object.
Description	Sets or returns a value indicating the locking that is in effect during editing.
Settings and Return Values	The setting or return value is a Boolean expression that indicates the type of locking. The data type is Boolean.

The possible settings or return values are:

Setting/Value	Description
True (-1)	(Default) Pessimistic locking is in effect. The 2K page containing the record you're editing is locked as soon as you use the **Edit** method.
False (0)	Optimistic locking is in effect for editing. The 2K page containing the record is not locked until the **Update** method is executed.

Remarks You can use the **LockEdits** property with dynaset- and Table-Type **Recordset** objects.

If a page is locked, no other user can edit records on the same page. If you set **LockEdits** to **True** and another user already has the page locked, an error occurs when you use the **Edit** method. Other users can read data from locked pages.

If you set the **LockEdits** property to **False** and later use **Update** method while the page is locked by another user, an error occurs. To see the changes made to your record by another user, set the **Bookmark** property of your **Recordset** object to itself. This approach results in your changes being lost.

When working with ODBC data sources, the **LockEdits** property is always set to **False**, or optimistic locking. The Microsoft Jet database engine has no control over the locking mechanisms used in external database servers.

See Also **Bookmark** Property; **Close** Method; **FindFirst**, **FindLast**, **FindNext**, **FindPrevious** Methods; **IsolateODBCTrans** Property; **MoveFirst**, **MoveLast**, **MoveNext**, **MovePrevious** Methods.

LockEdits Property 171

Example

This example opens a Dynaset-Type **Recordset** and sets its **LockEdits** property to **False**. This enables optimistic locking so other users can change the database records at any time. Your application triggers a trappable error if the data changes before you use the **Update** method.

```
Sub ShowLockStatus()
Dim dbsNorthwind As Database, rstCustomers As Recordset

Set dbsNorthwind = DBEngine.Workspaces(0).OpenDatabase("Northwind.mdb")
Set rstCustomers = dbsNorthwind.OpenRecordset("Customers", dbOpenDynaset)
rstCustomers.LockEdits = True
OnError Goto ErrorHandler
rstCustomers.Edit              ' Start editing.
    On Error GoTo 0
    rstCustomers.CancelUpdate
    rstCustomers.Close
    dbsNorthwind.Close
    Exit Sub

ErrorHandler:
    If Err = 3197 Then
        Debug.Print "data changed"
        Resume Next
    Else
        Debug.Print "some other error"
        Resume Next
    End If
End Sub
```

Example (Microsoft Access)

The following example opens a Dynaset-Type **Recordset** object and sets its **LockEdits** property to **False** (0). This enables optimistic locking so other users can change the database records at any time. Microsoft Access triggers a trappable error if the data changes before you use the **Update** method.

```
Sub ShowLockStatus()
    Dim dbs As Database, rst As Recordset

    ' Return Database variable that points to current database.
    Set dbs = CurrentDb
    Set rst = dbs.OpenRecordset("Customers", dbOpenDynaset)
    rst.LockEdits = False
    On Error Goto ErrorHandler
    ' Enable editing.
    rst.Edit
    .                                  ' Change records.
    .
    .
    rst.Update                         ' Try to post changes.
    rst.Close
```

```
            Exit Sub
        ErrorHandler:
            If Err.Number = 3197 Then
                MsgBox "Data changed by another user."
                Resume Next
            Else
                MsgBox "Some other error."
            End If
End Sub
```

Example (Microsoft Excel)

This example locks the Customer recordset in the NWINDEX.MDB database before updating the value in the CUSTMR_ID field of the first record with the value in cell A1 on Sheet1. Locking the recordset ensures that no other user modifies the record while it is being updated.

To create the NWINDEX.MDB database, run the Microsoft Excel example for the **CreateDatabase** method.

```
Dim db As Database, rs As Recordset
Sheets("Sheet1").Cells(1, 1).Value = "ACRIM"
databasePath = Application.Path & "\NWINDEX.MDB"
Set db = DBEngine.Workspaces(0).OpenDatabase(databasePath)
Set rs = db.OpenRecordset("Customer")
valueToAdd = Sheets("Sheet1").Cells(1, 1).Value
rs.LockEdits = False
rs.Edit
rs.fields("CUSTMR_ID").Value = valueToAdd
rs.Update
MsgBox "The new value of CUSTMR_ID is " & rs.fields("CUSTMR_ID").Value
rs.Close
db.Close
```

LoginTimeout Property

Applies To **DBEngine** Object.

Description Sets or returns the number of seconds before an error occurs when you attempt to log in to an ODBC database.

Settings and Return Values The setting or return value is an **Integer** representing the number of seconds before a login timeout error occurs. The default **LoginTimeout** property setting is 20 seconds. When the **LoginTimeout** property is set to 0, no timeout occurs.

LoginTimeout Property 173

Remarks

When you're attempting to log into an ODBC database, such as SQL Server, the connection can fail as a result of network errors or because the server isn't running. Rather than waiting for the default 20 seconds to connect, you can specify how long the Microsoft Jet database engine waits before it produces an error. Logging on to the server happens implicitly as part of a number of different events, such as running a query on an external server database.

The default timeout value is determined by the current setting of the **LoginTimeout** property entry in the HKEY_LOCAL_MACHINE\SOFTWARE\Jet\3.0\ODBC key of the Windows Registry.

See Also

ODBCTimeout Property, **QueryDef** Object, **QueryTimeout** Property.

Example

This example sets the **LoginTimeout** property to 120 seconds and then creates and runs a query on a database on an ODBC server.

```
Dim dbsNorthwind As Database
Dim qdfCustomers As QueryDef, rstCustomers As Recordset
DBEngine.LoginTimeout = 120           ' Timeout in 2 minutes.
Set dbsNorthwind = DBEngine.Workspaces(0).OpenDatabase("Northwind.mdb")
                                      ' Create query.
Set qdfCustomers = dbsNorthwind.CreateQueryDef("All Cust", _
    "SELECT * FROM Customers;")
qdfCustomers.Connect = "ODBC;DSN=Human Resources; " & _
    "DATABASE=HRSRVR; UID=Smith; PWD=Sesame"
                                      ' Log in to server and run query.
Set rstCustomers = qdfCustomers.OpenRecordset()
```

Example (Microsoft Access)

The following example sets the **LoginTimeout** property to 120 seconds, then creates a query, and runs it on a database on an ODBC server.

```
Sub Login()
    Dim dbs As Database
    Dim qdf As QueryDef, rst As Recordset

    ' Set timeout to 120 seconds.
    DBEngine.LoginTimeout = 120
    ' Return Database variable that points to current database.
    Set dbs = CurrentDb
    ' Create query.
    Set qdf = dbs.CreateQueryDef("All Employees", _
        "SELECT * FROM Employees;")
    qdf.Connect = "ODBC;DSN=Human Resources; " & _
        "DATABASE=HRSRVR; UID=Smith; PWD=Sesame"
    ' Log in to server and run query.
    Set rst = qdf.OpenRecordset()
End Sub
```

LogMessages Property

Applies To **QueryDef** Object.

Description Sets or returns a value that specifies if the messages returned from an ODBC database are recorded. This property is user-defined and is read/write once created and installed.

> **Note** The user must install this property using the **CreateProperty** method on a **QueryDef** object.

Settings and Return Values The setting or return value is a Boolean expression that specifies whether messages are recorded. The data type is Boolean. **True** indicates that ODBC-generated messages are recorded.

Remarks Some pass-through queries can return messages in addition to data. If you set the **LogMessages** property to **True** (-1), the Microsoft Jet database engine creates a table that contains returned messages. The table name is the user name concatenated with a hyphen (-) and a sequential number starting at 00. For example, because the default user name is ADMIN, the tables returned would be named ADMIN-00, ADMIN-01, and so on.

If you expect the query to return messages, create and append a user-defined **LogMessages** property for the **QueryDef** object, and set its type to Boolean and its value to **True**.

Once you've processed the results from these tables, you may want to delete them from the database along with the temporary query used to create them.

MakeReplica Method

Applies To **Database** Object.

Description Makes a new replica based on the current replicable database using the supplied filename.

Syntax *database*.**MakeReplica** *replica, description* [, **dbRepMakeReadOnly**]

The **MakeReplica** Method syntax has the following parts.

Part	Description
database	An existing, replicable **Database** object variable.
replica	The path and file name to be given the new replica. If replica is an existing filename, then the method fails and returns an error message.
description	Text string describing the replica to be created.

If **dbRepMakeReadOnly** is supplied, then the replicable elements of the newly created database will not be modifiable.

Remarks As with most of the replication methods and properties, the database has to be a replicable database for this method to work.

Note The **MakeReplica** method can be used only if your application has Microsoft Access with Briefcase Replication installed.

Move Method

Applies To Dynaset-Type **Recordset** Object, **Recordset** Object, Snapshot-Type **Recordset** Object, Table-Type **Recordset** Object.

Description Moves the position of the current record in a **Recordset** object.

Syntax *recordset*.**Move** *rows*[, *start*]

The **Move** method syntax has these parts.

Part	Description
recordset	The name of the **Recordset** object whose current record position is being moved.
rows	A signed **Long** value specifying the number of rows the position will move. If *rows* is greater than 0, the position is moved forward (toward the end of the file). If *rows* is less than 0, the position is moved backward (toward the beginning of the file).
start	A **String** value identifying a bookmark. If *start* is specified, the move begins relative to this bookmark. If *start* is not specified, **Move** begins from the current record.

176   Move Method

Remarks   If using **Move** would move the position of the current record to a position before the first record, the position is moved to the beginning-of-file (BOF) position. If the **Recordset** contains no records and its **BOF** property is set to **True**, using this method to move backward produces a trappable run-time error. If either the **BOF** or **EOF** property is **True** and you attempt to use the **Move** method without a valid bookmark, a trappable error is triggered.

If using **Move** would move the position of the current record to a position after the last record, the position is moved to the end-of-file (EOF) position. If the **Recordset** is based on a query, then this approach forces the query to be run on the specified number of rows. If the **Recordset** contains no records and its **EOF** property is set to **True**, then using this method to move forward produces a trappable run-time error.

Notes

- When you use **Move** on a forward-only scrolling snapshot, the *rows* argument must be a positive integer and bookmarks aren't allowed. This means you can only move forward.

- To make the first, last, next, or previous record in a **Recordset** the current record, use the **MoveFirst**, **MoveLast**, **MoveNext**, or **MovePrevious** method.

See Also   **BOF**, **EOF** Properties; **Bookmark** Property; **MoveFirst**, **MoveLast**, **MoveNext**, **MovePrevious** Methods.

Specifics (Microsoft Access)   When you use a bookmark in a Microsoft Access module, you must include an **Option Compare Binary** statement in the Declarations section of the module. A bookmark is a **Variant** array of **Byte** data, so the string comparison method for the module must be binary. If a bookmark is evaluated with a text-based string comparison method, such as the **Option Compare Text** statement or the default setting for the **Option Compare Database** statement, the current record may be set to an incorrect record.

Example   This example creates a function that moves the current record position in a **Recordset** forward or back a specified number of records and provides an optional offset.

```
Sub MoveRelative (lngDistance As Long, strDirection As String, _
    rstTarget As Recordset, varRelativeMark As Variant)
    Dim strHere As String
    strHere = rstTarget.Bookmark
    strDirection = UCase(strDirection)
    Select Case strDirection
        Case "FWD":  lngDistance = Abs(lngDistance)
        Case "BACK": lngDistance = Abs(lngDistance) * -1
        Case Else: MsgBox "Incorrect calling argument"
    End Select
    If UCase(varRelativeMark) = "HERE" Then
```

```
            rstTarget.Move lngDistance    ' Move current record position.
        Else
            ' Move relative to bookmark.
            rstTarget.Move lngDistance, varRelativeMark
        End If
        ' Move may not have been completed.
        If rstTarget.EOF Or rstTarget.BOF Then Beep
    End Sub
```

Example (Microsoft Access)

The following example uses the **Move** method to move forward two rows in a **Recordset** object.

```
Sub MoveForward()
    Dim dbs As Database, rst As Recordset
    Dim strCriteria As String

    ' Return Database variable pointing to current database.
    Set dbs = CurrentDb
    ' Open Dynaset-Type Recordset object.
    Set rst = dbs.OpenRecordset("SELECT * FROM Orders " & _
        "ORDER BY [ShipCountry];")
    rst.MoveFirst
    ' Check number of records in Recordset object.
    If rst.RecordCount > 2 Then
        ' Move forward two rows.
        rst.Move 2
        Debug.Print rst!ShipCountry
    End If
End Sub
```

Example (Microsoft Excel)

This example prompts the user to select a record number. The example then copies the selected record from the Customer recordset in the NWINDEX.MDB database onto Sheet1.

```
Dim db As Database, rs As Recordset
Set db = Workspaces(0).OpenDatabase(Application.Path & "\NWINDEX.MDB")
Set rs = db.OpenRecordset("SELECT [CUSTMR_ID], [CONTACT], [REGION] " _
    & "FROM Customer")
Sheets("Sheet1").Activate
aDistance = Application.InputBox("What record # you want to copy", Type:=2)
If aDistance = False Then     ' user cancelled InputBox
    Exit Sub
End If
rs.MoveFirst
rs.Move aDistance
For i = 0 To 2
    ActiveCell.Offset(, i).Value = rs.Fields(i).Value
Next
rs.Close
db.Close
```

MoveFirst, MoveLast, MoveNext, MovePrevious Methods

Applies To Dynaset-Type **Recordset** Object, **Recordset** Object, Snapshot-Type **Recordset** Object, Table-Type **Recordset** Object.

Description Move to the first, last, next, or previous record in a specified **Recordset** object and make that record the current record.

Syntax *object*.{**MoveFirst** | **MoveLast** | **MoveNext** | **MovePrevious**}

The *object* placeholder represents an object expression that evaluates to the name of an open **Recordset** object.

Remarks Use the Move methods to move from record to record without applying a condition. Use the Find methods to locate records in a dynaset- or Snapshot-Type **Recordset** object that satisfy a certain condition. To locate a record in a Table-Type **Recordset** object, use the **Seek** method.

> **Caution** If you edit the current record, be sure you save the changes using the **Update** method before you move to another record. If you move to another record without updating, your changes are lost without warning.

When you open the recordset named by *recordset*, the first record is current and the **BOF** property is set to **False**. If the recordset contains no records, the **BOF** property is set to **True**, and there is no current record.

If the first or last record is already current when you use **MoveFirst** or **MoveLast**, the current record doesn't change.

If you use **MovePrevious** when the first record is current, the **BOF** property is set to **True**, and there is no current record. If you use **MovePrevious** again, an error occurs; **BOF** remains **True**.

If you use **MoveNext** when the last record is current, the **EOF** property is set to **True**, and there is no current record. If you use **MoveNext** again, an error occurs; **EOF** remains **True**.

If *recordset* refers to a Table-Type **Recordset**, movement follows the current index. You can set the current index using the **Index** property. If you don't set the current index, the order of returned records is undefined.

If you use **MoveLast** on a **Recordset** object based on an SQL query or **QueryDef**, the query is forced to completion and the **Recordset** object is fully populated.

Notes

- You can't use the **MoveFirst**, **MoveLast**, or **MovePrevious** methods with a forward-only scrolling snapshot.
- To move the position of the current record in a **Recordset** object a specific number of records forward or backward, use the **Move** method.

See Also **AbsolutePosition** Property; **BOF**, **EOF** Properties; **FindFirst**, **FindLast**, **FindNext**, **FindPrevious** Methods; **Index** Property; **Move** Method; **RecordCount** Property; **Seek** Method.

Example This example changes the job title of all sales representatives in a table named Employees. After opening the table, it uses **MoveFirst** to locate the first record and **MoveNext** to move to the next record. For each record satisfying the title condition, the example changes the title and saves the change using the **Update** method.

It's far more efficient to use the WHERE clause of an SQL statement to request the records you want to update than to test each record one at a time. The whole operation could be accomplished by using a single UPDATE statement, as shown in the following example.

```
Dim dbsNorthwind As Database, rstEmployees As Recordset
Dim strSelect as String
Set dbsNorthwind = DBEngine.Workspaces(0).OpenDatabase("Northwind.mdb")
strSelect = "Select * FROM Employees WHERE Title = 'Sales Representative' "
' Open recordset.
Set rstEmployees = dbsNorthwind.OpenRecordset(strSelect)
Do Until rstEmployees.EOF                ' Begin loop.
    With rstEmployees
    .Edit                                ' Enable editing.
    !Title = "Account Executive"         ' Change title.
    .Update                              ' Save changes.
    .MoveNext                            ' Locate next record.
    End With
Loop                                     ' End of loop.
rstEmployees.Close                       ' Close table.
dbsNorthwind.Close
```

Tip Using an update query to change job titles might be more efficient. For example, you could use the following code to achieve the same results:

```
Dim strSelect as String
strSelect = "Update Employees Set Title = 'Account Executive' " _
    "WHERE Title = 'Sales Representative' "
dbsNorthwind.Execute strSelect
```

**Example
(Microsoft Access)**

The following example uses the **MoveLast** method to populate the **Recordset** object so the number of records can be counted. The **MoveFirst** method then moves the current record pointer to the first record in the **Recordset** object. The procedure prompts the user to enter a record number, then sets a bookmark for that record.

```
Sub MoveToRecord()
    Dim dbs As Database, rst As Recordset, intI As Integer
    Dim strNumber As String, strBookmark As String
    ' Return Database variable pointing to current database.
    Set dbs = CurrentDb
    Set rst = dbs.OpenRecordset("Orders")
    ' Populate Recordset object.
    rst.MoveLast
    ' Return to first record.
    rst.MoveFirst
    strNumber = InputBox("Please enter record number.")
    ' Check that number is within Recordset object.
    If strNumber <= rst.RecordCount And rst.Bookmarkable Then
        For intI = 1 To strNumber
            rst.MoveNext
        Next intI
        strBookmark = rst.Bookmark
    End If
End Sub
```

**Example
(Microsoft Excel)**

This example replaces values in the CON_TITLE field of the records in the Customer recordset in the NWINDEX.MDB database, and then it displays how many replacements were made.

To create the NWINDEX.MDB database, run the Microsoft Excel example for the **CreateDatabase** method.

```
Dim db As Database, rs As Recordset, sQLText As String
Set db = Workspaces(0).OpenDatabase(Application.Path & "\NWINDEX.MDB")
sQLText = "SELECT * FROM  Customer WHERE " _
    & "CON_TITLE =  'Sales Representative';"
Set rs = db.OpenRecordset(sQLText)
i = 0
Do Until rs.EOF
    With rs
        .Edit
        .Fields("CON_TITLE").Value = "Account Executive"
        .Update
        .MoveNext
    End With
    i = i + 1
Loop
MsgBox i & " replacements were made."
rs.Close
db.Close
```

Name Property

Applies To **Container** Object, **Database** Object, **Document** Object, Dynaset-Type **Recordset** Object, **Field** Object, **Group** Object, **Index** Object, **Parameter** Object, **Property** Object, **QueryDef** Object, **Recordset** Object, **Relation** Object, Snapshot-Type **Recordset** Object, Table-Type **Recordset** Object, **TableDef** Object, **User** Object, **Workspace** Object.

Description Sets or returns a user-defined name for a data access object. For an object not appended to a collection, this property is read/write.

Settings and Return Values The setting or return value is a string expression that specifies a name. The name must start with a letter and can contain a maximum of 64 characters. It can include numbers and underscore characters (_) but can't include punctuation or spaces. The data type is **String**.

Remarks **TableDef** and **QueryDef** objects can't share the same name, nor can **User** and **Group** objects.

The **Name** property of a **Recordset** object opened using an SQL statement is the first 256 characters of the SQL statement.

You can use an object's **Name** property with the **Dim** statement in code to create other instances of the object.

Note For many of the **Database** objects, the **Name** property reflects the name as known to the **Database** object, as in the name of a **TableDef**, **Field**, or **QueryDef** object. There is no direct link between the name of the **Database** object and the object variable used to reference it.

The read/write usage of the **Name** property depends on the type of object it applies to, and whether or not the object is has been appended to a collection.

Object	Usage
Container	Read-only
Database	Read-only
Document	Read-only
Field	
Unappended	Read/write
Appended to **Index**	Read-only
Appended to **QueryDef**	Read-only
Appended to **Recordset**	Read-only
Appended to **TableDef** (native)	Read/write

Object	Usage
Field	
Appended to **TableDef** (linked)	Read-only
Appended to **Relation**	Read-only
Group	
Unappended	Read/write
Appended	Read only
Index	
Unappended	Read/write
Appended	Read only
Parameter	Read-only
Property	
Unappended	Read/write
Appended	Read-only
Built-in	Read-only
QueryDef	
Unappended	Read/write
Temporary	Read-only
Appended	Read/write
Recordset	Read-only
Relation	
Unappended	Read/write
Appended	Read-only
TableDef	Read/write
User	
Unappended	Read/write
Appended	Read-only
Workspace	
Unappended	Read/write
Appended	Read-only

See Also   **CreateDatabase** Method, **CreateField** Method, **CreateIndex** Method, **CreateQueryDef** Method.

Example   This example creates a **TableDef** object and then names it Parts ID.

```
Dim dbsNorthwind As Database, tdfPartsID As TableDef
Set dbsNorthwind = DBEngine.Workspaces(0).OpenDatabase("Northwind.mdb")
Set tdfPartsID = dbsNorthwind.CreateTableDef()
```

Name Property

```
tdfPartsID.Name = "Parts ID"
...                              ' Create fields.
dbsNorthwind.TableDefs.Append tdfPartsID
```

Example (Microsoft Access)

The following example creates two new **TableDef** objects and names them. The name of the first **TableDef** object is included as an argument to the **CreateTableDef** method. The name of the second **TableDef** object is set using the **Name** property, after the **TableDef** object has been created.

Note that you must define fields in the table before the **TableDef** object can be appended to the **TableDefs** collection.

```
Sub NameNewTables()
    Dim dbs As Database
    Dim tdfDefinitions As TableDef, tdfSynonyms as TableDef

    ' Return Database variable that points to current database.
    Set dbs = CurrentDb
    ' Create and name TableDef object.
    Set tdfDefinitions = dbs.CreateTableDef("Definitions")
    ' Create second TableDef object.
    Set tdfSynonyms = dbs.CreateTableDef("")
    ' Set Name property for second TableDef object.
    tdfSynonyms.Name = "Synonyms"
    .                                            ' Create fields.
    .
    .

    dbs.TableDefs.Append tdfDefinitions
    dbs.TableDefs.Append tdfSynonyms
End Sub
```

Example (Microsoft Excel)

This example enters in the active cell on Sheet1 the name of the first recordset in the NWINDEX.MDB database.

To create the NWINDEX.MDB database, run the Microsoft Excel example for the **CreateDatabase** method.

```
Dim db As Database, td As TableDef
Set db = Workspaces(0).OpenDatabase(Application.Path & "\NWINDEX.MDB")
Set td = db.TableDefs(0)
Sheets("Sheet1").Activate
ActiveCell.Value = td.Name
db.Close
```

NewPassword Method

Applies To **Database** Object, **User** Object.

Description Changes the password of an existing user account or Jet version 3.0 database.

Syntax *object*.**NewPassword** *oldpassword, newpassword*

The **NewPassword** method syntax has these parts.

Part	Description
object	A variable of an object data type that represents the **User** object or a Jet 3.0 **Database** object whose **Password** property you want to change.
oldpassword	A string expression that is the current setting of the **Password** property of the **User** or Jet 3.0 **Database** object.
newpassword	A string expression that is the new setting of the **Password** property of the **User** or Jet 3.0 **Database** object.

Remarks The *oldpassword* and *newpassword* strings can be up to 14 characters long and can include any characters except the ASCII character 0 (null). To clear the password, use a zero-length string ("") for *newpassword*.

Passwords are case-sensitive.

If *object* refers to a **User** object that is not an element of a **Users** collection, an error occurs. To set a new password, you must either be logged on as the user whose user account you're changing, or you must be a member of the Admins group. The **Password** property of a **User** object is write-only—users can't read the current value.

If *object* refers to a Jet version 3.0 **Database** object, this method offers a limited form of security in the form of password protection. When creating or opening a version 3.0 .mdb file, part of the **Connect** string describes the password; thus, no work is required of your DAO code.

If a database has no password, one will be created automatically by passing "" for the old password. If you lose your password, you can never open the database again.

See Also **Name** Property, **PID** Property.

Example This example changes the password of the existing user Pat Smith from My Secret to msMSApw. The user must be logged on as Pat Smith or as a member of the Admins group.

```
Workspaces(0).Users("Pat Smith").NewPassword "My Secret", "msMSApw"
```

NoMatch Property

Applies To
Dynaset-Type **Recordset** Object, **Recordset** Object, Snapshot-Type **Recordset** Object, Table-Type **Recordset** Object.

Description
Returns a value indicating whether a particular record was found using the **Seek** method or one of the Find methods. **True** (-1) indicates that the desired record was not found.

Remarks
You can use the **NoMatch** property with **Recordset** objects.

When you open or create a **Recordset** object, its **NoMatch** property is set to **False** (0).

To locate a record, use the **Seek** method on a Table-Type **Recordset** object or one of the **Find** methods on a dynaset- or Snapshot-Type **Recordset** object. Check the **NoMatch** property setting to see whether the record was found.

If the **Seek** or **Find** method is unsuccessful and the **NoMatch** property is **True**, the current record will no longer be valid. Be sure to obtain the current record's bookmark before using the **Seek** method or a **Find** method if you'll need to return to that record.

Note Using any of the Move methods on a **Recordset** object won't affect its **NoMatch** property setting.

See Also
BOF, **EOF** Properties; **FindFirst**, **FindLast**, **FindNext**, **FindPrevious** Methods; **Seek** Method.

Example
This example changes the job title of all sales representatives in an Employees table. It creates a Dynaset-Type **Recordset** and then uses **FindFirst** and **FindNext** to locate every record satisfying the criteria for the title. It prepares each record for editing, changes the title, and saves the change with the **Update** method.

```
Dim strCriteria As String, varSaveHere As Variant
Dim dbsNorthwind As Database, rstEmployees As Recordset
strCriteria = "Title = 'Sales Representative'"    ' Define search
                                                  ' criteria.
Set dbsNorthwind = DBEngine.Workspaces(0).OpenDatabase("Northwind.mdb")
' Create Recordset.
Set rstEmployees = dbsNorthwind.OpenRecordset("Employees", dbOpenDynaset)
varSaveHere = rstEmployees.Bookmark        ' Save Bookmark.
rstEmployees.FindFirst strCriteria         ' Locate first occurrence.
Do Until rstEmployees.NoMatch              ' Loop until no matching
                                           ' records.
```

NoMatch Property

```
            With rstEmployees
                .Edit                           ' Enable editing.
                !Title = "Account Executive"    ' Change title.
                .Update                         ' Save changes.
                .FindNext strCriteria           ' Locate next record.
            End With
        Loop                                    ' End of loop.
        rstEmployees.Bookmark = varSaveHere
```

Tip In some situations, using an update query is faster.

Example (Microsoft Access)

The following example uses the **NoMatch** property to determine whether a **FindFirst** method process has been successful.

```
Function FindCountry() As Integer
    Dim intI As Integer, varRecord() As Variant
    Dim dbs As Database, rstOrders As Recordset
    Dim strCountry As String

    ' Return Database variable that points to current database.
    Set dbs = CurrentDb
    ' Create Dynaset-Type Recordset object.
    Set rstOrders = dbs.OpenRecordset("Orders", dbOpenDynaset)
    strCountry = InputBox("Please enter country name.")
    intI = 0
    rstOrders.FindFirst "[ShipCountry] = '" & strCountry & "'"
    If rstOrders.NoMatch Then
        FindCountry = False
        Exit Function
    Else
        Debug.Print rst!OrderID
    End If
    FindCountry = True
End Function
```

Example (Microsoft Excel)

This example adds all the names of contacts for the state of Washington to a list box on a new dialog sheet and then runs the dialog box. The data is drawn from the Customer recordset in the NWINDEX.MDB database.

To create the NWINDEX.MDB database, run the Microsoft Excel example for the **CreateDatabase** method.

```
Dim db As Database
Dim rs As Recordset
Set db = Workspaces(0).OpenDatabase(Application.Path & "\NWINDEX.MDB")
Set rs = db.OpenRecordset("SELECT * FROM Customer")
criteria = "[REGION] = 'WA'"
Set customDialog = DialogSheets.Add
```

```
Set list1 = customDialog.ListBoxes.Add(78, 42, 84, 80)
rs.FindFirst criteria
Do Until rs.NoMatch
    list1.AddItem (rs.fields("CONTACT").Value)
    rs.FindNext criteria
Loop
customDialog.Show
rs.Close
db.Close
```

Number Property

Applies To	**Error** Object.
Description	Returns a numeric value specifying an error. The **Number** property is the **Error** object's default property.
Return Values	The returned value is a **Long Integer** representing an error number.
Remarks	Use the **Number** property to determine the error that occurred. The value of the property corresponds to a unique trap number that corresponds to an error condition.
See Also	**Description** Property; **HelpContext**, **HelpFile** Properties; **Source** Property.
Example	See the **Description** property example.

ODBCTimeout Property

Applies To	**QueryDef** Object.
Description	Sets or returns the number of seconds the Microsoft Jet database engine waits before a timeout error occurs when a query is run on an ODBC database.
Settings and Return Values	The setting or return value is an integer representing the number of seconds that the Jet database engine waits before a timeout error occurs. The data type is **Integer**.
Remarks	When you're using an ODBC database, such as SQL Server, delays can occur because of network traffic or heavy use of the ODBC server. Rather than waiting indefinitely, you can specify how long the Jet database engine waits before it produces an error.

188 ODBCTimeout Property

The default timeout value is 60 seconds. When the **ODBCTimeout** property is set to -1, the default value is used. When the **ODBCTimeout** property is set to 0, no timeout occurs.

The **QueryTimeout** property setting for a **Database** object overrides the default setting.

Setting the **ODBCTimeout** property of a **QueryDef** object overrides the values specified by the **QueryTimeout** property setting of the **Database** object containing the **QueryDef** object, but only for that **QueryDef** object.

See Also   **QueryTimeout** Property.

Example   This example sets the **ODBCTimeout** property to 120 seconds and then creates a query and runs it on a database on an ODBC server.

```
Dim dbsNorthwind As Database
Dim qdfCustomers As QueryDef, rstCustomers As Recordset
Set dbsNorthwind =  DBEngine.Workspaces(0).OpenDatabase("Northwind.mdb")
' Create query.
Set qdfCustomers = dbsNorthwind.CreateQueryDef("All Cust", _
    "SELECT * FROM Customers;")
qdfCustomers.Connect = "ODBC;DSN=Human Resources; SERVER=HRSRVR: " & _
    "UID=Smith; PWD=Sesame"
' Log in to server and run query.
qdfCustomers.ODBCTimeout = 120
Set rstCustomers = qdfCustomers.OpenRecordset()
```

Example (Microsoft Access)   The following example sets the **ODBCTimeout** property to 120 seconds, creates a query, and runs it on a database on an ODBC server.

```
Sub SetTimeout()
    Dim dbs As Database
    Dim qdfCustomers As QueryDef, rstCustomers As Recordset

    ' Return Database variable that points to current database.
    Set dbs = CurrentDb
    ' Create QueryDef.
    Set qdfCustomers = dbs.CreateQueryDef("All Cust", _
        "SELECT * FROM Customers;")
    qdfCustomers.Connect = "ODBC;DSN=HumanResources;SERVER=HRSRVR: " & _
        "UID=Smith; PWD=Sesame"
    ' Log in to server and run query.
    qdfCustomers.ODBCTimeout = 120
    Set rstCustomers = qdfCustomers.OpenRecordset()
End Sub
```

OpenDatabase Method

Applies To **Workspace** Object.

Description Opens a specified database in a session and returns a reference to the **Database** object that represents it. The open database is automatically added to the **Databases** collection.

Syntax **Set** *database* = [*workspace*.]**OpenDatabase**(*dbname*[, *exclusive*[, *read-only*[, ↳ *source*]]])

The **OpenDatabase** method syntax has these parts.

Part	Description
database	A variable of a **Database** object data type that references the **Database** object that you're opening.
workspace	A variable of a **Workspace** object data type that references the existing **Workspace** object that will contain the database.
dbname	A string expression that is the name of an existing database file. Some considerations apply when using *dbname*: • If it refers to a database that is already open for exclusive access by another user, an error occurs. • If it doesn't refer to an existing database or valid ODBC data source name, an error occurs. (See Remarks for more information on opening ODBC databases.) • If it's a zero-length string ("") and *source* is "ODBC;", a dialog box listing all registered ODBC data source names is displayed so the user can select a database. (See Remarks for more information on opening ODBC databases.)
exclusive	A Boolean expression that is **True** if the database is to be opened for exclusive (nonshared) access and **False** if the database is to be opened for shared access. If you omit this argument, the database is opened for shared access.
read-only	A Boolean value that is **True** if the database is to be opened for read-only access and **False** if the database is to be opened for read/write access. If you omit this argument, the database is opened for read/write access.
source	A string expression used for opening the database, including databases with passwords. Note that the **NewPassword** method, when used on a **Database** object, changes the password parameter that appears in the "PWD=..." part of this argument. You must supply the *exclusive* and *read-only* arguments to supply a source string. See the **Connect** property for syntax, and see Remarks for more information on opening ODBC databases.

190 OpenDatabase Method

Remarks To close a database, and thus remove its **Database** object from the **Databases** collection, use the **Close** method on the object.

Because attached tables on ODBC databases improve performance, it's preferable to use them rather than opening ODBC databases directly. To open an ODBC database directly, you must specify a registered ODBC data source name. If the filename has an extension, it's required. If your network supports it, you can also specify a network path, such as:

```
"\\MYSERVER\MYSHARE\MYDIR\MYDB.mdb"
```

For more information about ODBC drivers, such as SQL Server, see the Help file provided with the driver.

Note The *source* argument is expressed in two parts: the database type, followed by a semicolon (;) and the optional arguments. The database type, such as "ODBC;" or "FoxPro 2.5" must be provided first. The optional arguments follow in no particular order, separated by semicolons. One of the parameters may be the password (if one is assigned). For example, .source = ("FoxPro 2.5; pwd=mypassword"). See the *source* argument, defined earlier in this topic, for more information.

See Also **Close** Method, **Connect** Property.

Specifics (Microsoft Access) In Microsoft Access, use the **CurrentDb** function to point a **Database** variable to the current database, rather than using the **OpenDatabase** method. For example, you can use the following code to get a variable that represents the current database.

```
Dim dbsCurrent as Database
set dbsCurrent = CurrentDb
```

Use the **OpenDatabase** method to open a database other than the current database.

Example This example opens the Employees table in the database in the default **Workspace** object. If the database can't be opened (for example, if it has already been opened for exclusive access by another user in a multiuser environment), an error occurs and a message is displayed. Then the example updates the Title field of the Employees table.

```
Function UpdateNorthwind () As Integer
    Dim wspDefault As Workspace, dbsNorthwind As Database
    Dim rstEmployees As Recordset
    Dim intErrorCondition As Integer, intUpdateNorthwind As Integer
    intUpdateNorthwind = True
    intErrorCondition = False
    On Error GoTo DBErrorHandler      ' Enable error trapping.
    Set wspDefault = DBEngine.Workspaces(0)
```

OpenDatabase Method   191

```
        ' Open database.
        Set dbsNorthwind = wspDefault.OpenDatabase("Northwind.mdb")
        If intErrorCondition = False Then
            On Error GoTo TableErrorHandler    ' Enable error trapping.
            ' Open table.
            Set rstEmployees = dbsNorthwind.OpenRecordset("Employees")
            If intErrorCondition = False Then
                On Error GoTo EditErrorHandler    ' Enable error trapping.
                Do Until rstEmployees.EOF
                    If rstEmployees![Title] = "Sales Representative" Then
                        rstEmployees.Edit' Enable editing.
                        rstEmployees![Title] = "Account Executive"
                        rstEmployees.Update      ' Save changes.
                    End If
                    rstEmployees.MoveNext' Move to next record.
                Loop
            End If
            dbsNorthwind.Close             ' Close database.
        End If
        On Error GoTo 0                    ' Disable error trapping.
        Exit Function
DBErrorHandler:
        intErrorCondition = True
        intUpdateNorthwind = False
        MsgBox "Can't open database.", vbExclamation
        Resume Next
TableErrorHandler:
        intErrorCondition = True
        intUpdateNorthwind = False
        MsgBox "Can't open Employees table.", vbExclamation
        Resume Next
EditErrorHandler:
        intErrorCondition = True
        UpdateDb = False
        MsgBox "Can't edit Employees table.", vbExclamation
        Resume Next
End Function
```

Example (Microsoft Access)

The following example returns a Database variable that points to the current database. Then it opens a different database called Another.mdb, using the **OpenDatabase** method. The procedure then enumerates all **TableDef** objects in both databases.

```
Sub OpenAnother()
    Dim dbs as Database, dbsAnother as Database
    Dim tdf as TableDef

    ' Return Database variable representing current database.
    Set dbs = CurrentDb
```

192 OpenDatabase Method

```
    ' Return Database variable representing Another.mdb.
    Set dbsAnother = DBEngine.Workspaces(0).OpenDatabase("Another.mdb")
    ' Enumerate all TableDef objects in each database.
    For Each tdf in dbs.TableDefs
        Debug.Print tdf.Name
    Next tdf
    For Each tdf in dbsAnother.TableDefs
        Debug.Print tdf.Name
    Next tdf
End Sub
```

Example (Microsoft Excel)

This example displays a custom dialog box containing a list of all databases with the filename extension .MDB that are located in the Microsoft Excel folder, and then it opens the database selected by the user.

```
Dim a(100), db As Database
i = 0
ChDrive "C"
ChDir Application.Path
a(i) = Dir("*.MDB")
If a(i) = "" Then
    MsgBox "You have no databases in the Microsoft Excel directory"
    Exit Sub
End If
Do
    i = i + 1
    a(i) = Dir()
Loop Until a(i) = ""
Set theDialog = DialogSheets.Add
Set list1 = theDialog.ListBoxes.Add(78, 42, 84, 80)
For counter = 0 To i - 1
    list1.AddItem a(counter)
Next
Application.ScreenUpdating = True
theDialog.Show
Set db = Workspaces(0).OpenDatabase(a(list1.Value - 1))
MsgBox "The " & db.Name & " database is now open"
' use database here
db.Close
```

OpenRecordset Method

Applies To Database Object, Dynaset-Type Recordset Object, QueryDef Object, Recordset Object, Snapshot-Type Recordset Object, Table-Type Recordset Object, TableDef Object.

Description Creates a new **Recordset** object and appends it to the **Recordsets** collection.

Syntax Set *variable* = *database*.**OpenRecordset**(*source*[, *type*[, *options*]])

Set *variable* = *object*.**OpenRecordset**([*type*[, *options*]])

The **OpenRecordset** method syntax has these parts.

Part	Description
variable	A variable that has been declared as an object data type **Recordset**.
database	The name of an existing **Database** object you want to use to create the new **Recordset**.
object	The name of an existing **QueryDef**, **Recordset**, or **TableDef** object you want to use to create the new **Recordset**. This argument can't be the name of a forward-only scrolling snapshot.
	If *object* refers to a dynaset or Snapshot-Type **Recordset** object, the type of the new object is the same as that of the **Recordset** specified by *object*. If *object* refers to a Table-Type **Recordset** object, the type of the new object is a Dynaset-Type **Recordset**.
source	A **String** specifying the source of the records for the new **Recordset**. The source can be a table name, a query name, or an SQL statement that returns records. For Table-Type **Recordset** objects, the source can only be a table name.
type	If you don't specify a type, **OpenRecordset** creates a Table-Type **Recordset** if possible. If you specify an attached table or query, **OpenRecordset** creates a Dynaset-Type **Recordset**. This value can be one of the following **Integer** constants:
	▪ **dbOpenTable**—to open a Table-Type **Recordset** object.
	▪ **dbOpenDynaset**—to open a Dynaset-Type **Recordset** object.
	▪ **dbOpenSnapshot**—to open a Snapshot-Type **Recordset** object.

Part	Description
options	Any combination (or none) of the following **Integer** constants specifying characteristics of the new **Recordset**, such as restrictions on other users' ability to edit and view it:

- **dbAppendOnly**—You can append only new records (Dynaset-Type **Recordset** only).
- **dbForwardOnly**—The **Recordset** is a forward-only scrolling snapshot. Note that **Recordset** objects created with this option cannot be cloned and only support the **MoveNext** method to move through the records.
- **dbSQLPassThrough**—SQL pass-through. Causes the SQL statement to be passed to an ODBC database for processing.
- **dbSeeChanges**—Generate a run-time error if another user is changing data you are editing.
- **dbDenyWrite**—Other users can't modify or add records.
- **dbDenyRead**—Other users can't view records (Table-Type **Recordset** only).
- **dbReadOnly**—You can only view records; other users can modify them.
- **dbInconsistent**—Inconsistent updates are allowed (Dynaset-Type **Recordset** only).
- **dbConsistent**—Only consistent updates are allowed (Dynaset-Type **Recordset** only).

Note The constants **dbConsistent** and **dbInconsistent** are mutually exclusive. You can use one or the other, but not both in a given instance of **OpenRecordset**.

Remarks

If *object* refers to a **QueryDef**, or a dynaset- or Snapshot-Type **Recordset**, or if *source* refers to an SQL statement or a **TableDef** that represents an attached table, you can't use **dbOpenTable** for the *type* argument; if you do, a trappable error occurs.

If you want to use an SQL pass-through query on an attached table, you must first set the **Connect** property of the attached table's database to a valid ODBC connect string. For more information on this, see the **Connect** property.

Use the **dbSeeChanges** flag if you want to trap changes made by another user or another program on your machine when you're editing or deleting the same record. For example, if two users start editing the same record, the first user to execute the **Update** method succeeds. When the **Update** method is executed by the second user, a run-time error occurs. Similarly, if the second user tries to use the **Delete** method to delete the record, and it has already been changed by the first user, a run-time error also occurs.

OpenRecordset Method 195

Typically, if the user gets this error while updating, your code should refresh the contents of the fields and retrieve the newly modified values. If the error occurs in the process of deleting, your code could display the new record data to the user and a message indicating that the data has recently changed. At this point, your code can request a confirmation that the user still wants to delete the record.

Tip Use the forward-only scrolling option (**dbForwardOnly**) to improve performance when your application makes a single pass through a **Recordset** opened from an ODBC data source.

When you close a **Recordset** using the **Close** method, it's automatically deleted from the **Recordsets** collection.

See Also   **Connect** Property, **Type** Property.

Example   See the **Edit** method example.

Example (Microsoft Access)   The following example opens a Dynaset-Type **Recordset** object and prints the number of records in the **Recordset** object.

```
Sub UKOrders()
    Dim dbs As Database, rst As Recordset
    Dim strSQL As String

    ' Return Database variable pointing to current database.
    Set dbs = CurrentDb
    strSQL = "SELECT * FROM Orders WHERE [ShipCountry] = 'UK'"
    Set rst = dbs.OpenRecordset(strSQL)
    rst.MoveLast
    Debug.Print rst.RecordCount
End Sub
```

Example (Microsoft Excel)   This example displays a custom dialog box containing a list of all available recordsets in the NWINDEX.MDB database. The example opens a new recordset based on the recordset selected by the user and then copies the records onto Sheet1.

To create the NWINDEX.MDB database, run the Microsoft Excel example for the **CreateDatabase** method.

```
Dim db As Database, rs1 As Recordset
Set db = Workspaces(0).OpenDatabase(Application.Path & "\NWINDEX.MDB")
Application.ScreenUpdating = False
Set theDialog = DialogSheets.Add
Set list1 = theDialog.ListBoxes.Add(78, 42, 84, 80)
Set label1 = theDialog.Labels.Add(78, 125, 240, 25)
label1.Text = "Recordsets for " & db.Name
i = 0
```

```
        Do Until i = db.TableDefs.Count
            list1.AddItem (db.TableDefs(i).Name)
            i = i + 1
Loop
Sheets("Sheet1").Activate
Application.ScreenUpdating = True
If theDialog.Show = True Then
    If list1.Value = 0 Then
        MsgBox "You have not selected an item from the list."
    Else
        Set rs1 = db.OpenRecordset(db.TableDefs(list1.Value - 1).Name)
        ActiveCell.CopyFromRecordset rs1
    End If
End If
rs1.Close
db.Close
```

OrdinalPosition Property

Applies To   **Field** Object.

Description   Sets or returns the relative position of a **Field** object within the **Fields** collection to which it is appended. For an object not yet appended to the **Fields** collection, this property is read/write.

Settings and Return Values   The setting or return value is an integer that specifies the numeric order of fields. The default is 0. The data type is **Integer**.

Remarks   For a **Field** object, use of the **OrdinalPosition** property depends on the object that contains the **Fields** collection that the **Field** object is appended to, as shown in the following table.

Object appended to	Usage
Index	Not supported
QueryDef	Read-only
Recordset	Read-only
Relation	Not supported
TableDef	Read/write

Generally, the ordinal position of an object that you append to a collection depends on the order in which you append the object. The first appended object is in the first position (0), the second appended object is in the second position (1), and so on. The last appended object is in ordinal position *count* –1, where *count* is the number of objects in the collection as specified by the **Count** property setting.

OrdinalPosition Property

Using the **OrdinalPosition** property, you can specify an ordinal position for new **Field** objects that differs from the order in which you append those objects to a collection. This enables you to specify a field order for your tables, queries, and recordsets when you use them in an application. For example, the order in which fields are returned in a SELECT * query would be determined by the current **OrdinalPosition** property values.

You can permanently reset the order in which fields are returned in recordsets by setting the **OrdinalPosition** property to any positive integer.

Two or more **Field** objects in the same collection can have the same **OrdinalPosition** property value, in which case they will be ordered alphabetically. For example, if you have a field named Age set to 4 and you set a second field named Weight to 4, Weight is returned after Age.

You can specify a number that is greater than the number of fields – 1. The field will be returned in an order relative to the largest number. For example, if you set a field's **OrdinalPosition** property to 20 (and there are only 5 fields) and you've set the **OrdinalPosition** property for two other fields to 10 and 30, respectively, the field set to 20 is returned between the fields set to 10 and 30.

After you change the **OrdinalPosition** property setting, you can use the property to return the current setting. However, the fields aren't reordered until the **Fields** collection is repopulated. For example:

```
TableDefs("Titles").Fields(0).OrdinalPosition = 3
```

This code changes which **Field** object is referenced in the fourth position (0 relative). Because **Field**(0) was Title, **Field**(2) now refers to Title, and **Field**(0) refers to the first (lowest) field in the sequence.

It is simpler to reference **Field** objects by their **Name** property. For example, this code assigns the AU_ID field to the third field position:

```
TableDefs("Titles").Fields("AU_ID").OrdinalPosition = 2
```

Note Changing the **OrdinalPosition** property setting of a **Field** object in the **Fields** collection will not immediately change its position in the collection. You will need to use the **Refresh** method on the collection to force the **Field** into its new position. Further, the **OrdinalPosition** setting is not the same as the field's index within a collection, although they may be equal.

See Also **Count** Property, **QueryDef** Object, **Refresh** Method.

**Example
(Microsoft Access)**

The following example changes the setting of the **OrdinalPosition** property for the first field in a Products table.

```
Sub SetPosition()
    Dim dbs As Database, tdf As TableDef
    Dim fldFirst As Field, fld As Field

    Set dbs = CurrentDb
    Set tdf = dbs.TableDefs!Products
    ' Return Field object pointing to first field in table.
    Set fldFirst = tdf.Fields(0)
    ' Set OrdinalPosition property to last position in collection.
    fldFirst.OrdinalPosition = tdf.Fields.Count
    ' Refresh Fields collection.
    tdf.Fields.Refresh
    ' Enumerate all fields and print ordinal position.
    For Each fld In tdf.Fields
        Debug.Print fld.Name, fld.OrdinalPosition
    Next fld
End Sub
```

Owner Property

Applies To **Container** Object, **Document** Object.

Description Sets or returns a value that specifies the owner of the object.

Settings and Return Values The setting or return value is a string expression that evaluates to either the name of a **User** object in the **Users** collection or the name of a **Group** object in the **Groups** collection. The data type is **String**.

Remarks The owner of an object has certain access privileges denied to other users. The **Owner** property setting can be changed at any time by any individual user account (represented by a **User** object) or group of user accounts (represented by a **Group** object) having the appropriate permissions.

See Also **Permissions** Property, **User** Object.

Example This example changes the **Owner** property setting of a **Document** object after determining whether the current user has the appropriate permissions to do so.

```
Dim dbsNorthwind As Database, docTest As Document
Set dbsNorthwind = DBEngine.Workspaces(0).OpenDatabase("Northwind.mdb")
Set docTest = dbsNorthwind.Containers(0).Documents(0)
If (docTest.Permissions And dbSecWriteOwner) <> 0 Then
    docTest.Owner = "SomebodyElse"
End If
```

Example (Microsoft Access)	The following example changes the **Owner** property setting of a Module **Document** object after determining whether the current user has the appropriate permissions to do so.

Note that the **And** operator performs a bitwise comparison to determine whether a certain permission is currently set.

```
Sub ChangeOwner()
    Dim dbs As Database, ctrModules As Container, docModule As Document

    ' Return Database variable that points to current database.
    Set dbs = CurrentDb
    ' Return Container variable that points to Modules container.
    Set ctrModules = dbs.Containers!Modules
    ' Return Document object that points to ValuableFunctions module.
    Set docModule = ctrModules.Documents!ValuableFunctions
    ' Compare current permissions with owner permissions.
    If (docModule.Permissions And dbSecWriteOwner) <> 0 Then
        docModule.Owner = "SomebodyElse"
    End If
End Sub
``` |

Parameter Object

Description	A **Parameter** object represents a parameter associated with a **QueryDef** object created from a parameter query.
Remarks	Using the properties of a **Parameter** object, you can set a query parameter that can be changed before the query is run. You can:

- Check the **Name** property setting to determine the name of a parameter.
- Check or set the **Value** property (default) of a parameter. For example:

    ```
    qdfNewHires.Parameters(0) = 5
    ```

- Check the **Type** property setting to determine the data type of the **Parameter** object.

The **Parameters** collection provides information only about existing parameters. You can't append objects to, or delete objects from, the **Parameters** collection.

The only method supported by the **Parameters** collection is the **Refresh** method. |
| **Properties** | **Name** Property, **Type** Property, **Value** Property. |
| **See Also** | Appendix, "Data Access Object Hierarchy." |

200   Parameter Object

Example

This example sets two query parameters for a hypothetical parameter query named "ParamQuery," executes the query by opening a **Recordset** from the **QueryDef**, and then prints the properties of each parameter. Note that this query does not actually exist in the Northwind sample database. The parameter data types are of type **Date**.

```
Dim dbsCurrent As Database
Dim qdfParam As QueryDef, prmEnum As Parameter
Dim rstParam As Recordset
Dim X As Integer
Set dbsCurrent = DBEngine.Workspaces(0).OpenDatabase("Northwind.mdb")
Set qdfParam = dbsCurrent.QueryDefs("ParamQuery")   ' Open existing
                                                    ' QueryDef.
qdfParam.Parameters("Order Date") = "10/11/94"      ' Set parameters.
qdfParam.Parameters("Ship Date") = "11/4/94"
Set rstParam = qdfParam.OpenRecordset()             ' Open Recordset.
For X = 0 To qdfParam.Parameters.Count - 1
    Set prmEnum = qdfParam.Parameters(X)
    Debug.Print prmEnum.Name            ' Print parameter properties.
    Debug.Print prmEnum.Type
    Debug.Print prmEnum.Value
Next X
rstParam.Close
```

Example (Microsoft Access)

The following example creates a new parameter query and supplies values for the parameters.

```
Sub NewParameterQuery()
    Dim dbs As Database, qdf As QueryDef, rst As Recordset
    Dim prm As Parameter, strSQL As String

    ' Return Database object pointing to current database.
    Set dbs = CurrentDb
    ' Construct SQL string.
    strSQL = "PARAMETERS [Beginning OrderDate] DateTime, " & _
        "[Ending OrderDate] DateTime; SELECT * FROM Orders " & _
        "WHERE ([OrderDate] Between[Beginning OrderDate] " & _
        "And [Ending OrderDate]);"
    ' Create new QueryDef object.
    Set qdf = dbs.CreateQueryDef("ParameterQuery", strSQL)
    ' Supply values for parameters.
    qdf.Parameters![Beginning OrderDate] = #4-1-95#
    qdf.Parameters![Ending OrderDate] = #4-30-95#
End Sub
```

Parameters Collection

Description	A **Parameters** collection contains all the **Parameter** objects of a **QueryDef** object.
Remarks	The **Parameters** collection provides information only about existing parameters. You can't append objects to or delete objects from the **Parameters** collection.
	The only method supported by the **Parameters** collection is the **Refresh** method.
Properties	**Count** Property.
Methods	**Refresh** Method.
See Also	Appendix, "Data Access Object Hierarchy."
Example	See the **Parameter** object example.
Example (Microsoft Access)	See the **Parameter** object example (Microsoft Access).

Password Property

Applies To	**User** Object.
Description	Sets the password for a user account. This property setting is write-only for new objects not yet appended to a collection, and is not available for existing objects.
Settings	The setting is a string expression that can be up to 14 characters long and can include any characters except the ASCII character 0 (null). The data type is **String**.
Remarks	Set the **Password** property along with the **PID** property when you create a new **User** object.
	Use the **NewPassword** method to change the **Password** property setting for an existing **User** object. To clear a password, set the *newpassword* argument of the **NewPassword** method to a zero-length string ("").
	Passwords are case-sensitive.
	Note If you don't have access permission, you can't change the password of any other user.
See Also	**NewPassword** Method, **Permissions** Property, **PID** Property, **UserName** Property.

Example

This example creates a new **User** object and sets the **Name**, **PID**, and **Password** properties for the new object before appending it to the **Users** collection.

```
Dim usrMyself As User, wrkDefault As Workspace
...
Set wrkDefault = DBEngine.Workspaces(0)    ' Get default workspace.
' Create, specify, and append new User object.
Set usrMyself = wrkDefault.CreateUser("Pat Smith")
usrMyself.PID = "abc123DEF456"
usrMyself.Password = "MySecret"
wrkDefault.Users.Append usrMyself
```

PercentPosition Property

Applies To

Recordset Object, Snapshot-Type **Recordset** Object, Table-Type **Recordset** Object.

Description

Sets or returns a value that indicates or changes the approximate location of the current record in the **Recordset** object based on a percentage of the records in the **Recordset**.

Settings and Return Values

The setting or return value is a number between 0.0 and 100.00. The data type is **Single**.

Remarks

To indicate or change the approximate position of the current record in a **Recordset** object, you can check or set the **PercentPosition** property. When working with a dynaset- or Snapshot-Type **Recordset** object, first populate the **Recordset** object by moving to the last record before you set or check the **PercentPosition** property. If you use the **PercentPosition** property before fully populating the **Recordset** object, the amount of movement is relative to the number of records accessed as indicated by the **RecordCount** property setting. You can move to the last record using **MoveLast** method.

Note Using the **PercentPosition** property to move the current record to a specific record in a **Recordset** object isn't recommended—the **Bookmark** property is better suited for this task.

Once you set the **PercentPosition** property to a value, the record at the approximate position corresponding to that value becomes current, and the **PercentPosition** property is reset to a value that reflects the approximate position of the current record. For example, if your **Recordset** object contains only five records, and you set its **PercentPosition** property value to 77, the value returned from the **PercentPosition** property may be 80, not 77.

PercentPosition Property

The **PercentPosition** property applies to all three types of **Recordset** objects, including tables without indexes. The only exceptions are that it does not apply to forward-only scrolling snapshots), or on a **Recordset** object opened from a pass-through query against a remote database.

You can use the **PercentPosition** property with a scroll bar on a form or text box to indicate the location of the current record in a **Recordset** object.

See Also

Bookmark Property; **Index** Property; **Move** Method; **MoveFirst**, **MoveLast**, **MoveNext**, **MovePrevious** Methods.

Example

This example displays the current position of a record in a **Recordset** in a message box.

```
Dim dbsNorthwind As Database, rstEmployees As Recordset
Set dbsNorthwind = DBEngine.Workspaces(0).OpenDatabase("Northwind.mdb")
' Open table.
Set rstEmployees = dbsNorthwind.OpenRecordset("Employees")
' Set current index.
rstEmployees.Index = "Last Name"
...
...     ' Move among the records.
...
' Display current position.
MsgBox("Current position is " & rstEmployees.PercentPosition & " %.")
```

Example (Microsoft Access)

The following example expresses the current position of a record in a recordset as a percent, then displays it in a message box.

```
Sub PercentOfRecords()
    Dim dbs As Database, rstProducts As Recordset
    Dim strInput As String, strSQL As String

    strSQL = "SELECT * FROM Products ORDER BY ProductName;"
    ' Return Database variable that points to current database.
    Set dbs = CurrentDb
    ' Open table.
    Set rstProducts = dbs.OpenRecordset(strSQL, dbOpenDynaset)
    ' Populate recordset.
    rstProducts.MoveLast
    ' Return to start of recordset.
    rstProducts.MoveFirst
    ' Prompt user to input name of product.
    strInput = InputBox("Please enter the full product name.")
    ' Find first occurrence.
    rstProducts.FindFirst "[ProductName] = '" & strInput & "'"
    ' Display current position as a percent.
    MsgBox("The current position in the Recordset is " & _
        rstProducts.PercentPosition & "%.")
End Sub
```

**Example
(Microsoft Excel)**

This example selects and changes records in the Customer recordset in the NWINDEX.MDB database, and then it copies the recordset onto Sheet1. The status bar shows the percentage of records changed.

To create the NWINDEX.MDB database, run the Microsoft Excel example for the **CreateDatabase** method.

```
Dim db As Database, rs As Recordset, sQLText as String
Set db = Workspaces(0).OpenDatabase(Application.Path & "\NWINDEX.MDB")
sQLText = "SELECT [CON_TITLE], [CONTACT], [COMPANY] FROM Customer " _
    & "WHERE [CON_TITLE] = 'Owner';"
Set rs = db.OpenRecordset(sQLText, dbOpenDynaset)
rs.MoveFirst
Sheets("Sheet1").Activate
Do While Not rs.EOF
    rs.Edit
    rs.Fields("CON_TITLE").Value = "Account Excecutive"
    rs.Update
    Application.StatusBar = rs.PercentPosition & "% of the" _
        & " records have been replaced."
    rs.MoveNext
Loop
Application.StatusBar = "Done"
rs.MoveFirst
numberOfRows = ActiveCell.CopyFromRecordset(rs)
MsgBox numberOfRows & " Records have been changed"
rs.Close
db.Close
```

Permissions Property

Applies To **Container** Object, **Document** Object.

Description Sets or returns a value that establishes the permissions for the user or group identified by the **UserName** property of the **Container** or **Document** object.

Settings and Return Values The setting or return value is a constant that establishes permissions. Possible settings or return values are:

Constant	Description
dbSecNoAccess	No access to the object.
dbSecFullAccess	Full access to the object.
dbSecDelete	Can delete the object.

Permissions Property

Constant	Description
dbSecReadSec	Can read the object's security-related information.
dbSecWriteSec	Can alter access permissions.
dbSecWriteOwner	Can change the **Owner** property setting.

For the Tables **Container** object or any **Document** object in a **Documents** collection, the possible settings or return values are:

Constant	Description
dbSecCreate	Can create new documents (valid only with a **Container** object).
dbSecReadDef	Can read the table definition including column and index information.
dbSecWriteDef	Can modify or delete the table definition including column and index information.
dbSecRetrieveData	Can retrieve data from the **Document** object.
dbSecInsertData	Can add records.
dbSecReplaceData	Can modify records.
dbSecDeleteData	Can delete records.

For the Databases **Container** object or any **Document** object in a **Documents** collection, the possible settings or return values are:

Constant	User or group
dbSecDBAdmin	Gives user permission to make a database replicable and change the database password.
dbSecDBCreate	Can create new databases (valid only on the databases **Container** object in the system database [Systen.mdw]).
dbSecDBExclusive	Exclusive access.
dbSecDBOpen	Can open the database.

Remarks

These constants are listed in the Data Access (DAO) object library in the Object Browser.

Use this property to establish or determine the type of read/write/modify permissions the user has for a **Container** or **Document** object.

A **Document** object inherits the permissions for users from its **Container** object, provided the **Inherited** property of the **Container** object is set for those users or for a group to which the users belong. By setting a **Document** object's **Permissions** and **UserName** properties later, you can further refine the access control behavior of your object.

206 Permissions Property

See Also **Inherited** Property, **UserName** Property.

Specifics (Microsoft Access) Microsoft Access defines four types of **Container** objects in addition to those defined by the Microsoft Jet database engine. These include the Forms, Reports, Scripts, or Modules **Container** objects. Individual Form, Report, Script and Module **Document** objects belong to the **Documents** collections of these **Container** objects. For these **Container** and **Document** objects, you can also set the **Permissions** property to the following constants.

Constant	User or group can
acSecFrmRptReadDef	Open the form or report in Design view but not make any changes.
acSecFrmRptWriteDef	Modify or delete the form or report in Design view.
acSecFrmRptExecute	Open the form in Form view or Datasheet view; print or open the report in Sample Preview or Print Preview.
acSecMacReadDef	Open the Macro window and view a macro without making changes.
acSecMacWriteDef	Modify or delete the macro in the Macro window.
acSecModReadDef	Open the module but not make any changes.
acSecModWriteDef	Modify or delete the contents of a module.
acSecMacExecute	Run the macro.

Example This example prints the **Permissions** property setting of a **Document** object for the current user.

```
Dim dbsNorthwind As Database, docTest As Document
Set dbsNorthwind = DBEngine.Workspaces(0).OpenDatabase("Northwind.mdb")
Set docTest = dbsNorthwind.Containers(0).Documents("MyDoc")
Debug.Print docTest.Permissions
```

Example (Microsoft Access) The following example adds a new user account by creating a **User** object and appending it to the **Users** collection of the default workspace. It then sets permissions for the new user for all tables in the database. The procedure first sets the **UserName** property of a Tables **Container** object to the name of the new user, then sets the **Permissions** property to the appropriate permissions. Note that the security constants used to set the **Permissions** property are **Integer** values, so the **+** (plus sign) operator is used to add them.

```
Sub SetPermissions()
    Dim dbs As Database, ctrTables As Container
    Dim wspDefault As Workspace, usrNew As User

    ' Return Workspace object pointing to default workspace.
    Set wspDefault = DBEngine.Workspaces(0)
    ' Create User object, specifying Name, PID, and Password.
```

```
        Set usrNew = wspDefault.CreateUser("Kevin Smith", "ABC123XYZ123",_
            "Password")
        ' Append to Users collection of default workspace.
        wspDefault.Users.Append usrNew
        ' Return Database variable pointing to current database.
        Set dbs = CurrentDb
        ' Return Container variable pointing to Tables Container object.
        Set ctrTables = dbs.Containers!Tables
        ctrTables.UserName = usrNew.Name
        ' Set new user's permissions for tables.
        ctrTables.Permissions = dbSecInsertData + dbSecReplaceData + _
            dbSecDeleteData
    End Sub
```

PID Property

Applies To   **Group** Object, **User** Object.

Description   Sets the personal identifier (PID) for either a group or a user account. This property setting is write-only for new objects not yet appended to a collection, and is not available for existing objects.

Settings   The setting is a string expression containing 4–20 alphanumeric characters. The data type is **String**.

Remarks   Set the **PID** property along with the **Name** property when you create a new **Group** object. Set the **PID** property along with the **Name** and **Password** properties when you create a new **User** object.

See Also   **Name** Property, **Password** Property.

Example   This example creates a new **User** object and sets the **Name**, **PID**, and **Password** properties for the new object before appending it to the **Users** collection.

```
Dim usrMyself As User, wrkDefault As Workspace
...
Set wrkDefault = DBEngine.Workspaces(0)    ' Get default workspace.
' Create, specify, and append new User object.
Set usrMyself = wrkDefault.CreateUser("Pat Smith")
usrMyself.PID = "abc123DEF456"
usrMyself.Password = "MySecret"
wrkDefault.Users.Append usrMyself
```

Primary Property

Applies To Index Object.

Description Sets or returns a value that indicates whether an **Index** object represents a primary index for a table. The **Primary** property setting is read/write for a new **Index** object not yet appended to a collection and read-only for an existing **Index** object in an **Indexes** collection. If the **Index** object is appended to the **TableDef** object but the **TableDef** object isn't appended to the **TableDefs** collection, the **Index** property is read-write.

Settings and Return Values The setting or return value is a Boolean expression that specifies a primary index. The data type is Boolean. **True** (-1) indicates that the **Index** object represents a primary index.

Remarks A primary index consists of one or more fields that uniquely identify all records in a table in a predefined order. Because the index field must be unique, the **Unique** property of the **Index** object is set to **True**. If the primary index consists of more than one field, each field can contain duplicate values, but each combination of values from all the indexed fields must be unique. A primary index consists of a key for the table and usually contains the same fields as the primary key.

> **Tip** You don't have to create indexes for tables, but in large, unindexed tables, accessing a specific record can take a long time. The **Attributes** property of each **Field** object in the **Index** object determines the order of records and consequently determines the access techniques to use for that index. When you create a new table in your database, it's a good idea to create an index on one or more fields that uniquely identify each record, and then set the **Primary** property of the **Index** object to **True**.

When you set a primary key for a table, the primary key is automatically defined as the primary index for the table.

See Also **Attributes** Property, **Clustered** Property, **Unique** Property.

Specifics (Microsoft Access) In Microsoft Access, when you set a primary key for a table in table Design view, the primary key is automatically defined as the primary index.

Example In the Biblio.mdb database, this example creates a new **Table** and primary key **Index** object and then adds the **Table** to the **TableDefs** collection of a **Database**.

```
Dim dbsBiblio As Database , tdfBookTypes As TableDef
Dim idxPrimaryKey As Index, fldTypeNum As Field, fldType As Field
    ' Open the Database.
Set dbsBiblio = DBEngine.Workspaces(0).OpenDatabase("Biblio.mdb")
Set tdfBookTypes = dbsBiblio.CreateTableDef("Book Types")
    ' Create and Set fldTypeNum field Set fldTypeNum =
    ' tdfBookTypes.CreateField("TypeNum",dbLong)
```

```
            ' Add fldTypeNum field to TableDef.
            tdfBookTypes.Fields.Append fldTypeNum
            ' Create and Set fldType field properties.
Set fldType = tdfBookTypes.CreateField("Type",dbText)
fldType.Size = 15           ' Set Size property of text field.
            ' Add fldType field to TableDef.
tdfBookTypes.Fields.Append fldType
Set idxPrimaryKey = tdfBookTypes.CreateIndex("PrimaryKey")
With idxPrimaryKey                 ' Set properties in new Index.
    .Name = "PrimaryKey"
    .Unique = True
    .Primary = True
    .Fields = "TypeNum"
End With
            ' Add Index to TableDefs collection.
idxPrimaryKey.fields.Append idxPrimaryKey.CreateField("TypeNum")
tdfBookTypes.Indexes.Append idxPrimaryKey
' Append TableDef to database.
dbsBiblio.TableDefs.Append tdfBookTypes
dbsBiblio.Close
```

Example (Microsoft Access)

The following example checks the **Primary** property of each index on a Products table, and prints the fields making up the primary key.

```
Sub SetIndex()
    Dim dbs As Database, tdf As TableDef, fld As Field
    Dim idx As Index

    ' Return Database variable that points to current database.
    Set dbs = CurrentDb
    Set tdf = dbs.TableDefs!Products
    ' Enumerate through Indexes collection of TableDef.
    For Each idx In tdf.Indexes
        ' Check Primary property of Recordset object.
        If idx.Primary Then
            For Each fld In idx.Fields
                Debug.Print fld.Name
            Next fld
            Exit Sub
        End If
    Next idx
    MsgBox "No primary key defined."
End Sub
```

Properties Collection

Description A **Properties** collection contains all the **Property** objects for a specific instance of an object.

Remarks Every data access object contains a **Properties** collection, which has certain built-in **Property** objects. These **Property** objects (which are often just called properties) uniquely characterize that instance of the object.

In addition to the built-in properties, some objects allow you to create and add your own user-defined properties. To add a user-defined property to an existing instance of an object, first define its characteristics with the **CreateProperty** method, then add it to the collection with the **Append** method.

You can use the **Delete** method to remove user-defined properties from the **Properties** collection, but you can't remove built-in properties.

Note A user-defined property (**Property** object) is associated only with the specific instance of the object whose **Properties** collection you append it to. The property isn't defined for all instances of objects of the selected type.

You can use the **Properties** collection of an object to enumerate the object's built-in and user-defined properties. You don't need to know beforehand exactly which properties exist or what their characteristics (**Name** and **Type** properties) are to manipulate them. However, if you try to read a write-only property, an error occurs.

You can refer to an existing built-in or user-defined property by its **Name** property setting using this syntax:

object.**Properties**("*name*")

For a built-in property, you can also use this syntax:

object.name

You can also reference properties by their ordinal position. For example, this syntax refers to the first member of the **Properties** collection:

object.**Properties**(0)

Note A user-defined property differs from a built-in property of a data access object in that you must refer to a user-defined property using the full **Properties**("*name*") syntax.

Properties **Count** Property.

Methods **Append** Method, **Delete** Method, **Refresh** Method.

See Also Appendix, "Data Access Object Hierarchy."

Specifics (Microsoft Access) Several types of properties exist in Microsoft Access. Each of these properties can be represented in Visual Basic code by a **Property** object variable, and each is a member of a **Properties** collection.

Properties that apply to data access objects

- Built-in properties are defined by the Microsoft Jet database engine for each data access object.

- User-defined properties can be added to some data access objects. These data access objects include **Database**, **Index**, **QueryDef**, and **TableDef** objects, and **Field** objects in the **Fields** collection of a **QueryDef** or **TableDef** object.

- Some properties defined by Microsoft Access apply to data access objects. These properties can generally be set either in the Microsoft Access window or from Visual Basic. The Jet database engine cannot recognize these properties until corresponding **Property** objects are specifically created and appended to the **Properties** collection. The data access objects to which such properties may apply are **QueryDef** and **TableDef** objects, and **Field** objects in the **Fields** collection of a **QueryDef** or **TableDef** object. For lists of these Microsoft Access-defined properties, see the Specifics (Microsoft Access) sections in the topics for the **TableDef**, **QueryDef**, and **Field** objects.

Microsoft Access-defined properties that apply to data access objects differ from properties defined by the Jet database engine in several ways.

To refer to a user-defined property or a property defined by Microsoft Access, you must explicitly refer to the **Properties** collection. The fastest way to refer to a Microsoft Access property is by the following syntax.

```
object.Properties!name
```

You can also use the following, slightly slower syntax.

```
object.Properties("name")
```

In contrast, to refer to properties defined by the Jet database engine, you can simply use the `object.name` syntax.

If you are setting the value of a Microsoft Access-defined property for the first time, you first need to create it using the **CreateProperty** method. For example, the **Caption** property of a **Field** object is a Microsoft Access-defined property. If you have not previously set the **Caption** property in table Design view, but are setting the property for the first time from Visual Basic code, you must first create that property using the **CreateProperty** method and append it to the **Properties** collection before you can set its value.

212 Properties Collection

A Microsoft Access-defined property is automatically appended to the **Properties** collection the first time it is set in the Microsoft Access window, so if you have already set a property in the user interface, you don't need to create and append the property in code. For example, you can set the **Caption** property for a table in Datasheet view by clicking Font on the Format menu. This property is then included in the **Properties** collection of a **TableDef** object that points to the table.

Until you have set a Microsoft Access-defined property either in table Design view or from Visual Basic code, that property will not appear in the **Properties** collection. When you set these properties from Visual Basic, you should include error-handling code that checks to see if the property exists in the **Properties** collection, and creates and appends the property if it does not.

Properties that apply to Microsoft Access objects

Like data access objects, every Microsoft Access object contains a **Properties** collection, which has built-in **Property** objects. For example, **Property** objects that apply to a form are members of the **Properties** collection of the **Form** object.

You can also create user-defined properties for Microsoft Access objects. For example, you might create a property called TextType that applies to a text box control.

Property objects in the **Properties** collections of **Form**, **Report**, and **Control** objects differ from data access **Property** objects in that they do not have an **Inherited** property.

You can enumerate the **Property** objects in the **Properties** collections of **Form**, **Report**, and **Control** objects. However, the Microsoft Access **Application** object and the **Screen** object have **Properties** collections that can't be enumerated. Additionally, the properties of these objects are read-only.

Example

This example creates a user-defined property for the current database, sets its **Type** and **Value** properties, and appends it to the **Properties** collection of the database. Then the example enumerates all properties in the database.

```
Function EnumerateProperty () As Integer
    Dim wrkDefault As Workspace, dbsExample As Database
    Dim prpUserDefined As Property, prpEnum As Property
    Dim I As Integer
    ' Get default workspace and current database.
    Set wrkDefault = DBEngine.Workspaces(0)
    Set dbsExample = wrkDefault.OpenDatabase("Northwind.mdb")
    ' Create user-defined property.
    Set prpUserDefined = dbsExample.CreateProperty()
    ' Set properties of new property.
    prpUserDefined.Name = "UserDefinedProperty"
    prpUserDefined.Type = dbText
    prpUserDefined.Value = "This is a user-defined property."
    ' Append property to current database.
```

```
        dbsExample.Properties.Append prpUserDefined
        ' Enumerate all properties of current database.
        Debug.Print "Properties of Database "; dbsExample.Name
        For I = 0 To dbsExample.Properties.Count - 1
            Set prpEnum = dbsExample.Properties(I)
            Debug.Print
            Debug.Print " Properties("; I; ")"
            Debug.Print "   Name: "; prpEnum.Name
            Debug.Print "   Type: "; prpEnum.Type
            Debug.Print "   Value: "; prpEnum.Value
            Debug.Print "   Inherited: "; prpEnum.Inherited
        Next I
        Debug.Print
        EnumerateProperty = True
End Function
```

This example shows how you can set an application-defined property (or any user-defined property that may not yet exist) without causing a run-time error. The example sets an arbitrary property of a **Field** object. The return value of the function is **True** if the value was properly set. The return value is **False** if an unexpected error occurs when the property is set.

```
Function SetFieldProperty (fldPropVal As Field, strName As String,
intType As Integer, varValue As Variant) As Integer
    Const ERR_PROPERTY_NONEXISTENT = 3270
    Dim prpUserDefined As Property
    On Error Resume Next ' Function handles errors.
    SetFieldProperty = True
    fldPropVal.Properties(strName) = varValue
    If Err <> 0 Then        ' Error occurred when value was set.
        If Err <> ERR_PROPERTY_NONEXISTENT
            On Error GoTo 0
            SetFieldProperty = False
        Else
            ' Create Property object, setting its Name, Type, and Value
            ' properties.
            On Error Resume Next
            Set prpUserDefined = fldPropVal.CreateProperty(strName, _
                intType, varValue)
            fldPropVal.Properties.Append prpUserDefined
            If Err <> 0 Then
                SetFieldProperty = False
            End If
            On Error GoTo 0
        End If
    End If
End Function
```

**Example
(Microsoft Access)**

The following example creates a new user-defined property, sets its initial value, and appends it to the **Properties** collection of a **TableDef** object.

```
Sub CreateNewProperty()
    Dim dbs As Database, tdf As TableDef
    Dim prp As Property
    ' Return Database object pointing to current database.
    Set dbs = CurrentDb
    Set tdf = dbs.TableDefs!Orders
    ' Create new property, denote type, and set initial value.
    Set prp = tdf.CreateProperty("LastSaved", dbText, "New")
    ' Append to Properties collection of TableDef object.
    tdf.Properties.Append prp
End Sub
```

The next example creates a property that is defined by Microsoft Access, but applies to data access objects. Because the Microsoft Jet database engine cannot recognize properties defined by Microsoft Access, you must create a new **Property** object and append it to the **Properties** collection if you are setting the property for the first time.

Note that you must specify the correct constant for the *type* argument when you create the property. If you're not certain which data type you should use, see the topic for the individual property.

```
Sub CreateAccessProperty()
    Dim dbs As Database, tdf As TableDef
    Dim prp As Property

    ' Return Database object pointing to current database.
    Set dbs = CurrentDb
    Set tdf = dbs.TableDefs!Orders
    ' Create property, denote type, and set initial value.
    Set prp = tdf.CreateProperty("DatasheetFontItalic", dbBoolean, True)
    ' Append Property object to Properties collection.
    tdf.Properties.Append prp
End Sub
```

Property Object

Description

A **Property** object represents a built-in or user-defined characteristic of a data access object.

Property Object 215

Remarks Every data access object contains a **Properties** collection, which has certain built-in **Property** objects. These **Property** objects (which are often just called properties) uniquely characterize that instance of the object. You specify built-in properties when you create a new data access object. You can set the properties of some existing data access objects using an assignment statement.

The **Property** object also has four built-in properties:

- The **Name** property, a **String** that uniquely identifies the property.
- The **Type** property, an **Integer** that specifies the property data type.
- The **Value** property, a **Variant** that contains the property setting.
- The **Inherited** property, a Boolean flag that indicates whether the property is inherited from another object. For example, a **Field** object in a **Fields** collection of a **Recordset** object can inherit properties from the underlying **TableDef** or **QueryDef** object.

In addition to these built-in properties, you can create and add your own user-defined properties to these objects:

- **Database**, **Index**, **QueryDef**, and **TableDef** objects
- **Field** objects in **Fields** collections of **QueryDef** and **TableDef** objects

To add a user-defined property, use the **CreateProperty** method to create a **Property** object with a unique **Name** property setting. Set the **Type** and **Value** properties of the new **Property** object, and then append it to the **Properties** collection of the appropriate object. The object to which you are adding the user-defined property must already be saved to disk (that is, it must be appended to a collection).

You can delete user-defined properties from the **Properties** collection, but you can't delete built-in properties.

Note A user-defined property (**Property** object) is associated only with the specific instance of the object whose **Properties** collection you append it to. The property isn't defined for all instances of objects of the selected type.

You can use the **Properties** collection of an object to enumerate the object's built-in and user-defined properties. You don't need to know beforehand exactly which properties exist or what their characteristics (**Name** and **Type** properties) are to manipulate them. However, if you try to read a write-only property (such as the **Password** property of a **Workspace** object), an error occurs.

You can refer to an existing built-in or user-defined property by its **Name** property setting using this syntax:

object.**Properties**("*name*")

For a built-in property, you can also use this syntax:

object.name

You can also reference properties by their ordinal position using this syntax, which refers to the first member of the **Properties** collection:

object.**Properties**(0)

A user-defined property differs from a built-in property of a data access object in the following ways:

- You must refer to a user-defined property using the full **Properties**("*name*") syntax.
- If you haven't previously set the property's value, you need to create it first using the **CreateProperty** method.

Properties	**Inherited** Property, **Name** Property, **Type** Property, **Value** Property.
See Also	**CreateProperty** Method; **Database** Object; Appendix, "Data Access Object Hierarchy."
Specifics (Microsoft Access)	See the **Properties** collection specifics (Microsoft Access).
Example	See the **Properties** collection example.
Example (Microsoft Access)	See the **Properties** collection example (Microsoft Access).

QueryDef Object

Description	A **QueryDef** object is a stored definition of a query in a Microsoft Jet database.
Remarks	The **QueryDef** object corresponds to a stored query definition in a database. You can think of a saved query as a compiled SQL statement.

You can use the properties of a **QueryDef** object to define a query. For example, you can:

- Check and modify the **SQL** property setting, set its parameters, and then run the query.
- Set query parameters using the **QueryDef** object's **Parameters** collection.
- Set or check the **Type** property to determine whether the query selects records from an existing table, makes a new table, inserts records from one table into another table, deletes records, or updates records.
- Retrieve data from an ODBC data source by setting the **ODBCTimeout** and **Connect** properties and, if the query isn't a select query, setting the **ReturnsRecords** property to **False**.
- Indicate the query is to be passed to an external ODBC server by setting the **Connect** property, making it an SQL pass through query.
- Use the **ReturnsRecords** property to indicate that the query returns records. The **ReturnsRecords** property is only valid on SQL pass through queries.
- Use the **ODBCTimeout** property to indicate how long to wait before the query returns records. The **ODBCTimeout** property applies to any query that accesses ODBC data.

Queries executed from **QueryDef** objects run faster than queries specified by the **OpenRecordset** method because the Microsoft Jet database engine doesn't need to compile the query before executing it.

The preferred way to use the native SQL dialect of an external database engine is by using **QueryDef** objects. For example, you can create a Transact SQL query (as used with Microsoft SQL Server) and store it in a **QueryDef** object. When you need to use a non-Jet database engine SQL query, you must provide a **Connect** property string that points to the external data source. Queries with valid **Connect** properties bypass the Jet database engine and pass the query directly to the external database server for processing.

To create a new **QueryDef** object, use the **CreateQueryDef** method.

Properties **Connect** Property; **DateCreated**, **LastUpdated** Properties; **KeepLocal** Property; **LogMessages** Property; **Name** Property; **ODBCTimeout** Property; **RecordsAffected** Property; **Replicable** Property; **ReturnsRecords** Property; **SQL** Property; **Type** Property; **Updatable** Property.

Methods **CreateProperty** Method, **Execute** Method, **OpenRecordset** Method.

See Also **CreateQueryDef** Method; Appendix, "Data Access Object Hierarchy."

218　QueryDef Object

Specifics (Microsoft Access)　　In addition to the properties defined by the Microsoft Jet database engine, a **QueryDef** object may also contain these Microsoft Access application-defined properties. For details on checking and setting these properties, see the topics for the individual properties and the **Property** object.

DatasheetFontHeight	**FrozenColumns**
DatasheetFontItalic	**LogMessages**
DatasheetFontName	**RecordLocks**
DatasheetFontUnderline	**RowHeight**
DatasheetFontWeight	**ShowGrid**
Description	

Example　　This example creates a new **QueryDef** object and appends it to the **QueryDefs** collection in the current database. Then the example enumerates all the **QueryDef** objects in the database and all the properties of the new **QueryDef**.

```
Function EnumerateQueryDef () As Integer
    Dim wrkCurrent As Workspace, dbsExample As Database, qdfTest As _
        QueryDef
    Dim I As Integer
    Set wrkCurrent = DBEngine.Workspaces(0)
    Set dbsExample = wrkCurrent.OpenDatabase("Northwind.mdb")
    Set qdfTest = dbsExample.CreateQueryDef("This is a test")
    Debug.Print
    ' Enumerate QueryDef objects.
    Debug.Print
    For I = 0 To dbsExample.QueryDefs.Count - 1
        Debug.Print dbsExample.QueryDefs(I).Name
    Next I
    ' Enumerate built-in properties of qdfTest.
    Debug.Print
    Debug.Print "qdfTest.Name: "; qdfTest.Name
    Debug.Print "qdfTest.DateCreated: "; qdfTest.DateCreated
    Debug.Print "qdfTest.LastUpdated: "; qdfTest.LastUpdated
    Debug.Print "qdfTest.SQL: "; qdfTest.SQL
    Debug.Print "qdfTest.ODBCTimeout: "; qdfTest.ODBCTimeout
    Debug.Print "qdfTest.Updatable: "; qdfTest.Updatable
    Debug.Print "qdfTest.Type: "; qdfTest.Type
    Debug.Print "qdfTest.Connect: "; qdfTest.Connect
    Debug.Print "qdfTest.ReturnsRecords: "; qdfTest.ReturnsRecords
    dbsExample.QueryDefs.Delete "This is a test"
    EnumerateQueryDef = True
End Function
```

**Example
(Microsoft Access)**

The following example checks to see if there is a query called RecentHires in the current database, and deletes it from the **QueryDefs** collection if it exists. Then the procedure creates a new **QueryDef** object and opens it in Datasheet view.

```
Sub NewQuery()
    Dim dbs As Database, qdf As QueryDef
    Dim strSQL As String

    ' Return Database object pointing to current database.
    Set dbs = CurrentDb
    ' Refresh QueryDefs collection.
    dbs.QueryDefs.Refresh
    ' If RecentHires query exists, delete it.
    For Each qdf in dbs.QueryDefs
        If qdf.Name = "RecentHires" Then
            dbs.QueryDefs.Delete qdf.Name
        End If
    Next qdf
    ' Create SQL string to select employees hired after 1-1-95.
    strSQL = "SELECT * FROM Employees WHERE HireDate >= #1-1-95#;"
    ' Create new QueryDef object.
    Set qdf = dbs.CreateQueryDef("RecentHires", strSQL)
    ' Open query in Datasheet view.
    DoCmd.OpenQuery qdf.Name
End Sub
```

QueryDefs Collection

Description	A **QueryDefs** collection contains all **QueryDef** objects in a **Database** object.
Remarks	The **QueryDef** object corresponds to a stored query definition in a database. When you create a **QueryDef** object, you can add it to the **QueryDefs** collection using the **Append** method so it will be saved when you close the **Database** object.
	To remove a **QueryDef** object from the collection, use the **Delete** method.
Properties	**Count** Property.
Methods	**Append** Method, **Delete** Method, **Refresh** Method.
See Also	Appendix, "Data Access Object Hierarchy."
Specifics (Microsoft Access)	See the **QueryDef** object specifics (Microsoft Access).
Example	See the **QueryDef** object example.

Example (Microsoft Access)	See the **QueryDef** object example (Microsoft Access).

QueryTimeout Property

Applies To	**Database** Object.
Description	Sets or returns a value that specifies the number of seconds the Microsoft Jet database engine waits before a timeout error occurs when a query is executed on an ODBC database.
Settings and Return Values	The setting or return value is an integer representing the number of seconds the Jet database engine waits before timing out and returning an error. The data type is **Integer**.
Remarks	When you're using an ODBC database, such as SQL Server, there may be delays due to network traffic or heavy use of the ODBC server. Rather than waiting indefinitely, you can specify how long to wait before the Jet database engine produces an error.
	When used with a **Database** object, the **QueryTimeout** property specifies a global value for all queries associated with the database.
	The timeout value is taken from the Windows Registry. If there is no Windows Registry setting, the default value is 60 seconds. Once this property is set, however, it overrides any Windows Registry setting or default value.
See Also	**ODBCTimeout** Property.
Example	This example opens the specified database and sets the **QueryTimeout** property to 120 seconds.

```
Dim dbsNorthwind As Database
Set dbsNorthwind = DBEngine.Workspaces(0).OpenDatabase("Northwind.mdb")
dbsNorthwind.QueryTimeout = 120
```

Example (Microsoft Access)	The following example opens the specified database and sets the **QueryTimeout** property to 120 seconds.

```
Sub SetTimeout()
    Dim dbs As Database
    ' Return Database variable that points to current database.
    Set dbs = CurrentDb
    dbs.QueryTimeout = 120
End Sub
```

RecordCount Property

Applies To Dynaset-Type **Recordset** Object, **Recordset** Object, Snapshot-Type **Recordset** Object, Table-Type **Recordset** Object, **TableDef** Object.

Description Returns the number of records accessed in a Dynaset-type or Snapshot-type **Recordset** object, or the total number of records in a Table-type **Recordset** or **TableDef** object. This property setting is read-only.

Return Values The return value is a **Long Integer**.

Remarks Use the **RecordCount** property to find out how many records in a **Recordset** or **TableDef** object have been accessed. The **RecordCount** property doesn't indicate how many records are contained in a dynaset- or snapshot-type **Recordset** object until all records have been accessed.

Once the last record has been accessed, the **RecordCount** property indicates the total number of undeleted records in the **Recordset** or **TableDef** object. To force the last record to be accessed, use the **MoveLast** method on the **Recordset** object. You can also use an SQL **Count** function to determine the approximate number of records your query will return.

As your application deletes records in a dynaset-type **Recordset** object, the value of the **RecordCount** property decreases. However, records deleted by other users aren't reflected by the **RecordCount** property until the current record is positioned to a deleted record. If you execute a transaction that affects the **RecordCount** property setting and subsequently rolls back the transaction, the **RecordCount** property won't reflect the actual number of remaining records.

The **RecordCount** property of a snapshot-type **Recordset** object isn't affected by changes in the underlying tables.

A **Recordset** or **TableDef** object with no records has a **RecordCount** property setting of 0.

When working with attached **TableDef** objects, the **RecordCount** property setting is always –1.

Using the **Requery** method on a **Recordset** object resets the **RecordCount** property just as if the query were re-executed.

See Also **MoveFirst**, **MoveLast**, **MoveNext**, **MovePrevious** Methods; **Requery** Method.

Example This example creates a **Recordset** object based on the Employees table and then determines the number of records in the **Recordset**.

```
Dim dbsNorthwind As Database, rstEmployees As Recordset
Dim lngTotal As Long
Set dbsNorthwind = DBEngine.Workspaces(0).OpenDatabase("Northwind.mdb")
```

222 RecordCount Property

```
Set rstEmployees = dbsNorthwind.OpenRecordset("Employees")
rstEmployees.MoveLast
lngTotal = rstEmployees.RecordCount
If lngTotal = -1 Then
    Debug.Print "Count not available."
End If
```

Example (Microsoft Access)

The following example creates a **Recordset** object based on the Orders table and then determines the number of records in the **Recordset** object.

```
Sub CountRecords()
    Dim dbs As Database, rstOrders As Recordset
    Dim lngTotal As Long

    ' Return Database variable that points to current database.
    Set dbs = CurrentDb
    ' Open table-type Recordset object.
    Set rstOrders = dbs.OpenRecordset("Orders")
    ' Fully populate Recordset object.
    rstOrders.MoveLast
    Debug.Print rstOrders.RecordCount
End Sub
```

Example (Microsoft Excel)

This example displays the number of records in the Customer recordset in the NWINDEX.MDB database.

To create the NWINDEX.MDB database, run the Microsoft Excel example for the **CreateDatabase** method.

```
Sub CountRecords()
    Dim db As Database, rs As Recordset
    Set db = Workspaces(0).OpenDatabase(Application.Path _
        & "\NWINDEX.MDB")
    Set rs = db.OpenRecordset("Customer")
    On Error GoTo errorHandler
    rs.MoveLast
    MsgBox "There are " & rs.RecordCount & " records in " _
        & rs.Name
    rs.Close
    db.Close
    Exit Sub
errorHandler:
    MsgBox "There are no records in " & rs.Name
    rs.Close
    db.Close
End Sub
```

RecordsAffected Property

Applies To **Database** Object, **QueryDef** Object.

Description Returns the number of records affected by the most recently invoked **Execute** method.

Return Values The return value is an integer from 0 to the number of records affected by the most recently invoked **Execute** method on either a **Database** or **QueryDef** object. The data type is **Long**.

Remarks The **RecordsAffected** property contains the number of records deleted, updated, or inserted when running an action query. When you use the **Execute** method to run a **QueryDef** object, the **RecordsAffected** property setting is the number of records affected.

Note The **RecordsAffected** property setting is the same as the value returned by the **ExecuteSQL** method.

Example This example prints the number of records updated by an action query.

```
Dim dbsBiblio As Database, lngResults As Long
Set dbsBiblio = DBEngine.Workspaces(0).OpenDatabase("Biblio.mdb")
dbsBiblio.Execute "Update Titles Set [Year Published] = 1994 " _
    & " WHERE Title = 'To Kill an SQL Query' "
lngResults = dbsBiblio.RecordsAffected
Debug.Print lngResults & " records were changed."
dbsBiblio.Close
```

Example (Microsoft Access) The following example prints the number of records updated by an action query.

```
Sub RecordsUpdated()
    Dim dbs As Database, qdf As QueryDef
    Dim strSQL As String

    ' Return Database variable that points to current database.
    Set dbs = CurrentDb
    strSQL = "UPDATE Employees SET Title = " & _
       "'Senior Sales Representative' " & _
       "WHERE Title = 'Sales Representative';"
    ' Create new QueryDef.
    Set qdf = dbs.CreateQueryDef("UpdateTitles", strSQL)
    ' Execute QueryDef object.
    qdf.Execute
    Debug.Print qdf.RecordsAffected
End Sub
```

Recordset Object

Description A **Recordset** object represents the records in a base table or the records that result from running a query.

Remarks When you use data access objects, you interact with data almost entirely using **Recordset** objects. All **Recordset** objects are constructed using records (rows) and fields (columns).

There are three types of **Recordset** objects:

- Table-type **Recordset**—a representation in code of a base table that you can use to add, change, or delete records from a single database table.
- Dynaset-type **Recordset**—the result of a query that can have updatable records. A dynaset-type **Recordset** object is a dynamic set of records that you can use to add, change, or delete records from an underlying database table or tables. A dynaset-type **Recordset** object can contain fields from one or more tables in a database.
- Snapshot-type **Recordset**—a static copy of a set of records that you can use to find data or generate reports. A snapshot-type **Recordset** object can contain fields from one or more tables in a database but can't be updated.

You can choose the type of **Recordset** object you want to create using the *type* argument of the **OpenRecordset** method. If you don't specify a *type*, the Microsoft Jet database engine attempts to create a table-type **Recordset** object. If this isn't possible, the Jet database engine attempts a dynaset-type and then a snapshot-type **Recordset** object.

When creating a **Recordset** object using a nonattached **TableDef** object, table-type **Recordset** objects are created. Only dynaset-type or snapshot-type **Recordset** objects can be created with attached tables or tables in external ODBC databases.

The **Type** property indicates the type of **Recordset** object created, and the **Updatable** property indicates whether you can change the object's records.

A new **Recordset** object is automatically added to the **Recordsets** collection when you open the object, and is automatically removed when you close it.

Information about the structure of a base table, such as the names and data types of each **Field** object and any **Index** objects, is stored in a **TableDef** object.

> **Note** If you use variables to represent a **Recordset** object and the **Database** object that contains the recordset, make sure the variables have the same scope, or lifetime. For example, if you declare a global variable that represents a **Recordset** object, make sure the variable that represents the database containing the recordset is also global, or is declared in a **Sub** or **Function** procedure using the **Static** keyword.

Your application can create as many Recordset object variables as needed. A Recordset object can refer to one or more tables or queries, or can be an SQL statement. You can also have a Recordset object that refers to some or all of the fields or records in other Recordset objects.

Dynaset- and snapshot-type **Recordset** objects are stored in local memory. If there isn't enough space in local memory to store the data, the Jet database engine saves the additional data to TEMP disk space. If this space is exhausted, a trappable error occurs.

The default collection of a **Recordset** object is the **Fields** collection, and the default property of a **Field** object is the **Value** property. You can simplify your code by using these defaults. For example, the following lines of code all set the value of the PubID field in the current record of a **Recordset** object.

```
rstPublishers!PubID = 99
rstPublishers("PubID") = 99
rstPublishers.Fields("PubID").Value = 99
```

When you create a **Recordset** object, the current record is positioned to the first record if there are any records. If there are no records, the **RecordCount** property setting is 0, and the **BOF** and **EOF** property settings are **True**.

You can use the **MoveNext**, **MovePrevious**, **MoveFirst**, and **MoveLast** methods to reposition the current record. For dynaset- and snapshot-type **Recordset** objects, you can also use the Find methods, such as **FindFirst**, to locate a specific record based on criteria. If the record isn't found, the **NoMatch** property is set to **True**. For table-type **Recordset** objects, you can scan records using the **Seek** function.

To cycle through all records, you can use the **BOF** and **EOF** properties to check for the beginning or end of the **Recordset** object. However, it may run faster to with an SQL query that performs operations that apply to an entire set of records.

Properties **AbsolutePosition** Property; **BOF**, **EOF** Properties; **Bookmark** Property; **Bookmarkable** Property; **CacheSize**, **CacheStart** Properties; **DateCreated**, **LastUpdated** Properties; **EditMode** Property; **Filter** Property; **Index** Property; **LastModified** Property; **LockEdits** Property; **Name** Property; **NoMatch** Property; **PercentPosition** Property; **RecordCount** Property; **Restartable** Property; **Sort** Property; **Transactions** Property; **Type** Property; **Updatable** Property; **ValidationRule** Property; **ValidationText** Property.

226 Recordset Object

Methods	**AddNew** Method; **CancelUpdate** Method; **Clone** Method; **Close** Method; **CopyQueryDef** Method; **Delete** Method; **Edit** Method; **FillCache** Method; **FindFirst**, **FindLast**, **FindNext**, **FindPrevious** Methods; **GetRows** Method; **Move** Method; **MoveFirst**, **MoveLast**, **MoveNext**, **MovePrevious** Methods; **OpenRecordset** Method; **Requery** Method; **Seek** Method; **Update** Method.
See Also	Dynaset-Type **Recordset** Object; **Index** Object; **OpenRecordset** Method; Snapshot-Type **Recordset** Object; Table-Type **Recordset** Object; Appendix, "Data Access Object Hierarchy."
Example	This example creates a new **Recordset** object and opens it (thereby appending it to the **Recordsets** collection) in the default database. Then the example enumerates all the **Recordset** objects in the current database and all the fields in each **Recordset** object and closes the new **Recordset**.

```
Function EnumerateRecordset () As Integer
    Dim dbsExample As Database, rstOrders As Recordset
    Dim rstTemp As Recordset
    Dim I As Integer, J As Integer
    Set dbsExample = _
        DBEngine.Workspaces(0).OpenDatabase("Northwind.mdb")
    Set rstOrders = dbsExample.OpenRecordset("Orders", dbOpenSnapshot)
    Debug.Print
    ' Enumerate all Recordset objects.
    For J = 0 To dbsExample.Recordsets.Count - 1
        Set rstTemp = dbsExample.Recordsets(J)
        Debug.Print
        Debug.Print "Enumeration of Recordset objects("; J; "): "; _
            rstTemp.Name
        Debug.Print
        ' Enumerate fields.
        Debug.Print "Fields: Name, Type, Value"
        For I = 0 To rstTemp.Fields.Count - 1
            Debug.Print "  "; rstTemp.Fields(I).Name;
            Debug.Print ", "; rstTemp.Fields(I).Type;
            If rstTemp.Fields(I).Type = dbText Then
                Debug.Print ", "; rstTemp.Fields(I).Value
            End if
        Next I
    Next J
    dbsExample.Close
    EnumerateRecordset = True
End Function
```

Example (Microsoft Access)	The following example opens a table-type **Recordset** object, a dynaset-type **Recordset** object, and a snapshot-type **Recordset** object. Then it displays the value of the **Updatable** property for the **Recordset** objects.

```
Sub NewRecordsets()
    Dim dbs As database, rst As Recordset
```

```
        Dim rstEmployees As Recordset, rstOrders As Recordset
        Dim rstProducts As Recordset, strSQL As String

        ' Return Database object pointing to current database.
        Set dbs = CurrentDb
        ' Create table-type Recordset object.
        Set rstEmployees = dbs.OpenRecordset("Employees", dbOpenTable)
        ' Construct SQL string.
        strSQL = "SELECT * FROM Orders WHERE OrderDate >= #1-1-95#;"
        ' Create dynaset-type Recordset object.
        Set rstOrders = dbs.OpenRecordset(strSQL, dbOpenDynaset)
        ' Create snapshot-type Recordset object.
        Set rstProducts = dbs.OpenRecordset("Products", dbOpenSnapshot)
        ' Print value of Updatable property for each Recordset object.
        For Each rst In dbs.Recordsets
            Debug.Print rst.Name; "   "; rst.Updatable
        Next rst
End Sub
```

Recordsets Collection

Description	The **Recordsets** collection contains all open **Recordset** objects in a **Database** object.
Remarks	When you use data access objects, you interact with data almost entirely using **Recordset** objects.
	A new **Recordset** object is automatically added to the **Recordsets** collection when you open the **Recordset** object, and is automatically removed when you close it.
	Your application can create as many Recordset object variables as needed. A Recordset object can refer to one or more tables, queries alone, or queries referenced by other Recordset objects in any combination. You can also have a Recordset object that refers to some or all of the fields or records in other Recordset objects.
Properties	**Count** Property.
Methods	**Refresh** Method.
See Also	Appendix, "Data Access Object Hierarchy."
Example	See the **Recordset** object example.
Example (Microsoft Access)	See the **Recordset** object example (Microsoft Access).

Refresh Method

Applies To	**Databases** Collection, **Documents** Collection, **Errors** Collection, **Fields** Collection, **Groups** Collection, **Indexes** Collection, **Parameters** Collection, **Properties** Collection, **QueryDefs** Collection, **Recordsets** Collection, **Relations** Collection, **TableDefs** Collection, **Users** Collection, **Workspaces** Collection.
Description	Updates the objects in a collection to reflect the current database's schema.
Syntax	*collection*.**Refresh**
Remarks	The **Refresh** method can't be used with collections that aren't persistent, such as **Databases**, **Recordsets**, or **Workspaces**.

> **Note** To determine the position that the Microsoft Jet database engine uses for **Field** objects in the **Fields** collection of a **QueryDef**, **Recordset**, or **TableDef** object, use the **OrdinalPosition** property of each **Field** object. The **Refresh** method may change the order of objects within the **Fields** collection, if the **OrdinalPosition** property of a **Field** object in the collection has been changed.

Use the **Refresh** method in multiuser environments in which other users may change the database. You may also need to use it on any collections that are indirectly affected by changes to the database. For example, if you change a **Users** collection, you may need to refresh a **Groups** collection before using the **Groups** collection.

> **Tip** A collection is filled with objects the first time it's referred to and won't automatically reflect subsequent changes made to it by other users. If it's likely that a collection has been changed by another user, use the **Refresh** method on the collection immediately before carrying out any task in your application that assumes the presence or absence of a particular object in the collection. This will ensure that the collection is as up-to-date as possible.

See Also	**Append** Method, **Close** Method, **Delete** Method, **OrdinalPosition** Property, **Requery** Method.
Example	This example refreshes the **Tables** collection in a database in a multiuser environment in case another user has made changes.

```
Dim wspDefault As Workspace, dbsNorthwind As Database
' Get default workspace.
Set wspDefault = DBEngine.Workspaces(0)
' Open database.
Set dbsNorthwind = wspDefault.OpenDatabase("Northwind.mdb")
...
```

```
                        ' Refresh possibly changed collection.
                        dbsNorthwind.Containers("Tables").Documents.Refresh
```

Example**(Microsoft Access)** The following example refreshes the **Indexes** collection of a **TableDef** object. In a database in a multiuser environment, you can use the **Refresh** method to show changes made by other users.

```
Sub RefreshIndex()
    Dim dbs As Database, tdf As TableDef
    Dim idx As Index, fld As Field

    ' Return Database variable pointing to current database.
    Set dbs = CurrentDb
    Set tdf = dbs.TableDefs!Employees
    tdf.Indexes.Refresh
    For Each idx In tdf.Indexes
        Debug.Print idx.Name; ":"
        For Each fld In idx.Fields
            Debug.Print "   "; fld.Name
        Next fld
    Next idx
End Sub
```

RefreshLink Method

Applies To **TableDef** Object.

Description Updates the connection information for an attached table.

Syntax *tabledef*.**RefreshLink**

The *tabledef* placeholder specifies the **TableDef** object representing the attached table whose connection information you want to update.

Remarks You change the connection information for an attached table by resetting the **Connect** property of the corresponding **TableDef** object and then using the **RefreshLink** method to update the information. When you use **RefreshLink**, the attached table's properties and **Relation** objects aren't changed.

To force this connection information to exist in all collections associated with the **TableDef** object that represents the attached table, you must also use the **Refresh** method on each collection.

See Also **Connect** Property, **Refresh** Method.

Example   This example attaches a Paradox table named PDX_Author to a database opened for exclusive use, moves the connection to a different directory, and then refreshes the connection information.

```
Dim dbsPublishers As Database, tdfPDX_Author As TableDef
' Open database.
Set dbsPublishers = DBEngine.Workspaces(0).OpenDatabase _
    ("C:\CONTACTS\Biblio.mdb")
Set tdfPDX_Author = dbsPublishers.CreateTableDef _
    ("PDX_Author", dbAttachExclusive)
tdfPDX_Author.SourceTableName = "Author"
tdfPDX_Author.Connect = "Paradox 3.x; " _
    & "DATABASE=C:\PDX\PUBS; PWD=books"
' Append to TableDefs collection.
dbsPublishers.TableDefs.Append tdfPDX_Author
' Move to new directory.
dbsPublishers.TableDefs!PDX_Author.Connect = "Paradox 3.x; " _
    & "DATABASE=N:\PDX\PUBS; PWD=books"
' Refresh connection information.
dbsPublishers.TableDefs!PDX_Author.RefreshLink
```

RegisterDatabase Method

Applies To   **DBEngine** Object.

Description   Enters connection information for an ODBC data source in the ODBC.INI file. The ODBC driver needs connection information when the Microsoft Jet database engine opens the data source during a session.

Syntax   **DBEngine.RegisterDatabase** *dbname*, *driver*, *silent*, *attributes*

The **RegisterDatabase** method syntax has these parts.

Part	Description
dbname	A string expression that is the name used in the **OpenDatabase** method that refers to a block of descriptive information about the data source. For example, if the data source is an ODBC remote database, it could be the name of the server.
driver	A string expression that is the name of the ODBC driver. This isn't the name of the ODBC driver DLL file. For example, SQL Server is a driver name, but SQLSRVR.dll is the name of a DLL file. You must have ODBC and the appropriate driver already installed.

Part	Description
silent	A numeric expression that is **True** if you don't want to display the ODBC driver dialog boxes that prompt for driver-specific information or **False** if you do want to display the ODBC driver dialog boxes. If *silent* is **True**, *attributes* must contain all the necessary driver-specific information or the dialog boxes are displayed anyway.
attributes	A string expression that is a list of keywords to be added to the ODBC.INI file. The keywords are in a carriage-return–delimited string.

Remarks

If the database is already registered (connection information is already entered) in the ODBC.INI file when you use the **RegisterDatabase** method, the connection information is updated.

In 32-bit installations, most of the ODBC registration information is maintained in the Windows registration database and not in the ODBC.INI file.

If the **RegisterDatabase** method fails for any reason, no changes are made to the ODBC.INI file, and an error occurs.

For more information about ODBC drivers such as SQL Server, see the Help file provided with the driver.

You are encouraged to use the Windows Control Panel ODBC setup icon to add new data sources, or to make changes to existing entries. However, if you choose to use the **RegisterDatabase** method, you are encouraged to set the *silent* option to **True**.

See Also

Database Object, **OpenDatabase** Method.

Example

This example registers a SQL Server data source named PtLudlow and then opens the database MySQLDb on that server.

Using the Windows ODBC control panel icon is the preferred way to create, modify, or delete data source names.

```
Dim dbsLudlow As Database
Dim strAttribs As String
' Build keywords string.
strAttribs = "Description=SQL Server on server PtLudlow" & _
    Chr$(13) & "OemToAnsi=No" & Chr$(13) & "Network=DBNMP3" & _
    Chr$(13) & "Address=\\PTLUDLOW\PIPE\SQL\QUERY" & Chr$(13) & _
    "Database=MySQLDb"
' Update ODBC.INI.
DBEngine.RegisterDatabase "PtLudlow", "SQL Server 32", True, strAttribs
' Open the database.
Set dbsLudlow = DBEngine.Workspaces(0).OpenDatabase("PtLudlow", _
    False, False, "ODBC;")
```

Relation Object

Description A **Relation** object represents a relationship between fields in tables or queries.

Remarks You can use the **Relation** object to create new relationships and examine existing relationships in your database. By setting the **Attributes** property, you can also use the Microsoft Jet database engine to enforce referential integrity.

Any changes you make to the database that violate the relationships established for the database result in a trappable error. If you request cascade update or cascade delete operations, the Jet database engine also modifies the primary or foreign key tables to enforce the relationships you establish.

An example of a typical relationship can be found between the NameAddress table and the ValidStateCodes table. The State field of the NameAddress table is the primary key, and the State field of the ValidStateCodes table is the foreign key. For a new record to be accepted in the NameAddress table, the Jet database engine searches the ValidStateCodes table for a match on the State field of the NameAddress table. If no match is found, the Jet database engine doesn't accept the new record, and a trappable error occurs.

Using a **Relation** object and its properties, you can:

- Specify an enforced relationship between fields in base tables (but not a relationship that involves a query or an attached table).
- Establish unenforced relationships between any type of table or query—native or attached.
- Use the **Name** property to refer to the relationship between the fields in the referenced primary table and the referencing foreign table.
- Use the **Attributes** property to determine whether the relationship between fields in the table is one-to-one or one-to-many and how to enforce referential integrity.
- Use the **Attributes** property to determine whether the Jet database engine can perform cascade update and cascade delete operations on primary and foreign tables.
- Use the **Attributes** property to determine whether the relationship between fields in the table is left join or right join.

- The **Name** property settings of all **Field** objects in the **Fields** collection of a **Relation** object represent the names of the fields in the primary key of the referenced table. The **ForeignName** property settings of the **Field** objects represent the names of the fields in the foreign key of the referencing table.
- When you enforce referential integrity, a unique index must already exist for the key field of the referenced table. The Jet database engine automatically creates an index with the **Foreign** property set to act as the foreign key in the referencing table.

To create a new **Relation** object, use the **CreateRelation** method.

Properties   **Attributes** Property, **ForeignTable** Property, **Name** Property, **Table** Property.

Methods   **CreateField** Method.

See Also   **CreateRelation** Method; **Foreign** Property; Appendix, "Data Access Object Hierarchy."

Example   This example creates a one-to-many relationship between single fields in two tables. Because referential integrity is enforced for the relationship, an index is created for the primary table.

```
Function EnumerateRelation () As Integer
    Dim dbsExample As Database
    Dim tdfReferenced As TableDef, tdfReferencing As TableDef
    Dim fldPrimeKey As Field, idxUnique As Index, relEnforced As _
        Relation
    Dim I As Integer
    ' Get database.
    Set dbsExample = _
        DBEngine.Workspaces(0).OpenDatabase("Northwind.mdb")
    ' Create referenced table with primary key.
    Set tdfReferenced = dbsExample.CreateTableDef("Referenced")
    Set fldPrimeKey = tdfReferenced.CreateField("PrimaryKey", dbLong)
    tdfReferenced.Fields.Append fldPrimeKey
    ' Create unique index for enforced referential integrity.
    Set idxUnique = tdfReferenced.CreateIndex("UniqueIndex")
    idxUnique.Primary = True    ' No Null values allowed.

    Set fldPrimeKey = tdfReferenced.CreateField("PrimaryKey")
    idxUnique.Fields.Append fldPrimeKey
    tdfReferenced.Indexes.Append idxUnique
    dbsExample.TableDefs.Append tdfReferenced
```

234   Relation Object

```
    ' Create referencing table with foreign key.
    Set tdfReferencing = dbsExample.CreateTableDef("Referencing")
    Set fldPrimeKey = tdfReferencing.CreateField("ForeignKey", dbLong)
    tdfReferencing.Fields.Append fldPrimeKey
    dbsExample.TableDefs.Append tdfReferencing
    ' Create one-to-many relationship and enforce referential integrity.
    Set relEnforced = dbsExample.CreateRelation("EnforcedOneToMany")
    relEnforced.Table = "Referenced"
    relEnforced.ForeignTable = "Referencing"
    ' Don't set either dbRelationUnique or dbRelationDontEnforce.
    relEnforced.Attributes = 0
    Set fldPrimeKey = relEnforced.CreateField("PrimaryKey")
    fldPrimeKey.ForeignName = "ForeignKey"
    relEnforced.Fields.Append fldPrimeKey
    dbsExample.Relations.Append relEnforced
    ' Enumerate relation and its fields.
    Debug.Print "Relation: "; relEnforced.Name
    Debug.Print "  Primary Table: "; relEnforced.Table
    Debug.Print "  Foreign Table: "; relEnforced.ForeignTable
    Debug.Print "  Attributes: "; relEnforced.Attributes
    Debug.Print "Fields in Relation: Primary, Foreign";
    For I = 0 To relEnforced.Fields.Count - 1
        Set fldPrimeKey = relEnforced.Fields(I)
        Debug.Print "  "; fldPrimeKey.Name;
        Debug.Print ", "; fldPrimeKey.ForeignName
    Next I
    Debug.Print
    dbsExample.Relations.Delete "EnforcedOneToMany"
    dbsExample.TableDefs.Delete "Referenced"
    dbsExample.TableDefs.Delete "Referencing"
    EnumerateRelation = True
End Function
```

**Example
(Microsoft Access)**

The following example creates a new **Relation** object representing the relationship between an Employees table and an Orders table.

To test the following example in Microsoft Access, open the Northwind sample database and choose Relationships from the Tools menu. Delete the relationship between the Employees table and the Orders table, and close the Relationships window. Then, run the following function from a standard module, and view the Relationships window again to see the new relationship.

```
Sub NewRelation()
    Dim dbs As Database
    Dim fld As Field, rel As Relation

    ' Return Database variable that points to current database.
    Set dbs = CurrentDb
```

```
        ' Create new relationship and set its properties.
        Set rel = dbs.CreateRelation("EmployeesRelation", "Employees", _
            "Orders")
        ' Set Relation object attributes to enforce referential integrity.
        rel.Attributes = dbRelationDeleteCascade + dbRelationUpdateCascade
        ' Create field in Fields collection of Relation.
        Set fld = rel.CreateField("EmployeeID")
        ' Provide name of foreign key field.
        fld.ForeignName = "EmployeeID"
        ' Append field to Relation and Relation to database.
        rel.Fields.Append fld
        dbs.Relations.Append rel
End Sub
```

Relations Collection

Description	A **Relations** collection contains stored **Relation** objects of a **Database** object.
Remarks	You can use the **Relation** object to create new relationships and examine existing relationships in your database. You can add a **Relation** object to the **Relations** collection using the **Append** method so it will be saved when you close the **Database** object. To remove a **Relation** object from the collection, use the **Delete** method.
Properties	**Count** Property.
Methods	**Append** Method, **Delete** Method, **Refresh** Method.
See Also	Appendix, "Data Access Object Hierarchy."
Example	See the **Relation** object example.
Example (Microsoft Access)	See the **Relation** object example (Microsoft Access).

RepairDatabase Method

Applies To	**DBEngine** Object.
Description	Attempts to repair a corrupted database that accesses the Microsoft Jet database engine.

RepairDatabase Method

Syntax

DBEngine.RepairDatabase *dbname*

The *dbname* placeholder represents a string expression that is the path and filename for an existing Jet engine database file. If you omit the path, only the current directory is searched. If your system supports the uniform naming convention (UNC), you can also specify a network path, such as: "\\MYSERVER\MYSHARE\MYDIR\MYDB.mdb".

Remarks

You must close the database specified by *dbname* before you repair it. In a multiuser environment, other users can't have *dbname* open while you're repairing it. If *dbname* isn't closed or isn't available for exclusive use, an error occurs.

This method attempts to repair a database that was marked as possibly corrupt by an incomplete write operation. This can occur if an application using the Jet database engine is closed unexpectedly because of a power outage or computer hardware problem. The database won't be marked as possibly corrupt if you use the **Close** method or if you quit your application in a usual way.

The **RepairDatabase** method also attempts to validate all system tables and all indexes. Any data that can't be repaired is discarded. If the database can't be repaired, a trappable error occurs.

When you attempt to open or compact a corrupted database, a trappable error usually occurs. In some situations, however, a corrupted database may not be detected, and no error occurs. It's a good idea to provide your users with a way to use the **RepairDatabase** method in your application if their database behaves unpredictably.

Some types of databases can become corrupted if a user ends an application without closing **Database** or **Recordset** objects and the Jet database engine; Microsoft Windows or MS-DOS® doesn't have a chance to flush data caches. To avoid corrupt databases, establish procedures for closing applications and shutting down systems that ensure that all cached pages are saved to the database. In some cases, power supplies that can't be interrupted may be necessary to prevent accidental data loss during power fluctuations.

Tip After repairing a database, it's also a good idea to compact it using the **CompactDatabase** method to defragment the file and to recover disk space.

See Also

Close Method, **CompactDatabase** Method, **Database** Object.

Example

This example attempts to repair a database named Northwind.mdb.

```
DBEngine.RepairDatabase "C:\Northwind.mdb"
```

Replicable Property

Applies To **Database** Object, **QueryDef** Object, **TableDef** Object.

Description Sets or returns a value that determines whether a database or object in a database can be replicated.

- On a **Database** object, this property adds fields, tables, and properties to a database.
- On a **TableDef** or **QueryDef** object, or table, query, form, report, macro, or module in a database, this property changes the object from local to replicable.

Setting and Return Values
- On a **Database** object, setting this property to the text string "T" makes the database replicable. Once the property is set to "T", it cannot be changed; setting the property to "F" (or any value other than "T") returns an error message.
- On an object in a database, setting this property to the text string "T" makes the object (and subsequent changes to the object) available at all replicas in the replica set. You can also set this property in the object's property sheet in Microsoft Access.

Remarks When you create a new table, query, form, report, macro, or module at a replica, the object is considered "local" and is stored only at that replica. If you want users at other replicas to be able to use the object, you must change it from local to replicable. Either create the object at, or import it into, the Design Master and then set the **Replicable** property to "T".

The object on which you are setting the **Replicable** property might have already inherited that property from another object. However, the value set by the other object has no affect on the behavior of the object you want to make replicable. You must directly set the property for each object.

See Also **KeepLocal** Property, **MakeReplica** Method.

ReplicaID Property

Applies To **Database** Object.

Description Returns a 16-byte, OLE 2 **GUID** that provides each database replica with a unique identification.

Setting and Return Values This property is read-only and the value is created by the Microsoft Jet database engine.

Remarks In addition to providing a unique identifier for each database replica, the **ReplicaID** property is used to identify the Design Master for the replica set. The **ReplicaID** property of the Design Master is stored in the MSysReplicas system table. Setting the **DesignMasterID** property gives a specific replica in the replica set design-master status. The **DesignMasterID** property can be set only if you are at the current Design Master. Under extreme circumstances, for example, the loss of the original Design Master, you can set the value at another replica. However, setting this value at a replica, when there is already another Design Master, might partition your replica set into two irreconcilable sets and prevent any further synchronization of data.

See Also **DesignMasterID** Property.

Requery Method

Applies To Dynaset-Type **Recordset** Object, **Recordset** Object, Snapshot-Type **Recordset** Object.

Description Updates the data in a **Recordset** object by re-executing the query on which the object is based.

Syntax *object*.**Requery** [**NewQuerydef**]

The **Requery** method syntax has the following parts.

Part	Description
object	The name of an existing table-type **Recordset** object that has a defined index as specified by the **Recordset** object's **Index** property.
NewQuerydef	A **Querydef** object, which is an optional parameter.

Remarks Use this method to make sure that a **Recordset** contains the most recent data. This method re-populates the current **Recordset** by either using the currrent query parameters or the new ones supplied by the **NewQuerydef** argument.

- If the original **Querydef** is supplied, then the **Recordset** is requeried using the parameters specified by the **Querydef** (for example, *myquerydef.OpenRecordset()*).

- If a **Querydef** was not used to create the recordset, or if a different **Querydef** is specified than what was originally used to create the **Recordset**, then the **Recordset** is essentially re-created from scratch.

When you use **Requery**, all changes made to the data in the underlying table by other users are displayed in the **Recordset**, and the first record in the **Recordset** becomes the current record.

You can't use the **Requery** method on dynaset- or snapshot-type **Recordset** objects whose **Restartable** property is set to **False**, nor can you use it on a table-type **Recordset**. However, if you supply the optional **NewQueryDef** argument, the **Restartable** property is ignored.

If both the **BOF** and **EOF** property settings of the **Recordset** object are **True** after you use the **Requery** method, the query didn't return any records and the **Recordset** will contain no data.

See Also   **BOF, EOF** Properties; **QueryDef** Object, **Requery** Method.

Example   This example determines the **Restartable** property setting of a dynaset-type **Recordset** and then uses the **Requery** method on the **Recordset**.

```
Dim dbsNorthwind As Database, rstChangeOften As Recordset
Set dbsNorthwind = DBEngine.Workspaces(0).OpenDatabase("Northwind.mdb")
Set rstChangeOften = dbsNorthwind.OpenRecordset _
    ("Table That Changes Often", dbOpenDynaset)
If rstChangeOften.Restartable = True Then
    rstChangeOften.Requery
End If
dbsNorthwind.Close
```

Example (Microsoft Access)   The following example checks the **Restartable** property setting of a dynaset-type **Recordset** object and then uses the **Requery** method on the **Recordset** object.

```
Sub RequerySource()
    Dim dbs As Database, rstOrders As Recordset

    ' Return Database variable that points to current database.
    Set dbs = CurrentDb
    Set rstOrders = dbs.OpenRecordset("Orders", dbOpenDynaset)
    If rstOrders.Restartable = True Then
        rstOrders.Requery
    Else
        rstOrders.Close
    End If
End Sub
```

Required Property

Applies To **Field** Object, **Index** Object.

Description Sets or returns a value that indicates whether a **Field** object requires a non-**Null** value or whether all the fields in an **Index** object must be filled in. For an object not yet appended to a collection, this property is read/write. For an **Index** object, this property setting is read-only for objects appended to **Indexes** collections in **Recordset** and **TableDef** objects.

Settings and Return Values The setting or return value is a Boolean expression indicating whether an object requires a non-**Null** value. True indicates that a **Null** value is not allowed.

Remarks For a **Field** object, use of the **Required** property depends on its parent object, as shown in the following table.

Parent Object	Usage
Index	Not supported
QueryDef	Read-only
Recordset	Read-only
Relation	Not supported
TableDef	Read/write

For a **Field** object, you can use the **Required** property along with the **AllowZeroLength**, **ValidateOnSet**, or **ValidationRule** property to determine the validity of the **Value** property setting for that **Field** object. If the **Required** property is set to **False** (0), the field can contain **Null** values as well as values that meet the conditions specified by the **AllowZeroLength** and **ValidationRule** property settings.

Tip When you can set this property for either an **Index** object or a **Field** object, set it for the **Field** object. The validity of the property setting for a **Field** object is checked before that of an **Index** object.

See Also **AllowZeroLength** Property, **QueryDef** Object, **Required** Property, **ValidateOnSet** Property, **ValidationRule** Property, **ValidationText** Property, **Value** Property.

Example (Microsoft Access) The following example creates a new **Index** object on an Employees table and sets the **Required** property for the index. The new index consists of two fields, LastName and FirstName.

```
Sub NewIndex()
    Dim dbs As Database, tdf As TableDef, idx As Index
    Dim fldLastName As Field, fldFirstName As Field, rst As Recordset
```

```
        ' Return Database variable that points to current database.
        Set dbs = CurrentDb
        Set tdf = dbs.TableDefs!Employees
        ' Return Index object that points to new index.
        Set idx = tdf.CreateIndex("FullName")
        ' Create and append index fields.
        Set fldLastName = idx.CreateField("LastName", dbText)
        Set fldFirstName = idx.CreateField("FirstName", dbText)
        idx.Fields.Append fldLastName
        idx.Fields.Append fldFirstName
        ' Ensure value is entered for each field in the index.
        idx.Required = True
        ' Append Index object.
        tdf.Indexes.Append idx
End Sub
```

Restartable Property

Applies To	Dynaset-Type **Recordset** Object, **Recordset** Object, Snapshot-Type **Recordset** Object, Table-Type **Recordset** Object.
Description	Returns a value that indicates whether a **Recordset** object supports the **Requery** method, which re-executes the query on which the **Recordset** object is based.
Return Values	The possible return values are:

Value	Description
True	The **Recordset** object supports the **Requery** method.
False	The **Recordset** object doesn't support the **Requery** method. Table-type **Recordset** objects always return **False** (0).

Remarks	Check the **Restartable** property before using the **Requery** method on a **Recordset** object. If the object's **Restartable** property is set to **False**, use the **OpenRecordset** method on the underlying **QueryDef** object to re-execute the query. You can use the **Requery** method to update a **Recordset** object's underlying parameter query after the parameter values have been changed.
See Also	**OpenRecordset** Method, **QueryDef** Object, **Requery** Method.
Example	See the **Requery** property example.
Example (Microsoft Access)	See the **Requery** property example (Microsoft Access).

RetunsRecords Property

Applies To **QueryDef** Object.

Description Sets or returns a value that indicates whether an SQL pass through query to an external database returns records.

Settings and Return Values A Boolean expression that indicates whether records are returned. The data type is Boolean. **True** (-1) (the default) indicates that a pass-through query returns records.

Remarks Not all SQL pass-through queries to external databases return records. For example, an SQL UPDATE statement updates records without returning records, while an SQL SELECT statement does return records. If the query returns records, set the **ReturnsRecords** property to **True**; if the query doesn't return records, set the **ReturnsRecords** property to **False** (0).

Note The **Connect** property must be set before the **ReturnsRecords** property is set.

See Also **Connect** Property, **QueryTimeout** Property, **SQL** Property.

Example The following example creates an SQL pass-through query that returns records from an external database.

```
Dim dbsNorthwind As Database, qdfPassThrough As QueryDef
Set dbsNorthwind = DBEngine.Workspaces(0).OpenDatabase("Northwind.mdb")
Set qdfPassThrough = dbsNorthwind.CreateQueryDef("October " & _
    "Orders","SELECT * From Orders WHERE ShipCity = 'London'")
dbsNorthwind.Connect = "ODBC; DSN=MySQLDBDSN; " _
    & " UID=Chrissy;PWD=FourOh;"
qdfPassThrough.ReturnsRecords = True
```

Example (Microsoft Access) The following example creates an SQL pass-through query that returns records from an external database.

```
Sub CreatePassThrough()
    Dim dbs As Database, qdfPassThrough As QueryDef

    ' Return Database variable that points to current database.
    Set dbs = CurrentDb
    Set qdfPassThrough = dbs.CreateQueryDef("OctoberOrders", _
        "SELECT * From Orders WHERE ShipCity = 'London'")
    dbs.Connect = "ODBC; DSN=MySQLDBDSN; " _
        & " UID=Chrissy;PWD=FourOh;"
    qdfPassThrough.ReturnsRecords = True
End Sub
```

Rollback Method

See BeginTrans, CommitTrans, Rollback Methods.

Seek Method

Applies To **Recordset** Object, Table-Type **Recordset** Object.

Description Locates the record in an indexed table-type **Recordset** object that satisfies the specified criteria for the current index and makes that record the current record.

Syntax *table***.Seek** *comparison*, *key1*, *key2*...

The **Seek** method syntax has the following parts.

Part	Description
table	The name of an existing table-type **Recordset** object that has a defined index as specified by the **Recordset** object's **Index** property.
comparison	One of the following string expressions: <, <=, =, >=, or >.
key1, *key2*...	One or more values corresponding to fields in the **Recordset** object's current index, as specified by its **Index** property setting.

Remarks You must set the current index with the **Index** property before you use **Seek**. If the index identifies a nonunique key field, **Seek** locates the first record that satisfies the criteria.

Caution If you edit the current record, be sure you save the changes using the **Update** method before you move to another record. If you move to another record without using **Update**, your changes are lost without warning.

The **Seek** method searches through the specified key fields and locates the first record that satisfies the criteria specified by *comparison* and *key1*. Once found, it makes that record current and the **NoMatch** property is set to **False**. If the **Seek** method fails to locate a match, the **NoMatch** property is set to **True**, and the current record is undefined.

If *comparison* is equal (=), greater than or equal (>=), or greater than (>), **Seek** starts at the beginning of the index. If *comparison* is greater than (<) or greater than or equal (<=), **Seek** starts at the end of the index and searches backward unless there are duplicate index entries at the end. In this case, **Seek** starts at an arbitrary entry among the duplicate index entries at the end of the index.

You must specify values for all fields defined in the index. If you use **Seek** with a multi-column index, and you don't specify a comparison value for every field in the index, then you cannot use the equal (=) operator in the comparison. That's because some of the criteria fields (key2, key3, and so on) will default to NULL, which will probably not match. Therefore, the equal operator will work correctly only if you have a record which is all NULL except the key you're looking for. It's recommended that you use the greater than or equal operator instead.

The *key1* argument must be of the same field data type as the corresponding field in the current index. For example, if the current index refers to a number field (such as Employee ID), *key1* must be numeric. Similarly, if the current index refers to a Text field (such as Last Name), *key1* must be a string.

There doesn't have to be a current record when you use **Seek**.

You can use the **Indexes** collection to enumerate the existing indexes.

Notes

- Always check the value of the **NoMatch** property setting to determine whether the **Seek** method has succeeded. If it fails, **NoMatch** is set to **True** and the current record is undefined.
- To locate a record in a dynaset- or snapshot-type **Recordset** that satisfies a specific condition, use the **Find** methods. To include all records, not just those that satisfy a specific condition, use the **Move** methods to move from record to record.

You can't use the **Seek** method on an attached table of any type because attached tables must be opened as dynaset- or snapshot-type **Recordset** objects, which don't support the **Seek** method. However, if you use the **OpenDatabase** method to directly open an installable ISAM database, you can use **Seek** on tables in that database.

See Also **AbsolutePosition** Property; **BOF**, **EOF** Properties; **FindFirst**, **FindLast**, **FindNext**, **FindPrevious** Methods; **Index** Object; **Index** Property; **Move** Method; **MoveFirst**, **MoveLast**, **MoveNext**, **MovePrevious** Methods; **NoMatch** Property; **OpenDatabase** Method.

Example This example uses **Seek** to locate the first record in the Publishers table where the PubID field is 3, using the existing primary key index.

```
Dim dbsBiblio As Database, rstPublishers As Recordset
' Open a database.
Set dbsBiblio = DBEngine.Workspaces(0).OpenDatabase("Biblio.mdb")
' Open a table.
Set rstPublishers = dbsBiblio.OpenRecordset("Publishers")
rstPublishers.Index = "PrimaryKey"    ' Define current index.
rstPublishers.Seek "=", 3             ' Seek record.
```

Seek Method 245

```
If rstPublishers.NoMatch Then...
```

This example uses the **OpenDatabase** method to directly open an installable ISAM database and then uses **Seek** to locate a record in a table in that database.

```
Dim dbsFoxData as Database, rstParts as Recordset
Dim varSaveHere as Variant
Set dbsFoxData = OpenDatabase("C:\FoxData", False, False,"Fox 2.5")
Set rstParts = dbsFoxData.OpenRecordset("PARTS.dbf", dbOpenTable)
' Choose record order and Seek index.
rstParts.Index = "PartNameIndex"
varSaveHere = rstParts.BookMark       ' Save current location.
' Search for first instance of a chosen part.
rstParts.Seek "=", "Framis Lever"
If rstParts.NoMatch then              ' Test for success.
    rstParts.BookMark = varSaveHere   ' Seek not successful.
    ...
Else                                  ' Seek worked; use current record.
    Debug.Print rstParts!PartName
End If
```

Example (Microsoft Access)

The following example creates a new **Index** object on an Employees table. The new index consists of two fields, LastName and FirstName. The procedure then uses the **Seek** method to find a specified record.

```
Sub NewIndex()
    Dim dbs As Database, tdf As TableDef, idx As Index
    Dim fldLastName As Field, fldFirstName As Field, rst As Recordset

    ' Return Database variable pointing to current database.
    Set dbs = CurrentDb
    Set tdf = dbs.TableDefs!Employees
    ' Return Index object that points to new index.
    Set idx = tdf.CreateIndex("FullName")
    ' Create and append index fields.
    Set fldLastName = idx.CreateField("LastName", dbText)
    Set fldFirstName = idx.CreateField("FirstName", dbText)
    idx.Fields.Append fldLastName
    idx.Fields.Append fldFirstName
    ' Append Index object.
    tdf.Indexes.Append idx
    ' Open table-type Recordset object.
    Set rst = dbs.OpenRecordset("Employees")
    ' Set current index to new index.
    rst.Index = idx.Name
    ' Specify record to find.
    rst.Seek "=", "Fuller", "Andrew"
    If rst.NoMatch Then
        Debug.Print "Seek unsuccessful!"
    Else
```

**Example
(Microsoft Excel)**

This example opens PRODUCT.DBF (a dBASE IV table located in the \Program Files\Common Files\Microsoft Shared\MSquery folder), locates a record, and then copies the values into cells B2:C2 on Sheet1. (On Windows NT™, PRODUCT.DBF is located in the WINDOWS\MSAPPS\MSQUERY folder.)

```
Const sourceDir = "C:\Program Files\Common Files\Microsoft Shared\" _
    & "MSquery"
Dim db As Database, rs As Recordset
Sheets("Sheet1").Activate
Set db = OpenDatabase(sourceDir, False, False, "dBASE IV")
Set rs = db.OpenRecordset("PRODUCT.DBF", dbOpenTable)
rs.Index = "PRODUCT"
rs.Seek "=", "1"
If rs.NoMatch Then
    MsgBox "Couldn't find any records"
Else
    ActiveSheet.Cells(2, 2) = rs.Fields("CATEGORY").Value
    ActiveSheet.Cells(3, 2) = rs.Fields("PROD_NAME").Value
End If
rs.Close
db.Close
```

Size Property

Applies To **Field** Object.

Description Returns a value that indicates the maximum size, in bytes, of a **Field** object. For Text fields, you can also use it to set the maximum size of data that the **Field** object can hold. For an object not yet appended to the **Fields** collection, this property is read/write.

Settings and Return Values The setting or return value indicates the maximum size of a **Field** object. The data type is **Long**. The setting depends on the **Type** property setting of the **Field** object and can be one of these integer values.

Type	Size	Description
dbBoolean	1	Boolean
dbByte	1	Byte

Size Property 247

Type	Size	Description
dbInteger	2	Integer
dbLong	4	Long
dbCurrency	8	Currency
dbSingle	4	Single
dbDouble	8	Double
dbDate	8	Date/Time
dbText	1–255	Text
dbLongBinary	0	Long Binary (OLE Object)
dbMemo	0	Memo
dbGUID	16	GUID

Remarks

These constants are listed in the Data Access (DAO) object library in the Object Browser.

Use of the **Size** property depends on the object that contains the **Fields** collection that the **Field** object is appended to, as shown in the following table.

Object appended to	Usage
Index	Not supported
QueryDef	Read-only
Recordset	Read-only
Relation	Not supported
TableDef	Read-only

When you create a **Field** object with a data type other than Text, the **Type** property setting automatically determines the **Size** property setting, and you don't need to set the **Size** property. For a **Field** object with the Text data type, however, **Size** can be set to any integer up to the maximum text size (for Microsoft Jet databases that maximum is 255). If you do not set the size, the field will be as large as the database allows.

For OLE Object and Memo **Field** objects, **Size** is always set to 0. Use the **FieldSize** method of the **Field** object to determine the size of the data in a specific record. The maximum size of an OLE Object or Memo field is limited only by your system resources or the maximum size that the database allows.

See Also

Attributes Property, **Index** Object, **QueryDef** Object, **Type** Property.

Specifics (Microsoft Access)

The **Size** property is equivalent to the **FieldSize** property in table Design view. You can't set the **FieldSize** property in Visual Basic; you must use the **Size** property instead.

In Microsoft Access, the Memo data type field can contain up to 1.2 gigabytes of information. However, Microsoft Access only displays the first 32K of data in a control on a form or report.

Example

This example creates a new **Field** object with a Text field type, sets its **Name** property to Fax Phone and its **Size** property to 20, and appends the new object to the **Fields** collection of the Employees table in the **TableDefs** collection of the database.

```
Function SizeType() As Integer
    Dim dbsNorthwind As Database
    Dim fldFaxPhone As Field, tdfEmployees As TableDef
    ' Open database.
    Set dbsNorthwind = _
        DBEngine.Workspaces(0).OpenDatabase("Northwind.mdb")
    ' Get existing table reference.
    Set tdfEmployees = dbsNorthwind.TableDefs("Employees")
    ' Create Field object.
    Set fldFaxPhone = tdfEmployees.CreateField("Fax Phone")
    ' Set field properties.
    fldFaxPhone.Type = dbText
    fldFaxPhone.Size = 20
    ' Append fldFaxPhone to Fields collection.
    tdfEmployees.Fields.Append fldFaxPhone
    SizeType = True
End Function
```

You can also use the **CreateField** method if you provide *name, type,* and *size* as arguments.

```
Set fldFaxPhone = tdfEmployees.CreateField("Fax Phone", dbText, 20)
```

Example (Microsoft Access)

The following example creates a new **Field** object and sets its **Size** and **Type** properties. The procedure then appends the new object to the **Fields** collection of the Employees table in the **TableDefs** collection of the database.

```
Sub NewField()
    Dim dbs As Database, tdf As TableDef
    Dim fld As Field

    ' Return Database object that points to current database.
    Set dbs = CurrentDb
    ' Return TableDef variable pointing to Employees table.
    Set tdf = dbs.TableDefs!Employees
    ' Create Field object.
    Set fld = tdf.CreateField("DaysOfVacation")
    ' Set field properties.
    fld.Type = dbText
    fld.Size = 20
```

Size Property 249

```
' Append fld to Fields collection.
tdf.Fields.Append fld
End Sub
```

You can also use the **CreateField** method to set the **Name**, **Type**, and **Size** properties if you provide *name, type,* and *size* as arguments.

```
Set fld = tdfEmployees.CreateField("DaysOfVacation", dbText, 20)
```

Example (Microsoft Excel)

This example copies onto Sheet1 all fields of the **Double** type from ORDDTAIL.DBF, a dBASE IV table located in the C:\Program Files\Common Files\Microsoft Shared\MSquery folder. (On Windows NT, ORDDTAIL.DBF is located in the \WINDOWS\MSAPPS\MSQUERY folder.)

```
Const sourceDir = "C:\Program Files\Common Files\Microsoft Shared\" _
    & "MSquery"
Dim db As Database, recordsToCopy As Recordset, tDef As Recordset
Dim fieldsToStore(1000), fileName As String
fileName = "ORDDTAIL.DBF"
Set db = Workspaces(0).OpenDatabase(sourceDir, _
    False, False, "dBASE IV")
Set tDef = db.OpenRecordset(fileName)
n = 0
Sheets("Sheet1").Activate
For i = 0 To tDef.Fields.Count - 1
    If tDef.Fields(i).Type = dbDouble Then
        fieldsToStore(n) = tDef.fields(i).Name
        n = n + 1
    End If
Next
If fieldsToStore(0) = "" Then
    MsgBox "There are no number fields in this table."
    Exit Sub
End If
For i = 0 To n - 1
    records = "SELECT " & "[" & fieldsToStore(i) & "]" _
        & " from " & db.Recordsets(fileName).Name & ";"
    Set recordsToCopy = db.OpenRecordset(records)
    With ActiveSheet.Cells(1, i + 1)
        .CopyFromRecordset recordsToCopy
        .ColumnWidth = recordsToCopy.fields(0).Size
    End With
Next
recordsToCopy.Close
tDef.Close
db.Close
```

Snapshot-Type Recordset Object

Description   A snapshot-type **Recordset** object is a static set of records that you can use to examine data in an underlying table or tables. A snapshot-type **Recordset** object can contain fields from one or more tables in a database but can't be updated.

Remarks   When you create a snapshot-type **Recordset** object, data values for all fields (except Memo and OLE Object field data types in .mdb files) are brought into memory. Once loaded, changes made to base table data aren't reflected in the snapshot-type **Recordset** object data. To reload the snapshot-type **Recordset** object with current data, use the **Requery** method, or re-execute the **OpenRecordset** method.

The order of snapshot-type **Recordset** object data doesn't necessarily follow any specific sequence. To order your data, use an SQL statement with an ORDER BY clause to create the **Recordset** object. You can also use this technique to filter the records so that only certain records are added to the **Recordset** object. For example, the following code selects only titles whose name contains the string "VBSQL" and sorts the resulting records by ISBN:

```
Dim dbsBiblio As Database, rstTitles As Recordset
Dim strSelect As String
Set dbsBiblio = Workspaces(0).OpenDatabase("Biblio.mdb")
strSelect = "SELECT * FROM Titles WHERE Title like '*VBSQL*' " & _
    "ORDER BY ISBN;"
Set rstTitles = dbsBiblio.OpenRecordset(strSelect,dbOpenSnapshot)
```

Using this technique instead of using the **Filter** or **Sort** properties or testing each record individually generally results in faster access to your data.

To create a snapshot-type **Recordset** object, use the **OpenRecordset** method on an open database, on another dynaset- or snapshot-type **Recordset** object, or on a **QueryDef** object.

Snapshot-type **Recordset** objects are generally faster to create and access than dynaset-type **Recordset** objects because their records are either in memory or stored in TEMP disk space, and the Microsoft Jet database engine doesn't need to lock pages or handle multiuser issues. However, snapshot-type **Recordset** objects use more resources than dynaset-type **Recordset** objects because the entire record is downloaded to local memory.

Properties   **AbsolutePosition** Property; **BOF**, **EOF** Properties; **Bookmark** Property; **Bookmarkable** Property; **Filter** Property; **Name** Property; **NoMatch** Property; **PercentPosition** Property; **RecordCount** Property; **Restartable** Property; **Sort** Property; **Transactions** Property; **Type** Property; **Updatable** Property; **ValidationRule** Property; **ValidationText** Property.

Snapshot-Type Recordset Object

Methods Clone Method; Close Method; CopyQueryDef Method; FindFirst, FindLast, FindNext, FindPrevious Methods; GetRows Method; Move Method; MoveFirst, MoveLast, MoveNext, MovePrevious Methods; OpenRecordset Method; Requery Method.

See Also OpenRecordset Method, Recordset Object; Appendix, "Data Access Object Hierarchy."

Example This example creates a new snapshot-type **Recordset** object and opens it, appending it to the **Recordsets** collection in the default database. It then finds a record and prints it.

```
Function ShowVBSQL () As Integer
    Dim dbsPublish As Database, rstTitles As Recordset
    Dim I As Integer, J As Integer
    Set dbsPublish = DBEngine.Workspaces(0).OpenDatabase("Biblio.mdb")
    Set rstTitles = dbsPublish.OpenRecordset("Titles", dbOpenSnapshot)
    If rstTitles.RecordCount > 0 Then
        rstTitles.FindFirst "Title Like '*VBSQL*'"   ' Any title on VBSQL
            Do until rstTitles.NoMatch = True
                Debug.Print rstTitles!Title
                rstTitles.FindNext "Title Like '*VBSQL*'"
            Loop
    Else
        Debug.Print "No such title"
    End If
    dbsPublish.Close
    ShowVBSQL = True
End Function
```

Example (Microsoft Access) The following example creates a snapshot-type **Recordset** object from an SQL statement, then prints the value of the **Updatable** property for the **Recordset** object. Since snapshot-type **Recordset** objects are never updatable, the value of this property will always be **False** (0).

```
Sub LongTermEmployees()
    Dim dbs As Database, qdf As QueryDef, rst As Recordset
    Dim strSQL As String

    ' Return Database object pointing to current database.
    Set dbs = CurrentDb
    strSQL = "SELECT * FROM Employees WHERE HireDate <= #1-1-95#;"
    Set rst = dbs.OpenRecordset(strSQL, dbOpenSnapshot)
    Debug.Print rst.Updatable
End Sub
```

Sort Property

Applies To Dynaset-Type **Recordset** Object, **Recordset** Object, Snapshot-Type **Recordset** Object.

Description Sets or returns the sort order for records in a **Recordset** object.

Settings and Return Values The setting or return value is a string expression that contains the ORDER BY clause of an SQL statement without the reserved words ORDER BY. (Data type is **String**.)

Remarks You can use the **Sort** property with dynaset- and snapshot-type **Recordset** objects.

When you set this property for an object, sorting occurs when a subsequent **Recordset** object is created from that object. The **Sort** property setting overrides any sort order specified for a **QueryDef** object.

The default sort order is ascending (A to Z or 0 to 100). The following examples show how you can set the sort order to ascending or descending (Z to A or 100 to 0):

```
rstOrders.Sort = "ShipCountry"            ' Defaults to ascending.
rstOrders.Sort = "ShipCountry Asc"        ' Ascending.
rstOrders.Sort = "ShipCountry Desc"       ' Descending.
```

The **Sort** property doesn't apply to table-type **Recordset** objects. To sort a table-type **Recordset** object, use the **Index** property.

Tip In many cases, it's faster to open a new **Recordset** object using an SQL statement that includes the sorting criteria.

See Also **Filter** Property, **Index** Property, **QueryDef** Object, **SQL** Property.

Example This example uses the **Sort** property to set the sort order of a dynaset-type **Recordset** based on an Orders table. The records in rstSorted will be in ascending Ship Country order.

```
Dim dbsNorthwind As Database
Dim rstOrders As Recordset, rstSorted As Recordset
Set dbsNorthwind = DBEngine.Workspaces(0).OpenDatabase("Northwind.mdb")
Set rstOrders = dbsNorthwind.OpenRecordset("Orders", dbOpenDynaset)
rstOrders.Sort = "ShipCountry"              ' Set sort order.
Set rstSorted = rstOrders.OpenRecordset()   ' Create second dynaset.
```

Tip In some situations, it may be more efficient to create the second **Recordset** object with the conditions you want in one step. As a general rule, when you know the data you want to select, it's usually more efficient to create a **Recordset** with an SQL statement. This example shows how you can create just one **Recordset** and obtain the same results as in the preceding example.

```
Dim dbsNorthwind As Database, rstOrders As Recordset
Dim strSelect As String
Set dbsNorthwind = DBEngine.Workspaces(0).OpenDatabase("Northwind.mdb")
strSelect = "SELECT * FROM Orders ORDER BY ShipCountry;"
Set rstOrders = dbsNorthwind.OpenRecordset(strSelect)
```

Example (Microsoft Access)

The following example uses the **Sort** property to set the sort order of a dynaset-type **Recordset** object based on an Orders table. The records in the rstSorted recordset variable will be ordered alphabetically by ship country.

Note that you first create a dynaset-type **Recordset** object and set its **Sort** property, then open a second dynaset-type **Recordset** object based on the first. Setting the **Sort** property of the first **Recordset** object doesn't actually affect the order of the records that it contains, so you need to create a second **Recordset** object in order to see the effects of the sort.

```
Sub SortByCountry()
    Dim dbs As Database
    Dim rstOrders As Recordset, rstSorted As Recordset

    ' Return Database variable that points to current database.
    Set dbs = CurrentDb
    ' Create dynaset-type Recordset object on Orders table.
    Set rstOrders = dbs.OpenRecordset("Orders", dbOpenDynaset)
    ' Set sort order.
    rstOrders.Sort = "ShipCountry"
    ' Create second dynaset-type Recordset object.
    Set rstSorted = rstOrders.OpenRecordset()
End Sub
```

Tip In most situations, it is more efficient to create the second **Recordset** object with the desired conditions in one step. As a general rule, when you know the data you want to select, it's usually more efficient to create a **Recordset** object with an SQL statement. The following example shows how you can create just one **Recordset** object and obtain the same results as in the preceding example.

```
Dim dbs As Database, rstOrders As Recordset
Dim strSelect As String
Set dbs = CurrentDb
strSelect = "SELECT * FROM Orders ORDER BY [ShipCountry];"
Set rstOrders = dbs.OpenRecordset(strSelect)
```

Example (Microsoft Excel)	This example creates a new recordset from the Supplier recordset in the NWINDEX.MDB database, and then it copies the new recordset onto Sheet1. The new recordset is sorted on the COUNTRY field, in ascending order.

To create the NWINDEX.MDB database, run the Microsoft Excel example for the **CreateDatabase** method.

```
Dim db As Database, rs As Recordset, sortedSet As Recordset
Set db = Workspaces(0).OpenDatabase(Application.Path & "\NWINDEX.MDB")
Set rs = db.OpenRecordset("Supplier", dbOpenDynaset)
rs.Sort = "[COUNTRY]"
Set sortedSet = rs.OpenRecordset()
Sheets("Sheet1").Activate
ActiveCell.CopyFromRecordset sortedSet
sortedSet.Close
rs.Close
db.Close
```

Source Property

Applies To	**Error** Object.
Description	Returns the name of the object or application that originally generated the error.
Return Values	The return value is a string expression representing the object or application that generated the error.
Remarks	The **Source** property specifies a string expression representing the object that originally generated the error; the expression is usually the object's class name or programmatic ID. Use the **Source** property to provide your users with information when your code is unable to handle an error generated in an accessed object. For example, if you access Microsoft Excel and it generates a Division by zero error, Microsoft Excel sets **Error.Number** to its error code for that error and sets the **Source** property to Excel.Application. Note that if the error is generated in another object called by Microsoft Excel, Microsoft Excel intercepts the error and sets **Error.Number** to its own code for Division by zero. However, it leaves the other **Error** object properties (including the **Source** property) as set by the object that generated the error. The **Source** property always contains the name of the object that originally generated the error—your code can try to handle the error according to the error documentation of the object you accessed. If your error handler fails, you can use the **Error** object information to describe the error to your user, using the **Source** property and the other **Error** properties to inform the user which object originally caused the error, its description of the error, and so forth.

SourceField, SourceTable Properties 255

> **Note** The **On Error Resume Next** construct may be preferable to **On Error GoTo** when dealing with errors generated during access to other objects. Checking the **Error** object property after each interaction with an object removes ambiguity about which object your code was accessing when the error occurred. Thus, you can be sure which object placed the error code in **Error.Number**, as well as which object originally generated the error (the one specified in **Error.Source**).

See Also	**Description** Property.
Specifics (Microsoft Access)	The data access **Source** property applies to the **Error** object and can be read only from Visual Basic.

> **Note** Don't confuse this property with the Microsoft Access **Source** property, which applies to a query and specifies the source connection string and source database for the query's input table or query.

Example	See the **Decription** property example.

SourceField, SourceTable Properties

Applies To   **Field** Object.

- **SourceField**—returns a value that indicates the name of the field that is the original source of the data for a **Field** object.
- **SourceTable**—returns a value that indicates the name of the table that is the original source of the data for a **Field** object.

This property is not available at design time and is read-only at run time.

Return Values   The return value is a string expression specifying the name of the field or table that is the source of data. The data type is **String**.

Remarks   For a **Field** object, use of the **SourceField** and **SourceTable** properties depends on the object that contains the **Fields** collection that the **Field** object is appended to, as shown in the following table.

Object appended to	Usage
Index	Not supported
QueryDef	Read-only

256 SourceField, SourceTable Properties

Object appended to	Usage
Recordset	Read-only
Relation	Not supported
TableDef	Read-only

These properties indicate the original field and table names associated with a **Field** object. For example, you could use these properties to determine the original source of the data in a query field whose name is unrelated to the name of the field in the underlying table.

See Also   **QueryDef** Object, **SourceTableName** Property.

Example   This example creates a **Recordset** object using an SQL statement that creates aliases for fields in two different tables in the database. The example then prints the name of the field, the original table, and the original field.

```
Function SourceInfo () As Integer
    Dim dbsNorthwind As Database
    Dim rstEmployCustID As Recordset, fldEnum As Field
    Dim strSelect As String, intStep As Integer
    ' Open database.
    Set dbsNorthwind = _
        DBEngine.Workspaces(0).OpenDatabase("Northwind.mdb")
    ' Construct SQL statement.
    strSelect = "SELECT EmployeeID As EmpID, CustomerID As " & _
        "CustID FROM Employees, Customers;"
    Set rstEmployCustID = dbsNorthwind.OpenRecordset(strSelect)
    For intStep = 0 To rstEmployCustID.Fields.Count - 1
        Set fldEnum = rstEmployCustID.Fields(intStep)
        Debug.Print fldEnum.Name         ' Print field name.
        Debug.Print fldEnum.SourceTable  ' Print original table name.
        Debug.Print fldEnum.SourceField  ' Print original field name.
    Next intStep
    SourceInfo = True
End Function
```

Example (Microsoft Access)   The following example creates a **Recordset** object using an SQL statement that creates aliases for fields in two different tables in the database. The example then prints the name of the field, the original table, and the original field.

```
Sub SourceInfo()
    Dim dbs As Database, rst As Recordset, fld As Field
    Dim strSQL As String

    ' Return Database object that points to current database.
    Set dbs = CurrentDb
    ' Construct SQL statement.
    strSQL = "SELECT ProductID As ProductCode, " & _
        "CategoryName As TypeOfProduct FROM Products, Categories;"
```

```
                Set rst = dbs.OpenRecordset(strSQL)
                For Each fld in rst.Fields
                    Debug.Print fld.Name          ' Print field name.
                    Debug.Print fld.SourceTable   ' Print original table name.
                    Debug.Print fld.SourceField   ' Print original field name.
                    Debug.Print
                Next fld
            End Sub
```

SourceTableName Property

Applies To	**TableDef** Object.
Description	Sets or returns a value that specifies the name of an attached table or the name of a base table. This property setting is read-only for a base table and read/write for an attached table or an object not appended to a collection.
Settings and Return Values	The setting or return value is a string expression that specifies a table name. For a base table, the setting is a zero-length string (""). The data type is **String**.
See Also	**Connect** Property; **OpenDatabase** Method; **RefreshLink** Method; **SourceField**, **SourceTable** Properties.
Example	See the **Connect** property example.
Example (Microsoft Access)	See the **Connect** property example (Microsoft Access).
Example (Microsoft Excel)	See the **Connect** property example (Microsoft Excel).

SQL Property

Applies To	**QueryDef** Object.
Description	Sets or returns the SQL statement that defines the query executed by a **QueryDef** object.
Settings and Return Values	The setting or return value is a string expression that contains an SQL statement. The data type is **String**.

258 SQL Property

Remarks The **SQL** property contains the SQL statement that determines how records are selected, grouped, and ordered when you execute the query. You can use the query to select records to include in a dynaset- or snapshot-type **Recordset** object. You can also define bulk queries to modify data without returning records.

Using the ORDER BY or WHERE clause to sort or filter a **Recordset** object is more efficient than using the **Sort** and **Filter** properties.

The SQL syntax used in a query must conform to the SQL dialect as defined by the Microsoft Jet database engine unless you create an SQL pass through query.

Using a **QueryDef** object is the preferred way to perform SQL pass through operations on ODBC databases. By setting the **QueryDef** object's **Connect** property to an ODBC data source, you can specify non-Microsoft Jet database SQL in the query passed to the external server. For example, you can use TRANSACT SQL statements (with Microsoft SQL Server or Sybase SQL Server databases) in the *value* argument, which won't be processed by the Jet database engine.

If the SQL statement includes parameters for the query, you must set these before you execute the query. Until you reset the parameters, the same parameter values are applied each time you execute the query. Set the parameters by accessing the **Parameters** collection of the **QueryDef** object using the following code.

```
qdfOrders.Parameters("Order Date") = "10/11/94"    ' Set parameters.
qdfOrders.Parameters("Ship Date") = "11/4/94"
```

See Also **CreateQueryDef** Method, **Filter** Property, **OpenRecordset** Method, **Parameter** Object, **Recordset** Object, **Sort** Property.

Example This example creates a query based on an Orders table. The query selects all orders that have a Freight value greater than 10.

```
Dim dbsNorthwind As Database, qdfLargeFrt As QueryDef
Dim rstFromQuery As Recordset
Set dbsNorthwind = DBEngine.Workspaces(0).OpenDatabase("Northwind.mdb")
Set qdfLargeFrt = dbsNorthwind.CreateQueryDef("Large Freight")
qdfLargeFrt.SQL = "SELECT * FROM Orders WHERE Freight > 10;"
Set rstFromQuery = qdfLargeFrt.OpenRecordset(dbOpenSnapshot)
```

Example (Microsoft Access) The following example creates a parameter query based on an Orders table. The query selects all orders for which the order date falls between the dates entered by the user.

```
Sub RangeOfOrders()
    Dim dbs As Database, qdf As QueryDef, rst As Recordset
```

```
                    ' Return Database variable that points to current database.
                    Set dbs = CurrentDb
                    Set qdf = dbs.CreateQueryDef("RangeOfOrders")
                    ' Construct SQL statement including parameters.
                    qdf.SQL = "PARAMETERS [Start] DATETIME, [End] DATETIME; " & _
                        "SELECT * FROM Orders WHERE [OrderDate] BETWEEN " & _
                        "[Start] AND [End];"
                    qdf.Parameters("Start") = #1/1/95#
                    qdf.Parameters("End") = #1/31/95#
                    ' Create snapshot-type Recordset object from QueryDef object.
                    Set rst = qdf.OpenRecordset(dbOpenSnapshot)
                End Sub
```

Example (Microsoft Excel) See the **CreateQueryDef** method example.

Synchronize Method

Applies To **Database** Object.

Description Synchronizes the current database object with the database in the .mdb file corresponding to *pathname*. Various types of exchanges can be performed as specified by the *exchange* argument. If no argument is provided, the exchange is bidirectional (import and export).

Syntax *database*.**Synchronize** *pathname* [,*exchange*]

The **Synchronize** method syntax has the following parts.

Part	Description
database	An existing, replicable **Database** object variable that you want synchronized.
pathname	Path to the target database with which *database* will be synchronized. The trailing .mdb can be optionally omitted.
exchange	A constant indicating which direction to synchronize changes between the two databases. This can be one of the following **Integer** constants: • **dbRepExportChanges**—Send changes from current database to *pathname*. • **dbRepImportChanges**—Receive changes from *pathname*. • **dbRepImpExpChanges**—(Default) Bidirectional exchange.

Remarks

This method causes an exchange of data and schema changes between the database and the .mdb identified by *pathname*. Schema changes are always done first. Both databases must be at the same schema level before data can be exchanged. For example, an exchange of type **dbRepExportChanges** might cause schema changes to be made at the current replica even though data changes flow only from the current replica to the designated target.

The replica identified in *pathname* must be part of the same replica set. If both replicas have the same **ReplicaID** property setting or have design-master status, the synchronization fails.

Note The **Synchronize** method can be used only if your application has Microsoft Access with Briefcase Replication installed.

Table Property

Applies To   **Relation** Object.

Description   Sets or returns a value that specifies the name of a **Relation** object's primary table. This name is the **Name** property setting of a **TableDef** or **QueryDef** object. The **Table** property setting is read/write for a new **Relation** object not yet appended to a collection and read-only for an existing **Relation** object in a **Relations** collection.

Settings and Return Values   The setting or return value is a string expression that evaluates to the name of a table in the **TableDefs** collection. The data type is **String**.

Remarks   Use the **Table** property with the **ForeignTable** property to define a **Relation** object, which represents the relationship between fields in two tables or queries. Set the **Table** property to the **Name** property setting of the primary **TableDef** or **QueryDef** object, and set the **ForeignTable** property to the **Name** property setting of the foreign (referencing) **TableDef** or **QueryDef** object. The **Attributes** property determines the type of relationship between the two objects.

For example, if you had a list of valid part codes (in a field named PartNo) and stored in a ValidParts table, you could establish a relationship with an OrderItem table such that if a part code was entered into the OrderItem table, it must exist in the ValidParts table. If the part code didn't exist in the ValidParts table and you had not indicated No Enforcement in the **Attributes** property, a trappable error would occur.

In this case, the ValidParts table is an example of a foreign table, so the **ForeignTable** property of the **Relation** object would be set to ValidParts and the **Table** property of the **Relation** object would be set to the OrderItem table. The **Name** property and **ForeignName** property of the **Field** object would both be set to PartNo.

The following illustration shows how the ValidParts table is primary because it's referenced by the OrderItem table.

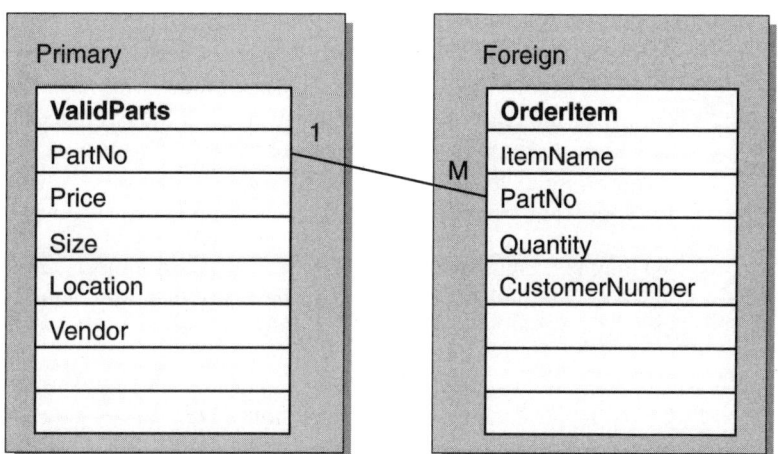

See Also   **Attributes** Property, **Field** Object, **ForeignTable** Property, **Name** Property, **QueryDef** Object.

Example   See the **ForeignName** property example.

Example (Microsoft Access)   See the **ForeignName** property example (Microsoft Access).

Table-Type Recordset Object

Description   A table-type **Recordset** object is a representation in code of a base table you can use to add, change, or delete records from a table. Only the current record is loaded into memory. A predefined index is used to determine the order of the records in the **Recordset** object.

262   Table-Type Recordset Object

Remarks	To create a table-type **Recordset** object, use the **OpenRecordset** method on an open **Database** object.
	A table-type **Recordset** object can be created with a base table of a Microsoft Jet database, but not with an ODBC or attached table. The table-type **Recordset** object can be used with ISAM databases (like FoxPro, dBASE, Paradox, or Btrieve) when opened directly.
	Unlike dynaset- or snapshot-type **Recordset** objects, the table-type **Recordset** object can't refer to more than one base table, and it can't be accessed using an SQL statement that filters or sorts the data. Generally, when you access a table-type **Recordset** object, you specify one of the predefined indexes for the table, which orders the data returned to your application. If the table doesn't have an index, the order of the data returned can't be guaranteed. If necessary, your application can create an index that returns records in a specific order. To choose a specific order for your table-type **Recordset** object, set the **Index** property to a valid index.
	To maintain data integrity, table-type **Recordset** objects are locked during the **Edit** and **Update** methods operations so that only one user can update a particular record at a time. When the Microsoft Jet database engine locks a record, it locks the entire 2K page containing the record.
	Two kinds of locking are used with non-ODBC tables—pessimistic and optimistic. ODBC-accessed tables always use optimistic locking. The locking conditions in effect during editing are determined by the **LockEdits** property.
Properties	**BOF**, **EOF** Properties; **Bookmark** Property; **Bookmarkable** Property; **DateCreated**, **LastUpdated** Properties; **EditMode** Property; **Index** Property; **LastModified** Property; **LockEdits** Property; **Name** Property; **NoMatch** Property; **PercentPosition** Property; **RecordCount** Property; **Restartable** Property; **Transactions** Property; **Type** Property; **Updatable** Property; **ValidationRule** Property; **ValidationText** Property.
Methods	**CancelUpdate** Method; **Clone** Method; **Close** Method; **Delete** Method; **Edit** Method; **GetRows** Method; **Move** Method; **MoveFirst**, **MoveLast**, **MoveNext**, **MovePrevious** Methods; **OpenRecordset** Method; **Seek** Method; **Update** Method.
See Also	**Index** Object; **OpenRecordset** Method; **Recordset** Object; Appendix, "Data Access Object Hierarchy."
Example	This example opens a table-type **Recordset** and selects an index for the **Recordset**. By setting an index, the Microsoft Jet database engine returns records in the order specified by the index. Without an index, table-type **Recordset** objects return records from the database table in no particular order.

```
Dim dbsExample As Database
Dim rstTitles as Recordset
' Get workspace and database.
```

```
                Set dbsExample = DBEngine.Workspaces(0).OpenDatabase("Biblio.mdb")
                Set rstTitles = dbsExample.OpenRecordset("Titles", dbOpenTable)
                rstTitles.Index = "MyIndex"
                ...
                ...
                ...
```

Example   The following example opens a table-type **Recordset** object, then prints the number
(Microsoft Access) of records in the **Recordset** object.

```
Sub CountEmployees()
    Dim dbs As Database, tdf As TableDef, rst As Recordset

    ' Return Database object pointing to current database.
    Set dbs = CurrentDb
    Set rst = dbs.OpenRecordset("Employees", dbOpenTable)
    rst.MoveLast
    Debug.Print rst.RecordCount
End Sub
```

TableDef Object

Description   A **TableDef** object represents the stored definition of a base table or an attached table.

Remarks   You manipulate a table definition using a **TableDef** object and its methods and properties. For example, you can:

- Examine the field and index structure of any local, attached, or external table in a database.
- Read or write the **Connect** and **SourceTableName** property settings for attached tables, and use the **RefreshLink** method to update connections to attached tables.
- Read (or write, if the **Updatable** property is set to **True** (-1)) the **ValidationRule** and **ValidationText** property settings to find (or specify) validation conditions.
- Use the **OpenRecordset** method to create a table-, dynaset-, or snapshot-type **Recordset** object, based on the table definition.

The default collection of a **Database** object is the **TableDefs** collection, and the default collection of a **TableDef** object is the **Fields** collection. You can simplify your code by using these defaults. For example, the following statements are identical in that they both print the number corresponding to the field data type of a **Field** object in a **TableDef** object:

```
Debug.Print dbsCurrent.TableDefs("Publishers").Fields("PubID").Type
Debug.Print dbsCurrent("Publishers")("PubID").Type
```

The **Name** property of a **TableDef** object isn't necessarily the same as the name of an object variable to which it's assigned.

For base tables, the **RecordCount** property contains the number of records in the specified database table. For attached tables, the **RecordCount** property setting is always -1.

You refer to a **TableDef** object that you create and append to a **TableDefs** collection by its **Name** property setting using this syntax:

TableDefs("*name***")**

To create a new **TableDef** object, use the **CreateTableDef** method.

You can delete a **Field** object from a **TableDefs** collection if it doesn't have any indexes assigned to it, but its underlying data is lost.

Properties	**Attributes** Property; **ConflictTable** Property; **Connect** Property; **DateCreated**, **LastUpdated** Properties; **KeepLocal** Property; **Name** Property; **RecordCount** Property; **Replicable** Property; **SourceTableName** Property; **Updatable** Property; **ValidationRule** Property; **ValidationText** Property.
Methods	**CreateField** Method, **CreateIndex** Method, **CreateProperty** Method, **OpenRecordset** Method, **RefreshLink** Method.
See Also	**CreateTableDef** Method; Appendix, "Data Access Object Hierarchy."
Specifics (Microsoft Access)	In addition to the properties defined by the Microsoft Jet database engine, a **TableDef** object may also contain the following Microsoft Access application-defined properties.

DatasheetFontHeight	**Description**
DatasheetFontItalic	**FrozenColumns**
DatasheetFontName	**RowHeight**
DatasheetFontUnderline	**ShowGrid**
DatasheetFontWeight	

TableDef Object   265

Example   This example creates a new **TableDef** object, adds a **Field** object to it, and appends the **TableDef** to the **TableDefs** collection in the current database. Then the example enumerates all the **TableDef** objects in the current database and all the properties of the new **TableDef**.

```
Function EnumerateTableDef () As Integer
    Dim dbsExample As Database
    Dim tdfEnum As TableDef
    Dim fldDate As Field
    Dim I As Integer
    Set dbsExample = _
        DBEngine.Workspaces(0).OpenDatabase("Northwind.mdb")
    Set tdfEnum = dbsExample.CreateTableDef("MyTable")
    Set fldDate = tdfEnum.CreateField("Date", dbDate)
    tdfEnum.Fields.Append fldDate
    dbsExample.TableDefs.Append tdfEnum
    ' Get database name.
    Debug.Print "Database Name: "; dbsExample.Name

    ' Enumerate all fields in tdfEnum.
    Debug.Print "TableDef: Name; Field: Name"
    For I = 0 To tdfEnum.Fields.Count - 1
        Debug.Print "  "; tdfEnum.Name;
        Debug.Print "; "; tdfEnum.Fields(I).Name
    Next I
    Debug.Print
    ' Enumerate all indexes in tdfEnum.
    Debug.Print "TableDef: Name; Index: Name"
    For I = 0 To tdfEnum.Indexes.Count - 1
        Debug.Print "  "; tdfEnum.Name;
        Debug.Print "; "; tdfEnum.Indexes(I).Name
    Next I
    Debug.Print
    ' Enumerate built-in properties of tdfEnum.
    Debug.Print "tdfEnum.Name: "; tdfEnum.Name
    Debug.Print "tdfEnum.Attributes: "; tdfEnum.Attributes
    Debug.Print "tdfEnum.Connect: "; tdfEnum.Connect
    Debug.Print "tdfEnum.DateCreated: "; tdfEnum.DateCreated
    Debug.Print "tdfEnum.LastUpdated: "; tdfEnum.LastUpdated
    Debug.Print "tdfEnum.RecordCount: "; tdfEnum.RecordCount
    Debug.Print "tdfEnum.SourceTableName: "; tdfEnum.SourceTableName
    Debug.Print "tdfEnum.Updatable: "; tdfEnum.Updatable
    Debug.Print "tdfEnum.ValidationRule: "; tdfEnum.ValidationRule
    Debug.Print "tdfEnum.ValidationText: "; tdfEnum.ValidationText
    EnumerateTableDef = True
End Function
```

**Example
(Microsoft Access)**

The following example creates a new **TableDef** object, defines a field within it, and appends it to the **TableDefs** collection of the current database.

```
Sub NewTable()
    Dim dbs As Database, tdf As TableDef, fld As Field

    ' Return Database object pointing to current database.
    Set dbs = CurrentDb
    Set tdf = dbs.CreateTableDef("Contacts")
    Set fld = tdf.CreateField("ContactName", dbText, 30)
    tdf.Fields.Append fld
    dbs.TableDefs.Append tdf
End Sub
```

TableDefs Collection

Description

A **TableDefs** collection contains all stored **TableDef** objects in a database.

Remarks

You manipulate a table definition using a **TableDef** object and its methods and properties.

The default collection of a **Database** object is the **TableDefs** collection.

You refer to a **TableDef** object that you create and append to a **TableDefs** collection by its **Name** property setting using this syntax:

TableDefs("*name*")

Methods

Append Method, **Delete** Method, **Refresh** Method.

See Also

Appendix, "Data Access Object Hierarchy."

**Specifics
(Microsoft Access)**

See the **TableDef** object specifics (Microsoft Access).

Example

See the **TableDef** object example.

**Example
(Microsoft Access)**

See the **TableDef** object example (Microsoft Access).

Transactions Property

Applies To Database Object, Dynaset-Type Recordset Object, Recordset Object, Snapshot-Type Recordset Object, Table-Type Recordset Object.

Description Returns a value that indicates whether an object supports the recording of a series of changes that can later be rolled back (canceled) or committed (saved). **True** (-1) indicates that the object supports transactions. Snapshot-type Recordset objects always return **False** (0).

Remarks You can use the **Transactions** property with dynaset- or snapshot-type Recordset objects.

If a dynaset or table is based on a Microsoft Jet database engine table, the **Transactions** property is **True** and you can use transactions. Other database engines may not support transactions. For example, you can't use transactions in a dynaset-type Recordset object based on a Paradox table.

Check the **Transactions** property before using the **BeginTrans** method on the Recordset object's Workspace object to make sure that transactions are supported. Using the **BeginTrans**, **CommitTrans**, or **Rollback** methods on a nonsupported object has no effect.

See Also **BeginTrans**, **CommitTrans**, **Rollback** Methods.

Type Property

Applies To Dynaset-Type Recordset Object, Field Object, Parameter Object, Property Object, QueryDef Object, Recordset Object, Snapshot-Type Recordset Object, Table-Type Recordset Object.

Description Sets or returns a value that indicates the operational type or data type of an object. For a **Field** or **Property** object, this property is read/write until the object is appended to a collection or to another object, after which it's read-only. For a **Parameter**, **QueryDef**, or **Recordset** object, the property setting is read-only.

Settings and Return Values The setting or return value is a constant that indicates an operational or data type. The data type is **Integer**.

For a **Field**, **Parameter**, or **Property** object, the possible settings and return values are:

Setting/Value	Description
dbBoolean	Boolean
dbByte	Byte
dbInteger	Integer
dbLong	Long
dbCurrency	Currency
dbSingle	Single
dbDouble	Double
dbDate	Date/Time
dbText	Text
dbLongBinary	Long Binary (OLE Object)
dbMemo	Memo
dbGUID	GUID

For a **QueryDef** object, the possible settings and return values are:

Setting/Values	Query type
dbQSelect	Select
dbQAction	Action
dbQCrosstab	Crosstab
dbQDelete	Delete
dbQUpdate	Update
dbQAppend	Append
dbQMakeTable	Make-table
dbQDDL	Data-definition
dbQSQLPassThrough	Pass-through
dbQSetOperation	Union
dbQSPTBulk	Used with **dbQSQLPassThrough** to specify a query that doesn't return records.

Note To create an SQL pass through query, don't set the **dbQSQLPassThrough** constant. This is set automatically by the Microsoft Jet database engine when you create a **QueryDef** object and set the **Connect** property.

For a **Recordset** object, the possible settings and return values are:

Setting	Recordset type
dbOpenTable	Table
dbOpenDynaset	Dynaset
dbOpenSnapshot	Snapshot

Remarks

These constants are listed in the Data Access (DAO) object library in the Object Browser.

Depending on the object, the **Type** property indicates:

Object	Type indicates
Field, Parameter, Property	Object data type
QueryDef	Type of query
Recordset	Type of **Recordset** object

When you append a new **Field**, **Parameter**, or **Property** object to the collection of an **Index**, **QueryDef**, **Recordset**, or **TableDef** object, an error occurs if the underlying database doesn't support the data type specified for the new object.

Specifics (Microsoft Access)

In Microsoft Access, you can set the data type for a field in table Design view, and you can set the data type for a parameter in the Query Parameters dialog box. These actions are equivalent to setting the data access **Type** property for a **Field** object or a **Parameter** object from Visual Basic.

The following table lists the **Type** property constants and the corresponding Microsoft Access settings for field and parameter data types if you are setting them from table Design view or the Query Parameters dialog box.

When creating a table field with data type Number, set the **FieldSize** property to specify which of the six numeric data types the field will be. By default this property is set to Long Integer. The other settings are Byte, Integer, Single, Double, and ReplicationID.

Constant	Table field setting	Query parameter setting
dbBoolean	Yes/No	Yes/No
dbByte	Number (**FieldSize** = Byte)	Byte
dbCurrency	Currency	Currency
dbDate	Date/Time	Date/Time

Constant	Table field setting	Query parameter setting
dbDouble	Number (**FieldSize** = Double)	Double
dbGUID	Number or AutoNumber (**FieldSize** = ReplicationID)	*Not supported*
dbInteger	Number (**FieldSize** = Integer)	Integer
dbLong	Number (**FieldSize** = Long Integer)	Long Integer
	AutoNumber (**FieldSize** = Long Integer)	*Not supported*
dbLongBinary	OLE Object	OLE Object
	Not supported	Binary
dbMemo	Memo	Memo
dbSingle	Number (**FieldSize** = Single)	Single
dbText	Text	Text
Not supported	*Not supported*	Value

Note The parameter data type **Value** doesn't correspond to a data type defined by the Microsoft Jet database engine. It corresponds to the SQL reserved word VALUE, which can be used to create a parameter query. In Microsoft Access or SQL queries, VALUE can be considered a valid synonym for the Visual Basic **Variant** data type.

Example　　See the **Size** property example.

Example (Microsoft Access)　　See the **Size** property example (Microsoft Access).

Example (Microsoft Excel)　　See the **Size** property example (Microsoft Excel).

Unique Property

Applies To **Index** Object.

Description Sets or returns a value that indicates whether an **Index** object represents a unique (key) index for a table. For an **Index** object, this property setting is read/write until the object is appended to a collection, after which it's read-only.

Settings and Return Values The setting or return value is a Boolean expression that specifies a unique index. The data type is Boolean. **True** (-1) indicates that the **Index** object represents a unique index.

Remarks A unique index consists of one or more fields that logically arrange all records in a table in a unique, predefined order. If the index consists of one field, values in that field must be unique for the entire table. If the index consists of more than one field, each field can contain duplicate values, but each combination of values from all the indexed fields must be unique.

If both the **Unique** and **Primary** properties of an **Index** object are set to **True**, the index is unique and primary: It uniquely identifies all records in the table in a predefined, logical order. If the **Primary** property is set to **False** (0), the index is a secondary index. Secondary indexes (both key and nonkey) logically arrange records in a predefined order without serving as an identifier for records in the table.

Tips

- You don't have to create indexes for tables, but in large, unindexed tables, accessing a specific record can take a long time.
- Records read from tables without indexes are returned in no particular sequence.
- The **Attributes** property of each **Field** object in the **Index** object determines the order of records and consequently determines the access techniques to use for that **Index** object.
- A unique index helps optimize finding records.
- Indexes don't affect the physical order of a base table—indexes affect only how the records are accessed by the table-type **Recordset** object when a particular index is chosen or when the Microsoft Jet database engine creates **Recordset** objects.

See Also **Attributes** Property, **Clustered** Property, **Primary** Property, **Unique** Property.

Example See the **Index** property example.

Example (Microsoft Access) See the **IgnoreNulls** property example (Microsoft Access).

Updatable Property

Applies To Database Object, Dynaset-Type **Recordset** Object, **QueryDef** Object, **Recordset** Object, Snapshot-Type **Recordset** Object, Table-Type **Recordset** Object, **TableDef** Object.

Description Returns a value that indicates whether changes can be made to a data access object. **True** (-1) indicates that the object can be changed or updated. (Snapshot-type **Recordset** objects always return **False** (0).)

Remarks Depending on the object, if the **Updatable** property setting is **True**, the specified:

- **Database** object can be changed.
- **QueryDef** object query definition can be changed.
- **Recordset** object records can be updated.
- **TableDef** object table definition can be changed.

You can use the **Updatable** property with all **Recordset** objects.

The **Updatable** property setting is always **True** for a newly created **TableDef** object and **False** for an attached **TableDef** object. A new **TableDef** object can be appended only to a database for which the current user has write permission.

Many types of objects can contain fields that can't be updated. For example, you can create a dynaset-type **Recordset** object in which only some fields can be changed. These fields can be fixed or contain data that increments automatically, or the dynaset can result from a query that combines updatable and nonupdatable tables.

If the object contains only nonupdatable fields, the value of the **Updatable** property is **False**. When one or more fields are updatable, the property's value is **True**. You can edit only the updatable fields. A trappable error occurs if you try to assign a new value to a nonupdatable field.

The **Updatable** property of a **QueryDef** object is set to **True** if the query definition can be updated, even if the resulting **Recordset** object isn't updatable.

Because an updatable object can contain nonupdatable fields, check the **Fields** collection of a **Recordset** object to check the **DataUpdatable** property of each field before you edit a record in the **Recordset** object.

See Also **Field** Object.

Example This example adds a record to a **Recordset** object if the object's **Updatable** property setting is **True**.

```
Dim dbsNorthwind As Database, rstUnknown As Recordset
Set dbsNorthwind = DBEngine.Workspaces(0).OpenDatabase("Northwind.mdb")
```

Updatable Property 273

```
    Set rstUnknown = dbsNorthwind.OpenRecordset("Unfamiliar Table")
    If rstUnknown.Updatable = True Then
        rstUnknown.AddNew
        rstUnknown("MyField") = "Some new data"
        rstUnknown.Update
    End If
    dbsNorthwind.Close
```

Example (Microsoft Access)

The following example adds a record to a **Recordset** object if the object's **Updatable** property setting is **True**.

```
Sub UpdateData()
    Dim dbs As Database, rstUnknown As Recordset

    ' Return Database variable that points to current database.
    Set dbs = CurrentDb
    Set rstUnknown = dbs.OpenRecordset("Unfamiliar Table")
    ' Check Updatable property before adding new record.
    If rstUnknown.Updatable = True Then
        With rstUnknown
            .AddNew
            !SomeField = "Some new data"
            .Update
        End With
    End If
    dbs.Close
End Sub
```

Example (Microsoft Excel)

This example prompts the user to select a cell that contains a value for the CONTACT field of the Customer recordset in the NWINDEX.MDB database. The example then checks to see whether the recordset can be updated. If so, the example adds a new record to the recordset, using the value in the selected cell.

To create the NWINDEX.MDB database, run the Microsoft Excel example for the **CreateDatabase** method.

```
Dim db As Database, rs As Recordset
Sheets("Sheet1").Activate
cellToCopy = Application.InputBox("What cell value do you want" _
    & " to update as contact?", Type:=8)
If cellToCopy = False Then      ' user cancelled InputBox
    Exit Sub
End If
Set db = Workspaces(0).OpenDatabase(Application.Path & "\NWINDEX.MDB")
Set rs = db.OpenRecordset("Customer")
If rs.Updatable = True Then
    rs.AddNew
    rs("CONTACT") = cellToCopy
    rs.Update
    rs.MoveLast
```

```
        MsgBox "The new contact is " & rs("CONTACT").Value
Else
        MsgBox "The recordset cannot be modified."
End If
rs.Close
db.Close
```

Update Method

Applies To Dynaset-Type **Recordset** Object, **Recordset** Object, Table-Type **Recordset** Object.

Description Saves the contents of the copy buffer to a specified dynaset- or table-type **Recordset** object.

Syntax *recordset*.**Update**

The *recordset* placeholder represents the name of an open, updatable dynaset- or table-type **Recordset** object.

Remarks Use **Update** to save the current record and any changes you've made to it.

Caution Changes to the current record are lost if:

- You use the **Edit** or **AddNew** method, and then move to another record without first using **Update**.
- You use **Edit** or **AddNew**, and then use **Edit** or **AddNew** again without first using **Update**.
- You set the **Bookmark** property to another record.
- You close the recordset referred to by *recordset* without first using **Update**.
- You cancel the Edit.
- You move off the record.

To edit a record, use the **Edit** method to copy the contents of the current record to the copy buffer. If you don't use **Edit** first, an error occurs when you use **Update** or attempt to change a field's value.

Update Method

When the **Recordset** object's **LockEdits** property setting is **True** (pessimistically locked) in a multiuser environment, the record remains locked from the time **Edit** is used until the **Update** method is executed or the edit is canceled. If the **LockEdits** property setting is **False** (optimistically locked), the record is locked and compared with the pre-edited record just before it is updated in the database. If the record has changed since you used the **Edit** method, the **Update** operation fails with a trappable error (3197). Note that optimistic locking is always used on external database formats such as ODBC or installable ISAM. To continue the **Update** operation with your changes, use the **Update** method again. To revert to the record as the other user changed it, refresh the current record using the **Move** methods, or set the **Bookmark** property to itself, as shown in the following example:

```
' Error 3197 detected: Restore record from database (as changed).
rstEmployees.BookMark = rstEmployees.Bookmark
```

To add a new record to a recordset, use the **AddNew** method.

See Also **AddNew** Method, **LockEdits** Property, **OpenRecordset** Method.

Specifics (Microsoft Access)

When you use a bookmark in a Microsoft Access module, you must include an **Option Compare Binary** statement in the Declarations section of the module. A bookmark is a **Variant** array of **Byte** data, so the string comparison method for the module must be binary. If a bookmark is evaluated with a text-based string comparison method, such as the **Option Compare Text** statement or the default setting for the **Option Compare Database** statement, the current record may be set to an incorrect record.

Example

See the **Edit** method example.

Example (Microsoft Access)

See the **AddNew** method example (Microsoft Access).

Example (Microsoft Excel)

This example opens PRODUCT.DBF (a dBASE IV table located in the \Program Files\Common Files\Microsoft Shared\MSquery folder), finds a record with the PRODUCT value 1, and then sets the CATEGORY field to the value in cell B2 on Sheet1. (On Windows NT, PRODUCT.DBF is located in the \WINDOWS\MSAPPS\MSQUERY folder.)

```
Const sourceDir = "C:\Program Files\Common Files\Microsoft " _
    & "Shared\MSquery"
Dim db As Database, rs As Recordset, categoryCell As Range
Sheets("Sheet1").Activate
Set categoryCell = ActiveSheet.Cells(2, 2)
categoryCell.Value = "BEVR"
Set db = OpenDatabase(sourceDir, False, False, "dBASE IV")
Set rs = db.OpenRecordset("PRODUCT.DBF", dbOpenTable)
With rs
    .Index = "PRODUCT"
    .Seek "=", "1"
```

```
            .Edit
            .Fields("CATEGORY").Value = categoryCell.Value
            .Update
End With
MsgBox "The field has been updated with " & categoryCell.Value
rs.Close
db.Close
```

User Object

Description A **User** object represents a user account that has access permissions when a **Workspace** object operates as a secure workgroup.

Remarks You use **User** objects to establish and enforce access permissions for the **Document** objects that represent databases, tables, and queries. Also, if you know the properties of a specific **User** object, you can create a new **Workspace** object that has the same access permissions as the **User** object.

You can append an existing **User** object to the **Users** collection of a **Group** object to give a user account the access permissions for that **Group** object. Alternatively, you can append the **Group** object to the **Groups** collection in a **User** object to establish membership of the user account in that group. If you use a **Users** or **Groups** collection other than the one to which you just appended an object, you may need to use the **Refresh** method.

Using the properties of a **User** object, you can:

- Check the **Name** property setting of an existing **User** object to determine its name. You can't check the **PID** and **Password** property settings of an existing **User** object.

- Set the **Name**, **PID**, and **Password** properties of a newly created, unappended **User** object to establish the identity of that **User** object. If you don't set the **Password** property, it's set to a zero-length string ("").

The Microsoft Jet database engine predefines two **User** objects named Admin and Guest. The user Admin is a member of the **Group** object named Admins and Users; the user Guest is a member only of the **Group** object named Guests.

You can refer to any other **User** object that you create and append to a **Users** collection by its **Name** property setting using this syntax:

Workspaces(*n*)|**Group.Users**("*name*")

To create a new **User** object, use the **CreateUser** method.

Properties **Name** Property, **Password** Property, **PID** Property.

User Object 277

Methods **CreateGroup** Method, **NewPassword** Method.

See Also **CreateUser** Method; Appendix, "Data Access Object Hierarchy."

Specifics (Microsoft Access) You can create **User** objects to establish and enforce permissions for Microsoft Access database objects as well as for data access objects. For example, you can set security for forms, reports, macros, and modules.

A **User** object has a **Name** property that you can use in setting permissions for a **Container** or **Document** object. For example, you can assign the value of a **User** object's **Name** property to the **UserName** property of a **Container** or **Document** object. You can then set the **Permissions** property of the **Container** or **Document** object to establish permissions for the user defined by the **UserName** property. Or you can read the **Permissions** property to determine existing permissions for that user.

Example See the **Group** object example.

Example (Microsoft Access) The following example creates a new **User** object and appends it to the **Users** collection of a **Workspace** object. It then creates a new **Group** object and appends it to the **Groups** collection of the **Workspace** object. The new **User** object is also appended to the **Users** collection of the **Group** object. The new user is then given retrieval permissions on tables.

Note that in order to assign users to groups, you must either append a **User** object to the **Users** collection of a **Group** object, or append a **Group** object to the **Groups** collection of a **User** object. It doesn't matter which option you choose; either will result in the specified user being included in the specified group.

```
Sub NewTablesUser()
    Dim wsp As Workspace, dbs As Database
    Dim usr As User, grp As Group, usrMember As User
    Dim ctr As Container, doc As Document

    Set wsp = DBEngine.Workspaces(0)
    ' Return Database object pointing to current database.
    Set dbs = CurrentDb
' Create User object and append to Users collection of Workspace object.
    Set usr = wsp.CreateUser("Chris Jones", "123abc456DEF", "Password")
    wsp.Users.Append usr
    ' Create Group object and append to Groups collection of Workspace
    ' object.
    Set grp = wsp.CreateGroup("Marketing", "321xyz654EFD")
    wsp.Groups.Append grp
    ' Append new User object to Users collection of new Group object.
    Set usrMember = grp.CreateUser("Chris Jones")
    grp.Users.Append usrMember
    ' Refresh Users collection of Group object.
```

```
        grp.Users.Refresh
        ' Return Container object.
        Set ctr = dbs.Containers!Tables
        ' Set UserName property of Container object.
        ctr.UserName = usrMember.Name
        ' Add retrieve permissions for new user on all tables.
        ctr.Permissions = ctr.Permissions Or dbSecRetrieveData
End Sub
```

UserName Property

Applies To **Container** Object, **Document** Object, **Workspace** Object.

Description Sets or returns a value that represents a user or group of users or the owner of a **Workspace** object. For **Container** and **Document** objects, this property setting is read/write. For a **Workspace** object, this property setting is read/write for an object not yet appended to a collection and read-only for an existing **Workspace** object.

Settings and Return Values The setting or return value is a string expression that evaluates to the name of a **User** object in the **Users** collection or a **Group** object in the **Groups** collection. (Data type is **String**.)

Remarks Depending on the type of object, the **UserName** property represents:

- A user or group of users when you manipulate the access permissions of a **Container** object or a **Document** object.
- The owner of a **Workspace** object. For **Container** and **Document** objects, you use the **UserName** property with the **Permissions** property to establish read or write permissions.

To find or set the permissions for a particular user or group of users, first set the **UserName** property to the user or group name that you want to examine. Then check the **Permissions** property setting to determine what permissions that user or group of users has, or set the **Permissions** property to change the permissions.

For a **Workspace** object, check the **UserName** property setting to determine the owner of the **Workspace** object. Set the **UserName** property to establish the owner of the **Workspace** object before you append the object to the **Workspaces** collection.

See Also **Append** Method, **Inherited** Property, **Password** Property, **Permissions** Property.

Example	This example sets the access permissions for a table named MyTable in the specified database for a user named Millicent to read-only. The code then checks to see if Millicent has permission to add records.
	
	``
	Dim wrkDefault As Workspace, dbsNorthwind As Database
	Dim docMyTable As Document
	...
	Set wrkDefault = DBEngine.Workspaces(0)
	Set dbsNorthwind = wrkDefault.OpenDatabase("Northwind.mdb")
	...
	Set docMyTable = dbsNorthwind.Containers("Tables")![MyTable]
	docMyTable.UserName = "Millicent"
	docMyTable.Permissions = dbSecRetrieveData
	If(docMyTable.Permissions and dbSecInsertData) > 0 Then
	    Debug.Print "Millicent can insert data."
	Else
	    Debug.Print "Millicent can't insert data."
	End If
	...
	``

Example (Microsoft Access)	See the **Permissions** property example (Microsoft Access)

Users Collection

Description	A **Users** collection contains all stored **User** objects of a **Workspace** or **Group** object.
Remarks	You can append an existing **User** object to the **Users** collection of a **Group** object to give a user account the access permissions for that **Group** object. Alternatively, you can append the **Group** object to the **Groups** collection in a **User** object to establish membership of the user account in that group. If you use a **Users** or **Groups** collection other than the one to which you just appended an object, you may need to use the **Refresh** method. The Microsoft Jet database engine predefines two **User** objects named Admin and Guest. The user Admin is a member of the **Group** object named Admins and Users; the user Guest is a member only of the **Group** object named Guests. You can refer to any other **User** object that you create and append to a **Users** collection by its **Name** property setting using this syntax: **Workspaces**(*n*)|**Group.Users**("*name*")
Properties	**Count** Property.

Methods	**Append** Method, **Delete** Method, **Refresh** Method.
See Also	Appendix, "Data Access Object Hierarchy."
Specifics (Microsoft Access)	See the **User** object specifics (Microsoft Access).
Example	See the **Group** object example.
Example (Microsoft Access)	See the **User** object example (Microsoft Access).

V1xNullBehavior Property

Applies To	**Database** Object.
Description	Sets or returns a value that indicates whether zero-length strings ("") used in code to fill Text or Memo fields are converted to **Null**. This property applies to Microsoft Jet database engine version 1.x databases that have been converted to Jet database engine version 2.0 or 3.0 databases.
	Note The Jet database engine automatically creates this property when it converts a version 1.*x* database to a version 2.0 or 3.0 database. A 2.0 database will retain this property when it is converted to a 3.0 database.
Settings and Return Values	The setting or return value is a Boolean expression that indicates whether zero-length strings are converted to **Null**. The data type is Boolean. **True** (-1) indicates that zero-length strings are converted to **Null**.
Remarks	If you change this property setting, you must close and then reopen the database for your change to take effect.
	For fastest performance, modify code that sets any Text or Memo fields to zero-length strings so that the fields are set to **Null** instead, and remove the **V1xNullBehavior** property from the **Properties** collection.
See Also	**Index** Property.

ValidateOnSet Property

Applies To	**Field** Object.

| | ValidationRule Property 281 |

Description	Sets or returns a value that specifies whether or not the value of a **Field** object is immediately validated when the object's **Value** property is set. Only **Field** objects in **Recordset** objects support the **ValidateOnSet** property as read/write.
Settings and Return Values	The setting or return value is a Boolean expression that indicates whether a value is validated, as described in Settings. The data type is Boolean. The possible settings or return values are:

Setting/Value	Description
True	Validate when the property is set.
False	Validate when the record is updated.

Remarks	When the **ValidateOnSet** property is set to **True** (-1), the validation rule specified by the **ValidationRule** property setting of the **Field** object is checked when you set the object's **Value** property.
	When the **ValidateOnSet** property is set to **False** (0), you can set the **Value** property of each field independently and perform validation using the final *value* settings when the record is updated.
See Also	**AllowZeroLength** Property, **QueryDef** Object, **Required** Property, **ValidationRule** Property, **ValidationText** Property, **Value** Property.

ValidationRule Property

Applies To	Dynaset-Type **Recordset** Object, **Field** Object, **Recordset** Object, Snapshot-Type **Recordset** Object, Table-Type **Recordset** Object, **TableDef** Object.
Description	Sets or returns a value that validates the data in a field as it's changed or added to a table. For an object not yet appended to the **Fields** collection, this property is read/write. See Remarks for the more specific read/write characteristics of this property.
Settings and Return Values	The settings or return values is a string expression that describes a comparison in the form of an SQL WHERE clause without the WHERE reserved word. The data type is **String**.
Remarks	The **ValidationRule** property determines whether or not valid data is in the associated field. If the data is not legal, a trappable run-time error occurs. The returned error message is the text of the **ValidationText** property, if specified, or the text of the expression specified by **ValidationRule**.

For a **Field** object, use of the **ValidationRule** property depends on the object that contains the **Fields** collection that the **Field** object is appended to, as the following table shows.

Object appended to	Usage
Index	Not supported
QueryDef	Read-only
Recordset	Read-only
Relation	Not supported
TableDef	Read/write

For a **Recordset** object, use of the **ValidationRule** property is read-only. For a **TableDef** object, use of the **ValidationRule** property depends on the status of the **TableDef** object, as the following table shows.

TableDef	Usage
Base table	Read/write
Attached table	Read-only

Validation is supported only for databases that use the Microsoft Jet database engine.

The string expression specified by the **ValidationRule** property of a **Field** object can refer only to that **Field**. The expression can't refer to user-defined functions, SQL aggregate functions, or queries. To set a **Field** object's **ValidationRule** property when its **ValidateOnSet** property setting is **True**, the expression must successfully parse (with the field name as an implied operand) and evaluate to **True**. If its **ValidateOnSet** property setting is **False**, the **ValidationRule** property setting is ignored.

The **ValidationRule** property of a **Recordset** or **TableDef** object can refer to multiple fields in that object. The restrictions noted earlier in this topic for the **Field** object apply.

For a table-type **Recordset** object, the **ValidationRule** property takes the value of the **ValidationRule** property setting of the **TableDef** object that you use to create the table-type **Recordset** object.

For a **TableDef** object based on an attached table, the **ValidationRule** property takes the value of the underlying base table. If the underlying base table doesn't support validation, the value of this property is a zero-length string ("").

See Also   **ValidateOnSet** Property, **ValidationText** Property.

Specifics (Microsoft Access)   Use the data access **ValidationRule** property to set validation rules for a **Field**, **Recordset**, or **TableDef** object from Visual Basic.

You can also set validation rules for a field or control in the Microsoft Access user interface. Set the Microsoft Access **ValidationRule** property for a field or a table in table Design view. Set the **ValidationRule** property of a control in the property sheet in form Design view.

In Microsoft Access, the string expression specified by the **ValidationRule** property of a **Field** object can't refer to user-defined functions, domain aggregate functions, SQL aggregate functions, the **CurrentUser** function, the **Eval** function, or queries.

Example (Microsoft Access)

The following example sets the **ValidationRule** and **ValidationText** properties for two fields in an Order Details table. Once these properties have been set, you can view them in table Design view as well.

```
Sub SetValidation()
    Dim dbs As Database, tdf As TableDef
    Dim fldQuantity As Field, fldDiscount As Field

    ' Return Database variable that points to current database.
    Set dbs = CurrentDb
    Set tdf = dbs.TableDefs![Order Details]
    Set fldQuantity = tdf.Fields!Quantity
    Set fldDiscount = tdf.Fields!Discount
    ' Set ValidationRule and ValidationText.
    fldQuantity.ValidationRule = ">= 4"
    fldQuantity.ValidationText = "Quantity must be four or more items."
    fldDiscount.ValidationRule = "Between .05 and .30"
    fldDiscount.ValidationText = "Discount must be between 5% and 30%."
End Sub
```

ValidationText Property

Applies To

Dynaset-Type **Recordset** Object, **Field** Object, **Recordset** Object, Snapshot-Type **Recordset** Object, Table-Type **Recordset** Object, **TableDef** Object.

Description

Sets or returns a value that specifies the text of the message that your application displays if the value of a **Field** object doesn't satisfy the validation rule specified by the **ValidationRule** property setting.

For an object not yet appended to a collection, this property is read/write. For a **Recordset** object, this property setting is read-only. For a **TableDef** object, this property setting is read-only for an attached table and read/write for a base table.

Settings and Return Values

The setting or return value is a string expression that specifies the text displayed if an entered value is invalid. The data type is **String**.

284 Value Property

Remarks	For a **Field** object, use of the **ValidationText** property depends on the object that contains the **Fields** collection that the **Field** object is appended to, as the following table shows.

Object appended to	Usage
Index	Not supported
QueryDef	Read-only
Recordset	Read-only
Relation	Not supported
TableDef	Read/write

See Also	**AllowZeroLength** Property, **QueryDef** Object, **Required** Property, **ValidateOnSet** Property, **ValidationRule** Property, **Value** Property.
Example (Microsoft Access)	See the **ValidationRule** property example (Microsoft Access).

Value Property

Applies To	**Field** Object, **Parameter** Object, **Property** Object.
Description	Sets or returns the value of an object.
Settings and Return Values	The setting or return value is an expression that evaluates to a value appropriate for the data type, as specified by the **Type** property of an object. The data type is **Variant**.
Remarks	Generally, the **Value** property is used to retrieve and alter data in **Recordset** objects.

The **Value** property is the default property of the **Field**, **Parameter**, and **Property** objects. Therefore, the following lines of code are equivalent (assuming Field1 is at the first ordinal position).

```
varX = rstProducts!Field1
varX = rstProducts!Field1.Value
varX = rstProducts(0)
varX = rstProducts(0).Value
varX = rstProducts("Field1").Value
varX = rstProducts("Field1")
F$ = "Field1" : varX = rstProducts(F$).Value
varX = rstProducts(F$)
```

See Also	**Name** Property, **Updatable** Property.

Version Property

Applies To **Database** Object, **DBEngine** Object.

Description Returns a value that indicates the version of the database or database engine associated with the object. This property setting is read-only.

Return Values The return value is a string expression that evaluates to a value, depending on the object specified:

- **Database** object—identifies the data format version of an open database.
- **DBEngine** object—identifies the version number of the Microsoft Jet database engine.

Remarks For a **Database** object, this property identifies the version of the Jet database engine that created the database.

The setting of the **Version** property represents the version number in the form "*major.minor*"; for example, "3.0". The product version number (for example, 3.0) consists of the version number (2), a period, and the release number (0).

See Also **CreateDatabase** Method.

Example This example checks the version number of the Microsoft Jet database engine and splits it into the version number and release number. The example doesn't check for an invalid string.

```
Dim strDBVersion As String, strJetVersion As String
Dim strJetRelease As String
Dim intDot As Integer
...
strDBVersion = DBEngine.Version
intDot = InStr(strDBVersion, ".")
strJetVersion = Left$(strDBVersion, intDot - 1)
strJetRelease = Right$(strDBVersion, Len(strDBVersion) - intDot)
...
```

Workspace Object

Description A **Workspace** object defines a session for a user. It contains open databases and provides mechanisms for simultaneous transactions and for a secure workgroup.

286 Workspace Object

Remarks

Use the **Workspace** object to manage the current session or to start an additional session. In a session, you can open multiple databases, manage transactions, and establish security based on user names and passwords. For example, you can:

- Create a **Workspace** object using the **Name** and **UserName** properties to establish a namcd, password-protected session. The session creates a scope in which you can open multiple databases and conduct one instance of nested transactions. Use the **Close** method to terminate a session.

- Use the **OpenDatabase** method to open one or more existing databases on that **Workspace**.

- Use the **BeginTrans**, **CommitTrans**, and **Rollback** methods to manage nested transaction processing within a **Workspace** and use several **Workspace** objects to conduct multiple, simultaneous, and overlapping transactions.

- Use the **IsolateODBCTrans** property to isolate multiple transactions that involve the same ODBC database.

When you start the Microsoft Jet database engine, you automatically create the default workspace, **DBEngine.Workspaces**(0). The settings of the **Name** and **UserName** properties of the default workspace are "#Default Workspace#" and "Admin," respectively. If security is enabled, the **UserName** property setting is the name of the user who logged on. If you use the **OpenDatabase** method without specifying a **Workspace** object, the default **DBEngine.Workspaces**(0) is used.

When you use transactions, all databases in the specified **Workspace** are affected—even if multiple **Database** objects are opened in the **Workspace**. For example, if you use a **BeginTrans** method, update several records in a database, and then delete records in another database, both the update and delete operations are rolled back when you use the **Rollback** method. You can create additional **Workspace** objects to manage transactions independently across **Database** objects.

Workspace objects are created using the **CreateWorkspace** method of the **DBEngine** object. After you create a new **Workspace** object, you must appended it to the **Workspaces** collection if you need to refer to it from the **Workspaces** collection. You can, however, use a newly created **Workspace** object without appending it to the **Workspaces** collection.

You can refer to any other **Workspace** object that you create and append to the collection by its **Name** property setting using this syntax:

Workspaces("*name*")

You can also refer to appended **Workspace** objects by their position in the **Workspaces** collection using this syntax (where *n* is the *n*th member of the **Workspaces** collection):

DBEngine.Workspaces(*n*)

Properties	**IsolateODBCTrans** Property, **Name** Property, **UserName** Property.
Methods	**BeginTrans**, **CommitTrans**, **Rollback** Methods; **Close** Method; **CreateDatabase** Method; **CreateGroup** Method; **CreateUser** Method; **OpenDatabase** Method.
See Also	**CreateWorkspace** Method; **Transactions** Property; Appendix, "Data Access Object Hierarchy."
Example	This example creates a new **Workspace** and appends it to the **Workspaces** collection. It assumes that the user JustAUser with a password of Secret has already been created. The example enumerates the collections of each **Workspace** object and finally closes the new **Workspace**. See the methods and properties of the **Workspace** object or **Workspaces** collection for additional examples.

```
Function EnumerateWorkspace () As Integer
    Dim wrkEnum As Workspace, wrkNew As Workspace
    Dim I As Integer, J As Integer
    ' Create new workspace and add it to collection.
    Set wrkNew = DBEngine.CreateWorkspace("NewWorkspace", "JustAUser", _
        "")
    DBEngine.Workspaces.Append wrkNew
    ' Enumerate all workspaces.
    For J = 0 To DBEngine.Workspaces.Count - 1
        Set wrkEnum = DBEngine.Workspaces(J)
        Debug.Print
        Debug.Print "Enumeration of Workspaces("; J; "): "; wrkEnum.Name
        Debug.Print
        ' Enumerate databases.
        Debug.Print "Databases: Name"
        For I = 0 To wrkEnum.Databases.Count - 1
            Debug.Print "  "; wrkEnum.Databases(I).Name
        Next I
        ' Enumerate all user accounts.
        Debug.Print "Users: Name"
        For I = 0 To wrkEnum.Users.Count - 1
            Debug.Print "  "; wrkEnum.Users(I).Name
        Next I
        Debug.Print
        ' Enumerate all group accounts.
        Debug.Print "Groups: Name"
        For I = 0 To wrkEnum.Groups.Count - 1
            Debug.Print "  "; wrkEnum.Groups(I).Name
        Next I
        Debug.Print
    Next J
    Debug.Print
    ' Enumerate built-in properties of wrkNew.
    Debug.Print "wrkNew.Name: "; wrkNew.Name
    Debug.Print "wrkNew.UserName: "; wrkNew.UserName
```

```
            Debug.Print
            wrkNew.Close
            EnumerateWorkspace = True
End Function
```

Workspaces Collection

Description The **Workspaces** collection contains all active, unhidden **Workspace** objects of the **DBEngine** object. (Hidden **Workspace** objects are not appended to the collection and referenced by the variable to which they are assigned.)

Remarks Use the **Workspace** object to manage the current session or to start an additional session.

When you start the Microsoft Jet database engine, you automatically create the default workspace, **DBEngine.Workspaces**(0).

New **Workspace** objects are created with the **CreateWorkspace** method of the **DBEngine** object. After you create a new **Workspace** object, you must appended it to the **Workspaces** collection if you need to refer to it from the **Workspaces** collection. You can, however, use a newly created **Workspace** object without appending it to the **Workspaces** collection.

You can refer to any other **Workspace** object that you create and append to the collection by its **Name** property setting using this syntax:

Workspaces("*name*")

You can also refer to appended **Workspace** objects by their position in the **Workspaces** collection using this syntax (where *n* is the *n*th member of the **Workspaces** collection):

DBEngine.Workspaces(*n*)

Properties **Count** Property.

Methods **Append** Method, **Refresh** Method.

See Also Appendix, "Data Access Object Hierarchy."

Example See the **Workspace** object example.

PART 2

SQL A–Z Reference

ALL, DISTINCT, DISTINCTROW, TOP Predicates

Description Specifies records selected with SQL queries.

Syntax SELECT [ALL | DISTINCT | DISTINCTROW | [TOP *n* [PERCENT]]]
       FROM *table*

A SELECT statement containing these predicates has the following parts.

Part	Description
ALL	Assumed if you don't include one of the predicates. The Microsoft Jet database engine selects all of the records that meet the conditions in the SQL statement. The following two examples are equivalent and return all records from the Employees table: SELECT ALL * FROM Employees ORDER BY EmployeeID; SELECT * FROM Employees ORDER BY EmployeeID;
DISTINCT	Omits records that contain duplicate data in the selected fields. To be included in the results of the query, the values for each field listed in the SELECT statement must be unique. For example, several employees listed in an Employees table may have the same last name. If two records contain Smith in the Last Name field, the following SQL statement returns only one record that contains Smith: SELECT DISTINCT LastName FROM Employees; If you omit DISTINCT, this query returns both Smith records. If the SELECT clause contains more than one field, the combination of values from all fields must be unique for a given record to be included in the results. The output of a query that uses DISTINCT isn't updatable and doesn't reflect subsequent changes made by other users.

Part	Description
DISTINCTROW	Omits data based on entire duplicate records, not just duplicate fields. For example, you could create a query that joins the Customers and Orders tables on the Customer ID field. The Customers table contains no duplicate Customer ID fields, but the Orders table does because each customer can have many orders. The following SQL statement shows how you can use DISTINCTROW to produce a list of companies that have at least one order but without any details about those orders: ``` SELECT DISTINCTROW CompanyName FROM Customers INNER JOIN Orders ON Customers.CustomerID = Orders.CustomerID ORDER BY CompanyName; ``` If you omit DISTINCTROW, this query produces multiple rows for each company that has more than one order. DISTINCTROW has an effect only when you select fields from some, but not all, of the tables used in the query. DISTINCTROW is ignored if your query includes only one table, or if you output fields from all tables.
TOP	Returns a certain number of records that fall at the top or the bottom of a range specified by an ORDER BY clause. Suppose you want the names of the top 25 students from the class of 1994: ``` SELECT TOP 25 FirstName, LastName FROM Students WHERE GraduationYear = 1994 ORDER BY GradePointAverage DESC; ``` If you don't include the ORDER BY clause, the query will return an arbitrary set of 25 records from the Students table that satisfy the WHERE clause. The TOP predicate doesn't choose between equal values. In the preceding example, if the twenty-fifth and twenty-sixth highest grade point averages are the same, the query will return 26 records.

ALL, DISTINCT, DISTINCTROW, TOP Predicates 293

Part	Description
TOP	You can also use the PERCENT reserved word to return a certain percentage of records that fall at the top or the bottom of a range specified by an ORDER BY clause. Suppose that, instead of the top 25 students, you want the bottom 10 percent of the class: SELECT TOP 10 PERCENT FirstName, LastName FROM Students WHERE GraduationYear = 1994 ORDER BY GradePointAverage ASC; The ASC predicate specifies a return of bottom values. The value that follows TOP must be an unsigned **Integer**. TOP doesn't affect the query's updatability.
table	The name of the table from which records are retrieved.

Specifics (Microsoft Access)

In Microsoft Access, using DISTINCT is equivalent to setting the **UniqueValues** property to Yes on the query property sheet in query Design view.

Using DISTINCTROW is equivalent to setting the **UniqueRecords** property to Yes (the default value) in the query property sheet in query Design view.

Using TOP is equivalent to setting the **TopValues** property on the query property sheet in query Design view, or entering a value in the Top Values list box on the toolbar in the Query window.

Using the PERCENT reserved word is equivalent to using the percent sign (%) with the **TopValues** property or in the Top Values list box.

Example

The following examples use two hypothetical tables, Customers and Orders.

Customers Table

First name	Customer ID
Bob	1
Adam	2
Beverly	3
Bob	4

Orders Table

Customer ID	Order ID
1	1
1	2

ALL, DISTINCT, DISTINCTROW, TOP Predicates

Customer ID	Order ID
2	3
2	4
2	5
4	6
4	7

```
SELECT ALL FirstName FROM Customers INNER JOIN Orders ON
Customers.CustomerID = Orders.CustomerID;
```

Result	Updatable
Bob	Yes
Bob	
Adam	
Adam	
Adam	
Bob	
Bob	

```
SELECT DISTINCT FirstName FROM Customers INNER JOIN Orders ON
Customers.CustomerID = Orders.CustomerID;
```

Result	Updatable
Bob	No
Adam	

```
SELECT DISTINCTROW FirstName FROM Customers INNER JOIN Orders ON
Customers.CustomerID = Orders.CustomerID;
```

Result	Updatable
Bob	Yes
Adam	
Bob	

```
SELECT TOP 5 FirstName FROM Customers INNER JOIN Orders ON
Customers.CustomerID = Orders.CustomerID ORDER BY Orders.OrderID;
```

Result	Updatable
Bob	Yes
Bob	
Adam	
Adam	
Adam	

ALTER TABLE Statement

Description Modifies the design of a table after it has been created with the CREATE TABLE statement.

Note The Microsoft Jet database engine doesn't support the use of ALTER TABLE, or any of the data definition language (DDL) statements, with non-Jet databases. Use the data access object Create methods instead.

Syntax ALTER TABLE *table* {ADD {COLUMN *field type*[(*size*)] [CONSTRAINT *index*] | CONSTRAINT *multifieldindex*} | DROP {COLUMN *field* | CONSTRAINT *indexname*} }

The ALTER TABLE statement has these parts.

Part	Description
table	The name of the table to be altered.
field	The name of the field to be added to or deleted from *table*.
type	The data type of *field*.
size	The field size in characters (Text and Binary fields only).
index	The index for *field*. See the CONSTRAINT clause topic for more information on how to construct this index.
multifieldindex	The definition of a multiple-field index to be added to *table*. See the CONSTRAINT clause topic for more information on how to construct this clause.
indexname	The name of the multiple-field index to be removed.

Remarks Using the ALTER TABLE statement, you can alter an existing table in several ways. You can:

- Use ADD COLUMN to add a new field to the table. You specify the field name, data type, and (for Text and Binary fields) an optional size. For example, the following statement adds a 25-character Text field called Notes to the Employees table:

```
ALTER TABLE Employees ADD COLUMN Notes TEXT(25)
```

You can also define an index on that field. For more information on single-field indexes, see the CONSTRAINT Clause Topic.

- Use the ADD constraint to add a multiple-field index. For more information on multiple-field indexes, see the CONSTRAINT Clause Topic.

- Use DROP COLUMN to delete a field. You specify only the name of the field.
- Use the DROP constraint to delete a multiple-field index. You specify only the index name following the CONSTRAINT reserved word.

Notes

- You can't add or delete more than one field or index at a time.
- You can use the CREATE INDEX statement to add a single- or multiple-field index to a table, and you can use ALTER TABLE or the DROP statement to delete an index created with ALTER TABLE or CREATE INDEX.

See Also

CONSTRAINT Clause, CREATE INDEX Statement, CREATE TABLE Statement, DROP Statement.

Example

The SQL statements shown below can be used on tables created with the CREATE TABLE statement.

This example adds a Salary field with a data type of Currency to the Employees table.

```
ALTER TABLE Employees ADD COLUMN Salary CURRENCY;
```

This example removes the Salary field from the Employees table.

```
ALTER TABLE Employees DROP COLUMN Salary;
```

This example adds a foreign key to the Orders table. The foreign key is based on the Employee ID field and refers to the Employee ID field of the Employees table. In this example, you don't have to list the Employee ID field after the Employees table in the REFERENCES clause because Employee ID is the primary key of the Employees table.

```
ALTER TABLE Orders ADD CONSTRAINT OrdersRelationship FOREIGN KEY
(EmployeeID) REFERENCES Employees (EmployeeID);
```

This example removes the foreign key from the Orders table.

```
ALTER TABLE Orders DROP CONSTRAINT OrdersRelationship;
```

Avg Function

Description

Calculates the arithmetic mean of a set of values contained in a specified field on a query.

Avg Function

Syntax

Avg(*expr*)

The *expr* placeholder represents a string expression identifying the field that contains the numeric data you want to average or an expression that performs a calculation using the data in that field. Operands in *expr* can include the name of a table field, a constant, or a function (which can be either intrinsic or user-defined but not one of the other SQL aggregate or domain aggregate functions).

Remarks

The average calculated by **Avg** is the arithmetic mean (the sum of the values divided by the number of values). You could use **Avg**, for example, to calculate average freight cost.

The **Avg** function doesn't include any **Null** fields in the calculation.

You can use **Avg** in a query expression and in the **SQL** property of a **QueryDef** object or when creating a **Recordset** object based on an SQL query.

See Also

SQL Aggregate Functions.

Specifics (Microsoft Access)

In Microsoft Access, you can use the **Avg** function in the query design grid, in an SQL statement in SQL view of the Query window, or in an SQL statement within Visual Basic code. You can also use the **Avg** function in a calculated control on a form or report.

The **Avg** function is most useful in totals queries and crosstab queries. It functions the same way whether you create the query in the query design grid or as an SQL statement in SQL view.

In the query design grid, you can create a new totals query by clicking the Totals button on the toolbar. The Total row is then inserted in the grid. You can set the Total cell beneath a field to the aggregate function to perform on the data in that field.

For example, suppose you have an Orders table that has both a Freight field and a ShipCity field. You can create a query that displays the average freight cost for orders sent to each city to which your company ships. Create a new totals query, and drag the ShipCity field to the query design grid. The Total cell beneath the ShipCity field should be set to Group By. Drag the Freight field to the query design grid, and set the Total cell beneath it to Avg. When you run the query, it will display the average freight cost by city.

You can view the SQL statement for this query by switching to SQL view. In this example, Microsoft Access creates the following SQL statement.

```
SELECT DISTINCTROW Avg(Orders.Freight) AS AvgOfFreight, Orders.ShipCity
FROM Orders
GROUP BY Orders.ShipCity;
```

298 Avg Function

You can also use an SQL statement such as this one within Visual Basic code. For example, using the following code you can create a **Recordset** object based on the query defined by this SQL statement.

```
Dim dbs As DatabAse, rst As Recordset, strSQL As String
Set dbs = CurrentDb
strSQL = "SELECT DISTINCTROW Avg(Orders.Freight) AS AvgOfFreight, "_
    "Orders.ShipCity FROM Orders GROUP BY Orders.ShipCity;"
Set rst = dbs.OpenRecordset(strSQL)
```

To use the **Avg** function in a calculated control, set the control's **ControlSource** property to an expression containing the **Avg** function. For example, to display the average freight cost for a set of orders in a text box, enter the following expression in the **ControlSource** property of the text box.

```
= Avg([Freight])
```

If you use the **Avg** function in a calculated control, you can restrict the set of records against which the function is performed by setting the form's **Filter** property.

Example

This example uses the Orders table to calculate the average freight charges for orders with freight charges over $100.

```
SELECT Avg(Freight) AS [Average Freight] FROM Orders WHERE Freight > 100;
```

Example (Microsoft Access)

The following example assumes that you have an Orders table that contains a field called Freight. You can use the **Avg** function to calculate the average freight charges for orders with freight charges over $100. Enter the following expression in SQL view in the Query window.

```
SELECT Avg([Freight]) AS [AverageFreight] FROM Orders WHERE [Freight] > 100;
```

The next example creates a calculated control that displays the average freight charges for all of the underlying records in a form based on the same Orders table. Open a new form and set its **RecordSource** property to Orders. Enter this expression in a the **ControlSource** property of a text box on the form. To apply a condition that limits the calculation to only some records, such as those for orders greater than $100, set the form's **Filter** property.

```
= Avg([Freight])
```

Between...And Operator

Description   Determines whether the value of an expression lies within a specified range of values. This operator can be used within SQL statements.

Syntax   *expr* [**Not**] **Between** *value1* **And** *value2*

The **Between...And** operator syntax has these parts.

Part	Description
expr	Expression identifying the field that contains the data you want to evaluate.
value1, *value2*	Expressions against which you want to evaluate *expr*.

Remarks   If the value of *expr* is between *value1* and *value2* (inclusive), the **Between...And** operator returns **True**; otherwise, it returns **False**. You can include the **Not** logical operator to evaluate the opposite condition (that is, whether *expr* lies outside the range defined by *value1* and *value2*).

You might use **Between...And** to determine whether the value of a field falls within a specified numeric range. The following example determines whether an order was shipped to a location within a range of ZIP codes. If the ZIP Code is between 98101 and 98199, the **IIf** function returns "Local." Otherwise, it returns "Nonlocal."

```
SELECT IIf(ZIP Between 98101 And 98199, "Local", "Nonlocal")
FROM Publishers
```

If *expr*, *value1*, or *value2* is **Null**, **Between...And** returns a **Null**.

Because wildcards, such as *, are treated as literals, you cannot use them with the **Between...And** operator. For example, you cannot use 980* and 989* to find all postal codes that start with 980 to 989. Instead, you have two alternatives for accomplishing this. You can add an expression to the query that takes the left three characters of the text field and use **Between...And** on those characters. Or you can pad the high and low values with extra characters—in this case, 98000 to 98999, or 98000 to 98999–9999 if using extended ZIP codes. (You must omit the –0000 off the low values because otherwise 98000 is dropped if some ZIP codes have extended sections and others do not.)

See Also   IN Clause, SQL Expressions.

Specifics (Microsoft Access)   In Microsoft Access, you can use the **Between...And** operator in a query expression or in a calculated control on a form or report.

You can use the **Between...And** operator in the Criteria field in the query design grid to create a parameter query. The **Between...And** operator enables you to prompt the user to enter a range of values by which the query is restricted. The expression supplied for the *value1* argument serves as the prompt for the beginning of the range, and the expression supplied for the *value2* argument serves as the prompt for the end of the range.

For example, suppose you have an Orders table that has an OrderDate field. Create a new query in the query design grid and drag the OrderDate field to the first Field cell in the grid. In the Criteria field, enter the following statement.

```
Between [Enter beginning date:] And [Enter ending date:]
```

When you run the query, you will first be prompted with a dialog box that says, "Enter the beginning date for the range." Once you enter a value in that dialog, you will be prompted by a second dialog box that says, "Enter the ending date for the range." Assuming you enter valid dates, your results will include all the values in the OrderDate field that either match or fall between the dates you specified as parameters.

You can also use the **Between...And** operator in a calculated control to determine whether the value of the control falls within a specified numeric range. The following example determines whether an order was shipped to a location within a range of zip codes. If the ZIP field is between 98101 and 98199, the **IIf** function returns "Local." Otherwise, it returns "Nonlocal."

```
= IIf([ZIP] Between "98101" And "98199", "Local", "Nonlocal")
```

If any of the arguments supplied for the **Between...And** expression is **Null**, **Between...And** returns a **Null**.

CONSTRAINT Clause

Description

A constraint is similar to an index, although it can also be used to establish a relationship with another table.

You use the CONSTRAINT clause in ALTER TABLE and CREATE TABLE statements to create or delete constraints. There are two types of CONSTRAINT clauses: one for creating a constraint on a single field and one for creating a constraint on more than one field.

Note The Microsoft Jet database engine doesn't support the use of CONSTRAINT, or any of the data definition language (DDL) statements, with non-Jet databases. Use the data access object Create methods instead.

Syntax

Single-field index:

CONSTRAINT *name* {PRIMARY KEY |
 UNIQUE |
 REFERENCES *foreigntable* [(*foreignfield1, foreignfield2*)]}

Multiple-field index:

CONSTRAINT *name*
 {PRIMARY KEY (*primary1*[, *primary2* [, ...]]) |
 UNIQUE (*unique1*[, *unique2* [, ...]]) |
 FOREIGN KEY (*ref1*[, *ref2* [, ...]]) REFERENCES *foreigntable*
 [(*foreignfield1* [, *foreignfield2* [, ...]])]}

The CONSTRAINT clause has these parts.

Part	Description
name	The name of the constraint to be created.
primary1, primary2	The name of the field or fields to be designated the primary key.
unique1, unique2	The name of the field or fields to be designated as a unique key.
ref1, ref2	The name of a foreign key field or fields that refer to fields in another table.
foreigntable	The name of the foreign table containing the field or fields specified by *foreignfield*.
foreignfield1, foreignfield2	The name of the field or fields in *foreigntable* specified by *ref1, ref2*. You can omit this clause if the referenced field is the primary key of *foreigntable*.

Remarks

You use the syntax for a single-field constraint in the field-definition clause of an ALTER TABLE or CREATE TABLE statement immediately following the specification of the field's data type.

You use the syntax for a multiple-field constraint whenever you use the reserved word CONSTRAINT outside a field-definition clause in an ALTER TABLE or CREATE TABLE statement.

Using CONSTRAINT, you can designate a field as one of the following types of constraints:

- You can use the UNIQUE reserved word to designate a field as a unique key. This means that no two records in the table can have the same value in this field. You can constrain any field or list of fields as unique. If a multiple-field constraint is designated as a unique key, the combined values of all fields in the index must be unique, even if two or more records have the same value in just one of the fields.
- You can use the PRIMARY KEY reserved words to designate one field or set of fields in a table as a primary key. All values in the primary key must be unique and not **Null**, and there can be only one primary key for a table.

Note Don't set a PRIMARY KEY constraint on a table that already has a primary key; if you do, an error occurs.

- You can use the FOREIGN KEY reserved words to designate a field as a foreign key. If the foreign table's primary key consists of more than one field, you must use a multiple-field constraint definition, listing all of the referencing fields, the name of the foreign table, and the names of the referenced fields in the foreign table in the same order that the referencing fields are listed. If the referenced field or fields are the foreign table's primary key, you don't have to specify the referenced fields—by default, the database engine behaves as if the foreign table's primary key is the referenced fields.

See Also   ALTER TABLE Statement, CREATE INDEX Statement, CREATE TABLE Statement, DROP Statement.

Example   This example creates a new table called ThisTable with two Text fields.

```
CREATE TABLE ThisTable (FirstName TEXT, LastName TEXT);
```

This example creates a new table called MyTable with two Text fields, a Date/Time field, and a unique index made up of all three fields.

```
CREATE TABLE MyTable (FirstName TEXT, LastName TEXT, DateOfBirth
    DATETIME, CONSTRAINT MyTableConstraint
    UNIQUE (FirstName, LastName, DateOfBirth));
```

This example creates a new table with two Text fields and an Integer field. The SSN field is the primary key.

```
CREATE TABLE NewTable (FirstName TEXT, LastName TEXT, SSN INTEGER
CONSTRAINT MyFieldConstraint PRIMARY KEY);
```

Count Function

Description Calculates the number of records returned by a query.

Syntax **Count**(*expr*)

The *expr* placeholder represents a string expression identifying the field that contains the data you want to count or an expression that performs a calculation using the data in the field. Operands in *expr* can include the name of a table field or function (which can be either intrinsic or user-defined but not other SQL aggregate functions). You can count any kind of data, including text.

Remarks You can use **Count** to count the number of records in an underlying query. For example, you could use **Count** to count the number of orders shipped to a particular country.

Although *expr* can perform a calculation on a field, **Count** simply tallies the number of records. It doesn't matter what values are stored in the records.

The **Count** function doesn't count records that have null fields unless *expr* is the asterisk (*) wildcard character. If you use an asterisk, **Count** calculates the total number of records, including those that contain null fields. **Count**(*) is considerably faster than **Count**([*Column Name*]). Don't enclose the asterisk in quotation marks (" "). The following example calculates the number of records in the Orders table:

```
SELECT Count(*)AS TotalOrders FROM Orders;
```

If *expr* identifies multiple fields, the **Count** function counts a record only if at least one of the fields is not **Null**. If all of the specified fields are **Null**, the record isn't counted. Separate the field names with an ampersand (&). The following example shows how you can limit the count to records in which either Shipped Date or Freight isn't **Null**:

```
SELECT Count('ShippedDate & Freight')
AS [Not Null] FROM Orders;
```

You can use **Count** in a query expression. You can also use this expression in the **SQL** property of a **QueryDef** object or when creating a **Recordset** object based on an SQL query.

See Also SQL Aggregate Functions, **Sum** Function.

Specifics (Microsoft Access) In Microsoft Access, you can use the **Count** function in the query design grid, in an SQL statement in SQL view of the Query window, or in an SQL statement within Visual Basic code. You can also use the **Count** function in a calculated control on a form or report.

The **Count** function is most useful in totals queries and crosstab queries. It functions the same way whether you create the query in the query design grid or as an SQL statement in SQL view.

In the query design grid, you can create a new totals query by clicking the Totals button on the toolbar. The Total row is then inserted in the grid. You can set the Total cell beneath a field to the aggregate function to perform on the data in that field.

The fastest way to count all the records in a query is to use the **Count(*)** function. You can use the **Count(*)** function in a calculated field in a query.

For example, suppose you have an Orders table that has both an OrderID field and a ShipCity field. You can create a query that displays the number of orders sent to each city. Create a new totals query, and drag the ShipCity field to the query design grid. Set the Total cell beneath the ShipCity field to Group By.

Next, create a calculated field by typing the following expression into a new Field cell.

```
CountOfOrders: Count(*)
```

Then, set the Total cell beneath this field to Expression. When you run the query, it will display the number of orders sent to each city.

You can view the SQL statement for this query by switching to SQL view. In this example, Microsoft Access creates the following SQL statement.

```
SELECT DISTINCTROW Count(*) AS CountOfOrders, Orders.ShipCity
FROM Orders
GROUP BY Orders.ShipCity;
```

You can achieve the same results by dragging the OrderID field to the query design grid, and choosing Count in the Total cell beneath it. This query will be slightly slower than the one that uses the **Count(*)** function. Note the differences between the following SQL statements.

```
SELECT DISTINCTROW Count(Orders.OrderID)
AS CountOfOrderID, Orders.ShipCity
FROM Orders
GROUP BY Orders.ShipCity;
```

You can also use an SQL statement such as this one within Visual Basic code. For example, using the following code you can create a **Recordset** object based on the query defined by this SQL statement.

```
Dim dbs As DatabAse, rst As Recordset, strSQL As String
Set dbs = CurrentDb
strSQL = "SELECT DISTINCTROW Count(*) AS CountOfOrders, Orders.ShipCity
FROM Orders GROUP BY Orders.ShipCity;"
```

```
Set rst = dbs.OpenRecordset(strSQL)
```

To use the **Count** function in a calculated control, set the control's **ControlSource** property to an expression containing the **Count** function. For example, to display the number of orders in a set of orders in a text box, enter the following expression in the **ControlSource** property of the text box.

```
= Count([OrderID])
```

If you use the **Count** function in a calculated control, you can restrict the set of records against which the function is performed by setting the form's **Filter** property.

Example

This example uses the Orders table to calculate the number of orders shipped to the United Kingdom.

```
SELECT Count(ShipCountry)AS [UK Orders] FROM Orders
WHERE ShipCountry = 'UK';
```

Example (Microsoft Access)

The following example assumes that you have an Orders table that contains a field called ShipCountry. You can use the **Count** function to calculate the number of orders shipped to the United Kingdom. Enter the following expression in SQL view in the Query window.

```
SELECT Count([ShipCountry]) AS [UKOrders] FROM Orders
WHERE [ShipCountry] = 'UK';
```

The next example creates a calculated control that displays the number of orders in the same Orders table. Open a new form and set its **RecordSource** property to Orders. Enter the following expression in the **ControlSource** property of a text box on the form. To apply a condition that limits the count to only some records, such as those for orders shipped to the United Kingdom, set the form's **Filter** property.

```
= Count([ShipCountry])
```

CREATE INDEX Statement

Description

Creates a new index on an existing table.

Note For non-Jet databases, the Microsoft Jet database engine doesn't support the use of CREATE INDEX (except to create a pseudo index on an ODBC attached table) or any of the data definition language (DDL) statements. Use the data access object **Create** methods instead. For more information, see the Remarks section.

CREATE INDEX Statement

Syntax

CREATE [UNIQUE] INDEX *index*
  ON *table* (*field* [ASC | DESC][, *field* [ASC | DESC], ...])
  [WITH { PRIMARY | DISALLOW NULL | IGNORE NULL }]

The CREATE INDEX statement has these parts.

Part	Description
index	The name of the index to be created.
table	The name of the existing table the index will be created on.
field	The name of the field or fields to be indexed. To create a single-field index, list the field name in parentheses following the table name. To create a multiple-field index, list the name of each field to be included in the index. To create descending indexes, use the DESC reserved word; otherwise, indexes are assumed to be ascending.

Remarks

To prohibit duplicate values in the indexed field or fields of different records, use the UNIQUE reserved word.

In the optional WITH clause, you can enforce data validation rules. You can:

- Prohibit **Null** entries in the indexed field or fields of new records by using the DISALLOW NULL option.
- Prevent records with **Null** values in the indexed field or fields from being included in the index by using the IGNORE NULL option.
- Designate the indexed field or fields as the primary key by using the PRIMARY reserved word. This implies that the key is unique, so you can omit the UNIQUE reserved word.

You can use CREATE INDEX to create a pseudo index on an attached table in an ODBC data source such as SQL Server that does not already have an index. You don't need permission or access to the remote server to create a pseudo index, and the remote database is unaware of and unaffected by the pseudo index. You use the same syntax for attached and native tables. This can be especially useful to create an index on a table that would ordinarily be read-only due to lack of an index.

You can also use the ALTER TABLE statement to add a single- or multiple-field index to a table, and you can use the ALTER TABLE statement or the DROP statement to remove an index created with ALTER TABLE or CREATE INDEX.

Note Don't use the PRIMARY reserved word when you create a new index on a table that already has a primary key; if you do, an error occurs.

See Also

ALTER TABLE Statement, CONSTRAINT Clause, CREATE TABLE Statement, DROP Statement.

Example

This example creates an index consisting of the fields Home Phone and Extension in the Employees table.

```
CREATE INDEX NewIndex ON Employees (HomePhone, Extension);
```

This example creates an index on the Employees table using the Social Security Number field. No two records can have the same data in the SSN field, and no **Null** values are allowed.

```
CREATE UNIQUE INDEX CustID ON Customers (CustomerID) WITH DISALLOW NULL;
```

This example creates an index on a hypothetical ODBC linked table. The table's remote database is unaware of and unaffected by the new index.

```
CREATE UNIQUE INDEX OrderID ON OrderDetails (OrderID);
```

CREATE TABLE Statement

Description

Creates a new table.

Note The Microsoft Jet database engine doesn't support the use of CREATE TABLE, or any of the data definition language (DDL) statements, with non-Jet database engine databases. Use the data access object Create methods instead.

Syntax

CREATE TABLE *table* (*field1 type* [(*size*)] [*index1*] [, *field2 type* [(*size*)] ↪ [*index2*] [, ...]] [, *multifieldindex* [, ...]])

The CREATE TABLE statement has these parts.

Part	Description
table	The name of the table to be created.
field1, *field2*	The name of field or fields to be created in the new table. You must create at least one field.
type	The data type of *field* in the new table.
size	The field size in characters (Text and Binary fields only).
index1, *index2*	A CONSTRAINT clause defining a single-field index. See the CONSTRAINT clause topic for more information on how to create this index.
multifieldindex	A CONSTRAINT clause defining a multiple-field index. See the CONSTRAINT clause topic for more information on how to create this index.

Remarks

You can use the CREATE INDEX statement to create indexes on existing tables.

308 DELETE Statement

See Also ALTER TABLE Statement, CONSTRAINT Clause, CREATE INDEX Statement, DROP Statement.

Example This example creates a new table called ThisTable with two Text fields.

```
CREATE TABLE ThisTable (FirstName TEXT, LastName TEXT);
```

This example creates a new table called MyTable with two Text fields, a Date/Time field, and a unique index made up of all three fields.

```
CREATE TABLE MyTable (FirstName TEXT, LastName TEXT, DateOfBirth DATETIME,
CONSTRAINT MyTableConstraint UNIQUE (FirstName, LastName, DateOfBirth));
```

This example creates a new table with two Text fields and an Integer field. The SSN field is the primary key.

```
CREATE TABLE NewTable (FirstName TEXT, LastName TEXT, SSN INTEGER
CONSTRAINT MyFieldConstraint PRIMARY KEY);
```

DELETE Statement

Description Creates a delete query that removes records from one or more of the tables listed in the FROM clause that satisfy the WHERE clause.

Syntax DELETE [*table*.*]
  FROM *table*
   WHERE *criteria*

The DELETE statement has these parts.

Part	Description
table	The optional name of the table from which records are deleted.
table	The name of the table from which records are deleted.
criteria	An expression that determines which records to delete.

Remarks DELETE is especially useful when you want to delete many records.

To drop an entire table from the database, you can use the **Execute** method with a DROP statement. If you delete the table, however, the structure is lost. In contrast, when you use DELETE, only the data is deleted; the table structure and all of the table properties, such as field attributes and indexes, remain intact.

You can use DELETE to remove records from tables that are in a one-to-many relationship with other tables. Cascade delete operations cause the records in tables that are on the many side of the relationship to be deleted when the corresponding record in the one side of the relationship is deleted in the query. For example, in the relationship between the Customers and Orders tables, the Customers table is on the one side and the Orders table is on the many side of the relationship. Deleting a record from Customers results in the corresponding Orders records being deleted if the cascade delete option is specified.

A delete query deletes entire records, not just data in specific fields. If you want to delete values in a specific field, create an update query that changes the values to **Null**.

Important

- After you remove records using a delete query, you can't undo the operation. If you want to know which records were deleted, first examine the results of a select query that uses the same criteria, and then run the delete query.
- Maintain backup copies of your data at all times. If you delete the wrong records, you can retrieve them from your backup copies.

See Also DROP Statement, FROM Clause, IN Clause, INNER JOIN Operation, SELECT Statement, UPDATE Statement, WHERE Clause.

Specifics (Microsoft Access) In Microsoft Access, no query output or datasheet is produced when you use the DELETE statement. If you want to know which records will be deleted, first view the datasheet of a select query that uses the same criteria, and then run a delete query.

Example Some of the following examples assume the existence of a hypothetical Payroll table.

This example deletes all records for employees whose title is Trainee. When the FROM clause includes only one table, you don't have to list the table name in the DELETE statement.

```
DELETE * FROM Employees WHERE Title = 'Trainee';
```

This example deletes all records for employees whose title is Trainee and who also have a record in the Payroll table. The Employees and Payroll tables have a one-to-one relationship.

```
DELETE Employees.* FROM Employees INNER JOIN Payroll
ON Employees.EmployeeID = Payroll.EmployeeID
WHERE Employees.Title = 'Trainee';
```

DISTINCT, DISTINCTROW Predicates

See ALL, DISTINCT, DISTINCTROW, TOP Predicates.

DROP Statement

Description Deletes an existing table from a database or deletes an existing index from a table.

Note The Microsoft Jet database engine doesn't support the use of DROP, or any of the data definition language (DDL) statements, with non-Jet databases. Use the data access object Create methods instead.

Syntax DROP {TABLE *table* | INDEX *index* ON *table*}

The DROP statement has these parts.

Part	Description
table	The name of the table to be deleted or the table from which an index is to be deleted.
index	The name of the index to be deleted from *table*.

Remarks You must close the table before you can delete it or remove an index from it.

You can also use ALTER TABLE to delete an index from a table.

You can use CREATE TABLE to create a table and CREATE INDEX or ALTER TABLE to create an index. To modify a table, use ALTER TABLE.

See Also ALTER TABLE Statement, CONSTRAINT Clause, CREATE INDEX Statement, CREATE TABLE Statement.

Example The following examples assume the existence of a hypothetical MyIndex index and a hypothetical Trainees table. Note that these objects do not actually exist in the Northwind database.

This example deletes the index MyIndex from the Employees table.

```
DROP INDEX MyIndex ON Employees;
```

This example deletes the Trainees table from the database.

```
DROP TABLE [Trainees];
```

First, Last Functions

Description Return a field value from the first or last record in the result set returned by a query.

Syntax **First**(*expr*)
Last(*expr*)

The *expr* placeholder represents a string expression identifying the field that contains the data you want to use or an expression that performs a calculation using the data in that field. Operands in *expr* can include the name of a table field, a constant, or a function (which can be either intrinsic or user-defined but not one of the other SQL aggregate or domain aggregate functions).

Remarks The **First** and **Last** functions can be thought of as analogous to the **MoveFirst** and **MoveLast** methods of a **Recordset** object. They simply return the value of a specified field in the first or last record, respectively, of the result set returned by a query. Since records are normally returned in no particular order (unless the query includes an ORDER BY clause), the records returned by these functions will be arbitrary.

See Also SQL Aggregate Functions.

Specifics (Microsoft Access) In Microsoft Access, you can use the **First** and **Last** functions in the query design grid, in an SQL statement in SQL view of the Query window, or in an SQL statement within Visual Basic code. You can also use the **First** and **Last** functions in a calculated control on a form or report.

The **First** and **Last** functions are most useful in calculated controls on a report. For example, if you have an Order report that is grouped on a ShipCountry field and sorted on an OrderDate field, you can use the **First** and **Last** functions in calculated controls to show the range of earliest to latest order dates for each grouping. To group on the ShipCountry field, click on the Sorting And Grouping button on the Reports toolbar. Choose ShipCountry in the Field/Expression column, and set the **GroupHeader** and **GroupFooter** properties to Yes. In Design view, create two new text boxes in the ShipCountry footer, and set the **ControlSource** property for both to the following expressions.

```
= First([OrderDate])
= Last([OrderDate])
```

When you switch to Print Preview, you will see the first and last order dates for each group of orders.

Note In previous versions of Microsoft Access, the **First** and **Last** functions returned the first and last record created, respectively. If you want to return the first or last record in a set of records in Microsoft Access for Windows 95, you should create a query sorted as either Ascending or Descending and set the **TopValues** property to 1. For more information, see the **TopValues** property topic. From Visual Basic, you can also create a sorted results set of the query, and use the **MoveFirst** or **MoveLast** method to return the first or last record in a set of records.

Example

This example uses the Employees table to return the values from the LastName field of the first and last records returned from the table.

```
SELECT First(LastName), Last(LastName) FROM Employees;
```

The next two examples compare using the First and Last functions with simply using the Min and Max functions to find the earliest and latest birth dates of Employees.

```
SELECT First(BirthDate), Last(BirthDate) FROM Employees;

SELECT Min(BirthDate), Max(BirthDate) FROM Employees;
```

FROM Clause

Description

Specifies the tables or queries that contain the fields listed in the SELECT statement.

Syntax

SELECT *fieldlist*
    FROM *tableexpression* [IN *externaldatabase*]

A SELECT statement containing a FROM clause has these parts.

Part	Description
fieldlist	The name of the field or fields to be retrieved along with any field-name aliases, SQL aggregate functions, selection predicates (ALL, DISTINCT, DISTINCTROW, or TOP), or other SELECT statement options.
tableexpression	An expression that identifies one or more tables from which data is retrieved. The expression can be a single table name, a saved query name, or a compound resulting from an INNER JOIN, LEFT JOIN, or RIGHT JOIN.
externaldatabase	The full pathname of an external database containing all the tables in *tableexpression*.

Remarks	FROM is required and follows any SELECT statement.
	The order of the table names in *tableexpression* isn't important.
	For improved performance and ease of use, it's recommended that you use an attached table instead of an IN clause to retrieve data from an external database.
	The following example shows how you can retrieve data from the Employees table:
	``
	SELECT LastName, FirstName
	FROM Employees;
	``
See Also	IN Clause; INNER JOIN Operation; LEFT JOIN, RIGHT JOIN Operations; SQL Aggregate Functions; WHERE Clause.
Specifics (Microsoft Access)	If you include a query or table name in the FROM clause of a SQL statement, that query or table will be automatically added to the Query window.
	Conversely, any table or query that you add to the Query window will be included in the FROM clause of the corresponding SQL statement.

GROUP BY Clause

Description	Combines records with identical values in the specified field list into a single record. A summary value is created for each record if you include an SQL aggregate function, such as **Sum** or **Count**, in the SELECT statement.
Syntax	SELECT *fieldlist* 　　FROM *table* 　　WHERE *criteria* 　　GROUP BY *groupfieldlist*
	A SELECT statement containing a GROUP BY clause has these parts.

Part	Description
fieldlist	The name of the field or fields to be retrieved along with any field-name aliases, SQL aggregate functions, selection predicates (ALL, DISTINCT, DISTINCTROW, or TOP), or other SELECT statement options.
table	The name of the table from which records are retrieved. For more information, see the FROM clause.

314　GROUP BY Clause

Part	Description
criteria	Selection criteria. If the statement includes a WHERE clause, the Microsoft Jet database engine groups values after applying the WHERE conditions to the records.
groupfieldlist	The names of up to 10 fields used to group records. The order of the field names in *groupfieldlist* determines the grouping levels from the highest to the lowest level of grouping.

Remarks　　GROUP BY is optional.

Summary values are omitted if there is no SQL aggregate function in the SELECT statement.

Null values in GROUP BY fields are grouped and aren't omitted. However, **Null** values aren't evaluated in any SQL aggregate function.

Use the WHERE clause to exclude rows you don't want grouped, and use the HAVING clause to filter records after they've been grouped.

Unless it contains Memo or OLE Object data, a field in the GROUP BY field list can refer to any field in any table listed in the FROM clause, even if the field isn't included in the SELECT statement, provided the SELECT statement includes at least one SQL aggregate function. The Jet database engine can't group on Memo or OLE Object fields.

All fields in the SELECT field list must either be included in the GROUP BY clause or be included as arguments to an SQL aggregate function.

See Also　　HAVING Clause, ORDER BY Clause, SELECT Statement, SELECT...INTO Statement, SQL Aggregate Functions.

Specifics (Microsoft Access)　　Including a GROUP BY clause in an SQL statement is equivalent to creating a totals query in the Query window and setting the Total cell to Group By for the appropriate field.

Example　　Some of the following examples assume the existence of a hypothetical Department field in an Employees table.

This example creates a list of unique department names and the number of employees in each of those departments.

```
SELECT Department, Count([Department]) AS Tally FROM Employees
GROUP BY Department;
```

For each unique job title, this example calculates the number of Sales department employees who have that title.

```
SELECT Title, Count(Title) AS Tally FROM Employees
WHERE Department = 'Sales' GROUP BY Title;
```

This example calculates the number of items in stock for each combination of item number and color.

```
SELECT Item, Sum(Units) AS Tally FROM ItemsInStock GROUP BY Item, Color;
```

HAVING Clause

Description Specifies which grouped records are displayed in a SELECT statement with a GROUP BY clause. After GROUP BY combines records, HAVING displays any records grouped by the GROUP BY clause that satisfy the conditions of the HAVING clause.

Syntax SELECT *fieldlist*
　　FROM *table*
　　WHERE *selectcriteria*
　　GROUP BY *groupfieldlist*
　　HAVING *groupcriteria*

A SELECT statement containing a HAVING clause has these parts.

Part	Description
fieldlist	The name of the field or fields to be retrieved along with any field-name aliases, SQL aggregate functions, selection predicates (ALL, DISTINCT, DISTINCTROW, or TOP), or other SELECT statement options.
table	The name of the table from which records are retrieved. For more information, see the FROM clause.
selectcriteria	Selection criteria. If the statement includes a WHERE clause, the Microsoft Jet database engine groups values after applying the WHERE conditions to the records.
groupfieldlist	The names of up to 10 fields used to group records. The order of the field names in *groupfieldlist* determines the grouping levels from the highest to the lowest level of grouping.
groupcriteria	An expression that determines which grouped records to display.

Remarks HAVING is optional.

HAVING is similar to WHERE, which determines which records are selected. After records are grouped with GROUP BY, HAVING determines which records are displayed:

```
SELECT CategoryID,Sum(UnitsIn Stock)
FROM Products
GROUP BY CategoryID
HAVING Sum(UnitsIn Stock) > 100 AND LIKE BOS*;
```

A HAVING clause can contain up to 40 expressions linked by logical operators, such as **And** and **Or**.

See Also GROUP BY Clause, SELECT Statement, SELECT...INTO Statement, SQL Aggregate Functions.

Example Some of the following examples assume the existence of a hypothetical Department field in an Employees table.

This example selects the job titles in the Production department assigned to more than 50 employees.

```
SELECT Title, Count(Title) FROM Employees
WHERE Department = 'Production' GROUP BY Title HAVING Count(Title) > 50;
```

This example selects departments with more than 100 employees.

```
SELECT Department, Count([Department]) FROM Employees
GROUP BY Department HAVING Count(Department) > 100;
```

IN Clause

Description Identifies tables in any external database to which the Microsoft Jet database engine can connect, such as a dBASE or Paradox database or an external Jet database.

Syntax To identify a destination table:

[SELECT | INSERT] INTO *destination*
 IN{*path* | ["*path*" "*type*"] | ["" [*type*; DATABASE = *path*]]}

To identify a source table:

FROM *tableexpression*
 IN {*path* | ["*path*" "*type*"] | ["" [*type*; DATABASE = *path*]]}

A SELECT statement containing an IN clause has these parts.

Part	Description
destination	The name of the external table into which data is inserted.
tableexpression	The name of the table or tables from which data is retrieved. This argument can be a single table name, a saved query, or a compound resulting from an INNER JOIN, LEFT JOIN, or RIGHT JOIN.
path	The full path for the directory or file containing *table*.
type	The name of the database type used to create *table* if a database isn't a Jet database (for example, dBASE III, dBASE IV, Paradox 3.*x*, Paradox 4.*x*, or Btrieve).

Remarks

You can use IN to connect to only one external database at a time.

In some cases, the path argument refers to the directory containing the database files. For example, when working with dBASE, FoxPro, or Paradox database tables, the path argument specifies the directory containing .dbf or .db files. The table filename is derived from the *destination* or *tableexpression* arguments.

To specify a non-Jet database, append a semicolon (;) to the name, and enclose it in single (' ') or double (" ") quotation marks. For example, either 'dBASE IV;' or "dBASE IV;" is acceptable.

You can also use the DATABASE reserved word to specify the external database. For example, the following lines specify the same table:

```
... FROM Table IN  "" [dBASE IV; DATABASE=C:\DBASE\DATA\SALES;];
... FROM Table IN "C:\DBASE\DATA\SALES" "dBASE IV;"
```

Notes

- For improved performance and ease of use, use an attached table instead of IN.
- You can also use the IN reserved word as a comparison operator in an expression. For more information, see the **In** operator.

See Also

FROM Clause, INSERT INTO Statement, SELECT Statement, SELECT...INTO Statement, SQL Aggregate Functions.

Example

The following table shows how you can use the IN clause to retrieve data from an external database. In each example, assume the hypothetical Customers table is stored in an external database.

External database	SQL statement

Microsoft Jet database. MYDATA.mdb is the name of the Jet database that contains the Customers table.	`SELECT CustomerID`
	`FROM Customers`
	`IN MYDATA.mdb`
	`WHERE CustomerID Like "A*";`

dBASE III or IV. To retrieve data from a dBASE III table, substitute "dBASE III" for "dBASE IV;".	`SELECT CustomerID`
	`FROM Customer`
	`IN "C:\DBASE\DATA\SALES" "dBASE IV;"`
	`WHERE CustomerID Like "A*";`

dBASE III or IV using DATABASE syntax. To retrieve data from a dBASE III table, substitute "dBASE III" for "dBASE IV;".	`SELECT CustomerID`
	`FROM Customer`
	`IN "" [dBASE IV;`
	`DATABASE=C:\DBASE\DATA\SALES;]`
	`WHERE CustomerID Like "A*";`

Paradox 3.x or 4.x. To retrieve data from a Paradox version 3.x table, substitute "Paradox 3.x;" for "Paradox 4.x;".	`SELECT CustomerID`
	`FROM Customer`
	`IN "C:\PARADOX\DATA\SALES" "Paradox 4.x;"`
	`WHERE CustomerID Like "A*";`

Paradox 3.x or 4.x using DATABASE syntax. To retrieve data from a Paradox version 3.x table, substitute "Paradox 3.x;" for "Paradox 4.x;".	`SELECT CustomerID`
	`FROM Customer`
	`IN "" [Paradox`
	`4.x;DATABASE=C:\PARADOX\DATA\SALES;]`
	`WHERE CustomerID Like "A*";`

In Operator

Description Determines whether the value of an expression is equal to any of several values in a specified list.

Syntax *expr* [**Not**] **In**(*value1, value2, . . .*)

In Operator

Remarks

The **In** operator uses the following arguments.

Argument	Description
expr	Expression identifying the field that contains the data you want to evaluate.
value1, *value2*	Expression or list of expressions against which you want to evaluate *expr*.

If *expr* is found in the list of values, the **In** operator returns **True** (−1); otherwise, it returns **False** (0). You can include the **Not** logical operator to evaluate the opposite condition (that is, whether *expr* is not in the list of values).

You might use **In** to determine which orders are shipped to a set of specified regions:

```
SELECT *
FROM Orders
WHERE ShipRegion In ('Avon','Glos','Som')
```

See Also

SQL Expressions.

Specifics (Microsoft Access)

In Microsoft Access, you can use the **In** operator in a query expression or in a calculated control on a form or report.

You can use the **In** operator in a query expression when you need to set a number of criteria. For example, suppose you have an Orders table with both a ShipCountry field and an OrderID field, and you want to create a query to show all orders sent to the United States, Canada, or the United Kingdom. Create a new query in the Query window and add the Orders table. Drag the OrderID field and the ShipCountry field to the query design grid. Enter the following expression in the Criteria cell below the ShipCountry field.

```
In('USA', 'Canada', 'UK')
```

When you run the query, you will see all orders shipped to one of these three countries.

You can achieve the same result by entering the following expression in the Criteria cell.

```
"USA" Or "Canada" Or "UK"
```

With a long list of criteria, it may be more convenient to use the **In** operator than the **Or** operator. In addition, the SQL statement for the expression containing the **In** operator is shorter.

You can use the **In** operator in a calculated control to determine whether the value of a field in the current record is within a set of values. For example, you might use the **In** operator with the **IIf** function to determine whether the value of a control is among a set of specified values. In the following example, if the ShipRegion is WA, OR, or ID, the **IIf** function returns "Local." Otherwise, it returns "Nonlocal."

```
= IIf([ShipRegion] In ('WA','OR','ID'), "Local", "Nonlocal")
```

Example

The following example uses the Orders table in the Northwind.mdb database to create a query that includes orders shipped to Avon, Gloucester, and Somerset.

```
SELECT * FROM Orders WHERE ShipRegion In ('Avon','Glos','Som');
```

INNER JOIN Operation

Description

Combines records from two tables whenever there are matching values in a common field.

Syntax

FROM *table1* INNER JOIN *table2* ON *table1.field1 compopr table2.field2*

The INNER JOIN operation has these parts.

Part	Description
table1, *table2*	The names of the tables from which records are combined.
field1, *field2*	The names of the fields that are joined. If they aren't numeric, the fields must be of the same data type and contain the same kind of data, but they don't have to have the same name.
compopr	Any relational comparison operator: =, <, >, <=, >=, or <>.

Remarks

You can use an INNER JOIN operation in any FROM clause. These are the most common type of join. They combine records from two tables whenever there are matching values in a field common to both tables.

You can use INNER JOIN with the Departments and Employees tables to select all the employees in each department. In contrast, to select all departments (even if some have no employees assigned to them) or all employees (even if some aren't assigned to a department), you can use a LEFT JOIN or RIGHT JOIN operation to create an outer join.

If you try to join fields containing Memo or OLE Object data, an error occurs.

You can join any two numeric fields of like types. For example, you can join on Counter and Long Integer fields because they are like types. However, you cannot join Single and Double types of fields.

INNER JOIN Operation

The following example shows how you could join the Categories and Products tables on the Category ID field:

```
SELECT CategoryName, ProductName
FROM Categories INNER JOIN Products
ON Categories.CategoryID = Products.CategoryID;
```

In the preceding example, Category ID is the joined field, but it isn't included in the query output because it isn't included in the SELECT statement. To include the joined field, include the field name in the SELECT statement—in this case, Categories.CategoryID.

You can also link several ON clauses in a JOIN statement, using the following syntax:

SELECT *fields*
   FROM *table1* INNER JOIN *table2*
   ON *table1.field1 compopr table2.field1* AND
   ON *table1.field2 compopr table2.field2*) OR
   ON *table1.field3 compopr table2.field3*)];

You can also nest JOIN statements using the following syntax:

SELECT *fields*
   FROM *table1* INNER JOIN
   (*table2* INNER JOIN [( ]*table3*
   [INNER JOIN [( ]*tablex* [INNER JOIN ...)]
   ON *table3.field3 compopr tablex.fieldx*)]
   ON *table2.field2 compopr table3.field3*)
   ON *table1.field1 compopr table2.field2*;

A LEFT JOIN or a RIGHT JOIN may be nested inside an INNER JOIN, but an INNER JOIN may not be nested inside a LEFT JOIN or a RIGHT JOIN.

See Also LEFT JOIN, RIGHT JOIN Operations; TRANSFORM Statement; UNION Operation.

Example This example creates two equi-joins: one between the Order Details and Orders tables and another between the Orders and Employees tables. This is necessary because the Employees table doesn't contain sales data, and the Order Details table doesn't contain employee data. The query produces a list of employees and their total sales.

```
SELECT DISTINCTROW Sum(UnitPrice * Quantity)
AS [Sales], FirstName & " " & LastName AS Name FROM Employees
INNER JOIN(Orders INNER JOIN [Order Details]
ON Orders.OrderID = [Order Details].OrderID)
ON Employees.EmployeeID = Orders.EmployeeID
GROUP BY FirstName & " " & LastName;
```

INSERT INTO Statement

Description Adds a record or multiple records to a table. This is referred as an append query.

Syntax Multiple-record append query:

INSERT INTO *target* [IN *externaldatabase*] [(*field1*[, *field2*[, ...]])]
    SELECT [*source*.]*field1*[, *field2*[, ...]
    FROM *tableexpression*

Single-record append query:

INSERT INTO *target* [(*field1*[, *field2*[, ...]])]
    VALUES (*value1*[, *value2*[, ...]])

The INSERT INTO statement has these parts.have this part.

Part	Description
target	The name of the table or query to append records to.
externaldatabase	The path to an external database. For a description of the path, see the IN clause.
source	The name of the table or query to copy records from.
field1, *field2*	Names of the fields to append data to, if following a *target* argument, or the names of fields to obtain data from, if following a *source* argument.
tableexpression	The name of the table or tables from which records are inserted. This argument can be a single table name or a compound resulting from an INNER JOIN, LEFT JOIN, or RIGHT JOIN operation or a saved query.
value1, *value2*	The values to insert into the specific fields of the new record. Each value is inserted into the field that corresponds to the value's position in the list: *value1* is inserted into *field1* of the new record, *value2* into *field2*, and so on. You must separate values with a comma, and enclose text fields in double quotation marks (" ").

Remarks You can use the INSERT INTO statement to add a single record to a table using the single-record append query syntax as shown above. In this case, your code specifies the name and value for each field of the record. You must specify each of the fields of the record that a value is to be assigned to and a value for that field. When you don't specify each field, the default value or **Null** is inserted for missing columns. Records are added to the end of the table.

You can also use INSERT INTO to append a set of records from another table or query by using the SELECT... FROM clause as shown above in the multiple-record append query syntax. In this case, the SELECT clause specifies the fields to append to the *target* table specified.

The source or target table may specify a table or a query. If a query is specified, the Microsoft Jet database engine appends to any and all tables specified by the query.

INSERT INTO is optional but when included, precedes the SELECT statement.

If your destination table contains a primary key, make sure you append unique, non-**Null** values to the primary key field or fields; if you don't, the Jet database engine won't append the records.

If you append records to a table with a Counter field and you want to renumber the appended records, don't include the Counter field in your query. Do include the Counter field in the query if you want to retain the original values from the field.

Use the IN clause to append records to a table in another database.

To create a new table, use the SELECT... INTO statement instead to create a make-table query.

To find out which records will be appended before you run the append query, first execute and view the results of a select query that uses the same selection criteria.

An append query copies records from one or more tables to another. The tables that contain the records you append aren't affected by the append query.

Instead of appending existing records from another table, you can specify the value for each field in a single new record using the VALUES clause. If you omit the field list, the VALUES clause must include a value for every field in the table; otherwise, the INSERT will fail. Use an additional INSERT INTO statement with a VALUES clause for each additional record you want to create.

See Also FROM Clause, WHERE Clause.

Specifics (Microsoft Access) If you create an INSERT INTO...VALUES query in SQL view, save and close the query, and then reopen it, you'll see that Microsoft Access has converted the VALUES clause to a SELECT clause. This doesn't alter the results of the query.

Using the INSERT INTO statement is equivalent to setting the **DestinationTable** property in the query property sheet in query Design view.

Example This example selects all records in a hypothetical New Customers table and adds them to the Customers table. (When individual columns are not designated, the SELECT table column names must match exactly those in the INSERT INTO table.)

```
INSERT INTO Customers SELECT [New Customers].* FROM [New Customers];
```

This example creates a new record in the Employees table.

```
INSERT INTO Employees (FirstName,LastName, Title)
VALUES ("Harry", "Washington", "Trainee");
```

This example selects all trainees from a hypothetical Trainees table who were hired more than 30 days ago and adds their records to the Employees table.

```
INSERT INTO Employees SELECT Trainees.* FROM Trainees
WHERE HireDate < Now() - 30;
```

LEFT JOIN, RIGHT JOIN Operations

Description Combines source-table records when used in any FROM clause.

Syntax FROM *table1* [LEFT | RIGHT] JOIN *table2*
ON *table1.field1 compopr table2.field2*

The LEFT JOIN and RIGHT JOIN operations have these parts.

Part	Description
table1, *table2*	The names of the tables from which records are combined.
field1, *field2*	The names of the fields that are joined. The fields must be of the same data type and contain the same kind of data, but they don't need to have the same name.
compopr	Any relational comparison operator: =, <, >, <=, >=, or <>.

Remarks Use a LEFT JOIN operation to create a left outer join. Left outer joins include all of the records from the first (left) of two tables, even if there are no matching values for records in the second (right) table.

Use a RIGHT JOIN operation to create a right outer join. Right outer joins include all of the records from the second (right) of two tables, even if there are no matching values for records in the first (left) table.

For example, you could use LEFT JOIN with the Departments (left) and Employees (right) tables to select all departments, including those that have no employees assigned to them. To select all employees, including those who aren't assigned to a department, you would use RIGHT JOIN.

The following example shows how you could join the Categories and Products tables on the Category ID field. The query produces a list of all categories, including those that contain no products:

```
SELECT CategoryName, ProductName
FROM Categories LEFT JOIN Products
ON Categories.CategoryID = Products.CategoryID;
```

In this example, Category ID is the joined field, but it isn't included in the query results because it isn't included in the SELECT statement. To include the joined field, enter the field name in the SELECT statement—in this case, Categories.CategoryID.

Notes

- To create a query that includes only records in which the data in the joined fields is the same, use an INNER JOIN operation.
- A LEFT JOIN or a RIGHT JOIN can be nested inside an INNER JOIN, but an INNER JOIN cannot be nested inside a LEFT JOIN or a RIGHT JOIN. See the discussion of nesting in the INNER JOIN topic to see how to nest joins within other joins.
- You can link multiple ON clauses. See the discussion of clause linking in the INNER JOIN topic to see how this is done.
- If you try to join fields containing Memo or OLE Object data, an error occurs.

See Also   INNER JOIN Operation, UNION Operation.

Example   These examples assume the existence of hypothetical Department Name and Department ID fields in an Employees table.

This example selects all departments, including those without employees.

```
SELECT [Department Name], FirstName & " " & LastName AS Name
FROM Departments LEFT JOIN Employees
ON Departments.[Department ID] = Employees.[Department ID]
ORDER BY [Department Name];
```

This example selects all employees, including those not assigned to a department.

```
SELECT LastName & ", " & FirstName AS Name, [Department Name]
FROM Departments RIGHT JOIN Employees
ON Departments.[Department ID] = Employees.[Department ID]
ORDER BY LastName & ", " & FirstName;
```

Like Operator

Description   Used to compare a string expression to a pattern in an SQL expression.

Syntax   Expression **Like** "*pattern*"

The **Like** operator syntax has these parts.

Part	Description
expression	SQL expression used in a WHERE clause.
pattern	String or character string literal against which *expression* is compared.

Remarks

You can use the **Like** operator to find values in a field that match the pattern you specify. For *pattern*, you can specify the complete value (for example, **Like** "Smith"), or you can use wildcard characters like those recognized by the operating system to find a range of values (for example, **Like** "Sm*").

In an expression, you can use the **Like** operator to compare a field value to a string expression. For example, if you enter **Like** "C*" in an SQL query, the query returns all field values beginning with the letter C. In a parameter query, you can prompt the user for a pattern to search for.

The following example returns data that begins with the letter P followed by any letter between A and F and three digits:

```
Like "P[A-F]###"
```

See Also

SQL Expressions.

Specifics (Microsoft Access)

In Microsoft Access, you can use the **Like** operator in a query expression, in a macro or module, or in a calculated control on a form or report.

The case sensitivity and character sort order of the **Like** operator depend on the setting of the New Database Sort Order box on the General tab of the Options dialog box, available by clicking Options on the Tools menu. By default, the New Database Sort Order is set to General, which specifies a case-insensitive sort order for the database.

You can alter the sort order for an individual Visual Basic module by changing the **Option Compare** statement in the Declarations section of a module. By default the Declarations section is set to **Option Compare Database**, which specifies the same sort order that currently applies to the rest of the database. If the module doesn't contain an **Option Compare** statement, the default string-comparison method is **Binary**, which is case-sensitive.

You can use the **Like** operator to specify inexact criteria in the query design grid. For example, if you type Like "C*" in the Criteria row of the query design grid, the query returns all field values beginning with the letter C.

In a parameter query, you can use the **Like** operator to prompt the user for a pattern to search for. For example, suppose you have an Employees table that includes a LastName field. In the Query window, create a new query by adding the Employees table and dragging the LastName field to the grid. Enter the following expression in the Criteria row.

```
Like [Enter first few letters of name:]&"*"
```

When the query is run, a dialog box prompts the user with "Enter first few letters of name:". If the user types **Sm** in the dialog box, the query looks for the pattern Sm* —that is, all names beginning with the letters Sm.

You can use **Like** in an expression as a setting for the **ValidationRule** property or as a macro condition. For example, you can restrict data entered in a text box control to an inexact specification. In the **ValidationRule** property of the text box, enter the following expression.

```
Like "P[A-F]###"
```

Data entered in this text box must now begin with the letter P, followed by any letter between A and F and three digits.

Example

This example returns a list of employees whose names begin with the letters A through D.

```
SELECT * FROM Employees WHERE LastName Like "[A-D]*"
```

The following table shows how you can use **Like** to test expressions for different patterns.

Kind of match	Pattern	Match (returns True)	No match (returns False)
Multiple characters	"a*a"	"aa", "aBa", "aBBBa"	"aBC"
	"*ab*"	"abc", "AABB", "Xab"	"aZb", "bac"
Special character	"a[*]a"	"a*a"	"aaa"
Multiple characters	"ab*"	"abcdefg", "abc"	"cab", "aab"
Single character	"a?a"	"aaa", "a3a", "aBa"	"aBBBa"
Single digit	"a#a"	"a0a", "a1a", "a2a"	"aaa", "a10a"
Range of characters	"[a-z]"	"f", "p", "j"	"2", "&"
Outside a range	"[!a-z]"	"9", "&", "%"	"b", "a"
Not a digit	"[!0-9]"	"A", "a", "&", "~"	"0", "1", "9"
Combined	"a[!b-m]#"	"An9", "az0", "a99"	"abc", "aj0"

Min, Max Functions

Description Return the minimum or maximum of a set of values contained in a specified field on a query.

Syntax **Min**(*expr*)

Max(*expr*)

The *expr* placeholder represents a string expression identifying the field that contains the data you want to evaluate or an expression that performs a calculation using the data in that field. Operands in *expr* can include the name of a table field, a constant, or a function (which can be either intrinsic or user-defined but not one of the other SQL aggregate or domain aggregate functions).

Remarks You can use **Min** and **Max** to determine the smallest and largest values in a field based on the specified aggregation, or grouping. For example, you could use these functions to return the lowest and highest freight cost. If there is no aggregation specified, then the entire table is used.

You can use **Min** and **Max** in a query expression and in the **SQL** property of a **QueryDef** object or when creating a **Recordset** object based on an SQL query.

See Also SQL Aggregate Functions.

Specifics (Microsoft Access) In Microsoft Access, you can use the **Min** and **Max** functions in the query design grid, in an SQL statement in SQL view of the Query window, or in an SQL statement within Visual Basic code. You can also use the **Min** and **Max** functions in a calculated control on a form or report.

The **Min** and **Max** functions are most useful in totals queries and crosstab queries. They function the same way whether you create the query in the query design grid or as an SQL statement in SQL view.

In the query design grid, you can create a new totals query by clicking the Totals button on the toolbar. The Total row is then inserted in the grid. You can set the Total cell beneath a field to the aggregate function to perform on the data in that field.

For example, suppose you have an Orders table that has both a Freight field and a ShipCity field. You can create a query that displays the minimum freight cost for orders sent to each city. Create a new totals query, and drag the ShipCity field to the query design grid. The Total cell beneath the ShipCity field should be set to Group By. Drag the Freight field to the query design grid, and set the Total cell beneath it to Min. When you run the query, it will display the minimum freight cost for orders sent to each city.

You can view the SQL statement for this query by switching to SQL view. In this example, Microsoft Access creates the following SQL statement.

```
SELECT DISTINCTROW Min(Orders.Freight) AS MinOfFreight, Orders.ShipCity
FROM Orders
GROUP BY Orders.ShipCity;
```

You can also use an SQL statement such as this one within Visual Basic code. For example, using the following code you can create a **Recordset** object based on the query defined by this SQL statement.

```
Dim dbs As DatabAse, rst As Recordset, strSQL As String
Set dbs = CurrentDb
strSQL = "SELECT DISTINCTROW Min(Orders.Freight) AS MinOfFreight, " _
    & "Orders.ShipCity FROM Orders GROUP BY Orders.ShipCity;"
Set rst = dbs.OpenRecordset(strSQL)
```

To use the **Min** and **Max** functions in a calculated control, set the control's **ControlSource** property to an expression containing either of these functions. For example, to display the minimum freight cost for a set of orders in a text box, enter the following expression in the **ControlSource** property of the text box.

```
= Min([Freight])
```

If you use the **Min** or **Max** function in a calculated control, you can restrict the set of records against which the function is performed by setting the form's **Filter** property.

Example

This example uses the Orders table to return the lowest and highest freight charges for orders shipped to the United Kingdom.

```
SELECT Min(Freight) AS [Low Freight], Max(Freight) AS [High Freight]
FROM Orders WHERE ShipCountry = 'UK';
```

Example (Microsoft Access)

The following example assumes that you have an Orders table that contains fields called Freight and ShipCountry. You can use the **Min** and **Max** functions to return the lowest and highest freight charges for orders shipped to the United Kingdom. Enter the following expressions in SQL view in the Query window.

```
SELECT Min([Freight]) AS [LowFreight] FROM Orders
WHERE [ShipCountry] = 'UK';
SELECT Max([Freight]) AS [HighFreight] FROM Orders
WHERE [ShipCountry] = 'UK';
```

The next example creates a calculated control that displays the lowest freight charge for all records in the same Orders table. Open a new form and set its **RecordSource** property to Orders. Enter the following expression in the **ControlSource** property of a text box on the form. To apply a condition that limits the search to only some records, such as those for orders shipped to the United Kingdom, set the form's **Filter** property.

```
= Min([Freight])
```

ORDER BY Clause

Description Sorts a query's resulting records on a specified field or fields in ascending or descending order.

Syntax SELECT *fieldlist*
   FROM *table*
   WHERE *selectcriteria*
   ORDER BY *field1* [ASC | DESC][, *field2* [ASC | DESC][, ...]]

A SELECT statement containing an ORDER BY clause has these parts.

Part	Description
fieldlist	The name of the field or fields to be retrieved along with any field-name aliases, SQL aggregate functions, selection predicates (ALL, DISTINCT, DISTINCTROW, or TOP), or other SELECT statement options.
table	The name of the table from which records are retrieved. For more information, see the FROM clause.
selectcriteria	Selection criteria. If the statement includes a WHERE clause, the Microsoft Jet database engine orders values after applying the WHERE conditions to the records.
field1, *field2*	The names of the fields on which to sort records.

Remarks ORDER BY is optional. However, if you want your data displayed in sorted order, then you must use ORDER BY.

The default sort order is ascending (A to Z, 0 to 9). Both of the following examples sort employee names in last name order:

```
SELECT LastName, FirstName
FROM Employees
ORDER BY LastName;
```

```
SELECT LastName, FirstName
FROM Employees
ORDER BY LastName ASC;
```

To sort in descending order (Z to A, 9 to 0), add the DESC reserved word to the end of each field you want to sort in descending order. The following example selects salaries and sorts them in descending order:

```
SELECT LastName, Salary
FROM Employees
ORDER BY Salary DESC, LastName;
```

If you specify a field containing Memo or OLE Object data in the ORDER BY clause, an error occurs. The Jet database engine doesn't sort on fields of these types.

ORDER BY is usually the last item in an SQL statement.

You can include additional fields in the ORDER BY clause. Records are sorted first by the first field listed after ORDER BY. Records that have equal values in that field are then sorted by the value in the second field listed, and so on.

See Also ALL, DISTINCT, DISTINCTROW, TOP Predicates; GROUP BY Clause; HAVING Clause; SELECT Statement; SELECT...INTO Statement; SQL Aggregate Functions.

Specifics (Microsoft Access) In Microsoft Access, an ORDER BY clause sorts the displayed data on a specified field or fields in ascending or descending order. Using an ORDER BY clause is equivalent to selecting Ascending or Descending in a Sort cell in the query design grid.

Example The SQL statements shown below use the ORDER BY clause to sort records alphabetically and then by category.

This example sorts the records by last name in descending order (Z to A).

```
SELECT LastName, FirstName FROM Employees ORDER BY LastName DESC;
```

This example sorts by category ID first, and then by product name.

```
SELECT CategoryID, ProductName, UnitPrice FROM Products
ORDER BY CategoryID, ProductName;
```

PARAMETERS Declaration

Description Declares the name and data type of each parameter in a parameter query.

Syntax PARAMETERS *name datatype* [, *name datatype* [, ...]]

The PARAMETERS declaration has these parts.

Part	Description
name	The name of the parameter. Assigned to the **Name** property of the **Parameter** object and used to identify this parameter in the **Parameters** collection. You can use *name* as a string that is displayed in a dialog box while your application runs the query. Use brackets ([ ]) to enclose text that contains spaces or punctuation. For example, [Low price] and [Begin report with which month?] are valid *name* arguments.
datatype	One of the primary Microsoft Jet SQL data types or their synonyms.

Remarks For queries that you run regularly, you can use a PARAMETERS declaration to create a parameter query. A parameter query can help automate the process of changing query criteria. With a parameter query, your code will need to provide the parameters each time the query is run.

The PARAMETERS declaration is optional but when included precedes any other statement, including SELECT.

If the declaration includes more than one parameter, separate them with commas. The following example includes two parameters:

```
PARAMETERS [Low price] Currency, [Beginning date] DateTime;
```

You can use *name* but not *datatype* in a WHERE or HAVING clause. The following example expects two parameters to be provided and then applies the criteria to records in the Orders table:

```
PARAMETERS [Low price] Currency,[Beginning date] DateTime;
SELECT OrderID, OrderAmount
FROM Orders
WHERE OrderAmount > [Low price]
AND OrderDate >= [Beginning date];
```

Specifics (Microsoft Access) With a parameter query, Microsoft Access prompts you for the criteria when the query is run. This eliminates the extra step of opening the query in Design view and changing the criteria.

The *name* argument that you supply with the PARAMETERS declaration provides the text that is displayed in a dialog box when you run the query. Microsoft Access automatically creates this dialog box for you.

Using the PARAMETERS declaration in SQL view is equivalent to defining parameters in the Criteria cell of the query design grid.

Example

This example requires you to provide an employee's last name and then uses that entry as the criteria for the query.

```
PARAMETERS [Enter a Last Name:] Text; SELECT * FROM Employees
WHERE LastName = [Enter a Last Name:];
```

This example requires you to provide a category ID and then uses that entry as the criteria for the query.

```
PARAMETERS [Enter a Category ID:] Value;
SELECT DISTINCTROW CategoryID, ProductName,
Count([Order Details].OrderID)
AS Tally FROM Products INNER JOIN [Order Details]
ON Products.ProductID = [Order Details].ProductID
GROUP BY CategoryID, ProductName
HAVING CategoryID = [Enter a Category ID:];
```

PROCEDURE Clause

Description Defines a name and optional parameters for a query.

Syntax PROCEDURE *name* [*param1 datatype*[, *param2 datatype*[, ...]]]

The PROCEDURE clause has these parts.

Part	Description
name	A name for the procedure. It must follow standard naming conventions.
param1, param2	One or more field names or parameters. For example: PROCEDURE Sales_By_Country [Beginning Date] DateTime, [Ending Date] DateTime; For more information on parameters, see PARAMETERS.
datatype	One of the primary Microsoft Jet SQL data types or their synonyms.

Remarks An SQL procedure consists of a PROCEDURE clause (which specifies the name of the procedure), an optional list of parameter definitions, and a single SQL statement. For example, the procedure Get_Part_Number might run a query that retrieves a specified part number.

Notes

- If the clause includes more than one field definition (that is, *param-datatype* pairs), separate them with commas.
- The PROCEDURE clause must be followed by an SQL statement (for example, a SELECT or UPDATE statement).

Specifics (Microsoft Access)

When you copy a PROCEDURE clause into SQL view, Microsoft Access removes the clause from the SQL statement when you switch to another view. Removing the PROCEDURE clause doesn't affect the result of the query. If the PROCEDURE clause includes parameters, Microsoft Access replaces PROCEDURE and *name* with the PARAMETERS reserved word. The defined parameters aren't removed.

Example

This example names the query "Category_List."

```
PROCEDURE Category_List; SELECT DISTINCTROW CategoryName, CategoryID
FROM Categories ORDER BY CategoryName;
```

This example names the query "Summary" and includes two parameters. The PROCEDURE clause is changed to the following PARAMETERS declaration:

```
PARAMETERS [Beginning Date] DateTime,
[Ending Date] DateTime;

PROCEDURE Summary [Beginning Date] DATETIME, [Ending Date] DATETIME;
SELECT DISTINCTROW ShippedDate, OrderID, EmployeeID,
Format(ShippedDate, "yyyy") AS Year FROM Orders
WHERE ShippedDate Between [Beginning Date] And [Ending Date];
```

RIGHT JOIN Operation

See LEFT JOIN, RIGHT JOIN Operations.

SELECT Statement

Description

Instructs the Microsoft Jet database engine to return information from the database as a set of records.

SELECT Statement

Syntax

SELECT [*predicate*] { * | *table*.* | [*table*.]*field1* [AS alias1] [, [*table*.]*field2* [AS alias2] [, ...]]}
FROM *tableexpression* [, ...] [IN *externaldatabase*]
[WHERE...]
[GROUP BY...]
[HAVING...]
[ORDER BY...]
[WITH OWNERACCESS OPTION]

The SELECT statement has these parts.

Part	Description
predicate	One of the following predicates: ALL, DISTINCT, DISTINCTROW, or TOP. You use the predicate to restrict the number of records returned. If none is specified, the default is ALL.
*	Specifies that all fields from the specified table or tables are selected.
table	The name of the table containing the fields from which records are selected.
field1, *field2*	The names of the fields to retrieve data from. If you include more than one field, they are retrieved in the order listed.
alias1, *alias2*	The names to use as column headers instead of the original column names in *table*.
tableexpression	The name of the table or tables containing the data you want to retrieve.
externaldatabase	The name of the database containing the tables in *tableexpression* if not in the current database.

Remarks

To perform this operation, the Jet database engine searches the specified table or tables, extracts the chosen columns, selects rows that meet the criterion, and sorts or groups the resulting rows into the order specified.

SELECT statements don't change data in the database.

SELECT is usually the first word in an SQL statement. Most SQL statements are either SELECT or SELECT... INTO statements.

The minimum syntax for a SELECT statement is:

SELECT *fields* FROM *table*

You can use an asterisk (*) to select all fields in a table. The following example selects all of the fields in the Employees table:

```
SELECT * FROM Employees;
```

If a field name is included in more than one table in the FROM clause, precede it with the table name and the . (dot) operator. In the following example, the Department field is in both the Employees table and the Supervisors table. The SQL statement selects Department from the Employees table and SupvName from the Supervisors table:

```
SELECT Employees.Department, Supervisors.SupvName
FROM Employees INNER JOIN Supervisors
WHERE Employees.Department = Supervisors.Department;
```

When a **Recordset** object is created, the Jet database engine uses the table's field name as the **Field** object name in the **Recordset** object. If you want a different field name or a name isn't implied by the expression used to generate the field, use the AS reserved word. The following example uses the title Birth to name the returned **Field** object in the resulting **Recordset** object:

```
SELECT BirthDate
AS Birth FROM Employees;
```

Whenever you use aggregate functions or queries that return ambiguous or duplicate **Field** object names, you must use the AS clause to provide an alternate name for the **Field** object. The following example uses the title Head Count to name the returned **Field** object in the resulting **Recordset** object:

```
SELECT COUNT(EmployeeID)
AS HeadCount FROM Employees;
```

You can use the other clauses in a SELECT statement to further restrict and organize your returned data. For more information, see the topic for the clause you're working with.

See Also   ALL, DISTINCT, DISTINCTROW, TOP Predicates; DELETE Statement, FROM Clause, GROUP BY Clause, HAVING Clause, IN Clause, INSERT INTO Statement, ORDER BY Clause, SELECT...INTO Statement, SQL Aggregate Functions, UNION Operation, UPDATE Statement, WHERE Clause, WITH OWNERACCESS OPTION Declaration.

Specifics (Microsoft Access)   In Microsoft Access, if you are working in SQL view in the Query window, field names (*field1, field2*) are used as column headings in Datasheet view. To display a different column heading for a column in the Datasheet, use the AS reserved word. If you use the AS reserved word, then the *alias1, alias2* arguments provide the column names to use in displaying the retrieved data in Datasheet view. Using the AS clause is equivalent to setting the **Alias** property in the field list property sheet in query Design view.

The following example uses the title "Birthday" to head the column in the resulting datasheet.

```
SELECT [BirthDate] AS Birthday FROM Employees;
```

When using aggregate functions or queries that return ambiguous or duplicate field names, you must use the AS clause to provide an alternate name for the field. The following example creates the column heading "Head Count" in Datasheet view.

```
SELECT COUNT([EmployeeID])
AS [HeadCount] FROM Employees;
```

If you are working with data access objects in Visual Basic code, the *field1, field2* arguments are used to name the **Field** objects in the **Recordset** object returned by the query. If you include the AS keyword, then the *alias1, alias2* arguments provide the column headings to return as **Field** object names in the resulting **Recordset** object.

Example

Some of the following examples assume the existence of a hypothetical Salary field in an Employees table.

This example selects the LastName and FirstName fields of all records in the Employees table.

```
SELECT LastName, FirstName FROM Employees;
```

This example selects all fields from the Employees table.

```
SELECT Employees.* FROM Employees;
```

This example counts the number of records that have an entry in the PostalCode field and names the returned field Tally.

```
SELECT Count(PostalCode) AS Tally FROM Customers;
```

This example shows what the salary would be if each employee received a 10 percent raise. It doesn't change the original salary amounts.

```
SELECT LastName, Salary AS Current, Salary * 1.1 AS Proposed
FROM Employees;
```

This example places the title Name at the top of the LastName column. The title Salary is displayed at the top of the Salary column.

```
SELECT LastName AS Name, Salary FROM Employees;
```

This example shows the number of employees and the average and maximum salaries.

```
SELECT Count(*) AS [Total Employees], Avg(Salary)
AS [Average Salary], Max(Salary) AS [Maximum Salary] FROM Employees;
```

For each record, this example shows the LastName and Salary in the first and last fields. The string "has a salary of" is returned as the middle field of each record.

```
SELECT LastName, 'has a salary of', Salary FROM Employees;
```

SELECT...INTO Statement

Description Creates a make-table query.

Syntax SELECT *field1*[, *field2*[, ...]] INTO *newtable* [IN *externaldatabase*]
FROM *source*

The SELECT...INTO statement has these parts.

Part	Description
field1, *field2*	The name of the fields to be copied into the new table.
newtable	The name of the table to be created. It must conform to standard naming conventions. If *newtable* is the same as the name of an existing table, a trappable error will result.
externaldatabase	The path to an external database. For a description of the path, see the IN clause.
source	The name of the existing table from which records are selected. This can be single or multiple tables or a query.

Remarks You can use make-table queries to archive records, make backup copies of your tables, or make copies to export to another database or to use as a basis for reports that display data for a particular time period. For example, you could produce a Monthly Sales by Region report by running the same make-table query each month.

Notes

- You may want to define a primary key for the new table. When you create the table, the fields in the new table inherit the data type and field size of each field in the query's underlying tables, but no other field or table properties are transferred.
- To add data to an existing table, use the INSERT INTO statement instead to create an append query.
- To find out which records will be selected before you run the make-table query, first examine the results of a SELECT statement that uses the same selection criteria.

See Also ALL, DISTINCT, DISTINCTROW, TOP Predicates; FROM Clause; IN Clause; SELECT Statement; UNION Operation; WHERE Clause.

SQL Aggregate Functions

Example

Some of the following examples assume the existence of a hypothetical Salary field in a Payroll table.

This example selects all records in the Employees table and copies them into a new table named Emp Backup.

```
SELECT Employees.* INTO [Emp Backup] FROM Employees;
```

This example creates a new table called Trainees that contains only employee records that have the title Trainee.

```
SELECT Employees.FirstName, LastName INTO Trainees FROM Employees
WHERE Title = 'Trainee';
```

This example makes a copy of the Employees table and places the new table in the hypothetical database BACKUP.MDB.

```
SELECT Employees.* INTO Employees IN "BACKUP.MDB" FROM Employees;
```

This example creates a new table that contains employee and payroll data for all trainees. The Employees and Payroll tables have a one-to-one relationship. The new table contains all of the data from the Employees table plus the Salary field from the Payroll table.

```
SELECT Employees.*, Salary INTO Trainees FROM Employees
INNER JOIN Payroll ON Employees.EmployeeID = Payroll.EmployeeID
WHERE Title = 'Trainee';
```

SQL Aggregate Functions

Description

Using the SQL aggregate functions, you can determine various statistics on sets of values. You can use these functions in a query and aggregate expressions in the **SQL** property of a **QueryDef** object or when creating a **Recordset** object based on an SQL query.

SQL Aggregate Functions

Avg Function

Count Function

Min, **Max** Functions

StDev, **StDevP** Functions

Sum Function

Var, **VarP** Functions

**Specifics
(Microsoft Access)**

The SQL aggregate functions are similar to the domain aggregate functions, but they are used in different contexts. In Microsoft Access, you can use the SQL aggregate functions in an SQL statement that you create in the SQL view of the Query window, or in an SQL statement within Visual Basic code. Conversely, domain aggregate functions can be called directly from Visual Basic code.

You can use both SQL aggregate and domain aggregate functions in query expressions in the query design grid. SQL aggregate functions are most useful in totals queries and crosstab queries.

You can also use both types of aggregate functions in a calculated control on a form or report.

SQL Expressions

Description

An SQL expression is a string that makes up all or part of an SQL statement. For example, the **FindFirst** method on a **Recordset** object uses an SQL expression, consisting of the selection criteria found in an SQL WHERE clause.

The Microsoft Jet Database Engine uses the Visual Basic for Applications (or VBA) expression service to perform simple arithmetic and function evaluation. All of the expressions operators used in Jet database engine SQL expressions (except **Between**, **In**, and **Like**) are defined by the VBA expression service. In addition, the VBA expression service offers over 100 VBA functions that can be used in SQL expressions. For example, an SQL query composed in the SQL View of the Microsoft Access Query Design window can use these VBA functions, and so can an SQL query used in the DAO **OpenRecordset** method in Microsoft Visual C++™, Microsoft Visual Basic, and Microsoft Excel code.

**Specifics
(Microsoft Access)**

You can use many Visual Basic functions in SQL strings while in Visual Basic code, in SQL view of the Query window, or in the query design grid.

For example, you can include Visual Basic functions in an SQL statement that you use to define a **QueryDef** object or a dynaset-type or snapshot-type **Recordset** object. In the Microsoft Access query design grid, you can include Visual Basic functions in criteria expressions, or in a calculated field expression.

**Example
(Microsoft Access)**

The following example creates a dynaset-type **Recordset** object from an SQL statement. The SQL statement includes the **Year** function in a WHERE clause to return only records for orders placed in 1995.

```
Sub Orders95()
    Dim dbs As Database, rst As Recordset, strSQL As String
    Dim fld As Field
```

```
        Set dbs = CurrentDb
        strSQL = "SELECT DISTINCTROW OrderID, OrderDate " & _
            "FROM Orders WHERE ((Year([OrderDate])=1995));"
        Set rst = dbs.OpenRecordset(strSQL, dbOpenDynaset)
        rst.MoveLast
        Debug.Print rst.RecordCount
End Sub
```

The next example shows how you can include a Visual Basic function in an SQL statement in SQL view in the Query window. The following SQL statement defines a query that displays the ShipName field from an Orders table, calculates the number of characters in that field for each record using the **Len** function, and displays that calculation in another column.

```
SELECT DISTINCTROW ShipName, Len([ShipName]) AS LengthOfShipName
FROM Orders;
```

You can create the same query in the query design grid. Create a new query and add the Orders table. Drag the ShipName field onto the Field cell in the first column in the grid. In another Field cell, create a calculated field expression by entering the following expression.

```
LengthOfShipName: Len([ShipName])
```

SQL Subqueries

Description   A subquery is a SELECT statement nested inside a SELECT, SELECT... INTO, INSERT...INTO, DELETE, or UPDATE statement or inside another subquery.

Syntax   You can use three forms of syntax to create a subquery:

comparison [ANY | ALL | SOME] (*sqlstatement*)

expression [NOT] IN (*sqlstatement*)

[NOT] EXISTS (*sqlstatement*)

A subquery has these parts.

Part	Description
comparison	An expression and a comparison operator that compares the expression with the results of the subquery.
expression	An expression for which the result set of the subquery is searched.
sqlstatement	A SELECT statement, following the same format and rules as any other SELECT statement. It must be enclosed in parentheses.

Remarks

You can use a subquery instead of an expression in the field list of a SELECT statement or in a WHERE or HAVING clause. In a subquery, you use a SELECT statement to provide a set of one or more specific values to evaluate in the WHERE or HAVING clause expression.

Use the ANY or SOME predicate, which are synonymous, to retrieve records in the main query that satisfy the comparison with any records retrieved in the subquery. The following example returns all products whose unit price is greater than that of any product sold at a discount of 25 percent or more:

```
SELECT * FROM Products
WHERE UnitPrice > ANY
(SELECT UnitPrice FROM OrderDetails
WHERE Discount >= .25);
```

Use the ALL predicate to retrieve only those records in the main query that satisfy the comparison with all records retrieved in the subquery. If you changed ANY to ALL in the above example, the query would return only those products whose unit price is greater than that of all products sold at a discount of 25 percent or more. This is much more restrictive.

Use the IN predicate to retrieve only those records in the main query for which some record in the subquery contains an equal value. The following example returns all products with a discount of 25 percent or more:

```
SELECT * FROM Products
WHERE ProductID IN
(SELECT ProductID FROM OrderDetails
WHERE Discount >= .25);
```

Conversely, you can use NOT IN to retrieve only those records in the main query for which no record in the subquery contains an equal value.

Use the EXISTS predicate (with the optional NOT reserved word) in true/false comparisons to determine whether the subquery returns any records.

You can also use table name aliases in a subquery to refer to tables listed in a FROM clause outside the subquery. The following example returns the names of employees whose salaries are equal to or greater than the average salary of all employees having the same job title. The Employees table is given the alias "T1."

```
SELECT LastName,FirstName, Title, Salary
FROM Employees AS T1
WHERE Salary >=(SELECT Avg(Salary)
FROM Employees
WHERE T1.Title = Employees.Title) Order by Title;
```

In the preceding example, the AS reserved word is optional.

Some subqueries are allowed in crosstab queries—specifically, as predicates (those in the WHERE clause). Subqueries as output (those in the SELECT list) are not allowed in crosstabs.

See Also INNER JOIN Operation; LEFT JOIN, RIGHT JOIN Operations; SELECT Statement; SELECT...INTO Statement; UNION Operation.

Example Some of the following examples assume the existence of a hypothetical Salary field in an Employees table.

This example lists the name, title, and salary of every sales representative whose salary is higher than that of all managers and directors.

```
SELECT LastName, FirstName, Title, Salary FROM Employees
WHERE Title LIKE "*Sales Rep*" AND Salary > ALL (SELECT Salary
FROM Employees
WHERE (Title LIKE "*Manager*") OR (Title LIKE "*Director*"));
```

This example lists the name and unit price of every product whose unit price is the same as that of Aniseed Syrup.

```
SELECT ProductName, UnitPrice FROM Products
WHERE UnitPrice = (SELECT UnitPrice FROM [Products]
WHERE ProductName = "Aniseed Syrup");
```

This example lists the company and contact of every customer who placed an order in the second quarter of 1995.

```
SELECT ContactName, CompanyName, ContactTitle, Phone
FROM Customers WHERE CustomerID IN (SELECT CustomerID FROM Orders
WHERE OrderDate BETWEEN #04/1/95# AND #07/1/95#);
```

This example lists employees whose salary is higher than the average salary for all employees.

```
SELECT LastName, FirstName, Title, Salary FROM Employees T1
WHERE Salary >= (SELECT AVG(Salary) FROM Employees
WHERE Employees.Title = T1.Title) ORDER BY Title;
```

This example selects the name of every employee who has booked at least one order. This could also be done with an INNER JOIN.

```
SELECT FirstName, LastName FROM Employees AS E
WHERE EXISTS (SELECT * FROM Orders AS O
WHERE O.EmployeeID = E.EmployeeID);
```

StDev, StDevP Functions

Description Return estimates of the standard deviation for a population or a population sample represented as a set of values contained in a specified field on a query.

Syntax **StDev**(*expr*)

StDevP(*expr*)

The *expr* placeholder represents a string expression identifying the field that contains the numeric data you want to evaluate or an expression that performs a calculation using the data in that field. Operands in *expr* can include the name of a table field, a constant, or a function (which can be either intrinsic or user-defined but not one of the other SQL aggregate or domain aggregate functions).

Remarks The **StDevP** function evaluates a population, and the **StDev** function evaluates a population sample.

If the underlying query contains fewer than two records (or no records, for the **StDevP** function), these functions return a **Null** (which indicates that a standard deviation can't be calculated).

You can use the **StDev** and **StDevP** functions in a query expression. You can also use this expression in the **SQL** property of a **QueryDef** object or when creating a **Recordset** object based on an SQL query.

See Also **Avg** Function, SQL Aggregate Functions, **Sum** Function.

Specifics (Microsoft Access) In Microsoft Access, you can use the **StDev** and **StDevP** functions in the query design grid, in an SQL statement in SQL view of the Query window, or in an SQL statement within Visual Basic code. You can also use the **StDev** and **StDevP** functions in a calculated control on a form or report.

The **StDev** and **StDevP** functions are most useful in totals queries and crosstab queries. They function the same way whether you create the query in the query design grid or as an SQL statement in SQL view.

In the query design grid, you can create a new totals query by clicking the Totals button on the toolbar. The Total row is then inserted in the grid. You can set the Total cell beneath a field to the aggregate function to perform on the data in that field.

For example, suppose you have an Orders table that has both a Freight field and a ShipCity field. You can create a query that displays the standard deviation of freight cost for orders sent to each city. Create a new totals query, and drag the ShipCity field to the query design grid. The Total cell beneath the ShipCity field should be set to Group By. Drag the Freight field to the query design grid, and set the Total cell beneath it to StDev. When you run the query, it will display the standard deviation of freight cost for orders sent to each city.

You can view the SQL statement for this query by switching to SQL view. In this example, Microsoft Access creates the following SQL statement.

```
SELECT DISTINCTROW StDev(Orders.Freight) AS StDevOfFreight,
Orders.ShipCity
FROM Orders
GROUP BY Orders.ShipCity;
```

You can also use an SQL statement such as this one within Visual Basic code. For example, using the following code you can create a **Recordset** object based on the query defined by this SQL statement.

```
Dim dbs As DatabAse, rst As Recordset, strSQL As String
Set dbs = CurrentDb
strSQL = "SELECT DISTINCTROW StDev(Orders.Freight) AS StDevOfFreight, "_
    & "Orders.ShipCity FROM Orders GROUP BY Orders.ShipCity;"
Set rst = dbs.OpenRecordset(strSQL)
```

To use the **StDev** and **StDevP** functions in a calculated control, set the control's **ControlSource** property to an expression containing either of these functions. For example, to display the standard deviation of freight costs for a set of orders in a text box, enter the following expression in the **ControlSource** property of the text box.

= StDev([Freight])

If you use the **StDev** or **StDevP** function in a calculated control, you can restrict the set of records against which the function is performed by setting the form's **Filter** property.

Example

This example uses the "Orders" table to estimate the standard deviation of the freight charges for orders shipped to the United Kingdom.

```
SELECT StDev(Freight) AS [Freight Dev] FROM Orders
WHERE ShipCountry = 'UK';

SELECT StDevP(Freight) AS [Freight DevP] FROM Orders
WHERE ShipCountry = 'UK';
```

Example (Microsoft Access)

The following example assumes that you have an Orders table that contains fields called Freight and ShipCountry. You can use the **StDev** and **StDevP** functions to return the standard deviation of freight charges for orders shipped to the United Kingdom. Enter the following expressions in SQL view in the Query window:

```
SELECT StDev([Freight]) AS [FreightDev] FROM Orders
WHERE [ShipCountry] = 'UK';
SELECT StDevP([Freight]) As [FreightDevP] FROM Orders
WHERE [ShipCountry] = 'UK';
```

The next example creates a calculated control that displays the standard deviation of freight charges for all records in the same Orders table. Open a new form and set its **RecordSource** property to Orders. Enter the following expression in the **ControlSource** property of a text box on the form. To apply a condition that limits the search to only some records, such as those for orders shipped to the United Kingdom, set the form's **Filter** property.

```
= StDev([Freight])
```

Sum Function

Description	Returns the sum of a set of values contained in a specified field on a query.
Syntax	**Sum**(*expr*)
	The *expr* placeholder represents a string expression identifying the field that contains the numeric data you want to add or an expression that performs a calculation using the data in that field. Operands in *expr* can include the name of a table field, a constant, or a function (which can be either intrinsic or user-defined but not one of the other SQL aggregate or domain aggregate functions).
Remarks	The **Sum** function totals the values in a field. For example, you could use the **Sum** function to determine the total cost of freight charges.
	The **Sum** function ignores records that contain **Null** fields. The following example shows how you can calculate the sum of the products of Unit Price and Quantity fields:
| | ```
SELECT Sum(UnitPrice * Quantity)
AS [Total Revenue] FROM [Order Details];
``` |
	You can use the **Sum** function in a query expression. You can also use this expression in the **SQL** property of a **QueryDef** object or when creating a **Recordset** based on an SQL query.
See Also	**Count** Function, SQL Aggregate Functions.
Specifics (Microsoft Access)	In Microsoft Access, you can use the **Sum** function in the query design grid, in an SQL statement in SQL view of the Query window, or in an SQL statement within Visual Basic code. You can also use the **Sum** function in a calculated control on a form or report.
	The **Sum** function is most useful in totals queries and crosstab queries. It functions the same way whether you create the query in the query design grid or as an SQL statement in SQL view.
```

In the query design grid, you can create a new totals query by clicking the Totals button on the toolbar. The Total row is then inserted in the grid. You can set the Total cell beneath a field to the aggregate function to perform on the data in that field.

For example, suppose you have an Orders table that has both a Freight field and a ShipCity field. You can create a query that displays the sum of freight costs for orders sent to each city. Create a new totals query, and drag the ShipCity field to the query design grid. The Total cell beneath the ShipCity field should be set to Group By. Drag the Freight field to the query design grid, and set the Total cell beneath it to Sum. When you run the query, it will display the sum of freight costs by city.

You can view the SQL statement for this query by switching to SQL view. In this example, Microsoft Access creates the following SQL statement.

```
SELECT DISTINCTROW Sum(Orders.Freight) AS SumOfFreight, Orders.ShipCity
FROM Orders
GROUP BY Orders.ShipCity;
```

You can also use an SQL statement such as this one within Visual Basic code. For example, using the following code you can create a **Recordset** object based on the query defined by this SQL statement.

```
Dim dbs As DatabAse, rst As Recordset, strSQL As String
Set dbs = CurrentDb
strSQL = "SELECT DISTINCTROW Sum(Orders.Freight) AS SumOfFreight, " _
    & "Orders.ShipCity FROM Orders GROUP BY Orders.ShipCity;"
Set rst = dbs.OpenRecordset(strSQL)
```

To use the **Sum** function in a calculated control, set the control's **ControlSource** property to an expression containing the **Sum** function. For example, to display the sum of freight costs for a set of orders in a text box, enter the following expression in the **ControlSource** property of the text box.

```
= Sum([Freight])
```

If you use the **Sum** function in a calculated control, you can restrict the set of records against which the function is performed by setting the form's **Filter** property.

Example

This example uses the Orders table to calculate the total sales for orders shipped to the United Kingdom.

```
SELECT Sum(UnitPrice*Quantity) AS [Total UK Sales] FROM Orders
INNER JOIN [Order Details] ON Orders.OrderID = [Order Details].OrderID
WHERE (ShipCountry = 'UK');
```

**Example
(Microsoft Access)**

The following example assumes that you have an Orders table that contains fields called OrderID and ShipCountry, and an OrderDetails table that contain fields called UnitPrice and Quantity. You can use the **Sum** function to calculate the total sales for orders shipped to the United Kingdom. Enter the following expression in SQL view in the Query window:

```
SELECT Sum([UnitPrice]*[Quantity]) AS [TotalUKSales]
FROM Orders INNER JOIN [OrderDetails]
ON Orders.[OrderID] = [OrderDetails].[OrderID]
WHERE ([ShipCountry] = 'UK');
```

The next example creates a calculated control that displays the total sales for records in the OrderDetails table. Open a new form and set its **RecordSource** property to Order Details. Enter the following expression in the **ControlSource** property of a text box on the form. To apply a condition that limits the search to only some records, such as those for orders shipped to the United Kingdom, set the form's **Filter** property.

```
= Sum([UnitPrice]*[Quantity])
```

TOP Predicate

See ALL, DISTINCT, DISTINCTROW, TOP Predicates.

TRANSFORM Statement

Description   Creates a crosstab query.

Syntax   TRANSFORM *aggfunction*
  selectstatement
  PIVOT *pivotfield* [IN (*value1*[, *value2*[, ...]])]

The TRANSFORM statement has these parts.

Part	Description
aggfunction	An SQL aggregate function that operates on the selected data.
selectstatement	A SELECT statement.
pivotfield	The field or expression you want to use to create column headings in the query's result set.
value1, *value2*	Fixed values used to create column headings.

TRANSFORM Statement 349

Remarks

When you summarize data using a crosstab query, you select values from specified fields or expressions as column headings so you can view data in a more compact format than with a select query.

TRANSFORM is optional but when included is the first statement in an SQL string. It precedes a SELECT statement that specifies the fields used as row headings and a GROUP BY clause that specifies row grouping. Optionally, you can include other clauses, such as WHERE, that specify additional selection or sorting criteria. You can also use subqueries as predicates—specifically, those in the WHERE clause—in a crosstab query.

The values returned in *pivotfield* are used as column headings in the query's result set. For example, pivoting the sales figures on the month of the sale in a crosstab query would create 12 columns. You can restrict *pivotfield* to create headings from fixed values (*value1*, *value2*) listed in the optional IN clause. You can also include fixed values for which no data exists to create additional columns.

See Also

FROM Clause, INNER JOIN Operation, ORDER BY Clause.

Example

This example creates a crosstab query that shows product sales by month for a user-specified year. The months are returned from left to right (pivoted) as columns, and the product names are returned from top to bottom as rows.

```
PARAMETERS [Sales for which year?] LONG;
TRANSFORM Sum([Order Details].Quantity * ([Order Details].UnitPrice -
    ([Order Details].Discount / 100) * [Order Details].UnitPrice))
AS Sales SELECT ProductName FROM Orders INNER JOIN(Products
INNER JOIN [Order Details]
ON Products.ProductID = [Order Details].ProductID)
ON Orders.OrderID = [Order Details].OrderID
WHERE DatePart("yyyy", OrderDate) = [Sales for which year?]
GROUP BY ProductName ORDER BY ProductName
PIVOT DatePart("m", OrderDate);
```

This example creates a crosstab query that returns product sales by quarter for each supplier for a user-specified year. The quarters are returned from left to right (pivoted) as columns, and the supplier names are returned from top to bottom as rows.

```
PARAMETERS [Sales for which year?] LONG;
TRANSFORM Sum([Order Details].Quantity * ([Order Details].UnitPrice -
    ([Order Details].Discount / 100) * [Order Details].UnitPrice)) AS Sales
SELECT CompanyName FROM Orders
INNER JOIN ((Suppliers INNER JOIN Products
ON Suppliers.SupplierID = Products.SupplierID)
INNER JOIN [Order Details]
ON Products.ProductID = [Order Details].ProductID)
ON Orders.OrderID = [Order Details].OrderID
WHERE DatePart("yyyy", OrderDate) = [Sales for which year?]
```

```
GROUP BY CompanyName ORDER BY CompanyName
PIVOT "Qtr " & DatePart("q", OrderDate) In ('Qtr 1', 'Qtr 2', 'Qtr 3',
'Qtr 4');
```

UNION Operation

Description

Creates a union query, which combines the results of two or more independent queries or tables.

Syntax

[TABLE] *query1* UNION [ALL] [TABLE] *query2*
    [UNION [ALL] [TABLE] *query1–n* [...]]

The UNION operation has this part.

Part	Description
query1–n	A SELECT statement, the name of a stored query, or the name of a stored table preceded by the TABLE keyword.

Remarks

You can merge the results of two or more queries, tables, and SELECT statements, in any combination, in a single UNION operation. The following example merges an existing table named New Accounts and a SELECT statement:

```
TABLE [New Accounts] UNION ALL
SELECT *
FROM Customers
WHERE OrderAmount > 1000;
```

By default, no duplicate records are returned when you use a UNION operation; however, you can include the ALL predicate to ensure that all records are returned. This also makes the query run faster.

All queries in a UNION operation must request the same number of fields; however, the fields don't have to be of the same size or data type.

Use aliases only in the first SELECT clause because they are ignored in any others. In the ORDER BY clause, refer to fields by what they are called in the first SELECT clause.

Notes

- You can use a GROUP BY and/or HAVING clause in each *query* argument to group the returned data.
- You can use an ORDER BY clause at the end of the last *query* argument to display the returned data in a specified order.

See Also	ALL, DISTINCT, DISTINCTROW, TOP Predicates; GROUP BY Clause; HAVING Clause; INNER JOIN Operation; LEFT JOIN, RIGHT JOIN Operations; ORDER BY Clause; SELECT Statement; SQL Subqueries; WHERE Clause.
Specifics (Microsoft Access)	In Microsoft Access, the arguments for the UNION operation (*query1, query2,...queryn*) can be a SELECT statement, the name of a stored Microsoft Access query, or the name of a stored Microsoft Access table preceded by the TABLE reserved word. You can view a union query only in SQL view, not in the query design grid.
Example	This example retrieves the names and cities of all suppliers and customers in Brazil.

```
SELECT CompanyName, City FROM Suppliers WHERE Country = "Brazil" UNION
SELECT CompanyName, City FROM Customers WHERE Country = "Brazil";
```

This example retrieves the names and cities of all suppliers and customers located in Brazil, using constants, an alias, and ordering by an alias.

```
SELECT CompanyName, City, "Supplier" AS Source FROM Suppliers
WHERE Country = "Brazil" UNION SELECT CompanyName, City, "Customer"
FROM Customers WHERE Country = "Brazil" ORDER BY City, Source;
```

This example retrieves the names and cities of all suppliers and customers in Brazil and the last names and cities of all employees in South America.

```
SELECT CompanyName, City FROM Suppliers WHERE Country = "Brazil" UNION
SELECT CompanyName, City FROM Customers WHERE Country = "Brazil" UNION
SELECT LastName, City FROM Employees WHERE Region = "South America";
```

This example retrieves the names and IDs of all suppliers and customers. This union assumes that there are the same number of columns in each table.

```
TABLE Customers UNION TABLE Suppliers;
```

UPDATE Statement

Description	Creates an update query that changes values in fields in a specified table based on specified criteria.

Syntax	UPDATE *table*
	    SET *newvalue*
	        WHERE *criteria*;

352 UPDATE Statement

The UPDATE statement has these parts.

Part	Description
table	The name of the table whose data you want to modify.
newvalue	An expression that determines the value to be inserted into a particular field in the updated records.
criteria	An expression that determines which records will be updated. Only records that satisfy the expression are updated.

Remarks

UPDATE is especially useful when you want to change many records or when the records that you want to change are in multiple tables.

You can change several fields at the same time. The following example increases the Order Amount values by 10 percent and the Freight values by 3 percent for shippers in the United Kingdom:

```
UPDATE Orders
SET OrderAmount = OrderAmount * 1.1,
Freight = Freight * 1.03
WHERE ShipCountry = 'UK';
```

UPDATE doesn't generate a result set. If you want to know which records will be changed, first examine the results of a select query that uses the same criteria, and then run the update query.

Specifics (Microsoft Access)

Since the UPDATE statement doesn't generate a result set, there is no query datasheet for Microsoft Access to display a when you use this statement.

If you want to confirm each change, you can use the Replace command on the Edit menu of the form or datasheet rather than an update query.

Example

This example changes values in the ReportsTo field to 5 for all employee records that currently have ReportsTo values of 2.

```
UPDATE Employees SET ReportsTo = 5 WHERE ReportsTo = 2;
```

This example increases the UnitPrice for all nondiscontinued products from supplier 8 by 10 percent.

```
UPDATE Products SET UnitPrice = UnitPrice * 1.1
WHERE SupplierID = 8 AND Discontinued = No;
```

This example reduces the UnitPrice for all nondiscontinued products supplied by Tokyo Traders by 5 percent. The Products and Suppliers tables have a many-to-one relationship.

```
UPDATE Suppliers INNER JOIN Products ON Suppliers.SupplierID =
Products.SupplierID SET UnitPrice = UnitPrice * .95
WHERE CompanyName = 'Tokyo Traders' AND Discontinued = No;
```

Var, VarP Functions

Description Return estimates of the variance for a population or a population sample represented as a set of values contained in a specified field on a query.

Syntax **Var**(*expr*)
VarP(*expr*)

The **VarP** function evaluates a population, and the **Var** function evaluates a population sample.

The *expr* placeholder represents a string expression identifying the field that contains the numeric data you want to evaluate or an expression that performs a calculation using the data in that field. Operands in *expr* can include the name of a table field, a constant, or a function (which can be either intrinsic or user-defined but not one of the other SQL aggregate or domain aggregate functions).

Remarks If the underlying query contains fewer than two records, the **Var** and **VarP** functions return a **Null** (which indicates that a variance can't be calculated).

You can use the **Var** and **VarP** functions in a query expression or in an SQL statement.

Specifics (Microsoft Access) In Microsoft Access, you can use the **Var** and **VarP** functions in the query design grid, in an SQL statement in SQL view of the Query window, or in an SQL statement within Visual Basic code. You can also use the **Var** and **VarP** functions in a calculated control on a form or report.

The **Var** and **VarP** functions are most useful in totals queries and crosstab queries. They function the same way whether you create the query in the query design grid or as an SQL statement in SQL view.

In the query design grid, you can create a new totals query by clicking the Totals button on the toolbar. The Total row is then inserted in the grid. You can set the Total cell beneath a field to the aggregate function to perform on the data in that field.

For example, suppose you have an Orders table that has both a Freight field and a ShipCity field. You can create a query that displays the variance of freight cost for orders sent to each city. Create a new totals query, and drag the ShipCity field to the query design grid. The Total cell beneath the ShipCity field should be set to Group By. Drag the Freight field to the query design grid, and set the Total cell beneath it to Var. When you run the query, it will display the variance of freight cost for orders sent to each city.

You can view the SQL statement for this query by switching to SQL view. In this example, Microsoft Access creates the following SQL statement.

```
SELECT DISTINCTROW Var(Orders.Freight) AS VarOfFreight, Orders.ShipCity
FROM Orders
GROUP BY Orders.ShipCity;
```

You can also use an SQL statement such as this one within Visual Basic code. For example, using the following code you can create a **Recordset** object based on the query defined by this SQL statement.

```
Dim dbs As DatabAse, rst As Recordset, strSQL As String
Set dbs = CurrentDb
strSQL = "SELECT DISTINCTROW Var(Orders.Freight) AS VarOfFreight, "_
    & "Orders.ShipCity FROM Orders GROUP BY Orders.ShipCity;"
Set rst = dbs.OpenRecordset(strSQL)
```

To use the **Var** and **VarP** functions in a calculated control, set the control's **ControlSource** property to an expression containing either of these functions. For example, to display the variance across freight costs in a text box, enter the following expression in the **ControlSource** property of the text box.

```
= Var([Freight])
```

If you use the **Var** or **VarP** function in a calculated control, you can restrict the set of records against which the function is performed by setting the form's **Filter** property.

Example

This example uses the Orders table to estimate the variance of freight costs for orders shipped to the United Kingdom.

```
SELECT Var(Freight) AS [UK Freight Variance] FROM Orders
WHERE ShipCountry = 'UK';

SELECT VarP(Freight) AS [UK Freight VarianceP] FROM Orders
WHERE ShipCountry = 'UK';
```

Example (Microsoft Access)

The following example assumes that you have an Orders table that contains a field called Freight. You can use the **Var** and **VarP** functions to estimate the variance of freight costs for orders shipped to the United Kingdom. Enter the following expressions in SQL view in the Query window:

```
SELECT Var([Freight]) AS [UKFreightVariance] FROM Orders
WHERE [ShipCountry] = 'UK';
SELECT VarP([Freight]) AS [UKFreightVarianceP] FROM Orders
WHERE [ShipCountry] = 'UK';
```

The next example creates a calculated control that displays the estimated variance for freight costs for records in the same Orders table. Open a new form and set its **RecordSource** property to Orders. Enter the following expression in the **ControlSource** property of a text box on the form. To apply a condition that limits the search to only some records, such as those for orders shipped to the United Kingdom, set the form's **Filter** property.

```
= Var([Freight])
```

WHERE Clause

Description Specifies which records from the tables listed in the FROM clause are affected by a SELECT, UPDATE, or DELETE statement.

Syntax SELECT *fieldlist*
   FROM *tableexpression*
   WHERE *criteria*;

A SELECT statement containing a WHERE clause has these parts.

Part	Description
fieldlist	The name of the field or fields to be retrieved along with any field-name aliases, selection predicates (ALL, DISTINCT, DISTINCTROW, or TOP), or other SELECT statement options.
tableexpression	The name of the table or tables from which data is retrieved.
criteria	An expression that records must satisfy to be included in the query results.

Remarks The Microsoft Jet database engine selects the records that meet the conditions listed in the WHERE clause. If you don't specify a WHERE clause, your query returns all rows from the table. If you specify more than one table in your query and you haven't included a WHERE clause or a JOIN clause, your query generates a Cartesian product of the tables.

WHERE is optional, but when included, follows FROM. For example, you can select all employees in the sales department (WHERE Dept = 'Sales') or all customers between the ages of 18 and 30 (WHERE Age Between 18 And 30).

If you don't use a JOIN clause to perform SQL join operations on multiple tables, the resulting **Recordset** object won't be updatable.

WHERE is similar to HAVING. WHERE determines which records are selected. Similarly, once records are grouped with GROUP BY, HAVING determines which records are displayed.

Use the WHERE clause to eliminate records you don't want grouped by a GROUP BY clause.

Use various expressions to determine which records the SQL statement returns. For example, the following SQL statements select all employees whose salaries are more than $21,000:

```
SELECT LastName, Salary
FROM Employees
WHERE Salary > 21000;
```

A WHERE clause can contain up to 40 expressions linked by logical operators, such as **And** and **Or**.

When you specify the *criteria* argument, date literals must be in U.S. format, even if you're not using the U.S. version of the Jet database engine. For example, May 10, 1994, is written 10/5/94 in the United Kingdom and 5/10/94 in the United States. Be sure to enclose your date literals with the number sign (#) as shown in the following examples.

To find records dated May 10, 1994 in a United Kingdom database, you must use the following SQL statement:

```
SELECT *
FROM Orders
WHERE ShippedDate = #5/10/94#;
```

You can also use the **DateValue** function which is aware of the international settings established by Microsoft Windows. For example, for code in the United States, you can use:

```
SELECT *
FROM Orders
WHERE ShippedDate = DateValue('5/10/94');
```

For code in the United Kingdom, use:

```
SELECT *
FROM Orders
WHERE ShippedDate = DateValue('10/5/94');
```

See Also IN Clause, ORDER BY Clause, SELECT Statement, SELECT...INTO Statement, SQL Aggregate Functions.

WHERE Clause 357

Specifics (Microsoft Access)

In Microsoft Access, the conditions that you establish in a WHERE clause in SQL view are the same as those you might enter in the Criteria field in the query design grid. If you enter criteria in the query design grid, you can change to SQL view to see the WHERE clause.

Conversely, if you enter a WHERE clause in an SQL statement in SQL view, you can change to Design view to see the criteria in the query design grid, unless you are creating a union query. Union queries can only be viewed in SQL view.

Example

Some of the following examples assume the existence of a hypothetical Salary field in an Employees table.

This example selects the LastName and FirstName fields of each record in which the last name is King.

```
SELECT LastName, FirstName FROM Employees WHERE LastName = 'King';
```

This example selects the LastName and FirstName fields for employees whose last names begin with the letter S.

```
SELECT LastName, FirstName FROM Employees WHERE LastName Like 'S*';
```

This example selects employees whose salaries are between $20,000 and $30,000, inclusive.

```
SELECT LastName, Salary FROM Employees
WHERE Salary Between 20000 And 30000;
```

This example selects employees whose last names fall in alphabetic order between Lon and Tol, inclusive. It doesn't retrieve Tolstoy because Tolstoy follows Tol and therefore is outside the specified range.

```
SELECT LastName, Salary FROM Employees
WHERE LastName Between 'Lon' And 'Tol';
```

This example selects orders placed during the first half of 1994.

```
SELECT OrderID, OrderDate FROM Orders
WHERE OrderDate Between #1-1-94# And #6-30-94#;
```

This example selects employees who live in Interlaken, New York, or Frankfurt.

```
SELECT LastName, FirstName, City FROM Employees
WHERE City In ('Interlaken', 'New York', 'Frankfurt');
```

WITH OWNERACCESS OPTION Declaration

Description In a multiuser environment with a secure workgroup, use this declaration with a query to give the user who runs the query the same permissions as the query's owner.

Syntax *sqlstatement*
    WITH OWNERACCESS OPTION

Remarks The WITH OWNERACCESS OPTION declaration is optional.

The following example enables the user to view salary information (even if the user doesn't otherwise have permission to view the Payroll table), provided that the query's owner does have that permission:

```
SELECT LastName,FirstName, Salary
FROM Employees
ORDER BY LastName
WITH OWNERACCESS OPTION;
```

If a user is otherwise prevented from creating or adding to a table, you can use WITH OWNERACCESS OPTION to enable the user to run a make-table or append query.

If you want to enforce workgroup security settings and users' permissions, don't include the WITH OWNERACCESS OPTION declaration.

This option requires you to have access to the System.mda file associated with the database. It's really useful only in secured multiuser implementations.

See Also SELECT Statement.

Specifics (Microsoft Access) You can include the WITH OWNERACCESS OPTION declaration in an SQL statement to allow users to run a query and view the results even if they don't have security permissions on the underlying tables. When this option is set, a user is granted the same permissions as the owner of the query.

For example, the owner of a query on an Employees table can include the WITH OWNERACCESS OPTION declaration in the definition of the query that returns all fields except those that give employees' addresses. A user who does not have read permissions on the Employees table can then run the query and view only those fields included in the query. Effectively, the user now has restricted read access to the table.

Using this declaration is equivalent to setting the **RunPermissions** property to Owner's in the query property sheet in query Design view. Omitting the declaration is equivalent to setting the **RunPermissions** property to User's, which is the default setting.

PART 3

Appendix

APPENDIX

Data Access Object Hierarchy

This appendix contains a graphical representation of the Data Access Objects object model. For detailed information on individual objects, see the topic for the object or collection in Part 1 of this book.

Data Access Objects

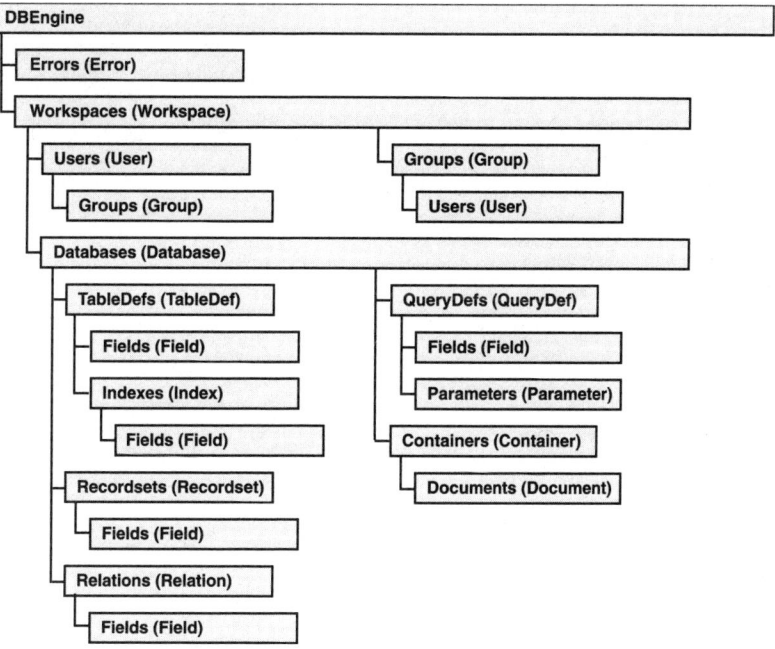

Your One-Stop Technical Resource for Microsoft® Word

The MICROSOFT WORD DEVELOPER'S KIT provides the technical information and tools you need to build practical solutions in and around Microsoft Word quickly and easily. You'll find everything you need to customize the operation of Microsoft Word, write powerful macros to streamline routine tasks, and build cross-application custom solutions. The kit contains complete documentation and program samples and covers the full scope of WordBasic, Microsoft Word's built-in programming language.

ISBN 1-55615-880-7, 1,000 pages, $49.95 U.S.A., $67.95 Canada

Sample programs show you how to:

- Automate repetitive tasks and complicated operations using WordBasic macros

- Build custom wizards to guide users step by step through complex tasks

- Extend the capabilities of Word by using WordBasic and Dynamic Data Exchange (DDE) to seamlessly communicate between applications

- Develop custom applications using the Microsoft Messaging API (MAPI) and Open Database Connectivity (ODBC)

- Create your own Word add-in libraries using the Word API

Microsoft Press

Microsoft Press® books are available wherever quality books are sold and through CompuServe's Electronic Mall—**GO MSP**.
Call **1-800-MSPRESS** for more information or to place a credit card order.* Please refer to **BBK** when placing your order. Prices subject to change.
*In Canada, contact Macmillan Canada, Attn: Microsoft Press Dept., 164 Commander Blvd., Agincourt, Ontario, Canada M1S 3C7, or call 1-800-667-1115.
Outside the U.S. and Canada, write to International Coordinator, Microsoft Press, One Microsoft Way, Redmond, WA 98052-6399, or fax +1-206-936-7329.

Microsoft® Office for Windows® 95 Resource Kit

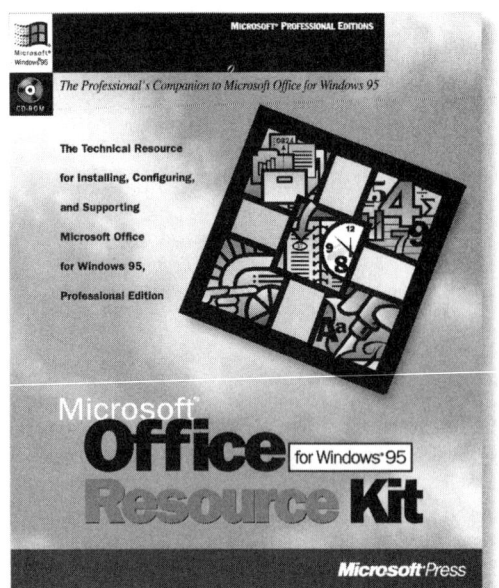

ISBN 1-55615-818-1, 942 pages
$49.95 U.S.A., $67.95 Canada

Complete Technical Information for the Support Professional

The MICROSOFT OFFICE FOR WINDOWS 95 RESOURCE KIT provides you with all of the information necessary to plan for and implement Microsoft Office for Windows 95 in your organization. This book includes coverage of all the Microsoft Office for Windows 95 Professional Edition applications, including Microsoft Word 95, Microsoft Excel 95, Microsoft PowerPoint® 95, and Microsoft Access 95. Details about how to install, configure, and support Microsoft Office for Windows 95 will save you hours of time and will help ensure that you get the most from your computing investment.

This exclusive Microsoft publication, written in cooperation with the Office for Windows 95 development team, is the perfect technical companion for network administrators, support professionals, systems integrators, consultants, advanced users, and other computer professionals. Whether you support Office for Windows 95 within an organization or just want to know more about it, the MICROSOFT OFFICE FOR WINDOWS 95 RESOURCE KIT is a valuable addition to your reference library.

Here are some of the topics you'll find covered in depth
in the MICROSOFT OFFICE FOR WINDOWS 95 RESOURCE KIT:

- Office for Windows 95 Architecture
- Installing Office for Windows 95
- Upgrading to Office for Windows 95
- Configuring for Optimal Performance
- Using Microsoft Office in a Workgroup
- Switching from Other Applications to Microsoft Office
- Support and Troubleshooting

Microsoft®Press

Microsoft Press® books are available wherever quality books are sold and through CompuServe's Electronic Mall—**GO MSP**.
Call **1-800-MSPRESS** for more information or to place a credit card order.* Please refer to **BBK** when placing your order. Prices subject to change.
*In Canada, contact Macmillan Canada, Attn: Microsoft Press Dept., 164 Commander Blvd., Agincourt, Ontario, Canada M1S 3C7, or call 1-800-667-1115.
Outside the U.S. and Canada, write to International Coordinator, Microsoft Press, One Microsoft Way, Redmond, WA 98052-6399, or fax +1-206-936-7329.

Register Today!

Return this
Microsoft® Office 95 Data Access Reference
registration card for:

✔ a Microsoft Press® catalog

✔ special offers on
Microsoft Press books

U.S. and Canada addresses only. Fill in information below and mail postage-free. Please mail only the bottom half of this page.

1-55615-942-0   *Microsoft Office 95 Data Access Reference*   *Owner Registration Card*

_____
NAME

_____
INSTITUTION OR COMPANY NAME

_____
ADDRESS

_____
CITY   STATE   ZIP

Microsoft® Press
Quality Computer Books

For a free catalog of
Microsoft Press® products, call
1-800-MSPRESS

BUSINESS REPLY MAIL
FIRST-CLASS MAIL   PERMIT NO. 53   BOTHELL, WA

POSTAGE WILL BE PAID BY ADDRESSEE

NO POSTAGE
NECESSARY
IF MAILED
IN THE
UNITED STATES

MICROSOFT PRESS REGISTRATION
MICROSOFT OFFICE 95
DATA ACCESS REFERENCE
PO BOX 3019
BOTHELL WA   98041-9946